SPORTING TRADITIONS
Since 1856

The Orvis Encyclopedia of
Fly Fishing

Your Ultimate A to Z Guide to Being a Better Angler

TOM ROSENBAUER

PHOTOS BY F-STOP FITZGERALD AND BRUCE CURTIS

FOREWORD: PERK PERKINS

THOMAS NELSON
Since 1798

NASHVILLE   DALLAS   MEXICO CITY   RIO DE JANEIRO

THE ORVIS ENCYCLOPEDIA OF FLY FISHING: *Your Ultimate A to Z Guide to Being a Better Angler*

Text copyright Tom Rosenbauer 2010.

Compilation copyright BAND-F Ltd. 2010 All rights reserved.

For photographic credits and copyrights, please see pages 311–312.

Produced by Band-f Ltd.

www.band-f.com

President: f-stop Fitzgerald

Production Director: Mie Kingsley

Cover and Interior Design and Typesetting: Maria Fernandez

Edited by Leigh Ronald Grossman. Special thanks to Dave Beattie, Ricky Coughlin, and Kim Lawson.

Published in Nashville, Tennessee, by Thomas Nelson. Thomas Nelson is a registered trademark of Thomas Nelson, Inc.

Any activities described herein undertaken by the reader are undertaken solely at the reader's sole risk. The publisher, packager, photographers, and authors, disclaim any and all liability from any injuries or damages therefrom.

Thomas Nelson, Inc., titles may be purchased in bulk for educational, business, fund-raising, or sales promotional use. For information, please e-mail SpecialMarkets@ThomasNelson.com.

Library of Congress Cataloging-in-Publication Data

Rosenbauer, Tom.

    The Orvis encyclopedia of fly fishing : your ultimate A to Z guide to being a better angler / Tom Rosenbauer ; photos by f-stop fitzgerald and Bruce Curtis, foreword Perk Perkins.

      p. cm.

    Includes bibliographical references and index.

    ISBN 978-1-4016-0370-0 (alk. paper)

    1. Fly fishing—Encyclopedias. I. Title.

SH456.R658 2010

799.12'4—dc22   2010032733

Printed in the United States of America

10 11 12 13 14 QG 6 5 4 3 2

CONTENTS

This is where it all begins; salmon eggs in a redd.

FOREWORD

BY PERK PERKINS, CEO,
THE ORVIS COMPANY, INC.

The two books that I can always find in my fly fishing book-shelves are A. J. McClane's *Standard Fishing Encyclopedia* and his *Encyclopedia of Fish Cookery*. Other books I've read once and store forever; these two books I refer to often. Now I can have an encyclopedia of fly fishing (McClane's was on all types of fishing) to answer questions, settle arguments, and enrich me with fly fishing trivia. For example, I didn't know that smallmouth bass were not native to Maine, Vermont, and New Hampshire.

This book is a huge gift to fly fishers and you probably cannot charge what it is worth. The research put into it is epic. I don't know how Tom found the time, because I know how hard he works at his "day job" at Orvis as marketing director for our Rod and Tackle division. This book is like dim sum to the inquiring mind.

Thanks from me and on behalf of all the anglers who will benefit from this book. I know it will sell like Prince Nymphs!

INTRODUCTION

BY TOM ROSENBAUER

Fly fishing has always been plagued with jargon. Like it or not, you'll trip across arcane terms in magazines and on websites, or you'll overhear them whispered in the back corner of a fly shop. If any of the sentences below leave you puzzled, this book is for you.

- When fishing the *Pteronarcyus* hatch, it's best to use a size 6 Stimulator or a size 4 bead head stonefly nymph fished on a 9-foot 3X leader under a strike indicator.
- The tarpon broke off because I didn't use a fluorocarbon shock tippet, was only using an 8-weight line, and didn't have enough backing.
- The swirly pocket water made it tough to get a dead drift, so he fished his Hendrickson subimago imitation on a braided leader with a 3-foot tippet.
- Traditionalists like to fish for steelhead with a Spey fly swung downstream.

- Halford would have approved of the way I fished my Trico spinner.
- To catch big Atlantic salmon in Ireland, it's best to fish spate rivers in February and March with a sink tip line.

The Orvis Encyclopedia of Fly Fishing is a reference book, and I wrote it so that you'd have something to keep on your desk when surfing websites or reading magazine articles. When a phrase you don't understand comes up, I think this will be the book you'll open to clear up the mystery and move on. I think you'll also find it fun to skim through it when you need a fly fishing fix and can't be on the water. In the dead of winter when even Florida redfish suffer lockjaw because of a series of cold fronts, you might find it fun to learn about the native range of Pacific salmon, where you might go to catch a muskellunge on a fly next year (and what tackle you need!), or the best places to go fly fishing in the southern hemisphere where it's high summer.

Encyclopedias, by nature, are not the best place to go for detailed information. For instance, if you have trouble with trout refusing your dry flies, this book will give you a few hypotheses to test. You might decide the culprit is line drag, and with further research here you would determine you need a dead drift. You might even find a few hints about how to get a drag-free presentation. You won't find a complete treatise on how to avoid drag; for that level of detail you will have to pursue your education with another book or through repeated web searches.

There are many things in this book you'll have trouble finding on the web, however. The web is miserly with basic unbiased information, because most websites are designed to sell you something, or get you to sign up for a magazine or join an organization. The web is particularly deceptive when looking for good information on new places to fish. You can plug "fly fishing for trout in Montana" into the Google box and get 125,000 entries to pick through. Many are lodges that want you to come to their little corner of the state and fish the rivers they float—regardless of whether they are the best in the state. You'll find people trying to sell you books and maps on fly fishing in Montana. Or you can

watch lots of bad videos on Youtube. But you'll be hard pressed to find an unbiased overview of the best rivers in the state, when to find the best fishing conditions, or what single drainage in Montana hosts true native rainbow trout.

In writing this book, I used a combination of sources for getting an evenhanded view of fishing various states and countries throughout the world. While I haven't fished all of the locations in this book, after 30 years in the fly fishing business I have a rich network of friends and guides throughout the world who I trusted to help me compile a list of the best fisheries in each location. While you might not want to plan a salmon fishing trip to the Kola Peninsula based *only* on the information in this book, you'll be able to start your planning knowing which rivers are considered the best ones, the time of year to plan your trip, and the tackle you might need.

In trying to give a broad overview for places to fish throughout the world, I had to make a lot of judgment calls. There is largemouth bass fishing in Kansas, and trout fishing in the mountains of Kenya. But I had to limit my coverage to those places fly fishers travel to expressly to fish—the best-known and best-loved places in the world for fly fishing. Otherwise I'd still be writing this book into my retirement, and I plan on spending *that* time traveling to the places listed in this book.

Alexandra

A

ACROSS-STREAM

In casting or presenting a fly, across-stream is used to describe a **fly line** angle that is directed toward the middle of the river at 90 degrees to the current. **Downstream** is the direction indicated when a fly line is cast parallel to the current, toward the direction the water is flowing, and **upstream** is parallel to the current toward where the water is flowing from. Quartering downstream is somewhere between across-stream and downstream, and quartering upstream is between across-stream and upstream. It's important to understand these directions when learning stream technique, as each direction makes the fly line and fly behave in a different manner and affects the sink rate of a sunken fly.

ACTION, FLY ROD

Few subjects in fly fishing are more confusing and subjective than **fly rod** action. "Action" is a way that anglers and manufacturers describe how a fly rod flexes when casting, but since there are many different casting styles, and casting style affects the way a rod flexes as much as anything, most descriptions of fly rod action are, at best, approximations. The way a rod flexes is important because to some degree it will determine how well a rod will perform on long casts, in the wind, for short, delicate fishing, or when playing a large fish.

A

Before discussing various actions it's useful to understand how different flex profiles are created. There are various grades of graphite with different stiffness ratings, but these are really negligible when determining the action of a rod—action is affected more by how the material is used than by what it is. (With **bamboo rods**, of course, material is irrelevant because bamboo is quite consistent.) Flex profiles can be lumped into two types—*progressive* and *compound*. A progressive taper is one where a rod starts at a given diameter at the butt and tapers at a constant rate to the tip. Compound tapers may decrease diameter at one rate for part of the rod, then change quickly into another taper. A rod with a compound taper could have as many as three different tapers over the length of a rod. Neither style is inherently better; whether a rod is progressive or compound just depends on what a rod designer has to do to get the rod to flex in the manner he or she wants.

Rod actions are usually categorized as fast, slow, or medium action. Of course this begs the question: "Fast as compared to what?" Orvis developed a flex index system that assigns a discrete number to a rod's action, so the similarity in action from one rod model to another can be determined by how close the flex index numbers are. Orvis uses the term tip-flex to describe what others would call fast action, mid-flex to define medium action, and full-flex to describe slow action. Some people associate slow action with a poor rod and fast action with a great one, but all action types actually have advantages and disadvantages.

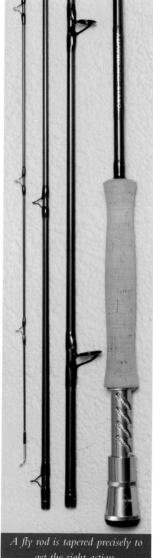

A fly rod is tapered precisely to get the right action.

TIP-FLEX (FAST ACTION)

These rods have fast tapers in the upper 25 percent or so (in other words, the diameter of the rod from the tip down decreases rapidly, so the tip bends more easily than the rest of the rod). The middle and the butt section remain relatively stiff compared to the tip of the rod. This action gives tip-flex rods a reserve of power for making long casts and for playing big fish, or for playing a strong fish in fast water. Tip-flex rods throw a tight casting loop, which drives the line better into the wind (and all other things being equal, throws the line farther), so they are the choice of tournament casters. Tip-flex rods are less forgiving of casting mistakes than other actions, though, so they can be difficult for beginners.

Scenarios where a tip-flex rod would be most useful include fishing on big, windy rivers and fishing in salt water. Both of these situations require long casts into the wind and the ability to play big fish quickly.

MID-FLEX (MEDIUM ACTION)

In this action, the rod flexes more down into the middle of its length than a tip-flex does. Mid-flex action is a great compromise between the strength of a tip-flex rod and the delicacy of a full-flex. It's the most common action sold today because it is easy to cast, yet relatively powerful. A mid-flex rod can move from one set of conditions to another without sacrificing the ability of the rod to present the fly properly.

FULL-FLEX (SLOW ACTION)

Full-flex action rods bend far into the butt of the rod, almost to the handle, under a moderate casting load. One of the reasons they are called *slow action* is because the casting stroke is longer than with other actions. (In other words, the angler has to wait longer in between the forward and back casts because the rod has to flex along a wider arc before maximum power is achieved.) Full-flex rods are terrific for small stream fishing, because these rods load well on the very short casts needed in small streams, and if a rod is not loaded fully, it won't present the line smoothly. A full-flex rod also acts as a shock absorber, so that very light **tippets** can be used without risking a fish breaking off. They are very accurate on short casts, generally poor on long casts, and don't do well in strong winds.

A term you may hear, especially when someone is discussing older **bamboo rods**, is *parabolic action*. Here, the rod is slightly stiffer in the middle than in the **butt** or **tip**, and is designed to throw the fly line like a catapult. This action throws a long line with the right casting style, but is not very efficient when throwing a short line.

ADAMS FLY

The Adams (along with its many variations) is the most popular dry fly in the world. The original fly, developed in **Michigan** in the 1920s to imitate either a deerfly or a **caddisfly**, is now used during all kinds of insect hatches, from **mayflies** to **midges**. Its mixed gray and brown colors seem to suggest a generalized aquatic insect well (or the colors may just appeal to trout). The traditional Adams uses upright wings and bushy **hackle**, like a traditional mayfly, but today the parachute version, with hackle that lays parallel to the surface of the water and a highly visible white wing, is easier to see on the water and seems to be equally inter-esting to trout. The Adams is also tied with spent wings to imitate a mayfly **spinner**, and with a yellow egg sack to imitate an egg-laying caddisfly or mayfly. The Adams is used from a large size 10 all the way down to a minuscule size 26, depending on what size insects local trout are feeding upon.

ALASKA

OVERVIEW

Alaska is North America's most remote fly fishing frontier; it offers an abundance of fish that are eager to take a fly, along with scenery that almost makes the fishing insignificant. Along with these blessings come the minor curses of thick mosquito swarms, wild weather that can change in instant, and frequent encounters with grizzly bears. Because of the bears and because most of Alaska's fishing travel is done by floatplane in sometimes stormy weather, it's best to hire an experienced outfitter and check references before heading to this fisherman's paradise.

Because Alaska's fish are big, flies are larger than normal trout flies, and because **sinking tips** are often used, most fly fishers travel to Alaska with tackle that is too light. The 9-foot 5-weight rod that serves you well in Montana won't be ade-quate for anything but fishing for **grayling** and small rainbows. A wise choice is a 7-weight rod for rainbow and grayling fishing, plus a 9-weight for **Pacific salmon** and **pike**. When fishing specifically for king salmon, which may weigh 40 pounds, a 10-weight light **tarpon** rod (along with a strong reel with plenty of **backing**) is not out of line.

Although dry-fly fishing for **rainbow trout** and grayling is superb during the summer, most Alaskan fishing is done with flies that imitate salmon eggs, simulate pieces of flesh torn off dying salmon on their spawning runs, or just with large, colorful attractor **streamers**. **Leaders** may be short and stout, because the fish are not leader shy and should be landed and released quickly.

A

Perhaps the most critical piece of gear on an Alaskan fishing trip is a reliable rain jacket, as southern Alaska is very wet in the summer and the weather can change in a heartbeat.

FISHERIES

Alaska's most famous fishery is the Bristol Bay/Lake Illiamna region, where the best fishing for large rainbow trout, Pacific salmon, grayling, pike, **arctic char**, and **Dolly Varden** is found. This fishing is almost entirely fly-in fishing, and may be done on long float trips where you camp overnight on the river, or fly out from a main lodge every day. Rivers like the Kvichak and Naknek are world famous for giant rainbow trout, but there are hundreds of smaller rivers and lakes in the Bristol Bay region that offer unparalleled fly fishing. Although chum, pink, sockeye, and king salmon can be taken on a fly rod, most fly fishers prefer the silver (coho) salmon, which takes a fly more aggressively than the other species. Top coho rivers are the Nushagak and Togiak, but as with the trout streams there are numerous excellent salmon rivers in this region.

Less remote and more crowded but still world-class fisheries can be found on the Kenai Peninsula south of Anchorage, where it is possible to drive to rivers like the Kenai for large king salmon and

Arctic char

rainbows, or to the Anchor River, which offers some of the finest accessible **steelhead** fishing in Alaska. Kodiak Island also has good fly fishing for king and silver salmon, because the rivers are short and the fish can be caught close to salt water, when they are more aggressive and eager to take a fly.

Southeastern Alaska offers a myriad of smaller coastal rivers, where fly fishing for both steelhead and silver salmon is productive and uncrowded. Most of the rivers here are short and have small runs of salmon and steelhead, but you'll see far fewer fishermen than on the Kenai Peninsula. Perhaps even better is fishing in the estuaries where salmon and steelhead stage before entering the rivers, because they are still feeding heavily. It's also possible to catch sea-run **cutthroats** or even a small halibut on a fly in this remote area.

Amazing scenery surrounds the angler in Alaska.

A

SEASON

Much of Alaska's fishing season is determined more by the ability to access its remote rivers than by the willingness of the fish to take a fly. Most lodges in the Bristol Bay area don't open until June, even though king salmon begin their runs earlier and rainbows, grayling, and arctic char are willing to take a fly much earlier. In the same light, probably the best month for catching big rainbows in Alaska is in September and October, but nearly all lodges close in September. Not only does the weather get uncomfortable, travel by float plane once the weather turns wintry is dangerous and unreliable. Of course, the rivers on the Kenai Peninsula can be accessed by car, and fly fishing in May and October can be productive in this area, at times when lodges in the interior of Alaska are closed.

For rainbow trout, arctic char, Dolly Varden, and grayling, best months for big fish are June and September. For taking these fish on a **dry fly**, midsummer, during hatches of aquatic insects, is best. King salmon begin running freshwater rivers in April, with the peak of the run in June and early July. The kings are followed by sockeyes in June and July, and best times to find fresh runs of silver, chum, and pink salmon are in August (although the silvers, the best of the fly rod salmon, will continue to run through October).

ALBRIGHT, JIMMIE (1916–1998)

Captain Jimmie Albright was a pioneer of **Florida** Keys fishing, and today is revered by guides and anglers alike as one of the finest saltwater guides who ever lived. He was responsible for developing a code of ethics and etiquette for shallow water fishing in the Keys, where crowded conditions and spooky fish would sometimes create pandemonium before his voluntary system where each boat respects the rights of others. Albright first came to Islamorada in the Keys in the 1940s, when the sport fishing industry there was in its infancy. He soon became a favorite guide of baseball great Ted

Williams, and together they caught the first **tarpon** over 100 pounds on a fly. He is most remembered today for his **Albright Knot**, used for joining lines of greatly different diameters.

ALBRIGHT KNOT

The Albright Knot is one of the best knots to join lines of widely different diameter or material. Developed by Captain **Jimmie Albright** in the 1940s, the knot is still widely used today. Common uses of the Albright Knot are joining heavy monofilament **shock tippet** to a **class tippet**, tying fly line to **backing**, or tying **monofilament** to single-strand **wire.** The Albright Knot is easy to tie and smooth when finished, but great care must be taken to tighten the knot carefully.

■ Fold the end of heavier material over itself, forming an open-ended loop (in this case the

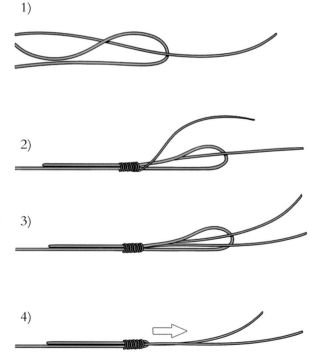

1)

2)

3)

4)

A

knot is shown joining a piece of single-strand wire, the heavier material, to monofilament tippet material). Pass the monofilament through the folded-over section and then begin to wrap it back over itself and the loop, toward the closed end of the loop (figure 1).

- Take 10 to 12 closely spaced, tight turns over the loop, ensuring that no turns overlap. Pass the end of the monofilament through the end of the closed loop so that it exits the loop on the same side it entered (figure 2).

- Tighten the knot by holding both ends of the wire in one hand and pulling on the tag end (the end that will be trimmed off) until it tightens (figure 3). Then pull on the standing end of the monofilament (the end that goes to the rest of the leader) until it tightens. Repeat once more with the tag end and then the standing end. Then pull tightly on only the standing end of the wire and the tippet (figure 4). Trim both tag ends. If the knot is to be used to attach fly line to backing, coat the knot with a waterproof flexible cement or super glue so that it slips through the guides easily.

AMERICAN MUSEUM OF FLY FISHING

Founded in 1968 and located in the town of Manchester, **Vermont**, the American Museum of Fly Fishing is a unique repository of fly fishing's historical past. Items on exhibit and in the collection include rods, reels, flies, manuscripts, artwork, and photography. The goals of the AMFF are to gather and preserve these objects as well as allowing the public to view and appreciate them.

ANGLERS OF THE AU SABLE

The Anglers of the Au Sable is a 600-member non-profit organization dedicated to the protection and preservation of **Michigan**'s **Au Sable** and Manistee River watersheds. Formed in 1987 to defend a catch-and-release section on the Au Sable, the organization soon became the watchdog of coldwater resources in this area. They have protected their river systems from many threats, and have taken on organizations from the National Guard to mining companies, as well as sponsoring telemetry studies of trout movement, studying the effects of canoes on fishing, and improving habitat by constructing in-stream structures.

ANT

Ants are favorite foods of trout and other freshwater fish. Fish seem to relish the taste of ants and will go out of their way to eat ants that fall into the water. Ants constantly patrol the banks of rivers during the warm months, and everything from large black cap carpenter ants to tiny brown ants may be eaten. Besides ordinary wingless ants falling into the water, during the summer and fall months

ant colonies grow wings and migrate, and when they do, they seem to be attracted to water, where they fall onto the surface, often in large quantities. At these times, trout feed with abandon and having a flying ant imitation is every bit as important as having the correct **mayfly** imitation during a hatch of aquatic insects.

Ants don't float very well, so imitations of these insects should float low in the water. Often tiny yarn or foam **indicators** are tied on top of ant flies so they can be seen by the angler. In addition, the slightest **riffle** can sink a floating natural ant, so sunken imitations of ants can be as deadly as those that float, but should be fished with a **strike** indicator so takes can be seen.

ANTI-REVERSE REELS
See Fly Reel.

ARCTIC CHAR
The arctic char, *Salvelinus alpinus*, is the northernmost of the salmonid family and lives in harsh freshwater environments from the Bering Sea to Labrador, though Greenland, **Iceland**, and Lapland to Siberia. Some populations ascend to the sea to grow fat and return to spawn, but there are landlocked varieties as well. The blueback trout of **Maine**, the Quebec red trout, and the extinct Sunapee trout of **New Hampshire** are all isolated relict populations from the last Ice Age.

Arctic char resemble **brook trout** but are slimmer and have a forked tail in contrast to the brookie's squared-off tail. Like brook trout, they are aggressive and easy to catch and are fond of bright-colored flies. When they are found in the same rivers as salmon they can be caught on egg imitations, but in most rivers the best flies are brightly colored **streamers**, especially those with hues of red, orange, and yellow. Arctic char are strong but not spectacular fighters. They are one of the best eating trout in the world.

ARGENTINA

Fly fishing the Lago Vintter in Patagonia, Argentina.

OVERVIEW
Argentina is a long, narrow country that ranges from subtropical in the north to subpolar in the south. Although trout are not native to Argentina, **brown trout** from Europe and **rainbow trout** from California were stocked in rivers at the base of the Andes around the turn of the twentieth century. Brown trout were also stocked in the southernmost rivers of Tierra del Fuego in the 1930s and soon established sea-run populations. **Brook trout** and landlocked **Atlantic salmon** from the eastern United States were also stocked, although they are not as common as rainbows or browns. Argentina's trout rivers run clean and cold and

A

have excellent food supply and spawning habitat, thus all trout fishing in Argentina is for wild, stream-bred fish.

Argentina's trout fishing is found from the central western part of the country south, along the spine of the Andes. Travel in the Argentine countryside can be difficult because rental cars are expensive and much of the land is tied up in large private *estancias*, so most fishing for visiting anglers revolves around the many fine lodges in the country, and is based around cities and towns with nearby airports. However, there are numerous national parks in the Andes with public water. The stream access laws in Argentina allow one to fish through private land on the banks of a river to the high-water mark, as long as access was obtained on public land, so a do-it-yourself trip is not out of line for the more adventurous angler.

Argentine trout rivers look and fish very much like the rivers of the American Rockies, except the trout are far less selective because they experience a lot lower fishing pressure. The rivers have the same groups of aquatic insects as trout streams anywhere in the world—**mayflies**, **caddisflies**, **stoneflies**, and **midges**—thus dry and **nymph** patterns are similar to those used in the American West. **Grasshoppers**, **ants**, and **beetles** are also abundant and eaten by the fish. Two prey items that are unique to Argentina are various species of large beetles, imitated by a size 6 or 8 Chernobyl Ant or similar foam terrestrial; and the *pancora*, a large river crustacean best imitated with a large olive **Woolly Bugger** or with local streamer patterns.

Besides introduced trout, Argentina offers another **fly rod** fish worth pursuing—the native *dorado*. This fish, which looks like a cross between a trout and a bass, averages 3 to 20 pounds, has very sharp teeth, hits as aggressively as any other freshwater fish, and makes frequent spectacular leaps when hooked. Dorado are restricted to subtropical northern Argentina.

FISHERIES

Argentine trout fishing is centered in northern Patagonia. The most famous area, near San Martin de los Andes, was popularized by anglers like **Joe**

Fly Fishing on the Rio Malleo in Argentina.

Brooks and **Ernest Schwiebert**, who extolled its praises in their books and magazine articles beginning in the 1960s. Rivers such as the Chimehuin, Calleufu, Malleo, and Alumine are known for their fabulous **dry fly** fishing, although trout can be caught on nymphs and **streamers** just as easily.

Moving further south toward the bigger town of Bariloche, which is the biggest tourist town in this part of Patagonia, the angler will encounter more services, easier transportation, and more public water in national parks. The most famous rivers in this area are the Rio Mansa and the Traful.

South of Bariloche is the Esquel area, which is more foothills than mountains (thus the stream valleys are more open and windswept). This area does not receive as much fishing pressure as the Bariloche area and the rivers are not as well known, but they are every bit as productive as those to the north. Best rivers in this area are the Corcovado and Frey, but there are numerous other rivers, lakes, and **spring creeks** in the area.

Tierra del Fuego, in the extreme south, is a land of windswept rivers and gigantic sea-run brown trout. Although the geography is barren and the wind blows constantly, there are a number of excellent lodges in this region because the sea-run brown trout in rivers like the Rio Grande and Gallegos run from 10 to 20 pounds and are spectacular fighters. Two-handed rods are almost a necessity because of the wind and long casts, and most fish are caught using **sinking** or **sink tip lines** on large streamers and wet flies. There are also smaller streams and spring creeks in the area with resident trout, but most traveling anglers are lured by the giant sea-run fish, despite the average catch of only one or two fish per day.

Dorado are found only on the pampas in northern Argentina. They are sometimes found in clear, rocky streams, but most fishing is in wide, slow river systems and marshes. The Rio Corriente and Rio Parana are the two most popular rivers for dorado. These fish require a stout 9- or 10-weight fly rod, heavy leaders with a wire bite **tippet**, and

sinking or sink tip lines. They will hit most large streamer flies and are very aggressive, so catching them is more a matter of finding the fish than selecting the right fly.

SEASON

Trout fishing in the northern Patagonia streams begins in November and ends in April, but prime fishing time is January through March. As with any high-mountain rivers, anglers need to be careful to avoid snow runoff, which varies river by river, but is typically in November and December. (Patagonia also has superb lake fishing, and lakes will have fine conditions during runoff.) The season for sea-run trout is January through March, and February is the prime month. January and March can be very cold in Tierra del Fuego. Although dorado can be caught year-round, the best fishing period is from January through April.

ARIZONA

OVERVIEW

Although most people think of Arizona as an arid state with brutally hot weather, it offers some excellent fly fishing throughout the year. From tiny wild trout in the White Mountains to **largemouth bass** in reservoirs and irrigation canals at the outskirts of Phoenix and Scottsdale, Arizona can give the fly fisher challenges when other states are locked into the dead of winter. Arizona is also the only place in the world to catch the rare Apache trout. This beautiful trout, *Oncorhynchus apache*, is related to the interior **rainbow** and **cutthroat trout,** and is native to the Salt River drainage.

FISHERIES

Trout fishing is very popular in Arizona, and the state has both wild and stocked populations of **brown**, rainbow, Apache, and **brook** trout. The closest high-quality stream to the Phoenix/Scottsdale megalopolis is Oak Creek in Sedona, a small stream that is stocked weekly with rainbows but also has a wild population of brown trout. Other good streams in the Sedona area include Beaver Creek, which has **smallmouth bass** as well as rainbows, and Verde River, which hosts largemouth bass and crappie as well as rainbows.

For the fly fisher looking for solitude and wild mountain trout in small streams and lakes, the White Mountains in the northeastern part of the state offer year-round fishing in cool rivers and lakes because of the average altitude of 8,000 feet. The Salt River is the native watershed of the Apache trout and wild fish are still found in its headwater areas, along with rainbow and brown trout. The East and West Forks of the Black River also offer very large trout; at lower altitudes there is good smallmouth bass fishing with a **fly rod**. Earl Park, Hawley Lake, and Big Lake also have excellent fishing for large trout. Trout in the White Mountains are not picky about their flies, and a selection of **Woolly Buggers,** Prince Nymphs, and attractor dries like **grasshoppers** and **Parachute Adams** will work well.

The premier trophy trout fishery in Arizona is the Colorado River below Lake Powell, near Lee's Ferry before the river enters the Grand Canyon. This river, in the extreme north central part of the state, has a dense population of very large, wild rainbow trout. Accessible only by float fishing, it is primarily a **nymph** river because the fish feed heavily on **scuds**, **midge** larvae, and aquatic **worms**. Some **dry fly** fishing to tiny midge adults is possible in slow backwaters all year long, though, and during the summer big dry fly imitations of grasshoppers and cicadas will bring the fish up from the depths.

Largemouth bass, panfish, and **carp** can be taken on a fly in nearly every body of water in Arizona. Pleasant, Alamo, and Bartlett Lakes are close to Phoenix, and fly fishing subsurface with minnow and **crayfish** imitations, as well as standard **poppers**

Smallmouth bass

work well in those lakes. Lake Pleasant and Roosevelt Lake in the Sonora Desert are also well known for fly fishing opportunities for largemouth bass, smallmouth bass, white bass, and crappie.

SEASON

Trout can be caught in Arizona 12 months a year and fish can even be caught with dry flies in the dead of winter. However, most winter fishing is done with nymphs and streamers, with heavy midge hatches beginning in March and lasting through the fall. During the summer, the lower altitude rivers and lakes warm too much for easy trout fishing, but the Colorado River at Lee's Ferry and the high-altitude streams of the White Mountains have great dry fly fishing with big attractor fries like grasshoppers, Stimulators, and **beetle** imitations. Bass fishing during the winter is primarily done with sinking lines as the fish are deep then, but by March bass and panfish enter the shallows to spawn and can be caught easily on poppers and streamers until the heat of summer sets in. During the summer, bass and panfish will still take a fly, but early morning and night fishing provide the most productive opportunities. In fall, bass return to the shallows and can again be caught on surface flies during the day, until they return to the depths for the winter.

ATHERTON, JOHN (1900–1952)

John Atherton wrote a single influential book, *The Fly and the Fish*, in which he applied his artist's training to fly tying and postulated that flies imitating aquatic insects should have an impressionistic look (in other words an impression of movement and life instead of exact copies of aquatic insects). He was a commercial artist and a friend and neighbor of Norman Rockwell while both of them lived in **Vermont** in the 1940s and 1950s.

ATLANTIC SALMON FEDERATION

The Atlantic Salmon Federation is an international nonprofit organization dedicated to the conservation and wise management of **Atlantic salmon** and their environment. Based in New Brunswick, it has regional councils throughout maritime **Canada** and the northeastern United States, and works through both a professional paid staff and about 40,000 grassroots volunteers.

Because of the highly migratory nature of Atlantic salmon, the Federation works with conservation and government agencies throughout the North Atlantic, and was instrumental in securing a conservation agreement with Greenland that protects salmon in their winter feeding grounds, while providing long-term economic alternatives for Greenlanders. The organization has also been instrumental in studying the movements of Atlantic salmon while at sea, and has developed telemetry gear to track salmon migrations.

In less than 300 years, wild Atlantic salmon populations have decreased by 90 percent, and the North American population reached an all-time low of only 418,000 adult fish in 2001. There is some hope for the future, thanks to this organization, but it will be a long struggle.

ATTRACTOR FLIES

Flies are often lumped into two groups, *attractors* and *imitators*. Imitators are those flies that are made to imitate a specific insect, whether it is a **mayfly**, **baitfish**, or **grasshopper**. Attractors don't imitate any specific prey, but are appealing to fish in other ways. In general, imitators are used when fish are seen feeding on a specific insect, crustacean, or baitfish, and attractors are used when no fish are seen feeding or it can't be determined what they are feeding upon.

Attractor flies may interest fish through the use of bright colors like red, yellow, or purple, which are not common in natural foods but are highly visible. Or they can be made with materials like rubber legs or marabou feathers that wiggle enticingly in the water and suggest something that is alive and trying to escape. Attractor flies are typically larger than imitators, so they can be noticed quickly by a hungry gamefish.

Since we don't know exactly why fish strike attractor flies, when a fish takes an attractor fly it might think our attractor looks just like one of its common prey items. In that case, the fly that was supposed to be an attractor immediately becomes an imitator without our knowledge!

Attractor dry flies

AUTOMATIC REELS

See Fly Reel.

AU SABLE RIVER (MICHIGAN)

The Au Sable River, located in northeastern **Michigan** and flowing east into Lake Huron, is one of the finest trout streams in the country. The river's mostly gentle flows offer easy wading and floating (especially in the iconic Au Sable River Boat, a long, canoelike craft that can be poled or paddled and excels in handling tight turns in shallow water). The many springs that feed the river keep summer water temperatures comfortable for trout and offer up an abundant supply of aquatic insects.

The Au Sable hosts all of the important eastern **mayflies**, **stoneflies**, and **caddisflies**, but its most famous insect is a giant mayfly of the genus *Hexagenia,* commonly called the **Hex**, which hatches after dark in June and brings normally reclusive giant **brown trout** to the surface. Thirty-inch brown trout can be caught on a dry fly during this hatch. The Au Sable also holds a healthy population of wild **brook** and **rainbow trout** in addition to the browns, and in its lower reaches just upstream from Lake Huron it offers superb fishing for **steelhead**.

The most famous stretch of the Au Sable is its fly fishing-only "Holy Water" stretch just downstream of Grayling, but excellent fly fishing in bigger water is available below this special regulations water, and much of it runs through the relative wilderness of the Huron National Forest. The Au Sable's North Branch and South Branch, major upstream tributaries, are easily fished and waded, and an angler on these waters will seldom encounter the recreational canoes that crowd the main river on summer days.

AUSABLE RIVER (NEW YORK)

New York's AuSable River (typically spelled as one word as opposed to **Michigan**'s **Au Sable**) is a classic mountain stream that runs near the rugged High Peaks region of New York State's Adirondack Mountains. The West Branch of this river is a far superior fishery to its East Branch, as the habitat on the East Branch has been greatly degraded by road development and channelization and trout fishing there is marginal. Access to the river is excellent as most of the river's West Branch is paralleled by paved roads, and there is no private, posted water until the river flows below the town of Wilmington. The river is a study in contrasts, with long, slow pools punctuated by fast pocket water. Wading the AuSable can be tricky in the fast-water stretches, as the riverbed is filled with round, slippery boulders, and felt soles with cleats plus a **wading staff** are recommended.

The West Branch of the AuSable's trout population is almost entirely hatchery-raised **brown** and **rainbow trout**, except for pockets of wild **brook trout** in its headwaters. No-kill regulations on parts of the river, however, ensure that plenty of trophy trout are available throughout the year. The river offers diverse hatches, including good populations of large **Green Drake** and *Isonychia* **mayflies** plus large **stoneflies**, so large (size 8 through 12) dry flies like the famous AuSable **Wulff** can be productive, especially in the river's fast water stretches. Best fishing is in May and June and again in September, as the river warms considerably in the middle of the summer.

Fall on New York's AuSable River.

Blue Sapphire

BACK CAST
See Overhead Cast.

BACKING
Backing is a thin, flexible line that is wound onto a **fly reel**, prior to the **fly line** proper. It fills up the arbor of a spool so that the fly line is wound around a larger diameter and is thus less likely to form annoying coils. But its most important purpose is to provide insurance against a fast-running fish. Fly lines are between 75 and 150 feet long, and fish like **salmon**, **steelhead**, and many saltwater species can run 150 feet or more before the angler can tire them enough to retrieve line. In fact, a large **tarpon**, **sailfish**, or **tuna** can run hundreds of yards on their first bolt for freedom. It's impractical to make a fly line longer than 120 feet as few people can cast that far, and the additional line would be too thick to add hundreds of yards of insurance—thus the reason for thin-diameter backing.

In some cases, like small stream trout fishing or when fishing for **largemouth bass**, no backing is needed, other than to keep the line from coiling too tightly on the spool. For large river trout fishing, where a 20-inch **rainbow** might get into fast current, 100 yards is plenty. Salmon, steelhead, **bonefish**, and **striped bass** anglers like to use 200 yards just in case that once-in-a-lifetime fish is

B

hooked. And blue water ocean fly fishers will sometimes use as much as 400 yards.

Good backing should be strong, abrasion-resistant (in case it gets dragged along coral or sharp rocks), limp, and small in diameter. Braided **Dacron**, a form of **nylon**, is the most common type as it is inexpensive. Breaking strength on Dacron is either 20- or 30-pound; the lighter type is used for most freshwater fishing and the larger diameter for saltwater, not so much for its greater strength as its larger diameter, to prevent coils of backing from binding on the spool.

Another type of backing is gel spun polyester, which is much stronger for a given diameter so that more backing can be put on the spool. It's useful when an angler wants to add a lot of backing to a smaller diameter reel. Gel spun breaks at between 35 and 50 pounds depending on the type used, and gives the angler around 60 percent more capacity on a spool. Because of gel spun's finer diameter, when a fish has run 100 yards the remaining spool has a wider diameter, so that spool rpms are slower and line pickup is quicker.

All fly reels are sold with a stated backing capacity, which shows how much backing a reel will take with a standard floating line. It's wise to fill the spool with the recommended amount of backing even if the angler won't encounter large fish, because it will fill up the spool and lessen line coils.

BAETIS
See Blue-Winged Olive.

BAHAMAS
The Bahamas consists of nearly 700 islands and 2,000 cays, but only about 40 of the islands are inhabited. With extensive saltwater flats, there are opportunities for fly fishing everywhere, but fishing areas are understandably limited to the islands with air service or those within a short boat ride from settled areas. There are opportunities to fish from lodges that have been popular retreats since Hemingway's day or to fish wilderness flats that have never seen a fly fisher—if you are lucky enough to own a seaplane or a boat that can travel for days without refueling.

Bonefish are the most abundant and popular **fly rod** fish in the Bahamas, but certain locations also offer superb fishing for **permit** and **tarpon**. Bonefish flats are also home to other species that are exciting to take on a fly rod, including jacks, blacktip and lemon **sharks**, **snook**, **barracuda**, and mutton snapper. Although the Bahamian offshore fly rod fishery is not well developed, there are **sailfish**, **marlin**, **wahoo**, dolphin, sierra and Spanish **mackerel**, and various species of **tuna**. Sometimes these fish are less than a mile from shore. Guiding is an important occupation in the Bahamas, often passed down from one generation to another, and guides there are some of the best in the world. Fishing opportunities in the Bahamas are year-round, but flats fishing becomes a morning and evening affair in July and August when water temperatures are at their maximum. In the summer, most Bahamian guides are commercial lobster fishermen, so finding a guide in midsummer can be difficult.

Andros Island is the premier bonefishing spot in the Bahamas. It's the largest island in the country yet sparsely populated and developed, and the flats are endless, from the more traveled ocean flats and bays on the east side to the endless channels of the Middle Bight that separates North from South Andros, to the uninhabited West Side. The West

Side requires a long boat ride, but it also hosts some of the best tarpon fishing in the Bahamas. The Joulter's Cays at the north end of the island are one of the best places in the Bahamas for permit fishing.

The Abaco Islands and surrounding cays including the famous Walker's Cay have abundant bonefishing, especially on the uninhabited west shore, called The Marls. Bonefish here run from very small to large, and schools can number in the hundreds. Because Abaco is further north than Andros, it fishes better during the summer, but winter cold fronts in December through February can make flats fishing uncertain.

Although Freeport on Grand Bahama Island is the second largest settlement in the country, both the east and west ends of the island offer some of the most famous bonefish flats in the world in unspoiled settings. Bimini has been famous for its offshore fishery since the 1930s, but it also harbors some of the largest bonefish in the Bahamas and several line-class world records have been set there. Eleuthera is home to both luxury resorts and miles of expansive white sand flats—and big bonefish. The Exumas have more stable weather than the northern Bahamas, many easily waded sand flats, and a good tarpon fishery.

B

Casting to bonefish in Andros Island, Bahamas.

BAITFISH

Baitfish is a generic term used to describe any fish a bigger one will eat. Typically it describes small minnows and related species, but 2-pound menhaden and 12-inch **mackerel** can be considered baitfish to a 40-pound **striped bass**. Some gamefish, like members of the **tuna** family, feed almost entirely on baitfish. Others, like striped bass, feed heavily on baitfish but will also prey upon crabs, squid, **shrimp**, and almost anything else they can swallow. Large trout consume a lot of baitfish, but smaller trout eat them infrequently, typically as a target of opportunity rather than a steady diet.

Gamefish prey upon baitfish by ambushing them. Some species, particularly saltwater fish, pursue schools of baitfish in schools of their own, herding the baitfish into reefs, shallow bays, or other obstructions where the baitfish are cornered. In open water, gamefish force schools of baitfish to the surface, where they are also trapped between the gamefish below them and sea birds above.

Gamefish seem to have an intuitive sense of when baitfish will be most vulnerable. A few small individual baitfish may be totally ignored by a larger fish because it knows it can be outmaneu-

vered by the quicker baitfish. However, the instant a smaller fish shows distress by changing its swimming pattern the larger fish will strike. This is why baitfish are most often eaten by trout on a rise of water when the smaller fish get disoriented, or after dark when the larger fish have the advantage of stealth.

Baitfish are imitated by **streamer flies**, which are long, skinny flies that mimic the shape and behavior of fleeing prey.

BAMBOO ROD

Until the late nineteenth century, **fly rods** were made from woods like lancewood, greenheart, or ash. These woods did not have the strength or resiliency to cast a **fly line** very far, and the only way to cast a longer line was to use an 11-foot-long rod. Those solid wood rods were heavy, warped frequently, and would break under the stress of playing a large fish. In the search for a stronger material, bamboo, with its strong and elastic outer skin, was used. At first only two strips were glued together, but later the six-strip construction used today was developed. (It is also possible to make a good bamboo rod with four or five strips, but six–strip construction has proven to be the most popular.)

Early bamboo rods were made from many types of bamboo such as "Calcutta cane" from India. Unfortunately, most species of bamboo do not have power fibers that are strong and resilient enough to construct a superior fly rod. Of the hundreds of species of bamboo in the world, only *Arundinaria amabilis* from southern China produces acceptable rod-making material, and it cannot be grown anywhere else in the world.

In making a bamboo rod (also called split cane, split bamboo, or cane rods), the six strips are cut from the outside layer of bamboo and then planed to exacting specifications to get the taper of the finished rod. These strips are then glued together. Rods made prior to World War II were made with animal glues. Because these glues would absorb moisture and warp the bamboo, the rods were varnished on the outside to keep out moisture. Wes Jordan of Orvis invented a process in the 1940s that would impregnate the bamboo and prevent water entry without the need to varnish the outside of the rod, but today bamboo rod makers use modern synthetic glues that negate the need for both varnishing or impregnation.

Bamboo rods generally have a slower action than **graphite rods**, but by carefully controlling the taper a rod maker can construct a bamboo rod with relatively fast action. Still, most anglers buy a

Early fly rod made from Calcutta cane

bamboo rod for its slow, delicate action; the rods are mostly used for small stream trout fishing, where they really shine. A well-made bamboo rod will cast small flies with equal or better accuracy and delicacy than a graphite rod as long as casts are short, winds are light, and the flies are smaller than size 12.

Not all bamboo rods found in yard sales are priceless heirlooms. Prior to World War II, nearly all fly rods were made from bamboo and many inexpensive rods were mass-produced with little thought to carefully controlling the tapers. Modern bamboo rods and a few brands that were made in the twentieth century are carefully crafted by hand with precise tapers.

Modern bamboo fly rod from Tonkin cane

BARB
See Hook.

BARRACUDA

Barracuda are found in tropical waters throughout the world and are especially common on saltwater flats. Although they are not as glamorous as **bonefish** or **tarpon**, they are exciting fish on a **fly rod**, and are often more difficult to catch because of their sharp eyesight. Once hooked, a barracuda in shallow water will make fast runs and will often clear the water numerous times in impressive leaps. Barracuda will often save the day for a fly fisher when a cold front passes through, as they aren't as sensitive to cooler water as other flats species.

Unlike most other flats gamefish, barracuda usually remain motionless, waiting in ambush for prey. They can be spotted along the edges of white sand patches, points of land, or near underwater obstructions, and because they aren't moving it's easier to set up a presentation. The best way to hook a barracuda is to make a long cast beyond a fish but in front of it, so the fly passes in front of the barracuda. Fast retrieves are necessary, as fast as the angler can strip, and it's often helpful to place the rod under your arm and strip with both hands. Both **streamers** and **poppers** can be effective for barracuda, especially long, green streamers that imitate needlefish, one of the barracuda's favorite foods. A short **wire tippet** is essential when fishing for barracuda, as their sharp teeth can easily cut through the thickest **monofilament**.

BARREL KNOT

See Blood Knot.

BASS FLY

Freshwater bass will take nearly any kind of fly imaginable, from tiny **dry flies** to giant saltwater flies, but the best flies for them are **floating** and **sinking flies** that range between one and five inches long, typically with bright colors and materials that wiggle in the water. Bass are opportunistic feeders and seldom selective, so the plan in choosing bass flies should be to show them something big enough to notice that looks alive. Bass are almost never selective feeders, and **largemouths** or **smallmouths** feeding on a hatch of **mayflies** will eat a **popper** or a **streamer** just as enthusiastically as an exact imitation of a mayfly.

As any plug caster will tell you, the most important aspects of a lure are the **action** and the depth at which it is retrieved. Flies are no different. Although color may not be critical, it pays to experiment with different colors if the bass aren't in a feeding mood. The best colors for bass flies are black, purple, red, yellow, chartreuse, white, and combinations of these colors. Counterintuitively, dark flies often draw more strikes in deep or dirty water, and at night and on dark days. Bright flies work best under strong sunlight.

The action of a fly is determined partly by the way the fly is retrieved and partly by the materials it's made of. Long, flowing **hackle** feathers give a good undulation in the water, and may suggest a snake or leech or skinny **baitfish** to the bass. Marabou is a fluffy feather that breathes in the water, and the slightest movement of current will make it shimmy like a plastic **worm**. Rabbit fur has similar action in the water. Rubber legs wiggle in a different manner than feathers and may imitate the helpless struggling legs of an insect or frog. By making a quick strip of the line followed by a long pause, a bass fly using these materials will look alive both when it is moving and when it stops because the material keeps moving even without action imparted by the angler. The effect of a fly that seems to escape and then stops but continues to wiggle as if crippled is often too much for a hungry bass to resist.

Bass streamer (top) and bass popper

Bass flies can be fished either right on the surface or up to about 25 feet below the surface. The most enjoyable is surface fishing with a popper, because **floating lines** are easier to cast and **strikes** on the surface are often explosive. Surface flies come in three basic shapes—poppers, sliders, and divers. Poppers have a concave forward surface and make a deep gurgling sound when pulled sharply. They are most effective when fished over deeper water or in dirty water, because the sound a popper makes can attract a bass from a much longer distance than just the sight of the fly itself. Poppers can also be effective in shallow water when bass are in a very aggressive mood, especially during the spring spawning period. Sliders have a pointed front surface and thus are much more subtle than poppers when pulled across the surface. Sliders work better when bass are shy, especially in very clear or shallow water, because sometimes the loud

sound of a popper can spook the fish. One of the most deadly and effective sliders is the Sneaky Pete. Divers will dive slightly under the surface when pulled, and are great at mimicking the struggles of a wounded baitfish or frog. The Dahlberg Diver is the most popular bass diver. Fish a diver by making a sharp pull so that it dives under the surface, then allow the fly to float back to the surface and let it sit motionless five to 30 seconds.

Floating bass flies can be made of painted cork, hard plastic, foam, or spun deer hair. Deer hair flies are softer and have a slightly different action on the water, so they may work for spooky fish or for fish that reject the fly quickly. Deer hair is most effectively used on divers. But deer hair gradually absorbs water and makes a fly difficult to cast, so most anglers opt for the less realistic but better-floating hard-bodied poppers and sliders.

Sinking flies for bass are generally variations on trout streamers and **nymphs**, but one of the most popular sinking flies for bass is the **Clouser Minnow**, typically considered more of a saltwater fly (although the original fly was invented by Bob Clouser as a smallmouth bass fly). A Clouser Minnow's weighted eyes sink the fly quickly, and it's an especially useful fly in deep lakes or fast rivers. Some sinking bass flies were actually tied to mimic more popular bass lures—the Gulley Worm is a fly fisherman's equivalent to the ubiquitous plastic worm used by spin and plug casters.

BASS, LARGEMOUTH

Largemouth bass, *Micropterus salmoides*, are the most popular gamefish in North America. Originally found in the Great Lakes and upper Mississippi drainage, they have been transplanted around the world and can be found from **California** to Kenya, because they thrive anywhere you find warm, shallow, weed-filled waters. Largemouths can be found within a 10-minute drive of most people in North America, yet they are nowhere near as popular a **fly rod** fish as trout. That's unfortunate, because largemouths smash a surface fly with spectacular enthusiasm, and even the tiniest farm ponds or golf course water traps have bass big enough to put up a spirited battle.

The most enjoyable way to catch largemouths is with a surface **popper**, hair bug, or diver because you can see the take. At most times of year, the best time to catch a largemouth on a surface fly is just before or after dawn and dusk, when light levels are low and the fish are on the prowl for food. Night fishing can also be very productive with a fly. To fish successfully for largemouths, a stout **leader** and weedless flies are needed, because the fish will seldom be found more than a few feet from brush piles, downed trees, or weed beds. Largemouth bass are not leader shy in the slightest, so a 3-foot leader of 15- to 20-pound test **monofilament** can be used, which makes it easy to turn over the large flies these fish prefer, and easier to horse them out of submerged cover. Rods from 7-weight to 9-weight are most popular.

The best way to catch a largemouth on a surface fly is to cast the fly right onto shore or into a tangle of brush or lily pads. Give the fly a twitch or two by stripping line until the fly is in a small open patch of water, not too far from cover. Then let the fly rest up to a full minute, as bass will often eyeball a fly for an agonizingly long time before finally pouncing on it. Give the fly another twitch, let it rest again, and continue until the fly is close to you.

Subsurface flies for largemouths in shallow water should be cast into the same heavy cover, but should be retrieved with slow, steady pulls. Although not as exciting as surface fishing, at times bass won't come to the surface for a fly, especially during the middle of the day. If no fish are found in shallow water, the last resort is to put on a full-**sinking line** and fish over submerged weed beds in deeper water offshore, which is often necessary during the heat of the summer. It's more work, but some of the biggest fly rod bass are caught this way.

Largemouth bass feed on frogs, **crayfish**, smaller fish, tadpoles, **dragonflies**, and anything else they can get their considerable jaws around. Flies for largemouth bass are typically larger than those used for **smallmouths**. Although they are active year-round, even in their northern range, the best time to fish for them is just before and during their spawning period, which happens when water temperatures reach 60 degrees. This can be as early as February in the south and as late as July in the extreme north.

BASS, SMALLMOUTH

Smallmouth bass, *Micropterus dolomieui*, are closely related to **largemouth bass** but have a smaller mouth (the lower jaw line does not extend past the eye), don't grow as large, and prefer cooler, rockier habitat than largemouths. In a lake with both species, you'll find the smallmouths closer to open water around rocky shores and gravel bottoms, and will find the large-mouths in weedy, muddy back bays. Smallmouths are more likely to be found in rivers and large lakes than in the smaller ponds that largemouths often thrive in. Smallmouths were originally native to the Great Lakes and upper Mississippi system, but they have been introduced throughout the northern United States. Smallmouths are found as far south as Oklahoma and northern Alabama, but only in large reservoirs with cooler water. They are now abundant and popular on the West Coast from

California to **Washington**, especially in the lower reaches of rivers.

Smallmouth bass will eat the same frogs, small fish, and tadpoles that largemouths eat, but they are especially fond of **crayfish**, hellgrammites, and **mayflies**. Thus, although smallmouth bass fishing with surface bugs is often very successful, more smallmouths will be taken on **streamer** flies, large **nymphs**, and large **dry flies** that imitate these prey items. A dark brown or black **Woolly Bugger** is an especially productive smallmouth fly, as it suggests crayfish, hellgrammites, and **sculpins**, three top small-mouth foods. A good fly box for smallmouths will include a few **poppers** and sliders in different colors (the Chartreuse Sneaky Pete is especially deadly), some dark streamers to imitate crayfish and hell-grammites, a few brighter streamers to imitate bait-fish, and a few large **stonefly** nymphs and attractor dry flies like the Stimulator, PMX, and White **Wulff** to imitate adult insects. Because they live in clear water and eat smaller food than largemouths, a longer, finer leader is necessary. A 7-foot or 9-foot leader with a 2X (10-12 pound) tippet is perfect for smallmouth fishing.

B

Smallmouths in rivers will be found along drop-offs, around rock piles, and in the shallow tails of pools. They often prefer to lie in slow water just on the edge of faster water. River smallmouths are active feeders all day long, even on bright days in the middle of summer, although evening is probably the best time. Nymphs and streamers can be fished **dead drift**, with an occasional twitch, but most often the best retrieve is fast and steady. If neither dead drift nor a fast retrieve work, try a few fast strips followed by a long pause.

In lakes, smallmouths will be found along rocky shores and submerged logs, but seldom over silt bottoms. They are not as likely to be found in weed beds as largemouth bass, although they will sometimes be found on the edges of weed beds feeding on **baitfish**. One of the best ways to find lake smallmouths in early morning is with a popper or slider, and during spawning time (May and June) they can be caught all day long with surface bugs. However, once summer heat sets in smallmouths in lakes are most often taken with a nymph or streamer and fished on a sinking or sink tip line in 5 to 20 feet of water, using a fairly slow and steady retrieve.

BATTENKILL

The Battenkill (technically calling it the Battenkill River is redundant since "kill" means river in Dutch) is a small wooded trout river that flows from southwestern **Vermont** into southeastern **New York** and finally into the Hudson River. The Battenkill is famous for difficult trout that are inordinately fond of small flies. **Hatches** are not abundant on this river except for the early season Hendrickson and late season Trico **mayflies**, and trout density is not high. However, the Battenkill's scenic valley, and its proximity to the headquarters of The Orvis Company, have ensured that it is well known throughout the world. All of the trout in the Vermont stretch of the Bat-

tenkill are wild **brook** and **brown trout**. After the river flows into New York State, a mix of wild and stocked trout will be found. The Battenkill is best fished in May and June, when fly hatches are most active and the water has recovered from spring snow melt but still has enough flow to make the fish easy to approach. Although it flows mostly through private land, there is access throughout the length of the river through the generosity of local farmers and landowners.

BEADHEAD FLIES

Beadhead flies were developed in Austria by Roman Mosher in the 1970s, and quickly found their way to trout streams throughout the world. The original flies used solid brass beads to imitate the emerging sparkle of a **caddis pupa,** but fly tiers soon found that heavy beads added sparkle, weight, and fish-catching appeal to **nymphs** used to imitate other insects as well as to **streamer** flies and saltwater flies. Beads are now also made from tungsten, which sinks more quickly than brass, or from glass, which adds sparkle but not as much weight as brass and tungsten. Thus by tying nymphs with glass, brass, and tungsten beads, the fly fisher can regulate the depth at which he is fishing without adding extra weight to the leader.

Metal beads for flies are made in the original brass color, as well as in silver, copper, red, and black. Glass beads are available in every color of the rainbow. A red bead might be used on an imitation of a bloodworm, which is a bright red **midge larva**. Black

beads are often used to give weight to a fly while still maintaining the subdued tones of a natural insect. The bright copper, brass, and silver beads are used for flies that will be used in turbulent or discolored water, because they are more visible to the fish. Similar to beads are metal cones, used most often on streamer flies.

The most popular Beadhead flies include the Beadhead Hare's Ear, Beadhead **Pheasant Tail**, Beadhead Prince, and Beadhead **Stonefly**. Most common conehead flies are the Conehead **Muddler** and Conehead **Woolly Bugger**.

BEAVERKILL RIVER

The Beaverkill is a medium-sized trout stream in the southern Catskill Mountains of **New York State**. Despite being a mere two-hour drive from New York City, it is a wooded mountain river with a high density of trout. The Beaverkill is formed by the junction of the Little Beaverkill and Willowemoc Rivers, and from this junction to where the Beaverkill flows into the East Branch of the Delaware River is almost entirely public water. The river occupies a classic **riffle**/pool floodplain, and both the larger pools and the riffles offer good trout fishing. The river is mostly a **brown trout** river, with a mixture of wild and stocked trout, but wild **rainbows** occasionally enter the Beaverkill from the Delaware, and there are wild **brook trout** in its upper tributaries.

The Beaverkill offers all the classic eastern **hatches**, partially because it is a productive river, but also because much of American fly-fishing entomology books were researched on the Beaverkill and surrounding rivers. Beginning with the **Quill Gordon mayflies** in April, through heavy hatches of Hendricksons and March Browns in May, **Green Drakes** and Sulphurs in June, and continuing with **Slate Drakes** and **Tricos** during the summer and fall, the Beaverkill offers **dry fly** fishing for the entire season. As belies its rich heritage, all of the pools on the Beaverkill are named,

with legendary names like Hendrickson's, Cairn's, Horse Brook Run, and Wagon Tracks.

The Beaverkill fishes well in spring and typically fishing remains superb until mid-June. Summer water temperatures often range into the 80s, which makes fishing slow and puts a lot of stress on the fish. In fall, water temperatures decline and fishing picks up, without the crowds that spring angling attracts.

BEETLE

Beetles are a common food of trout and **panfish**, both the terrestrial beetle varieties that fall into the water and aquatic species that live underwater. Aquatic beetles are more common in ponds than in rivers; trout, panfish, and small bass in lakes feed on them constantly because aquatic beetles are quite active throughout the day. Sunken beetles fished in lakes should be cast out, allowed to sink slightly, and retrieved with a slow but steady retrieve.

Although beetles are active along trout streams from the first warm days through late fall, it is during the summer months, when aquatic hatches dwindle, that they become of paramount importance to trout—and to trout anglers. Beetles tumble, crawl, or fly into the water by mistake, and a trout stream will have a dozen species along its banks at any given time. Trout typically eat terrestrial beetles with a subtle, determined sip and seldom with a splashy rise. Because beetles float low in the water it's sometimes difficult to guess when a feeding trout is eating them. Presume any trout feeding quietly along the banks or under trees in midsummer is a beetle-eater.

Most beetles are brown, black, or tan and between size 12 and 20. Imitations should be chosen accordingly, and the best patterns are made from closed-cell foam, which floats well and simulates the hard exoskeleton of a beetle very well. A **parachute** wing, a tuft of yarn, or a piece of bright foam on top of the fly can also help you track the fly's progress in the water and detect strikes.

B

BELLY BOAT

A belly boat (or float tube) is a small watercraft perfect for fishing small lakes and ponds. Powered by swim fins and kicked along by the angler, it can get to places unreachable by larger boats, and can be launched anyplace. Because they are light enough to be carried in a backpack, belly boats are excellent for high mountain lakes. A belly boat consists of a large inner tube covered by a fabric layer that protects the tube and offers pockets, backrest (inflated by a separate tube for emergency flotation), and a stripping skirt, which keeps coils of **fly line** from tangling around the angler's legs.

The original belly boat was circular and difficult to enter and exit, especially with swim fins. Current designs are more U-shaped, which give the same flotation but much easier access to the seat. However, the round types are less wind-resistant, so on windy lakes most anglers prefer the older style. No belly boat should be used in places with very strong winds or current, because they are slow to paddle and can get an angler into a dangerous situation.

BERGMAN, RAY (1891–1968)

Ray Bergman was fishing editor of *Outdoor Life* magazine for most of the middle of the twentieth century, and his book *Trout* (1932) was the basic fly fishing reference book for several generations of anglers. Although Bergman was first and foremost an expert on Catskill trout fishing, he traveled throughout North America during his tenure at *Outdoor Life* and wrote about fly fishing from **Maine** to **California**. Bergman was not a big believer in matching the **hatch**, and preferred to concentrate on presenting a fly to a fish instead of worrying about what was on the end of the **leader**.

BERNERS, DAME JULIANA

Although fishing with a feather hook is known to have existed for over 2,000 years, the first English reference book on fishing with a fly, *The Treatyse of Fysshynge with an Angle,* was purported to have been written by an abbess of a convent named Dame Juliana Berners. First published in 1496 (although it may have existed in manuscript form as early as 1450) there is scant evidence that Berners wrote it, but most popular angling litera-

The easiest way to catch trout on the Bighorn is with a pair of **nymphs** and an **indicator**. Best nymphs are small imitations of scuds and midge larvae. Fish can be caught on these flies all day long, all season long. On warm winter days and throughout spring, summer, and fall, a close examination of slow backwaters will often reveal scores of trout feeding quietly on small mayflies, midges, or caddisflies. These fish are a challenging target for the wading angler, as it's difficult to work these pods of fish while floating by in a **drift boat**. **Streamers** are also very effective on the Bighorn, particularly in fall and winter, and many large trout are taken each year on imitations of baitfish or **crayfish**.

B

ture prefers this more romantic attribution. Regardless of its author, the *Treatyse* described fishing methods, fly patterns, and the seasonal progression of fly hatches. The dozen flies mentioned in her book were so good that fly fishers were still using them hundreds of years later.

BIGHORN RIVER

The Bighorn River is one of the most famous and productive trout rivers in the world. The Bighorn begins in **Wyoming** as the Wind River. Below "The Wedding of the Waters" it exits the Wind River and becomes the Bighorn. The most famous stretch of the Bighorn is the 13 miles below Yellowtail Dam in **Montana**, where the water runs clear, cold, and stable 12 months a year. Wild **brown** and **rainbow trout** here grow quickly on a diet of **midge larvae**, **scuds**, **baitfish**, **mayflies**, and **caddisflies**. Fishing is open year-round and the fly fisher, given the right conditions, can enjoy **dry fly** fishing every month of the year.

BIMINI TWIST

The Bimini Twist is a knot used to double a section of finer diameter line before tying it to a much thicker piece, or tying **monofilament** to wire. It is most often used in saltwater **class tippets**, where the finer class tippet is joined to a very heavy piece of **shock tippet**. The Bimini Twist is a knot that retains 100 percent of the strength of the line. Because no other knot is quite that effective, the Bimini gives the angler a bigger diameter section to knot that will be twice as strong as the tippet itself. Bimini Twists also offer some elasticity to a section

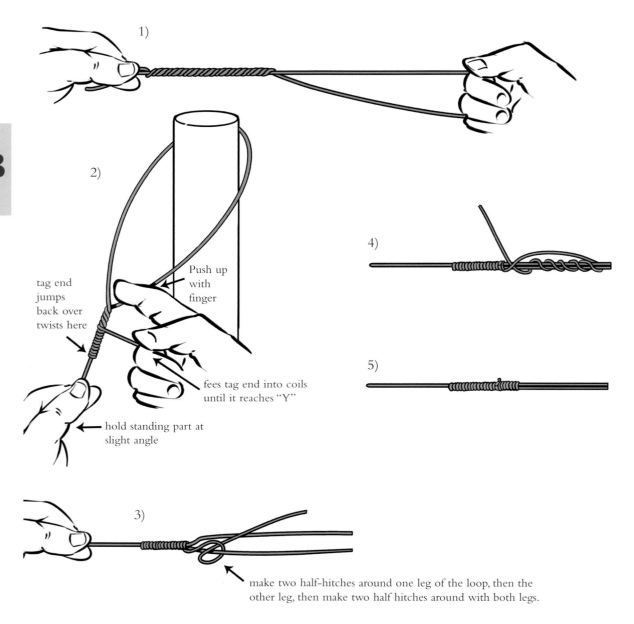

1)

2)

tag end
jumps
back over
twists here

Push up
with
finger

fees tag end into coils
until it reaches "Y"

hold standing part at
slight angle

4)

5)

3)

make two half-hitches around one leg of the loop, then the
other leg, then make two half hitches around with both legs.

of line, further protecting the **leader** from breaks due to quick **strikes**.

Start with a section of line that is about two feet longer than the single-strand tippet section you desire. If a Bimini twist will be tied in both ends of the tippet, add four feet. Double about 14 inches of the tippet over itself. Pinch the tag end to the standing part with one hand and rotate your other hand inside the loop 20 times to form 20 twists in the loop (figure 1).

■ Place the end of the loop over a nail or cleat. Cradle the standing part of the line with one hand. Place the forefinger of your other hand inside the loop and up against the twists. Hold the standing part with your other fingers. Cock the standing part of the line slightly to the side while pushing up against the twists with your forefinger. Begin to feed the standing part onto the twists, moving down toward your forefinger. Make sure these turns are smooth, don't overlap, and are immediately adjacent to each other (figure 2).

■ When the standing part has reached the bottom of the twists close to your forefinger, bring the fingers of your other hand down and pinch the junction. Take a single half hitch around one strand of the loop and tighten. Then take a single half hitch around both strands of the loop and tighten (figure 3).

■ Make a three-turn hitch around both legs of the loop, starting away from the knot and working back toward it. Work this hitch tight by slowing drawing the turns down, pulling away from the knot slightly, and then tightening again (figure 4). It make take several repetitions of this to draw the hitch tightly against the twists without overlapping them. Trim the tag end (figure 5).

end away from the crossing point over the standing part three to four times. Carefully open the fingers of the other hand and insert the tag end at the point where the standing parts of each line cross. Re-pinch this area with the other hand to hold this tag end in place (figure 2).

■ Wind the other tag end away from the crossing point in the same manner. Open the loop slightly and bring this tag end back through the loop that was formed at the crossing point, but from the opposite direction as the first tag end (figure 3).

■ Carefully pull on both standing ends to tighten the knot. Make sure the tag ends do not slip back through the loop and ensure that the standing ends are at 180 degrees to each other when the knot is tightened. (Otherwise it will not hold properly.) Trim the tag ends as close to the knot as possible (figure 4).

B

BLOOD KNOT

The blood knot is the slimmest possible knot for joining two pieces of **monofilament**. It is used in **leader** construction for fish like trout that may be spooked by bulky knots in leaders. Although it is a very strong knot, the difference between the two diameters joined should be no greater than .003" in smaller diameters and no greater than .005" in sizes above .020". If two pieces of monofilament with a larger difference in diameter are joined, an improved blood knot should be used, where the finer diameter piece is doubled on itself before tying the knot.

■ Cross the two sections over each other, forming an X, leaving about two inches of each tag end beyond the crossing point (figure 1).

■ Pinch the thumb and forefinger of one hand around the crossing point and wind one tag

1)
2)
3)
4)

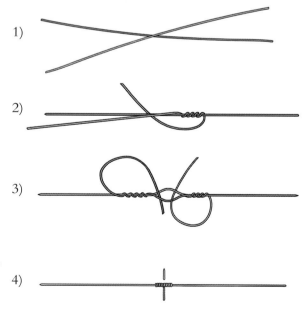

BLUEFISH

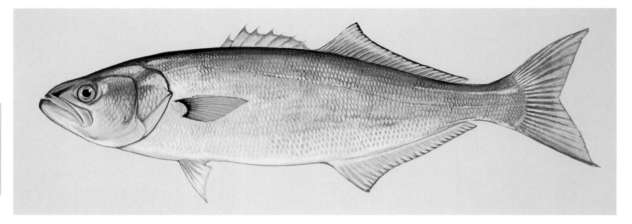

B

Bluefish, *Pomatomus saltatrix,* are an aggressive inshore fish found on the Atlantic Coast south of Nova Scotia. They travel in large schools of like-sized individuals; because bluefish are one of the most aggressive fish that swims they are a terrific target for the novice saltwater fly rodder. Bluefish can be found almost anywhere, from open oceans to inshore harbors, but they won't enter brackish water or move as far up estuaries as **striped bass**. Schools move quickly and will almost always have gulls or terns hovering over them. Bluefish feed primarily on **baitfish** and squid, although they will feed on crabs or **shrimp** if available.

Bluefish sport small but very sharp teeth and have been known to attack swimmers. They can be landed without a wire **shock tippet**, but without wire only about one in ten fish will be landed before cutting the line. Anglers pursuing bluefish should always attach the fly to a 4- to 8-inch piece of **wire** between the **leader** and the fly. Bluefish will inhale almost anything that moves but veer away from flies that stop moving or slow down, so the retrieve should be a very fast strip with no pauses in between. Some anglers put the rod under their arm and strip with both hands to get a fast, steady retrieve. Bluefish will take both subsurface flies and **poppers**, and fishing for them with an explosive popper is one of the most exciting ways to take them, as three or four indi-

viduals may compete for the same fly. Bluefish are strong fighters and fast runs of about 50 yards and a few leaps are common when they are hooked. Average size ranges from about 4 to 12 pounds, depending on location and time of year.

BLUE-WINGED OLIVE

The term Blue-Winged Olive refers to both species of **mayflies** with a gray wing and olive-brown abdomen as well as the artificial fly that imitates them. The term is most often used for mayflies in the genus *Baetis*, which range from size 16 through size 24 and hatch throughout the year, especially in spring and fall. However, a number of other common mayflies in the genus *Ephemerella* exhibit the same coloration and some fly fishers call them Blue-Winged Olives, Slate-Winged

Olives, or sometimes just "Olives." The *Ephemerella* species are larger (size 12-16) and **hatch** during the summer.

In the **United Kingdom**, the *Baetis* species are called "Duns" or "Olives," while the *Ephemerella* species are properly called Blue-Winged Olives. *Baetis* mayflies are the most common and widely distributed genus in the world.

Imitations of these mayflies are just as diverse. The most common imitations of the adult duns include the hackled Blue-Winged Olive, the Olive **Parachute**, Olive No-Hackle, Olive **Comparadun**, Olive Thorax, and Olive Sparkle **Dun**. Nymphs of this genus are slim and brownish-olive, and are best imitated by the **Pheasant Tail nymph** or Olive Pheasant Tail nymph.

BONEFISH

Bonefish, *Albula vulpes*, are the most popular **fly rod** fish on tropical flats. Although they don't look fierce, bonefish are more aggressive predators than the **sharks** or **barracuda** they share shallow water flats with—they are just far more wary and when frightened can speed into deep water at more than 25 miles per hour. This speed, combined with their wariness, is why they are such a popular challenge for fly fishers.

Bonefish spend low tide periods in deep channels, moving onto shallow water as the tide washes over the productive saltwater flats and eel grass, making the myriad of crabs, **shrimp**, mollusks, and **baitfish** that live in tide pools accessible. Bonefish are almost always in motion when feeding, swimming along a flat singly or in schools of up to hundreds of individuals. They root along the bottom, flush their prey from hiding, chase them down, then inhale and crush them with specialized granular plates between their tongues and upper jaws.

Bonefish have reflective scales that make them difficult to spot, even in clear, shallow water. Sunlight produces a shadow that is easier to spot than the fish, which sometimes helps; cloudy days make

spotting them almost impossible except to the most experienced guides and anglers. The best bonefish spotters don't look for the whole fish, but rather something moving that just doesn't look right. Often a fin or tail will be spotted long before the entire fish is seen. Another way to detect bonefish is to look for waking fish in shallow water. Bonefish make a hesitant, v-shaped wake and occasionally their dorsal fins or forked tails will also appear. A school of fish in deeper water might show

"nervous water," which is a shaky look on the surface made by many fish swimming together. Fly fishers may also spot tailing fish, where a bonefish in around 20 inches of water tips its body upward to root something off the bottom and the tail pokes through the surface. On a calm day, the silvery glint of their tails can be seen from 100 yards away. A school of bonefish in deep water will also make a "mud," when many fish root together in a silty bottom.

B

Bonefish can be pursued from a flats boat carefully poled through the shallows or on foot, wading those flats that have hard sand or coral bottoms. (Many flats, such as those in the **Florida** Keys or on the lee side of most **Bahamian** islands, have such deep silt beds that wading is impossible.) The best scenario is to have the bonefish moving toward the angler at a leisurely pace, because a bonefish is used to seeing its prey dart away from it, not toward it. Bonefish can be spooked by a single **false cast** overhead, so casting should be kept to a minimum and never over the top of a school. If many fish are in a school, always cast to the outside of the school, never inside it; even if only one fish is frightened, the entire school will bolt along with it.

For fish cruising the flats, the fly is cast far enough ahead of the bonefish's expected path to sink almost to the bottom, and as the fish approaches the fly it is given a series of short strips until the bonefish shows interest. When a bonefish seems to hover over the fly or tip down the fly is usually not moved, and then one long strip is given, which serves not only as a strike, but also if the bonefish has not eaten the fly the sudden dart won't spook the fish as a fly lifted from the water would. For a fish that has not taken, the long strip may also make the fish show renewed interest.

For tailing bonefish, the fly should be cast right next to the fish and allowed to sink. (Tailing fish won't notice a fly that is more than a few feet away.) Sometimes a bonefish will take a fly as it sinks, so if the fish suddenly moves in the direction of your fly it's best to make a long strip in case the fly was taken. If there is no initial take, the fly should be moved in short, sharp strips to catch a fish's attention. For mudding bonefish, a fly with a fast sink rate should be chosen, and the fly should be cast right into the middle of the mud. Fish in a mud are not as spooky and you can seldom spot individual fish. The fly should be allowed to sink, and then stripped quickly through the mud.

Tackle for bonefish can be anything from a 6-weight outfit for small fish, small flies, and light winds, to a 9-weight for bigger flies and windy days. Floating lines are all that is needed, as the sink rate of the presentation is determined by fly choice. One of the most important parts of bonefish tackle is a smooth, fast-retrieve fly reel that holds 200 yards of backing, as a large bonefish in shallow water can quickly strip well over a hundred yards of line on its first run. After the initial run, bonefish often change direction and run toward the angler, thus the need for a **large arbor fly reel** with its fast retrieve to keep the line under control.

Bonefish are found in tropical waters around the world, but fly fishing is limited to places where there are extensive saltwater flats and the fish feed in shallow water. The best places in the world are the Florida Keys, Bahamas, Puerto Rico, the Cayman Islands, Cuba, Honduras, Belize, Los Roques in Venezuela, Mexico's Yucatan Peninsula, Christmas Island in the South Pacific, the coast of Mozambique, and the Seychelles off the coast of Kenya.

BONEFISH FLY

Bonefish are not very discriminating in their selection of food, and will eat almost anything they can stir up while rooting along the bottom. Many of the foods they eat, such as snails, clams, oysters, and **worms**, are difficult to imitate

with a fly. Thus most bonefish flies are tied to imitate the bonefish foods that flee when disturbed: crabs, **shrimp**, and small **baitfish**. Many popular bonefish flies are impressionistic imitations that just suggest the movement of a shrimp or baitfish, such as the Crazy Charlie or Gotcha. Other flies, like the Bonefish Scampi, Flexo Crab, Mantis Shrimp, and Bonefish Minnow imitate specific prey.

Bonefish flies are tied in sizes 2 through 8, with 4 and 6 the most popular sizes. Bonefish will eat bigger and smaller creatures, but seem to readily eat these sizes, which are easy to imitate and easy to cast. In general, bigger bonefish seem to prefer the larger sizes, while small individuals in large schools are less likely to be spooked with a smaller fly. Fly size can also vary by location. Bonefish flies in the **Florida** Keys and the **Bahamas** are more often fished in sizes 2 and 4, yet the smaller fish of Mexico or Christmas Island prefer size 6 and even size 8 flies.

The most important aspect of a bonefish fly is its sink rate: The fly should sink quickly to the bottom, where bonefish do most of their feeding, but should not be so heavy as to cause a big splash in shallow water. Thus, bonefish flies for deep water are tied with solid metal eyes to sink them quickly; flies for knee-deep water are tied with hollow bead-chain eyes; and flies for shallow water have no eyes, or if eyes are desired they are made from lightweight plastic. Because bonefish feed close to the bottom, often in coral or grass beds, bonefish flies are either tied to ride point-up or incorporate a **weed guard**, as a fly that snags on the bottom will ruin a presentation.

Bonefish flies should also match the shade of the bottom, as bonefish prey are well camouflaged and a fleeing object that stands out too much from the bottom will make a bonefish suspicious. Over white sand bottoms, white, light tan or pink flies work best. On medium colored marl or coral bottoms, light browns, tans, and olives are favored. Over dark turtle grass, dark brown or olive flies will draw the most strikes.

BONITO

The most common species of bonito pursued with a fly rod are the Pacific bonito, *Sarda chiliensis*, and the Atlantic bonito, *Sarda sarda*. They are common in inshore water along both coasts, but in Gulf of Mexico waters the **little tunny** or **false albacore** (*Euthynnus alletteratus*) is also called a bonito. Both fish often occur together throughout their range, but the bonito has diagonal stripes along its dorsal side while the little tunny has wormlike markings. Bonito are small members of the **tuna** family and although often used as bait by offshore fishermen, they are a terrific fish on a **fly rod**.

Bonito feed by forcing **baitfish** to the surface and then slashing through the bait. They often leap clear of the water

B

when feeding but never leap after being hooked. They travel in small schools of a few to a dozen individuals, and the schools move quickly, so it's necessary to position a boat in the expected path of a feeding school and wait for the school to surface nearby. Shore anglers in the surf and along jetties can also catch bonito. Schools tend to run the same places along a jetty or channel, so shore fishing involves picking a spot where a school has been seen before and waiting for another pack of fish.

Bonito prefer small, slim flies from two to four inches long. An 8- or 9-weight rod provides the backbone to land these tough fighters, and gives the ability to make long casts to a cruising school quickly. Although bonito feed close to the surface, flies fished with **sinking lines** will draw far more strikes than **floating lines**. A smooth saltwater reel with 150 to 200 yards of backing is required as bonito make long, fast runs and can swim up to 30 miles per hour.

BROOK TROUT

The American brook trout, *Salvelinus fontinalis*, is technically not a trout at all but a **char**. Also known as the brook char or speckled trout, is more closely related to the **lake trout, Dolly Varden, arctic char,** and **bull trout** than it is to **brown, rainbow,** and **cutthroat trout.** Early European colonists, not known for their taxonomic precision, found it living in great numbers in rivers and lakes of northeastern North America, and because it looked and acted just like the European brown trout they named it accordingly. Char have finer scales than trout, and the scales in brook trout are so small that the skin appears smooth (scales are present, but micro-

scopic in size). Also unlike trout, char do not have teeth on the bone in the center of the upper jaw, called the vomer.

Brook trout are positively identified by the small red spots along their flanks, usually with a blue halo around them. Larger, more irregular spots along their flanks are off-white, yellow, or pale olive. Their backs are olive or bluish gray, with wormlike markings called vermiculations both across the back and on the dorsal fin. No other char has these vermiculations. Fins along the bottom of brook trout have stark white leading edges, followed by a black stripe with the rest of the fin orange or red.

Brook trout, like most salmonids, have been transported to **New Zealand**, **Argentina**, **Chile**, Europe, and mountainous regions of Africa like Kenya, as well as western North America. Their original range was from Hudson Bay south to **Georgia**, and west as far as the Great Lakes, although the populations south of **Pennsylvania** were and still are restricted to colder streams high in the Appalachians. Although all trout can exhibit stunted populations of many tiny individuals when food and living space is at a premium but reproduction is optimal, brook trout seem particularly successful in exploiting a resource in this manner. Thus, although brook trout of any size are prized in the wilds of **Maine** and the **Virginia** mountains,

an alpine lake in **Montana** overrun with six-inch brookies are more a source of frustration to fishermen than happy acceptance of this pretty little outsider. Luckily, brook trout are perhaps the finest eating fish found in fresh water, with the tiny ones being especially sweet and delicate.

Brook trout, like most salmonids, can form anadromous populations, using the ocean (or large bodies of fresh water like Lake Superior) to fatten, then returning to freshwater rivers to spawn. Sea-run brook trout are known as coasters or salters. Small populations of oceangoing brook trout remain on Cape Cod and Maine in the United States, and are relatively common in the Maritime Provinces of **Canada**. Coaster populations are also still found in Lake Superior.

Brook trout are sensitive indicators of environmental quality. They must have cold spring water percolating through clean, pea-sized gravel to spawn successfully. Among the trout and chars, they require the coldest water and will migrate when water temperatures rise above 68 degrees. If they are unable to migrate, water temperatures in the low 70s for extended periods can kill them. For that reason, brook trout today are restricted to spring-fed rivers in lowlands and cooler, shaded, high-altitude mountain rivers. They are better adapted than brown or rainbow trout to the acidic conditions found in high-altitude brooks, so they may actually have an edge in tiny headwater streams.

Brook trout spawn in the fall and young hatch in mid-winter. If adults live close to a source of spring water they may travel only a few yards to spawn, but if suitable spawning gravel and spring water are not close to their summer feeding spots they may travel many miles, usually upstream, to spawn. Brook trout do not live as long as most other salmonids and a 4-year-old fish is an old-timer. Because most of the places they inhabit are not rich in food, brook trout do not often reach a size much over a pound in weight, and in many tiny mountain streams the largest fish and oldest fish in the population might not exceed 6 inches.

However, in lakes and huge rivers where brook trout have an abundant supply of **baitfish** like smelt or large **mayflies** like the *Hexagenia*, they can grow as big as 8 pounds. The world record brook trout was caught in the Nipigon River in Ontario in 1915 on a **fly rod** (but with a live minnow as bait) and weighed 14 pounds 9 ounces.

Where they occur alongside other trout species, brook trout can be caught using the same techniques used to catch browns, rainbows, or cutthroats. Brook trout eat the same insects, baitfish, and crustaceans that other trout eat, but seem to be a little less picky about their diet. In other words, brookies are easier to catch than most other trout species. Having evolved in environments where food is scarce, brook trout will eat first and ask questions later, even when transplanted into richer waters where food is more abundant than in typical brook trout habitat. They are known to be fonder of bright-colored flies like the Royal Coachman or Parmachene Belle than browns or rainbows, but I suspect this idea comes more from fly fishers who frequent infertile wilderness rivers, where the fly that is the most visible will draw trout from a longer distance. However, they are not always pushovers. A brook trout feeding on mayflies on the surface of a calm lake or one taking **midges** from the surface film in a weedy spring creek can test all the skills an experienced fly fisher possesses. And a brook trout lying in a shallow pool in a mountain stream will be as aware of the motion of a predator along the banks as a deer in a cornfield. So approaching a brook trout without spooking it is more important than having the perfect fly pattern.

Brook trout are not spectacular fighters and seldom jump or make long runs. A hooked brook trout typically makes a couple of short runs and then thrashes and twists and turns right up to the

B

net. Although they are not known as leapers, in some rivers they jump when hooked. What they lack in fighting spirit is made up in beauty, however, as there is no freshwater fish more brilliant than a brook trout in fall spawning colors, with orange belly and fins on fire contrasted against the greens and blues of its upper body, punctuated by the bright red spots haloed in blue.

BROOKS, JOE (1900–1972)

Joe Brooks was one of the most popular and beloved fishing writers of the twentieth century. He was a pioneer of saltwater fly fishing in the 1940s in **Florida**, and also was more responsible than anyone for making the fabulous trout fishing of **Argentina** common knowledge. He was fishing editor of *Outdoor Life* magazine for many years, and also hosted the *American Sportsman* TV show in the 1960s, where he often appeared with Bing Crosby, Ted Williams, Curt Gowdy, and **Lee Wulff**. His most popular book, entitled simply *Trout Fishing* (1972), was the definitive reference book for an entire generation of fly fishers.

BROWN TROUT

Brown trout, *Salmo trutta*, are native to Europe and Central Asia, and native populations range from **Iceland** south to Portugal and east through Afghanistan. Many local races are found that differ in shape and color, from the snail eating Gillaroo of Scottish lochs to the marble trout of Slovenia to the Aral sea trout of Uzbekistan, but they are all the same species. British colonists transported fertilized brown trout eggs throughout the empire and beyond in the late nineteenth century, and today wild, reproducing populations can be found from Tierra del Fuego to British Columbia and from **New Zealand** to the mountains of Kenya.

Brown trout can live their entire lives in a small stream or pond, but if a stream has access to a large lake or the ocean, some members of a population

will head **downstream** for bigger water where they live and grow fat on the abundant food, then return to rivers in the fall to spawn. Brown trout that spend part of their life in the ocean are called **sea trout** and become silvery, looking very much like their relative the **Atlantic salmon**. Sea trout do not enter the open ocean like Atlantic salmon, but while in salt water typically stay in large bays and estuaries. Brown trout can be distinguished from Atlantic salmon by their thicker caudal peduncle (the area just in front of the tail), an eye that is forward of the jawbone, and two rows of teeth on the vomer instead of the one row in Atlantic salmon (the vomer is the central bone on the upper inside of a fish's mouth).

The coloration of stream-dwelling brown trout ranges from an overall buttery yellow to olive to brown. Spots are irregular and black, and there may be a few large dark spots or many fine spots. Most individuals have large black or red spots encircled by white along their sides, and many have a red tip on the adipose fin (the single small fin on the dorsal side just in front of that tail). The dorsal fin is usually spotted, and the ventral fins are yellow with white edges.

Brown trout spawn in the fall and young hatch in late winter. They grow slower than **rainbow trout**, but tend to live longer, up to 10 or 12 years. Brown trout seem to be more tolerant of pollution and high water temperatures than other species, and thus are often found well down into the lower reaches of large rivers, where they feed on the more abundant **baitfish** and **crayfish** populations found in the warmer waters. Brown trout can tolerate water temperatures in the low 70s (about 22°C) well, and can stand water temperatures close to 80 (27°C) for short periods if there are cold-water refuges nearby. But brown trout are not as acid-tolerant as **brook trout**, and in eastern rivers where browns and brookies exist together, fewer brown trout are found in the upper, more acidic headwaters of mountain rivers.

The one thing most anglers agree upon is that browns are the most difficult trout to catch, and appear to be more wary of an angler's approach, sloppy casts, and the wrong fly than any other trout. To most, there is no greater accomplishment than a large brown trout on a **dry fly**. In a stream that has equal numbers of brown trout and another species of trout, catch rates of browns will be far below that of rainbows, **cutthroats**, or brook trout. Large brown trout also become nocturnal, living in tangles of roots or undercut banks and prowling at night for crayfish, mice, and baitfish.

When brown trout were first introduced in the United States, anglers thought they were more likely to feed on the surface than the native brook trout, but in many rivers today brown trout are reluctant to rise to the surface unless a heavy **hatch** is in progress. Nineteenth-century anglers also vilified the brown trout because they

turn into cannibals after they reach about 14 inches, preferring to feed on minnows, other trout, and crayfish once they get large. No one today disputes that thought, and although large brown trout can be caught on a dry fly or **nymph**, the odds of a very large brown are in favor of the angler who sticks to **streamer flies**—especially one who fishes into the dark or before the morning sun touches the water.

When hooked, brown trout are determined fighters and no species of trout is more likely to head for a submerged log or rock than a panicked brown trout. Although large brown trout are not typically spectacular fighters, a 17-inch brown trout in good condition at the optimum water temperature of 58 to 65 degrees can make long runs and leaps that, although not as spirited as those of a rainbow, are nonetheless magnificent. And a 15-pound sea-run brown trout from Tierra del Fuego in **Argentina** will fight a battle as spectacular as an Atlantic salmon.

BUCKTAIL
See Streamer Fly.

BULL TROUT
The bull trout, *Salvelinus confluentus*, is a member of the **char** genus (closely related to **brook trout**, **lake trout**, **arctic char**, and **Dolly Varden**) and thus it has tiny, almost microscopic scales, and also

B

does not have teeth on the vomer, or the bone in the middle of the upper jaw. Bull trout are often confused with the more common Dolly Varden (until 1978 they were considered the same species), but bull trout have a broader head and a slightly longer lower jaw. Although both species occupy Pacific Coast rivers from **Alaska** south to **Oregon**, the bull trout range extends as far inland as Great Slave Lake.

Bull trout eat some insects when younger, but their diet quickly switches over to **whitefish**, trout, and salmon—as well as any other fish that gets in their way. Because of their diet, bull trout can grow as big as 30 pounds. Bull trout prefer slow, deep pools in large rivers. They need a constant supply of very cold, clean water and migrate long distances in the fall to spawn, so it's not surprising that bull trout habitat is declining. In fact, although bull trout take large streamers aggressively, their status is considered threatened and it is illegal to even target them with a fishing rod in most places. If a bull trout is accidentally hooked when fishing for other species, it should be carefully released as quickly as possible.

BUTT
See Leader, Fly Rod.

BUZZER
See Midge.

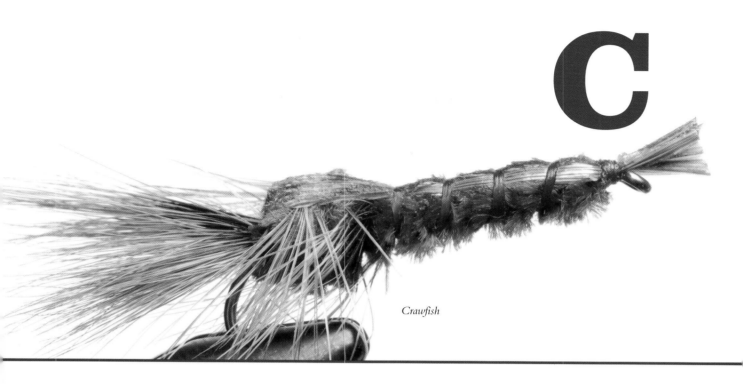

C

Crawfish

CADDISFLY

Caddisflies are some of the most important insects in trout streams around the world. At least one or two species will be found in any stream that holds trout, and some rivers may host dozens of different kinds. Caddisflies are members of the order Tricoptera, and have a complete metamorphosis, including a **larva**, **pupa**, and adult stage. The larva and pupa are aquatic stages and the adult is a winged **terrestrial**. Trout eat the larvae off the bottoms of streams and in drifting current, and are especially fond of pupae as they drift in the current and rise to the surface, as in this stage they are helpless and easy prey. One the pupa rises to the surface and hatches into a winged adult trout will eat them, but often adult caddisflies leave the water quickly or skitter across the surface, making them more difficult targets. After living for a few days as a winged adult, caddisflies return to the surface of a river or lake where they mate in midair, finally entering the water a final time where females lay their eggs and both sexes die. Trout are almost as

fond of this egg-laying stage as they are of the pupae.

The most familiar caddisfly larvae are the case-making variety. The larva constructs a case out of twigs or small pebbles, which acts as both protection and ballast. However, many species of caddisflies are free-living and without the typical cases. Free-living caddisfly larvae can be identified by their caterpillarlike shape but with three prominent legs at the thorax and a pair of tiny hooks at the end of the abdomen. Pupae have a distinctive curved shape with prominent wing cases along the sides and legs and antennae tucked along the curve of the body. Adults look similar to moths, especially in flight, but at rest their wings are held tentlike along the body. Caddisflies typically have tan or gray wings and tan, gray, black, or green bodies. Most are between size 14 and 18.

In most trout streams and lakes, caddisflies **hatch** between April and October, with the heaviest hatches in May, June, and July. At times, these insects will cover the surface of the water and the air above it, creating a feeding bonanza for the trout and other fish. It's not necessary to carry many different kinds of caddisfly imitation, but it is important to have imitations of the larva, pupa, and adult stages in size 14, 16, and 18 as trout can often key in on only the pupa or only the egg-laying adult. Popular imitations of the larva include the **Hare's Ear Nymph**, Czech Mate Nymph, and Oliver Edwards Hydrophyche Nymph. Pupae are best imitated by the LaFontaine Sparkle Pupa or Bead-Head Hare's Ear Nymph. Adults are best imitated with the Henryville Special or **Elk Wing Caddis**. Many times an emerging pupa will be the best fly of all, fished just under the surface, and some of the best flies for this stage are the CDC Emerging Caddis and the X-Caddis.

Caddis larvae and pupae are best imitated with a **dead drift** presentation, although during a hatch a slight twitch added to the drift, or a presentation that allows the nymph to swing to the surface will turn the trick. **Emergers** are best fished dead drift, the same as a **dry fly**. If adults are seen skittering across the surface with trout chasing them, a dry fly can be skated by raising the rod **tip** and stripping line while wiggling the rod tip from side to side.

CALIFORNIA

OVERVIEW

California offers a vast menu of fly fishing opportunities, from small wild trout streams high in the snow-capped Sierras to subtropical saltwater species like **barracuda** of the southern coast. With the largest population of fly fishers in the United States, California's fisheries have been more thoroughly explored than most. Although the **rainbow trout**, **steelhead**, **Pacific salmon**, and all the saltwater species along the coast are native to California, **striped bass**, **largemouth bass**, **smallmouth bass**, and **shad** were all introduced from the eastern U.S. around the turn of the twentieth century.

California offers a wide variety of fly fishing opportunities.

FISHERIES

Although remnant populations of steelhead can be found as far south as Los Angeles, the major steelhead rivers of California are all found north of San Francisco. The northernmost steelhead river in California, the Smith, is probably the most famous and productive river in the state. This massive and majestic near-wilderness river offers the chance at a giant record-breaking fish. It also tends to clear more quickly after rainstorms than other rivers, so it is in fishable condition at most times. The Klamath and its tributary the Trinity are also known worldwide for their steelhead and king salmon fishing. They don't host big fish like the Smith, but they are less crowded and offer more fish.

California offers a vast menu of fly fishing opportunities, and the largest population of fly fishers in the United States.

C

The Eel and Sacramento Rivers also have good runs of steelhead, as well as many of the smaller coastal rivers like Redwood Creek, Mad River, Noyo River, and Alder Creek. The lower reaches of most of the bigger steelhead rivers also have runs of American shad (especially in the Feather, American, and Yuba Rivers) and striped bass from the estuaries, as well as resident trout and smallmouth bass.

Although California does not have an extensive estuary system like the Northeast or prolific saltwater flats like the Gulf Coast, saltwater fly fishing is very popular in California, with good fishing and many species to target. Humboldt Bay in the north has estuary salmon and steelhead, as well as leopard **sharks** and surfperch. San Francisco Bay is one of the best striped bass fisheries on the West Coast. Beaches and estuaries in southern California give the fly fisher the opportunity to catch surfperch, calico bass, sand bass, barracuda, and challenging sight-fishing opportunities for corbina. Less than 10 miles offshore, especially in the San Diego area, mako sharks, **tunas**, yellowtail, and **dolphin** are pursued with **fly rods**.

Southern California is fast becoming one of the best places in the world to catch giant largemouth bass, and unlike many places, fly rods are often used to pursue them. Lakes such as Casitas, Castaic, and Cahuma near Ventura have become famous for their **Florida** strain largemouth bass. However, there are largemouth bass in lakes throughout California, and the giant Florida strain has also been introduced in Clear Lake in the northern part of the state.

Despite the scarcity of water in parts of California, the state is blessed with many excellent trout streams. In the Sierras, high above any dams that collect water for the cities and agricultural areas, small mountain streams fed by snowmelt abound. Here the backpacking angler may find the rare **golden trout**, the state fish of California. These fish are making a comeback in the Golden Trout Wilderness Area in the southern Sierras, thanks to work by the U.S. Forest Service, **Trout Unlimited**, and **California Trout** (CAL Trout). Closer to roads, rainbow trout or rainbows that have hybridized with the goldens are more abundant, as well as introduced brown and brook trout.

North-central California has the highest concentration of quality trout rivers. Here you'll find the spring-fed Upper Sacramento River, and the lower Sacramento below Lake Shasta, a giant **tailwater** that produces the largest stream trout in the state. The Fall River, although mostly on private land, is a large spring creek best fished by boat and famous for its **dry fly** fishing. Hat Creek is another stream with abundant flat water and challenging trout, but it is easily waded and has far more public access. The McCloud River is more of a wilderness stream dashing through a lush canyon, with hard-fighting wild rainbows. The Pit River is another tumbling river known for its abundant trout population, difficult wading, and trout that prefer **nymphs** fished deep.

The other main trout-fishing area in California is the eastern slope of the Sierras. Rivers like the Truckee, Carson, Owens, and Hot Creek are waters of a different character, more high desert than temperate rain forest in character, with rich soils that encourage aquatic insect growth (and thus great trout fishing) but also the occasional high winds common in this landscape.

SEASONS

Steelhead season in California runs from September through April. Whether fish will be in any given river depends on rainfall amounts. Rain brings fish into rivers from the ocean but also makes them too high and dirty to fish for days to weeks after, so catching steelhead when they are moving through a river when it is clear enough to fish with a fly is always planning combined with luck. Typically, smaller "half-pounder" fish (smaller steelhead that actually average several pounds) come into rivers early in the season and the bigger mature fish of over 10 pounds follow later in the season.

Trout fishing is open in some California Rivers year-round, but the best fishing is in spring and fall, when rivers warm up enough to encourage trout feeding and insect activity but are not too hot to depress feeding. In the heat of summer, it's best to either fish the small streams of the Sierras or spring-fed rivers like Fall River.

Shad season is May 15 through the end of July, when adult fish ascend rivers from the ocean. Striped bass fishing is best in June and then again in

fall, when larger fish are entering rivers and estuaries and feeding actively. However, where striped bass are found, small resident fish can be caught on a fly year-round. Largemouth bass can also be caught on a fly year-round in California, but the best fly fishing is in March through June, when the big fish come into the shallows to spawn and can be caught by sight-fishing in the thin water.

CALIFORNIA TROUT

California Trout, or CAL Trout, is an organization of both professional conservation workers and grass-roots members dedicated to protecting and restoring wild trout and **steelhead** waters throughout California. It was formed in 1970 as a splinter organization of **Trout Unlimited** when many members of Trout Unlimited in California did not agree with the policies of the national organization. Today, both organizations often work together.

Typical projects undertaken by CAL Trout include making sure that dam re-licensing is done with mitigation for migratory fish (or perhaps removed entirely), stopping the spread of invasive organisms in trout rivers, working to maintain minimum summer flows in rivers to protect aquatic insects and spawning trout, and helping to maintain the threatened **golden trout** in the High Sierras.

CANADA

OVERVIEW

With a vast land mass, sparse population, and extensive coastline on both the Atlantic and Pacific oceans, Canada offers a myriad of fly fishing opportunities. Many North American traditions in both **steelhead** fishing and **Atlantic salmon** fishing were established in Canada, and eastern Canada has long been the place to go for the world's largest **brook trout**. More recent developments include the pursuit of large northern **pike** on a **fly rod**, as well as the Great Lakes fishery for introduced **Pacific salmon** and steelhead.

Atlantic Salmon

FISHERIES

Eastern Canada offers some of the best Atlantic salmon fishing in the world, and many of the famous rivers in Nova Scotia, Newfoundland, Labrador, New Brunswick, and Quebec can be fished on a relatively modest budget, without having to stay in an expensive lodge. Most of the rivers in Nova Scotia and Newfoundland are shorter "spate" rivers, which fill with salmon on high water and then quickly drop to low water conditions where salmon are difficult to catch. A fishing trip timed with a period of moderate water levels can be quite productive. Notable salmon rivers in Nova Scotia include Cape Breton's Margaree and Cheticamp, and productive and famous rivers in the lower peninsula include the St. Mary's and LeHarve. Newfoundland hosts over 200 mostly small salmon rivers but has over 60 percent of the salmon rivers in North America. New Brunswick has perhaps the most famous salmon river in North America, the Miramichi, and its reputation is justified: Half of the rod-caught Atlantic salmon in North America are hooked in this massive river. The Gaspe Peninsula of Quebec and Labrador contains the Cascapedia, known for its extremely large salmon, as well as many other productive Atlantic salmon rivers like the Moise, York, Gander, Eagle, and Matapedia.

British Columbia is known for some of the largest steelhead in the world, and these fish can sometimes be taken on a **dry fly**. Fish from the Dean River and its tributary the Thompson are thought to be the strongest in the world. The other legendary British Columbia river is the Skeena, with its equally famous tributaries the Kispiox, Bulkley, and Babine. Many of the steelhead rivers in British Columbia are remote and can be accessed only by a long drive down gravel roads or by fly-in trips from a lodge. Besides the chance of a 30-pound fish, much of the appeal of British Columbia steelhead fishing is because the rivers are untainted by dams or hatchery fish.

Steelhead can now also be found in eastern Canada as well. Hatchery transplants of steelhead as well as chinook and coho salmon to the Great Lakes has transformed rivers that were once home to **smallmouth** bass and pike into premier salmonid fisheries. Rivers worth noting are the Nipigon, Cypress, Nottawasaga, Maitland, Credit, and Ganaraska, all in Ontario.

Not all of the great fly fishing in Canada is for its migratory salmon and steelhead. Kamloops, a race of lake-dwelling rainbow trout, thrives in thousands of fertile lakes in British Columbia's interior. The Elk River in British Columbia is known for its very productive **cutthroat trout** fishery. Alberta's Bow, Crowsnest, and Oldman rivers are known throughout the world for their fine insect **hatches** and productive fly fishing. Ontario's Grand River is a **tailwater** that rivals many of the famous trout streams south of the United States border.

Eastern and central Canada have thousands of rivers with brook trout in them, but most of these

Atlantic salmon fishing on the Miramichi River in New Brunswick

fish are small, averaging less than a pound. However, certain wilderness rivers produce brook trout that average over four pounds—and often much larger. Areas like the Minipi River, Eagle River, and Lake Mistassini regions of Quebec and Labrador, as well as the God's River watershed in Manitoba have a long history of giving up trophy brook trout, and many fine lodges and fly-in operations to access these fisheries. Most salmon rivers of eastern Canada also hold populations of sea-run brook trout.

Great fly rod fishing for northern pike can be found throughout Canada, from above the Arctic Circle to the United States border, but the biggest fish are found in the central provinces, where food is more abundant and growing seasons are longer. Island Lake, Little Churchill Lake, and Reindeer Lake in Manitoba are famous for their large pike in shallow water. Lake Athabasca in Saskatchewan and Great Slave Lake in the Northwest Territories are also noted for very large pike that can be taken on a fly rod.

SEASON

Given its northern latitudes, most of Canada's best fishing is in the summer months, particularly for nonmigratory trout in the interior of the country. Atlantic salmon season begins with ice-out in early spring for "black" salmon, or those fish that remained in rivers over the winter and are returning to salt water. The season for fresh-run Atlantic salmon varies river by river, but the best fishing is from June through September, although midsummer fishing can be difficult during periods of drought. British Columbia steelhead are found in rivers throughout the year, but the best fishing for fresh, aggressive fish is from July through September. Fishing for steelhead in the Great Lakes streams runs later, from September throughout the winter and into May. Pike season in Canada runs from May through September, but the best chance of catching a large pike in shallow water is in June.

CANOE

Canoes are traditional fly fishing craft, particularly in eastern **Canada** and the United States. They are quiet, have a shallow draft, and modern canoes made with composites can easily be portaged several miles without requiring muscles of iron. Although the popularity of canoes for fly fishing has been overshadowed by increased interest in **belly boats**, **kayaks**, and **drift boats**, in some conditions a canoe is still the best craft. For long-distance hauling of camping gear and large amounts of fishing gear, nothing beats a canoe. Canoes are faster and more maneuverable than belly boats and pontoon boats, particularly in the wind. And when chasing cruising fish in a large lake, a tandem canoe, with one angler paddling and the other casting, is a most efficient and deadly method.

CARP

Carp, *Cyprinus carpio*, are large members of the minnow family that were introduced into Europe and the United States in the late nineteenth century as a food fish. Popular with anglers in Europe, they were originally maligned as alien invaders by sport fishermen in the United States (because they are not particularly attractive fish and they can muddy clear waters with their constant rooting on the bottom). However, fly fishers have found them superb gamefish, particularly in shallow water. Carp are spooky, selective, and very strong fighters— exactly the same qualities found in **bonefish**, **permit**, and **brown trout**. Yet carp are found almost anywhere, except in the coldest streams and

lakes. They can thrive in muddy lakes with low oxygen content as well as in pristine trout streams, so the chances of being able to pursue a large, hard-fighting game fish with a **fly rod** a few miles from home is within the reach of most fly fishers.

Carp will eat almost anything, from cottonwood tufts and berries falling into the water to **mayflies hatching** in a river (where they can be caught on **dry flies**), but their most common prey is aquatic insects and crustaceans. They prefer to feed in shallow water, in mud or sand flats along weed beds, in shallow covers, and in the tails of large pools in rivers. They cruise along the bottom slowly, watching for prey that might flush out in front of them, or for puffs of silt as a **crayfish** or large aquatic insect bolts for cover. Pods of carp can often be found by looking for clouds of mud or silt that are stirred up as they are feeding, or by looking for their fins breaking the surface as they prowl the shallows. On sunny days they can be sight-fished at midday, like bonefish on the flats, in clear lakes and rivers.

Carp should be approached with caution. Splashes or wakes made by a boat or wading angler can spook them, and once a carp is spooked it gives off a chemical fright signature that will be sensed by other carp in the area. Polarized **sunglasses** and a long-brimmed **hat**, plus drab clothing are impor-

tant for sighting and approaching carp. An accurate cast must be made, so try to approach a cruising or feeding carp within 30 or 40 feet before making a cast. The fly should be presented slightly beyond and off to the side of a carp, but it should be within a foot of the fish. Carp often take a fly as it sinks, but if not, let the fly sink to the bottom and make a single short strip, preferably so it makes a slight puff of silt that attracts the fish. If the carp moves toward the fly, wait until it stops moving and then make another short strip—if the carp has taken the fly it will be hooked; if not the small movement of the fly may convince the fish to inhale your fly.

Floating lines are best for carp fishing, and unless the fish are feeding on berries, aquatic insects, or other floating food the fly should sink relatively quickly but without a large splash that may frighten a wary carp. Flies that ride inverted, like Crazy Charlie bonefish flies with metal eyes, are preferred by some anglers because they can be drawn along the bottom without hanging up. Large **nymphs** such as a weighted **Hare's Ear Nymph** in size 10 or 12 are also popular, as are crayfish and leech imitations like the **Woolly Bugger**.

Stout tackle is important for carp fishing, as they are dogged fighters that will strain most trout rods. Fish over 20 pounds are not uncommon. An outfit suited for light saltwater fishing, such as an 8- or 9-weight rod plus a reel with a strong drag and with at least 100 yards of **backing** capacity is need for all but the smallest carp. **Leaders** should be about 12-pound-test, which is strong enough to land most carp but light enough to present the fly in a natural manner.

CATSKILL FLY FISHING CENTER AND MUSEUM

It is fitting that the "Birthplace of American Fly Fishing" has a museum in its midst, the Catskills Fly Fishing Center and Museum in Livingston Manor, **New York**. The CFFCM has a threefold goal: to conserve and display angling artifacts, to teach fly fishing to the next generation, and to protect the lakes and streams which are home to myriad fish species. The Catskill Fly Fishing Center and Museum was organized in 1978, with Elsie Darbee as its first president. In 1982 the center bought a 35-acre site along the banks of the Willowemoc Creek. The next year it opened a storefront museum on the main street of Roscoe ("Trout Town, USA") to exhibit its collection of angling material; a new museum opened in 1995. In 1998, the center increased its size to 53 acres, along a mile of accessible, prime trout water.

CENTRAL AMERICA

OVERVIEW

Fly fishing in Central America is centered on areas that combine good fishing with an infrastructure that provides lodging, food, boats, and guides. Much of the coast is inaccessible; while it probably offers good fishing for various saltwater species, much of this coastline has not been explored by fly fishers. Central America is an attractive destination for fly fishers because it offers year-round fishing, especially in the December through February period when the **Bahamas** and **Florida** experience cold fronts that send the fish off the flats and into deep water. In addition, Panama and Costa Rica are below the normal hurricane belt so fishing from June through October is a safer bet than more northern tropical fisheries. The Caribbean side of Central America is where the shallow water flats fishing for **bonefish**, **permit**, and **tarpon** are found, while on the Pacific side it is mainly deep water fishing for **sailfish**, **marlin**, roosterfish, and other offshore species.

FISHERIES

With more extensive flats and offshore islands than other Central American countries, Belize offers a greater opportunity for fly fishing than most. The two most popular areas are Ambergris Cay and Turneffe Islands. Ambergris offers more amenities and the flats fishing there is mainly boat fishing, and while Turneffe Islands have extensive wading flats, there are few amenities other than fishing or diving. Bonefish are smaller in Belize (and in the rest of Central America) than in most other popular destinations. They average two pounds, but what they lack in size they make up in numbers and it is common to see schools of hundreds of bonefish at one time. The fish are also easier to catch than in most parts of the world. Fish over 6 pounds are not common, and bonefish over 10 pounds are very rare.

It is permit fishing that is one of the primary draws of Belize to the fly fisher, as this is probably

Casting to a bonefish, Mangrove Cay, Bahamas.

sport fishery for offshore species, although compared to other parts of the world the fishing pressure is very light. The current off the coast of Guatemala brings a great variety of gamefish and **baitfish** close to shore, thus **sailfish**, dolphin, **tuna**, and various species of marlin can be taken quite close to the shore. Although the Pacific coast drops off quickly with little opportunity for flats fishing, there are roosterfish and jack crevalle within casting distance of shore.

Honduras has few commercial operations but good potential for fly fishing for the adventurous traveler. The best flats fishing is in the Bay Islands, on the central Caribbean coast. Here the fishing is similar to Belize, with good wading flats for bonefish, permit, and some resident tarpon, particularly in deep channels and around docks and pilings near villages. Offshore, a fly fisher can chase **wahoo**, **dolphin**, tuna, king **mackerel**, and sailfish.

Costa Rica is famous for its giant tarpon. Much of this fishing is different from that you'd find in Belize or in the **Florida** Keys, as the tarpon are found in large river mouths (that are almost always muddy) or offshore in clear water where they can be spotted rolling. Tarpon here are large, with an average size of around 80 pounds and it is not uncommon to hook tarpon of 120 to 160 pounds. Anglers going to Costa Rica should be prepared with fast-sinking lines or shooting heads and flies with heavy metal eyes, which are needed to get down into the fast current of the river mouths. The tarpon fishing here is not difficult, but does not often have the visual thrills of sight-casting for tarpon on clear shallow flats. Like Guatemala, Costa Rica's Pacific coast is a productive fishery for sailfish, marlin, dolphin, and roosterfish, and these species are taken regularly on the **fly rod**.

Panama's saltwater fishery is mainly for offshore species because it has no extensive inshore flats. Sailfish, marlin, dolphin, yellowfin tuna, roosterfish, and wahoo can also be taken on a fly rod. And although few travelers go to Panama for freshwater fishing, it offers many opportunities for catching

the best place in the world to catch one on a fly in shallow water. Tarpon are also common in Belize, with resident fish of 10 to 30 pounds all year long, plus migratory giants that run between 100 and 200 pounds from May through October. Given the large numbers of permit, Belize is the best place in the world for the opportunity of a Grand Slam (a permit, bonefish, and tarpon in the same day) because the permit is always the toughest piece of the puzzle.

Most of Guatemala's shoreline is on the Pacific Coast, and this country has established a thriving peacock bass, jaguar guapote, and many other tropical freshwater fish that have been introduced in Panama, particularly Gatun Lake.

SEASON

All Central American counties have a year-round fishing season. The rainy season is July through November, but in Belize, especially in the Turneffe Islands region, the rain typically hovers over the mainland so the rainy season does not hinder fishing. March is the windiest month but also offers the best chance of a cloud-free sky, which helps in sight fishing. Because permit are less spooky and easier to catch with a **riffled** surface, March is the best time of year to catch one. Best months for large migratory tarpon in Belize are May through October, and the giant tarpon fishing in Costa Rica is best from July through November. August and September are the most likely times to be caught in a hurricane in this part of the world, but only Belize and northern Honduras are in the hurricane belt.

CHAR

See Artic Char, Brook Trout, Lake Trout, and Bull Trout.

CHEST PACK

Chest packs are minimalist alternatives to fishing **vests** or jackets. They are typically made from lightweight, quick-drying synthetic materials combined with **nylon** straps. Chest packs can be as simple as two or three pockets or they can be made into modular systems, with almost as many pockets as a vest. Their main benefit is reduced fabric around the shoulders and back, so they are lighter and cooler than a conventional fishing vest. Chest packs are most often used by fly fishers who hike a long way into spots; **bass** anglers who walk the shores of small ponds; or saltwater anglers who want to keep cool and don't need to carry a lot of gear.

CHILE

OVERVIEW

Most Chilean fly fishing, especially for the traveling angler, is fishing for trout in Patagonian rivers and lakes. Chilean fly fishing is some of the best in the world, although not as well known as the fishing in nearby **Argentina**. Part of the reason is that, when Argentine fly fishing was being developed in the late twentieth century, Chile's government and economy were not as stable as Argentina. With a strong economy and democratic government, Chile has become much more inviting to the visiting angler.

Chile is a long, narrow maritime country, and its southern half is rugged wilderness with the Andes descending quickly to the Pacific ocean. No salmonids are native to Chile, but Europeans brought **rainbow trout**, **brown trout**, and **brook trout** in the early twentieth century and lately extensive salmon farming in Chile's vast fjords has introduced escapee silver, king, and **Atlantic salmon** that provide an additional anadromous fishery that is welcomed by some and reviled by trout purists.

Like Argentina, most of Chile's fly fishing is centered around places with airports, and the main airport and center of angling in Chile is the small city of Puerto Montt. With a fine airport, anglers can head north to the Lake District of Chile and Argentina, or south to the more remote lodges in Chaiten and Coyhaique. Some fishing is available for the driving do-it-yourself angler, particularly in the Vicente Varas National Park near Puerto Varas, but most visiting anglers

Spectacular Andean scenery is home to big brown and rainbow trout.

C

fish this area with local lodges, or in one case a luxury yacht that travels the coastline and takes guests inland to remote rivers by helicopter.

FISHERIES

The most accessible fishing in Chile is in the Puerto Varas area, about an hour north of Puerto Montt. Rivers here include the Petrohue, Puelo, and Maullin, as well as many other smaller streams and tributaries. The Petrohue especially is known for its large brown and rainbow trout, plus the potential of large sea-run brown trout later in the season, all in spectacular Andean scenery in the shadow of the spectacular snow-capped Osorno volcano.

Further south, near the town of Chaiten and close to the Argentine border are rivers such as the Yelcho and Futaleufu, large rivers known for their large stream trout as well as king salmon up to 40 pounds and the occasional steelhead or silver salmon. Lago Yelcho also produces very large trout for the stillwater angler. Chaiten can be reached by car and boat from Esquel in Argentine Patagonia or by a short commuter flight from Puerto Montt.

The southernmost area of developed fishing is the Coyhaique region, which can be reached via a commuter flight to Balmaceda airport and then about a two-hour drive. This area offers big rivers like the Rio Baker and Rio Cochrane, as well as the Rio Nireguao—the only catch-and-release river in Chile.

All of the areas in Chile offer fly fishing in big lakes and also in small ponds called lagunas, which are often lined with thick reeds along their banks and are typically shallow so sight fishing to cruising fish or **dry fly** fishing are very effective. These lagunas often grow very fat trout that will leap with abandon onto dry **damselfly** imitations and can be fished almost like one would fish for **large-mouth bass**.

Most Chilean fishing is done with large dry flies, **streamers**, and **nymphs**. The rivers have abundant **grasshopper** populations in February and March, and also see mating flights of damselflies and large

C

indigenous **beetles**, so large hairwing dries like the Stimulator or foam dries like Chernobyl Ants are very popular. **Stoneflies** are common as well as the pancora, a small freshwater crab that big trout love, thus large nymphs and streamers like the Olive **Woolly Bugger** and its many variations are widely used. Small hatch-matching dries and nymphs will also produce earlier in the season, when **mayfly** and **caddisfly hatches** are heavy.

SEASON

Although the trout fishing in Chile opens in mid-October, this early season can be very cold and rainy. By December, most spring runoff has tapered and during December and January the aquatic insect hatches are in full swing. In February and March, there will still be insects hatching, but the better fishing can be had with large attractor dry flies that imitate hoppers and beetles and big horseflies. April brings the onset of colder weather, but also the opportunity for big spawning brown trout from the lakes or even sea-run browns from the Pacific.

CHIRONOMID
See Midge.

CLASS TIPPET

When fishing for record catches, the class tippet is the weakest link between the angler and the fly. According to **International Game Fishing Association** (IGFA) rules, the class **tippet** must be at least 15 inches long between the knots at either end. Records are awarded for 2, 4, 6, 8, 12, 16, and 20-pound class tippets in the fly-fishing category. The IGFA tests all lines submitted for world records, and because the records are actually classified in metric equivalents, a fish submitted for the 8-pound class record can actually be caught on a line that tests up to 8.81 pounds because it is a 4 kg class.

Because only the unknotted section of the class tippet is measured, it's important that the knots connecting the class tippet to the **leader** be as strong as possible. All knots are a fraction weaker than an unbroken strand, and the greater the difference in diameter between two lines, the weaker the knot. Thus when an 8-pound class tippet is attached to a 60-pound **shock tippet**, a **Bimini twist** is used to double the class tippet so the knot is more secure. A Bimini twist is also used at the other end of the class tippet, where it is attached to the **butt** section of the leader, for the same reason. Thus the 15 inches in a class tippet is usually the measurement between the Bimini twist knots at both ends.

CLINCH KNOT

The Clinch Knot is the most common knot used to attach the **tippet** to the fly. It is best when the diameter of the wire used for the eye of a **hook** is no more than twice the diameter of the tippet. If there is a large difference between the two, some type of **loop knot** is stronger and more practical. The Clinch Knot is rated at 90 to 98 percent of the line's strength when knotted, depending on how well the knot is tied.

- Pass the tag end of the tippet through the eye of the fly (figure 1).

1)

- Wrap the tag end around the standing part of the tippet, away from the fly, in five close turns (figure 2).

2)

■ Pass the tag end back through the loop formed in front of the eye. Tighten the knot by pulling on the standing part of the tippet and the fly—never pull on the tag end (figure 3).

3)

The Improved Clinch Knot is a version where the tag end is then passed through the loop in front of the eye and then also through the loop just made along the standing part of the tippet. It is more difficult to tie and tests have shown that it is no stronger than a properly tied standard clinch knot. One variation on the Clinch Knot that is very reliable, especially when a light tippet is tied to a heavy wire hook, is the **Trilene Knot**.

CLOUSER MINNOW

The Clouser Minnow is the most popular fly used in saltwater fly fishing. Developed originally by Pennsylvanian Bob Clouser as a fly for **smallmouth bass**, its utility as a **baitfish** imitation has far surpassed the original purpose and it is used around the world for everything from **bonefish** to **tarpon** to **carp** to **tuna**. In smaller sizes (size 4 and smaller), it is also a deadly fly for large trout.

The Clouser Minnow is a simple and durable fly—basically three bunches of **bucktail** or synthetic hair and a pair of metal dumbbell eyes tied to a hook. Sometimes a few strands of tinsel are used to add flash. Typically the fly is two-toned, with a darker color over a lighter color. The metal eyes are lashed to the **hook** so that the fly rides with the hook point upright, which means it is less likely to snag on the bottom. Popular colors are olive-and-white, brown-and-white, yellow-and-white, all-chartreuse, and all-black, however nearly every color of the rainbow has been used. Most common sizes are from size 2/0 down to size 8 for trout and bonefish.

The fly is fished by stripping line and then pausing slightly, so the heavy metal eyes make the fly dart up and down as it is fished, similar to the action of a jig used in spin fishing. Because of the heavy eyes, the fly can be fished quite deep without resorting to a **sinking fly line**.

C

COLORADO

OVERVIEW

Although Colorado has excellent **pike** and **bass** fishing in high plains lakes and reservoirs, plus **panfish** and **carp** in warmer waters, fly fishing in Colorado is almost entirely trout-oriented. Colorado offers some of North America's best and most famous trout waters, and there are many public easements on Colorado rivers and lakes. This is fortunate because in Colorado the landowner owns the bottom of the river, unlike many other states, where you can wade through private land in the stream or up to the high water mark. Thus, the angler fishing without a guide has to be careful—just because your feet are wet does not mean you can enter private land.

Most of Colorado's better trout streams are **tailwaters**, with uniform flows regulated below water supply reservoirs. Because of the uniform temperatures and flows, fishing can be excellent on Colorado trout streams even in the dead of winter, and some anglers combine ski trips with fishing trips. Tailwaters also encourage the growth of **caddisflies** and **midges**; in fact the primary source of food in many rivers in the state is midge **larvae** and **pupae**. As a result, Colorado leads the world in the design of tiny flies and the methods used to fish them. Although there are times (especially during **grasshopper** season, during **stonefly hatches**, or on ponds when **damselflies** hatch) when big flies are effective. But day in and day out, fly fishers in Colorado count on tiny dries and especially nymphs in sizes 18 through 26 for consistent success.

FISHERIES

All of Colorado's better trout streams are in the western part of the state, west of Interstate 25. Here, springs and snowmelt from both sides of the continental divide flow cold and relatively pristine to the lowlands below. In the far north, the two most notable trout streams are the North Platte, which flows north into **Wyoming**, and the Cache la Poudre, which flows east into the Platte. The North Platte is mostly slower meadow water flowing through dry grassland, and the Cache la

Fly fishing in Colorado is almost entirely trout-oriented.

Fishing a nymph on Colorado's Arkansas River

Poudre is one of the few undammed trout streams left in Colorado.

Close to Aspen are two of the best streams in Colorado, the Frying Pan and the Roaring Fork. The Frying Pan is an intimate little tailwater that grows huge **brown** and **rainbow trout**. The Roaring Fork is a larger river that is better fished by floating, and although not as well known as some of Colorado's other trout streams, it is very productive, especially with **nymphs**. It also has an excellent population of scrappy **whitefish**, and some of them grow quite large. In the Steamboat Springs area is another wonderful trout stream, the Yampa, known for its large trout and great **dry fly** fishing. Unfortunately, there are just a few small stretches of public water on this river.

The mighty Colorado River flows through a patchwork of public and private land. The river above Kremmling is best fished by wading, and its excellent tributaries the Blue River and Williams Fork are both worth exploring. Below Kremmling, the river is best fished from a raft or **drift boat**, and good trout water extends to well below Glenwood Springs. Unlike most Colorado Rivers, this river fishes well with bigger dries, **streamers**, and nymphs. Flowing in the opposite direction, toward the Mississippi drainage, the Arkansas River is a wonderful brown trout river with a very dense population of mostly smaller brown trout. Further south, the Dolores River gives fly fishers a taste of selective tailwater fish with tiny flies and light **tippets**, while its major tributary, the San Miguel offers 50 miles of trout fishing over less selective fish in a beautiful and unspoiled canyon setting.

The two southernmost trout streams of note are the Rio Grande and the Animas. The Rio Grande is less technical than most other Colorado Rivers, and its brook, brown, rainbow, and **cutthroat trout** rise well to big dry flies. The Animas is a large, meandering river that flows south through Durango and into **New Mexico**. Because of its lower elevation and southern location, it often fishes well during the winter.

A little over an hour from Denver, the famous South Platte is a heavily fished but very productive river. Water types range from intimate meadow water in the South Park area to canyon water with giant boulders and spectacular scenery in the Cheeseman Canyon stretch to classic riffle-and-pool water below the canyon. Regardless of the water type, though, on the South Platte tiny flies and light tippets will be needed most days, and the fish here, although large, are never easy, as Denver has one of the largest populations of fly fishers in the country.

Not all fly fishing in Colorado is on famous waters. Many of the smaller lakes, mountain streams, and beaver ponds of Rocky Mountain National Park have excellent fly fishing for smaller trout in pristine and isolated settings. Although these tiny waters have introduced brook, brown, and rainbow trout, the real thrill here is to catch wild cutthroat trout, Colorado's only native species.

SEASON

Early spring on Colorado's trout streams means low, clear water and hatches of small **mayflies** and midges. Once runoff starts in May, many rivers will be in full flood, muddy and unfishable (and often crowded with whitewater rafters). Runoff usually clears by mid-June, when insect activity really picks up with warming water temperatures and lower flows. July, August, and September are the prime fishing months on Colorado Rivers, especially September, when cooler temperatures make fishing during the day more pleasant. Most of Colorado's rivers fish well into the fall, and some even offer great fly fishing with nymphs and midge imitations in the dead of winter, especially the Frying Pan, Roaring Fork, Colorado, Yampa, Animas, and South Platte Rivers.

COMPARADUN FLY

The Comparadun is a popular style of **dry fly** tied without **hackle**. Developed by Al Caucci and Bob Nastasi in the 1970s, it is based on an older Adirondack pattern called the Haystack, originated by Francis Betters. Comparaduns can be tied to imitate any species of **mayfly dun** by merely varying the color and size of the fly.

Comparaduns are durable and are highly visible on the water, and they provide a very realistic mayfly profile to the trout. Effective in both fast and slow water, they are one of the best **hatch**-matching flies ever developed. They are also quite easy to tie and require just a half-dozen hackle fibers, a pinch of fur, and a tuft of hair from the leg or face of a deer. The **Sparkle Dun**, created by Craig Matthews of **Montana**, is a similar fly that utilizes a small amount of sparkle yarn at the tail to imitate the **emerging** shuck of a mayfly in the process of hatching.

CONEHEAD FLY

Conehead flies are **streamer** flies made with a metal cone that is threaded onto the **hook** before the fly is tied. Cones add weight and sparkle to a fly and also make it very durable. Cones are most often machined from brass or cast from tungsten (which adds about twice as much weight as brass) and are commonly brass, copper, silver, or black depending

upon the color impression a fly dresser wants to make.

Conehead flies are best for fishing deep, fast current because they sink the fly so quickly. Conehead flies used in calm or shallow water may spook more fish than they attract, so a more subtle streamer pattern should be used. Conehead variations of the **Muddler Minnow**, **Woolly Bugger**, and Zonker streamers are the most common types used.

COTTON, CHARLES (1630–1687)

Charles Cotton met **Isaak Walton** in 1655 and added 12 chapters to *The Compleat Angler* entitled "Instructions how to angle for trout or **grayling** in a clear stream." Written with the Derbyshire streams he was familiar with in mind, although the chapters deal with fly fishing, they also teach an angler how to fish with bait. Cotton devoted a whole chapter to a list of flies that could be used all months of the year, and even described a natural **stonefly** in great detail. He was the originator of the famous (and still valid) advice to "fish fine and far off."

CRAB FLIES

Gamefish love crustaceans because they are full of fat and protein, and crabs are seldom passed up by a gamefish, even when it is not actively feeding. Fish prey on crabs on the bottom of sand and mud flats, drifting in tidal currents, and even just under

the surface when crabs are molting or frightened off the bottom.

Although crab flies can be fished blind over wrecks in deep water or in tidal currents, most often they are cast to fish that are seen in the water, like **bonefish**, **permit**, **redfish**, or **striped bass** on shallow flats. The fly is cast relatively close to the fish and allowed to sink. A sinking crab fly looks like a real crab darting to the bottom for cover and most fish will take the fly as it sinks. If a fish does not take the fly after it sinks, it should be twitched once or twice along the bottom to interest the fish.

The best crab flies are Del's Merkin, Chernobyl Crab, Flexo Crab, and the Epoxy Crab. These flies are bulky and not easy to cast, thus a 9- or 10-weight rod with at least a 12-pound **tippet** should be used. Most of the crab fly patterns used today are between the diameter of a nickel and the diameter of a half-dollar in size, with the smaller sizes used for bonefish and the larger ones for permit, striped bass, and redfish.

CRANEFLY

Craneflies are aquatic insects in the order *Tipulidae*. They are found in trout streams and lakes around the world, and are most common in streams with silt or mud bottoms. The legless **larvae** look like drab-colored grubs and burrow in moist sand just along the edges of streams and lakes. When high water increases a river's velocity, the larvae

are often washed into the current and are eaten eagerly by trout and **smallmouth bass**. Good imitations for the larva include a large **Hare's Ear Nymph** or a small tan **Woolly Bugger**, although specific cranefly nymphs can sometimes be found in fly shops.

The adults look like giant mosquitoes and are from one-half inch to three inches in length. Most are tan, cream, or gray and can be identified by the single pair of wings and long spindly legs. Adults are often blown into the water on windy days, and they also return to the water to make and lay their eggs in early morning. Trout often take these insects as they skate across the surface, and when a trout rises for a cranefly the rise is often explosive, with the fish leaping completely clear of the water. Large **hackled** dry flies are the best imitations of adult craneflies, and the fly is best presented by greasing the **leader** and skating the fly across the surface.

CRAYFISH

Crayfish are freshwater crustaceans of the order *Decapoda*; they are extremely common in streams and lakes throughout the world. Gamefish, especially trout and **smallmouth bass**, relish the lobsterlike creatures and where crayfish are abundant the average size of a trout or bass will be larger than normal because crayfish are a large and highly nutritious meal. Over 250 species of crayfish live in North America. They are most common in cold, rocky streams but can be found in almost any type of clean water. Crayfish eat detritus off the bottom and are most active from dusk to dawn, although

younger and smaller crayfish will often be active during the day as well. Crayfish are most vulnerable to trout, bass, and other gamefish during their periodic molts because their shells are softer, but fish will seldom pass one up, regardless of its shell hardness.

Crayfish in streams and lakes grow to about three inches at maturity, but fish will eat any size they can get, from a tiny just-hatched specimen to a full-sized adult. Crayfish can be orange or bright blue, but the most common ones range from a rusty brown to a dark olive. There are flies tied specifically to imitate crayfish, but a **Woolly Bugger**, Tequeely, or **Conehead** Marabou **Muddler** will also do an effective job of imitating the larger adult crayfish. A small dark **stonefly nymph** is an acceptable imitation of a young crayfish as well.

Crayfish imitations can be fished with an active strip, because frightened crayfish scull backward quickly with their flat tails. Sometimes an active strip combined with a long pause can also be effective, and even a **dead drift** presentation, with a fly fished through a deep pool under a **strike indicator**, can fool a wary trout or bass that just can't resist a lobster dinner.

CRICKET

Crickets are active along all trout streams and often fall or jump into the water, becoming a quick meal for a trout. Crickets are active for a much longer period than **grasshoppers**, as they hatch in early spring and are available to trout throughout the season. Unlike grasshoppers, crickets are more active in early morning and late evening than during the heat of the day, so these flies can be used during times when grasshopper imitations won't be as effective.

Not many cricket imitations are needed. The famous Letort Cricket is as good an imitation as any, and it's only needed in a size 10 or 12. Cricket flies should be fished along banks with heavy vegetation, and can either be fished as a **dry fly** or sunk and fished like a **nymph**, as natural crickets don't float very well. A **dead drift** with an occasional twitch is the best way to present these flies.

CUTTHROAT TROUT

The cutthroat trout is the native salmonid of most of the Rocky Mountains. Before the introduction of **rainbows** from California, **brook trout** from the East, and **brown trout** from Europe, it was the trout that lived in most of the famous rivers of the American West. Unfortunately, cutthroats don't compete well with other species and hybridize easily with rainbows (to which they are closely related), so in many watersheds they have been pushed into small tributaries and remote creeks and lakes high in the mountains. There are also dozens of subspecies of cutthroats, but man's tinkering with transplanted fish has diluted many of these pure strains.

Cutthroats can all be identified by the bright red slash just under the lower jaw. On some subspecies like the Yellowstone cutthroat, this mark is prominent, whereas in the coastal cutthroat of the Northwest, it is almost invisible in some specimens.

The main subspecies of cutthroats are the **Col-orado** River cutthroat of the southern Rockies, the Lahontan of the Nevada desert, the Yellow-stone cutthroat of the **Yellowstone River** drainage, the **Snake River** fine-spotted cutthroat of the Snake River watershed, and the coastal cut-throat of the Northwest. The best places to catch a cutthroat trout today, outside of high mountain areas, are the Yellowstone River in Yellowstone Park, the Snake River in **Wyoming** and **Idaho**, and the coastal rivers of Washington and British Columbia for the coastal cutthroat, where they are often caught in estuaries or just above the tide line. Cutthroats do not transplant well to waters where they are not native, but token populations sup-ported by hatchery stocking exist in Maryland's North Branch of the Potomac River and Arkansas's North Fork of the White River.

Cutthroats prefer the softer water at the edge of fast currents, especially along deep banks. Although they don't often live right in the foamy water that rainbows seem to like, when insect **hatches** are thick they will move into shallow **riffles** and gravel bars, into water so thin their backs may stick out of the water. In fact, it is this predilection for eating insects that endears them to anglers—cutthroats, even the biggest specimens, continue to eat small insects their entire lives. Cut-throats also tend not to be as spooky as brown trout or rainbows, and when they are actively feeding will tolerate a lot more commotion by the angler.

This is not to say that cutthroats are always pushovers. In shallow mountain streams they can get very spooky, and in big rivers like the Yellowstone or Snake, where insect hatches are abun-dant, cutthroats can get extremely selec-tive to size, shape, and color. Add to this a big cutthroat's tendency to rise and inhale an insect in slow motion movie-style, and most anglers' inclination to **strike** too quickly, and fishing over a pod of big cutthroats at the height of a hatch can be a frustrating (but exciting) experience.

Cutthroat trout don't fight with the spectacular leaps of a rainbow or strong runs of a brown trout. But what they lack in fighting sprit they more than make up for in their eagerness to take **dry flies** and their spectacular beauty, a true symbol of Rocky Mountain wilderness.

C

Dragon nymph

DACRON
See Backing.

DAMSELFLY
Damselflies are aquatic insects of the order *Odonata*. The **larvae** are most commonly found in shallow weedy ponds and lakes, but can also be found in rivers with slow current and abundant aquatic vegetation. The adults **hatch** by crawling onto emergent vegetation, splitting their exoskeleton, and flying away. Adults return to the surface of the water to lay their eggs.

Because damselflies don't hatch on the surface of the water, fly fishers don't fish damselfly hatches. However, the larvae are active, fast-swimming insects and are eagerly eaten by trout, bass, and **panfish**. Most are about a size 10 or 12 and brownish olive in coloration, with a long slender abdomen and thorax. The larvae propel themselves through the water by expelling water from their abdomen, and can move quickly. Slim **nymphs**

with an olive color, fished with a steady strip through the water, are most effective in imitating the larvae.

Adults do get blown into the water on windy days and also return to the water to mate and lay their eggs, so a **dry fly** imitation is effective at times. Damselfly dry flies are quite large for trout flies, size 8 or 10, and are usually bright green or blue to imitate the colors of the naturals. Dry flies should be cast near cruising or rising fish and allowed to sit motionless, although an occasional brief twitch may catch a fish's attention.

DEAD DRIFT
Getting a dead drift is an essential component of many fly fishing techniques in moving water. The term implies that a fly is moving in the current as though it were not attached to anything else or able to move under its own power. More a result than a technique, getting a dead drift can be accomplished in many different ways. Most aquatic insects that

D

it hits the water. Thus, casting **across-stream** gives a brief moment of dead drift followed by drag. (How quickly the drag begins depends on the speed of the current between the angler's position and the fly.)

There are ways to accomplish a dead drift even in conflicting currents. Typically, an angler casts into slow current against the far bank, and across faster current in the middle of a river. The fly line in the middle of the river is pushed downstream faster than the line and leader in the slower water. Thus a bow forms in the middle of the line and pulls the fly downstream. This can be lessened by either making an upstream **reach cast** or an upstream **mend**, which puts a bow with an upstream curve into it. This curve will invert before the fly is dragged downstream.

Another way to accomplish a dead drift is to throw deliberate slack into a presentation. By aiming high and overpowering a cast, the line and leader fall into loose coils, which allow the fly to drift downstream without hindrance until the coils straighten out. Yet another method, usually used with a sinking fly and weight on the leader, is called *high sticking*. Here, all of the fly line and most of the leader are kept off the water by holding the tip of the rod in the air, with a straight line to the point where the leader enters the water. By following the fly's progress downstream while keeping the rod high, very little drag is induced into the drift. The high stick method works only on short casts where the fly drifts almost directly under the rod tip.

live in moving water are only capable of crawling along the bottom and have feeble movements when they break loose from the bottom. Eggs of fish deposited during spawning and terrestrial insects that fall into the water also exhibit weak movement, if any at all. Thus getting a dead drift on a fly is important for a lifelike presentation, whether the fly floats or sinks.

Drag on a fly is the opposite of dead drift. If a floating fly is cast onto moving water, currents of varying speed soon pull on the **leader** and **fly line** and yank the fly across the surface, creating a motorboatlike wake behind the fly. From below, this movement is magnified to the fish, so at times, even though the fly does not appear to be dragging from above and seems to have a perfect dead drift, it may still be dragging enough to alert the fish to its fraudulent nature. Underwater, a fly swimming across or against the current is also suspect, and even though it does not create that surface wake, unless something is done to accomplish a dead drift fish may refuse the fly.

The most basic way to get a dead drift is to stand in the same current lane as the fish (or where you suspect a fish may be) and cast the fly directly **upstream**. Because the line, leader, and fly all drift in the same current there should be no drag on the fly. Casting a fly directly **downstream** creates exactly the opposite effect—the fly drags as soon as

DECEIVER FLY

The Deceiver is a style of saltwater fly first developed by Lefty Kreh for striper fishing in Chesapeake Bay in the 1960s. It is one of the oldest saltwater fly patterns but remains one of the most popular. The Deceiver has the right combination of action in the water, durability, and a **baitfish** shape and profile when wet. This fly has caught every

species of saltwater fish that will take a fly, and is also used in fresh water for bass, **pike**, and even large trout.

Deceivers can be tied in any color imaginable, but the most popular colors are all-black (especially for night fishing), all-white, olive-and-white, blue-and-white, and red-and-white. Most popular hook sizes are from 2 to 2/0. The Deceiver is best fished with a steady pulsing **retrieve**, to get the most action out of its long **hackle** feather wing and to imitate a crippled baitfish.

DESCHUTES RIVER

The Deschutes River, flowing through central **Oregon** north along the eastern slope of the Cascades, is Oregon's finest trout and summer **steelhead** river, and considered by some one of the finest fly fishing rivers in North America. The most popular and productive section of the Deschutes is the lower section, from Pelton Dam north of Bend to the river's confluence with the Columbia River. This is a massive river, flowing through arid canyons and high desert, with 100 miles of beautiful **riffles**, runs, and pools. Native redsides **rainbow trout** averaging 12 to 16 inches can be caught throughout the year on **dry flies** and **nymphs**, with an abundance of **hatches** from May through October. The most popular hatch is the emergence of large **stoneflies** called Salmonflies in late May and early June, but the river offers great **caddisfly** and **mayfly** hatches as well throughout the summer.

In late July, large numbers of summer steelhead between 4 and 12 pounds enter the river from the Columbia, and fishing for these fish is productive through November. Deschutes steelhead, unlike many strains, rise well to a fly on a **floating line**, so the most common method is to fish classic **wet flies** on a **downstream** swing. Such famous steelhead flies as the Mack's Canyon, Freight Train, and Signal Light were developed for Deschutes River steelhead.

The upper and middle stretches of the Deschutes south of Bend offer excellent fishing for **brown**, **rainbow**, and **brook trout** in a more forested and intimate setting than the lower river. Access to the entire Deschutes can be tricky because it flows across a combination of public land, private land, and tribal land, and the river can also be dangerous to wade and float. Fishing out of a boat is also illegal. Anglers unfamiliar with the area should invest in a reliable local guide.

DIRECT DRIVE REELS

See Fly Reel.

DOLLY VARDEN

The Dolly Varden, *Salvelinus malma*, was named by early explorers of western North America after a colorful character in a Dickens novel. A member of the **char** genus, it is more closely related to **brook trout**, **arctic char**, and **lake trout** than it is to **rainbow trout**, **brown trout**, or salmon. Char can be identified by lack of teeth on the vomer (the bone in the middle of the upper roof of the mouth)

and by their tiny, almost microscopic scales. Dolly Varden can be distinguished from brook trout by a lack of vermiculations (wormlike markings along the dorsal side), and from the similar-looking arctic char by a tail that is not forked, and by smaller and more numerous spots than an arctic char. Dolly Varden are also broader and more slablike than other trout and char.

Dolly Varden are a Pacific char, found from **Alaska** south to **Oregon** and on the other side of the Bering Sea in Kamchatka. Both freshwater and anadromous populations occur. Those that migrate to sea spend 3 to 4 years in saltwater estuaries, returning to rivers in midsummer and spawning in the fall. As spawning time approaches, Dolly Varden change color from pale olive and blue to a dark olive back and bright red bellies and spots. Their fins turn red as well, with a white leading edge.

In salt water, Dolly Varden feed on **baitfish** and crustaceans. When sea-run Dolly Varden enter freshwater, they feed on the same foods that their landlocked relatives eat, including salmon eggs, insect **larvae**, and small baitfish. Dolly Varden are not difficult to catch, which endears them to anglers when salmon or other trout are not cooperating. **Streamers**, **nymphs**, and even **dry flies** are very effective on Dollies; just finding the fish is more important than the correct fly. Typically, Dollies will be found in deeper pools and runs in a stream. Where sea-run Dolly Varden are found, they will be in lake outlets, stream mouths, and beaches in April and May, and then primarily in estuaries from May through July. In August, they will be found further **upstream** in rivers and lakes, most often behind spawning salmon.

DOLPHIN

Dolphin or mahi-mahi (*Coryphaena hippurus*) are a pelagic fish of tropical oceans that may range as far north as the coast of **Rhode Island** during years when warm ocean currents run close to shore. They are an excellent fish to catch on a **fly rod**

since dolphin are aggressive feeders that are attracted to flies that resemble squid or **baitfish**. The best way to catch them is to look for pieces of debris in tropical ocean waters. Weed lines are especially productive, but floating buoys and even turtles may have dolphin lurking under them. When one fish is hooked the rest of the school will stay in the vicinity, so one dolphin is often hooked by trolling a fly, or a **popper** is cast to a school with a spinning rod. While this fish is played, a fly can be cast near the hooked fish with an almost instant hookup guaranteed. Large, brightly colored flies with lots of flash and big poppers are preferred; dolphin have sharp teeth, so a 40- to 60-pound **monofilament shock tippet** is recommended.

DOUBLE HAUL

The double haul is a variation on the **overhead cast** that increases **fly line** speed by forcing the **fly rod** to bend more (and thus build up more energy) than it would with a standard overhead cast. Its purpose is to cast a line further, because a fly line traveling faster has more momentum, and also to cast more efficiently when the wind is blowing hard. It is extremely difficult to cast more than 60 feet with a single-handed fly rod without utilizing the double haul. The double haul should not be attempted without first obtaining some proficiency with the overhead cast and shooting line.

To perform a double haul, begin with the rod tip held low to the water as in a normal overhead cast, with stripping hand held close to the rod (figure 1). As the rod tip moves to the vertical, the stripping hand should also move in the opposite direction, and with a brisk motion, the stripping hand should be hauled down to the side, to about waist level (figure 2). As soon as the stripping hand reaches waist level, it should immediately drift back to the rod, letting the line between the two hands feed back into the **back cast**. The moment the rod stops dead at the end of the back cast, the line hand should be next to the rod (figure 3).

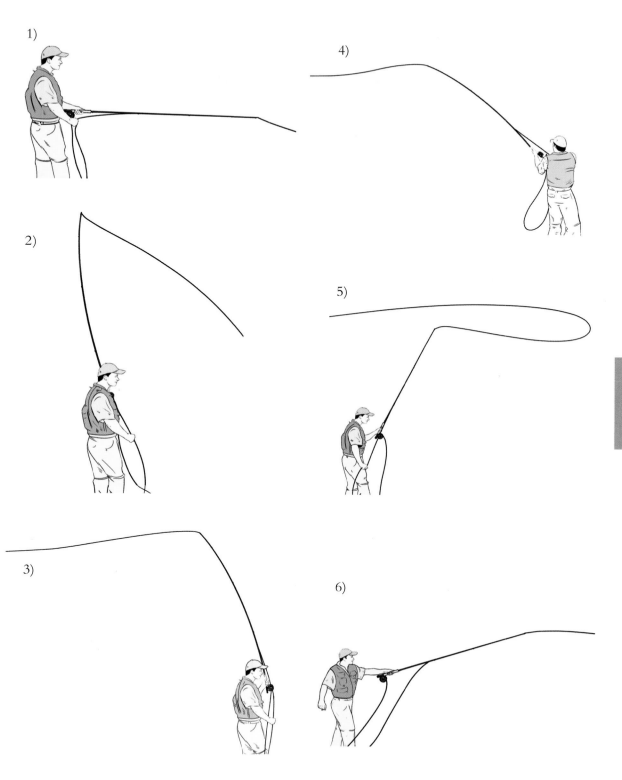

1)

2)

3)

4)

5)

6)

D

On the **forward cast**, the line hand again hauls down as soon as the rod motion begins (figure 4). In the same motion as the forward cast, the line hand hauls down and then the line is released (figures 5 & 6). It helps to imagine your casting and line hands moving apart at about the same speed, and it also help to recite *downup...downup* as you cast.

By utilizing the double haul, 20 feet or more of line can be shot through to guides to obtain extra distance. It's useful to have the slack line neatly coiled at your feet, or coiled in a special **stripping basket** that allows line to shoot through the guides without tangling or added resistance. It's difficult to practice the double haul with less than 40 feet of line, because with shorter casts there is not enough fly line to properly load the rod.

Use the double haul any time you are casting over 50 feet, when faced with a wind blowing at you, or when throwing big, wind-resistant flies. The higher line speed you generate will help drive your fly line better than a normal over-head cast. It's also much easier to use the double haul with a weight-forward **fly line** or **shooting head** than it is with a double taper fly line.

DOWNSTREAM
See Across-Stream.

DRAG, LINE
See Dead Drift.

DRAG, REEL
See Fly Reel.

DRAGONFLY
Dragonflies are large aquatic insects of the order *Odonata*. They live in freshwater lakes and ponds and in the slow stretches of rivers. The adults look similar to **damselflies,** but are typically larger and fatter. The **nymphs** do not look at all like damselfly nymphs, though, as they are much wider and flatter than damselfly nymphs. Although dragonfly **larvae** live in the same places as damselfly larvae, they are not eaten as often by trout and bass because they are less likely to swim in open water and prefer crawling among weed growth. Because dragonflies emerge by crawling up the stems of emergent vegetation, the adults are not often

available to trout and bass, but during mating flights in midsummer or on windy days they are often blown into the water, where they are eaten by fish in explosive rises.

The best fly to imitate a dragonfly nymph is a drab, heavy-bodied fly like a size 8 or 10 **Hare's Ear Nymph**. Adults are imitated by large foam-bodied or deer hair flies especially designed to imitate dragonflies, but in a pinch a large Stimulator or other **attractor dry fly** will work.

DRIFT BOAT
A drift boat is the most stable and elegant way to fly fish in moving water. Fly fishers can fish in rivers from **canoes** (slower water current only), inflatable rafts, **kayaks**, and pontoon boats, but

none of these craft can match the comfort and maneuverability of a McKenzie-style dory or drift boat.

Drift boats have upturned ends at both bow and stern, which lowers the profile of the boat below the waterline and aids in turning quickly in fast current. Drift boats are mainly propelled by the current, while the boatman rows backward to slow the boat in the current, making the boat more stable and making it easier for fly anglers to hit all the likely spots while drifting. The oarsman or guide sits in the middle of the boat, manning the oars and watching for dangerous currents and likely places to find fish. At his feet is a line that can be easily released to drop the anchor, which hangs off the stern while the boat is moving.

There are typically anglers at both the bow and stern of the boat. They can cast while seated, or in calmer water they can stand and brace their thighs

in braces located just in front of the seats. Standing gives the angler an easier cast and a better view of the water. The anglers in bow and stern should cast parallel to each other to avoid tangling; it's the responsibility of the stern angler to watch where the bow angler is casting. An experienced guide will quickly notice the most comfortable casting distance for his or her clients and will position the boat so that it runs parallel to the fishing water at this comfortable distance.

Drift boats can be high profile for heavy water or lower profile for less wind resistance in wide-open rivers. They are made from aluminum (rugged but heavy and hard to turn), fiberglass (tough and light), or wood. Classic wood drift boats are a beautiful sight on a river.

DROPPER

A dropper is a secondary piece of **tippet** that hangs off the main **leader**. Although droppers are used to attach **strike indicators** or weight to a leader, they are most commonly used to attach multiple flies to a single leader. Although fly fishers in the nineteenth century seeking wilderness **brook trout** often fished as many as a dozen flies on a single leader, modern fly fishers seldom fish more than two flies at once—one attached to the main leader and one attached to a dropper. In some regulated rivers, only one fly at a time is allowed to reduce the possibility of inadvertently (or purposely) snagging a fish, so it's best to check regulations before adding a second fly.

Droppers are used to try two different patterns at the same time (often a big **nymph** and a smaller one), for visibility (a large **dry fly** plus a smaller nymph or dry), or to excite aggressive fish into striking (two **streamers** at the same time). Droppers always offer the potential for tangling in the wind, in a net, on the bottom, or in a finger, plus they make casting more difficult, so the added benefits of adding a second fly should be weighed against the annoyances.

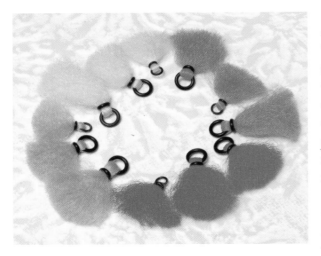

At one time. special dropper loops were added to the main leader and then flies pre-tied on a looped piece of tippet were looped to the main leader. However, fly anglers today favor cleaner and easier methods to attach a second fly. One way is to leave one tag end of a **blood knot** just above the tippet extra long, from three to six inches.

Because the tag end of a blood knot stands at right angles to the leader, this arrangement helps keep the fly from tangling. Another way, perhaps the easiest and most common method, is to tie on the first fly normally, then tie a second piece of tippet material to the bend of the **hook** of this fly and tie the second fly on the end of this piece. This arrangement keeps both flies in line and is the least likely to tangle.

DRY FLY

A dry fly is simply a fly that floats on the surface film of a river or lake. It could be argued that **poppers**, cork or plastic lures used for bass, **pike**, and saltwater species are also dry flies, but the term usually refers to an imitation of an insect. **Emergers**, flies that float in or just under the surface film, can also be considered dry flies but most anglers consider them a different style of fly—even though the line between a dry fly and an emerger is often very slight.

Dry flies, unless they are constructed from closed-cell foam, are actually heavier than water. The **hooks** used to construct dry flies are made from lighter wire than that used for sinking flies, with floatation assisted by the use of stiff, bushy chicken **hackles**, lightweight hair from a deer or elk, or downy duck feathers. Most dry flies need some help in flotation from waterproofing treatments called **fly flotants**, which are most often made from silicone compounds.

Dry flies have been used since the mid-nineteenth century. Until then, hooks were not light enough and **fly rods** were not stiff enough to dry the water from flies between casts. Around the turn of the twentieth century, an Englishman named **Frederick Halford** worked hard to codify dry fly technique and fly construction, but in the process made dry fly fishing quite rigid and exclusionary, with generations of anglers throughout the world feeling that fishing with a dry fly was a superior method. Modern anglers are a more flexible lot, and regularly switch between dry and **wet flies** as conditions dictate.

Dry flies take many shapes and forms, and all have their purpose. Most imitate **mayflies**, **caddisflies**, **stoneflies**, **midges**, and various land-bred insects that fall into the water like **ants**, **beetles**, **crickets**, **grasshoppers**, and moths. Some anglers like to classify dry flies as attractors, those flies that just appeal to the fish in a general sense, and imitators, flies that imitate a specific insect. However, a fly that is an imitator today might work as an attractor tomorrow.

TRADITIONAL DRY FLIES

A traditional dry fly is a fly with wings that stick up perpendicular to the water's surface, float by virtue of stiff hackles, and have either hackle fiber or hair tails. Most of them are designed to imitate adult mayflies. The **Royal Wulff**, **Adams**, **Light Cahill**, and Humpy are some of the most popular traditional dry flies. These patterns float very well in fast water, are easy to see on the water, and work best when adult mayflies are fluttering on the surface. They are also superb attractor flies in fast water when no fish are rising.

DOWNWINGS

Unlike adult mayflies, caddisflies, stoneflies, and midges carry their wings parallel to their bodies when resting on the surface. Thus, flies to imitate these insects have wings that are lower in profile and lie parallel to the water. The wings on this kind of fly are often made from buoyant hair from deer or elk, although duck feathers are also used. Downwings can utilize hackle for floatation, or they can rely on the floating properties of animal hair. Many downwings, particularly imitations of larger stoneflies and caddisflies, use closed-cell foam for both bodies and wings, which makes them very durable and keeps them floating all day. Downwings should be used when stoneflies or caddisflies are seen on the water, but they also make superb attractor flies. Popular downwings include the **Elk Hair Caddis**, Stimulator, and Henryville Special.

COMPARADUNS, SPARKLE DUNS, AND NO-HACKLES

These dry flies are very similar in that although they have upright wings and imitate adult mayflies, they don't use hackle for floatation. The theory is that hackle obscures the clean outline of an adult insect in slower water where the fish gets a better look at a fly. These flies rely more upon proper balance, a delicate delivery, and wings that act as outriggers for flotation. They are deadly flies during mayfly **hatches** and are often more effective on selective fish than traditional dry flies.

PARACHUTES

Parachute dries are similar to traditional dry flies, but the hackle is wound around the wing so that it sits parallel to the water's surface instead of perpendicular to it. Parachutes land softly, float very well, and present a more realistic profile to fish in flat water. Parachutes are a great utilitarian fly, as they work well during hatches, as attractor flies, in fast water, and in slow water. The most popular dry fly in the world is the Parachute Adams.

MIDGES

Any fly smaller than a size 20 is considered a midge by some, but tiny flies can also imitate small mayflies. Typically, midges are simple flies with just a bit of hackle or wing and a thin body. For instance, the Black Midge is just a whisp of black hackle with a black fur body, and the Griffith's Gnat is simply a piece of peacock herl for a body with a speckled hackle wound through it. Midges are almost never used as attractors, but are fished over trout lurking quietly in slow water.

TERRESTRIALS

Terrestrials are imitations of ants, beetles, grasshoppers, and other land-bred insects. Because terrestrial insects float low in the water, terrestrials are usually tied without hackle, or in the case of some ant patterns, just a small amount to imitate the legs of an ant. Terrestrials can range from size 6 foam grasshoppers that are two inches long to tiny ants and beetles in size 20 or 22. Terrestrials can be made from feathers and hair, but the most popular styles today are tied from a combination of closed-cell foam and other materials, so they land with the characteristic splat of a land insect, yet float well in the surface film without added treatment. They are most often used in summer months on windy days, especially close to deep banks.

DUN

See Mayfly.

Elk with caddistan

ELK HAIR CADDIS

The Elk Hair Caddis, also known as the Elk Wing Caddis, is one of the most useful and popular **dry flies**. Developed by **Montana** fishing guide Al Troth, it is a high-floating, durable imitation of an adult **caddisfly** fluttering on the surface. The fly is made with a wing of elk body hair, with a fur body to match the color of the prevalent caddisflies, plus a stiff chicken **hackle** wound over the entire body to aid in flotation and to imitate the twitching legs of the insect. Elk hair caddis can be tied in any color, but the most popular combinations are a tan wing combined with a tan, cream, or olive body. An Elk Hair Caddis in these three colors in sizes 12 through 18 will imitate 90 percent of the adult caddisflies found on a trout stream.

ELK WING CADDIS

See Elk Hair Caddis.

EMERGER

An emerger is a cross between a **wet fly** and a **dry fly** and is designed to imitate an immature aquatic insect at the moment it reaches the surface of the water and splits its skin to hatch into a winged adult. A **nymph** can be treated with fly flotant or a dry fly can be left untreated to serve as an emerger, but the most effective emergers are those designed specifically to imitate this stage of an insect's life cycle. At first glance it seems fussy to simulate such a brief moment in an insect's life cycle, but it's an extremely deadly approach to matching the **hatch**. At the moment an insect emerges, it is at the most vulnerable part of its life, as it can neither hide under a rock nor fly away. At the height of a hatch, trout may feed selectively on emerging insects, ignoring nymphs underwater and adult flies on the surface, choosing only the flies drifting just under the surface.

Flies designed to imitate emergers look much like dry flies. They are tied on light **wire hooks**, and the biggest difference is that they don't have the bushy **hackle** of a traditional dry fly. One feature often used on emergers is a trailing shuck of translucent yarn to imitate the adult fly wiggling out of its exoskeleton. Wings on an emerger can be anything from straight upright to parallel to the body of the fly, depending on the insect being imitated and the amount of visibility needed (upright wings are not as realistic but are easier for the angler to see).

Popular and effective emerger patterns for mayflies include the Sparkle Dun, Rabbit's Foot Emerger, RS2, and Para Emerger. Caddisfly emergers include the X-Caddis and LaFontaine Emergent Sparkle Pupa. Emerging midges are imitated by a myriad of specific patterns, although a smaller size of the previously mentioned flies can also be used.

Trout eating emergers can be identified by splashy rises that do not produce bubbles. When a trout takes an insect on the surface, it inhales air that is then expelled through its gills during the rise. A trout taking an insect just under the surface may break the surface with its back or the momentum of rising for an insect may produce a splash, but the lack of bubbles is a dead giveaway. In slower water, fish taking emergers can be identified by a rise that shows the back and dorsal fin above the surface but

not the head—and again the lack of bubbles. However, often the first clue that trout are taking emergers is that they appear to be rising but completely ignore a well-presented dry fly.

The best way to fish emerger imitations is **dead drift**, with any added drag or movement of the fly, because emerging insects are so helpless. However, sometimes just a short twitch of the fly will induce reluctant trout to inhale the fraud.

ENGLAND

Overview

England is a small country with a dense population, but because of careful resource management and a rich tradition in fly fishing, the opportunities for a fly fisher are plentiful. Much of the early development of fly fishing happened in England, including the foundations of **dry fly** fishing, **nymph** fishing, and **Atlantic salmon** fishing. Thus a fishing trip to England is almost a pilgrimage to the places to which we owe much of our tradition today.

Unlike many places in the world, there is little public fishing in England. Less than 2 percent of the rivers in England have public access. A landowner owns the riverbed, so access to a river in a public area does not mean the angler can wade through private property. Whatever your personal views on private ownership of rivers, this has enabled a country that has been civilized and developed for thousands of years to offer relatively high quality fishing, because the landowners maintain and protect their waters beyond what the government could accomplish.

Stretches of the most famous trout rivers in England are tied up by private clubs or syndicates, and the visiting fly fisher would never be able to fish these areas. However, "day tickets" are available through various anglers associations, municipalities, tackle shops, and especially through inns and hotels. Even the most famous chalk streams have day tickets available in certain stretches; prices for

River Bourne, in the English county of Berkshire.

these vary from hundreds of dollars to as little as $20. In addition, fishing in well stocked and maintained reservoirs can be had for even less.

FISHERIES

To a fly fisher, the most revered fishing is on an English chalk stream, and to fish a day on the River Test or Itchen is like visiting the Louvre to an artist. Chalk streams magnify everything that produces a healthy trout population—stable cold temperatures are nourished by groundwater held in the sponge-like chalk deposits, and rich insect life is encouraged by the chemicals dissolved from the chalk, primarily calcium carbonate. Chalk streams run through gentle lowlands that have been cultivated for thousands of years. Not only the main rivers but also the "carriers," side channels that divert water used to fertilize water meadows and keep them

from freezing during the winter, host dense populations of trout.

Because of the clear, shallow flows of these rivers, most fishing on English chalk streams is sight-fishing with dry flies and nymphs. In some rivers, fishing **downstream** is not even allowed. Most of these streams are not fished by **wading**, but by carefully stalking trout from manicured banks and meadows. Benches are often placed at strategic spots to observe the river or wait for the rise, and fisherman's huts provide respite from rainy days with an afternoon tea.

There is a great concentration of chalk streams south and west of London, particularly in Hampshire. Rivers like the Test, Itchen, Avon, Wylye, Bourne, and Anton are found here. Further west in Dorset are less famous chalk streams like the Frome and Piddle, and north of London is a belt of chalk

E

streams that runs through the center of East Anglia to the coast, with names like the Tas, Nar, Cam, and Granta. There is also an isolated pocket of chalk deposits and chalk streams in the Eastern Wolds of Yorkshire and Lincolnshire, where rivers are known as "becks." Two of the better rivers there are the Bain and the Driffield.

Trout can be found in rivers other than chalk streams. The Yorkshire Dales and the Peak District offer many small streams where the fish will not be as large as those in the chalk streams, but the settings are more remote and the fish are likely to be wild. In Devon, the fly fisher will find the classic Dartmoor spate rivers (more prone to rising and falling waters than chalk streams), with good insect life and frequent **hatches**, as well as the opportunity to catch sea-run **brown trout** or **sea trout**. The Teign, Taw, and Exe are some of the better rivers in this region.

Brown trout are the native trout of the English rivers and lakes, and you will find a mix of wild and stocked fish in most rivers. In addition, native **grayling** are found in most trout rivers. These beautiful salmonids will rise to a dry fly, but are easier to catch on small **nymphs**. They are more difficult than trout to catch and in chalk streams can be as large as two pounds, so they are a wonderful and challenging **fly rod** fish.

Rainbow trout are often not welcome in English rivers. These easier-to-catch North American transplants are sometimes stocked in chalk streams where anglers with less skill require an easier quarry. And on some waters the angler is required to kill all rainbow trout caught. However, rainbows are the mainstay of the stillwater or reservoir fishery in England, because these fisheries require stocking and rainbow trout grow much faster than browns in a hatchery, and are far easier to catch once released into a reservoir. Reservoirs such as Chew Valley and Blagdon in the southwest, Rutland Water in central U.K., and Bewl in the southwest are known for their huge trout. Competitions are popular on most stillwater fisheries.

Pike can be caught on a fly in many slower, warmer rivers and canals in England, as well as the stillwater fisheries. Pike of over 20 pounds are frequently caught on flies in Blagdon. Although most of English coastal waters are too cold to produce viable sport fisheries, there is a thriving fishery for Atlantic sea bass along the southern coast, with a number of guides who specialize in fishing for them with a fly rod.

SEASONS

The season for river trout fishing in England runs from March through October. The very best fishing is in late May and early June, when a large species of **mayfly** (*Ephemera danica*) known in England as The Mayfly or **Green Drake** hatches in abundance and brings every trout in the river to the surface in an orgy of feeding that makes it easy for even the novice fly fisher to catch a large brown trout on a fly. Midsummer can bring warmer water temperatures and heavy aquatic weed growth to both rivers and stillwater trout fisheries, but summers are seldom warm enough in the U.K. to ruin the fishing. Fall is also a prime

time on chalk streams, and although it's easier to get a booking in September and October, the aquatic insects are often tiny and the fishing is challenging. After the trout season closes anglers may still legally fish for grayling all winter long. The season for sea bass is from April through October.

ENTOMOLOGY

Entomology, the study of insects, has been responsible for scaring more would-be fly fishers away from the sport than almost anything else. To avoid confusion of what insects they are imitating, experienced fly fishers often use the genus and even the species of the insect they are referring to when communicating with fly fishers from another river system. Casual fly fishers, upon hearing these conversations, often feel they need a graduate degree in entomology to have success in fly fishing for trout.

It is true that knowing that the **mayfly** species *Drunella inermis* will **hatch** in midmorning on western rivers throughout the summer, and being able to identify the adult will tell the angler the color of the immature **nymphs** and what type of water they inhabit, and that the egg-laying **spinners** are tan and will return to the water the next day to lay eggs. However, the angler that approaches a stream and notices that a creamy yellow bug in size 18 is hatching and proceeds to tie on a yellow **dry fly** will perhaps catch just as many fish.

It is important, however, to recognize the different *orders* of aquatic insects because each order has a distinct life cycle and behavior, and this knowledge can be useful to any fly angler. The most important orders of aquatic insects to the fly fisher include the mayflies, **caddisflies**, **midges**, and **stoneflies**, and each of these can be identified quite easily, either in their **larval** stage or as winged adults.

Any study of aquatic entomology as it relates to fly fishing must first begin with the life cycles of aquatic insects. Eggs are laid by adults, and are either dropped in the water like tiny bombs or are carried underwater to the surface of vegetation or rocks. After a few weeks, the tiny larvae hatch. These larvae, often called nymphs, grow and go through various subsurface molts over the course of about 11 months. Some larvae are predators, but most graze or filter-feed on algae, diatoms, and decaying plant matter. Midges and caddisflies have complete metamorphosis and also enter a dormant **pupa** stage prior to hatching, but the more primitive mayflies and stoneflies hatch directly from the larval stage without transforming into pupae.

Just prior to hatching, nymphs and pupae become more active and eventually release their hold on the river bottom and drift in the current, rising quickly to the surface, splitting their nymphal or pupal exoskeleton, and emerging as a winged adult. In most cases, insects of one species will hatch within a period of weeks or even days and almost always at the same time of day, ensuring that the adults can easily find mates. This is referred to as a hatch and can be predicted with some accuracy within a week or two, especially if periodic water temperatures are taken. (The long-term trigger for hatching is photoperiod but the short-term trigger is probably both light levels and water temperature.) Most aquatic insects hatch as water temperatures are gradually rising, and are more abundant on cloudy days than bright sunny days. Many species also hatch in early morning or evening when direct sun is not on the water.

Adult insects live anywhere from 24 hours to several weeks before forming mating flights over the water, laying eggs, and falling spent to the surface. Mating flights are often called "spinner falls" when referring to mayflies. Regardless of the insect order, mating insects falling to the water create feeding frenzies by trout that are just as impressive as when the insects hatch.

E

Flying Ant

FALKUS, HUGH (1917–1995)

Hugh Falkus was a legendary British fly fisherman, but was also a colorful filmmaker, fighter pilot, naturalist, and television host, among other professions. His book *Salmon Fishing and Sea Trout Fishing* revolutionized **sea trout** fishing in particular, by establishing that sea trout did most of their feeding at night. However, he is probably best known today for being an early authority on the modern use of two-handed rods and **Spey casting**, before double-handed rods came back into vogue for both **Atlantic salmon** and **steelhead** fishing. His 1994 book *Spey Casting: A New Technique* helped usher in this revival.

FALSE ALBACORE

The false albacore, *Euthynnus alletteratas,* is a small member of the tuna family highly prized by fly fishers for its fighting ability and its willingness to take a fly. The fish is also known as the **little tunny**, fat albert, albacore, and on the Gulf Coast of Florida, **bonito**, which is the name of a similar small tuna. False albacore can be distinguished from other tuna by the wormlike vermiculations along the dorsal side. Reaching 20 pounds with the average size around 10 pounds, this streamlined aquatic bullet has a reputation for taking 100 yards of **backing** or more on its first run.

False albacore are found from Cape Cod to the **Florida** Keys on the Atlantic Coast, and also along the Gulf Coast. In their northern range, they begin to feed in shallow water close to shore in August and by November the migration has peaked off the **North Carolina** coast. False albacore are most often caught by chasing fast-moving schools as they crash into bait at the surface, but they will also be found trailing shrimp trawlers, feeding on the by-catch thrown overboard. Best flies are slim, light-colored **baitfish** imitations like the **Clouser Minnow** or **Deceiver**, but false albacore will also take surface **poppers** when conditions are right.

FALSE CAST
See Overhead Cast.

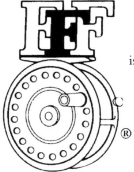

FEDERATION OF FLY FISHERS

The Federation of Fly Fishers is an affiliation of independent fly fishing clubs formed in 1965 by **Lee Wulff** and other influential fly fishers of that era. The Federation now has over 300 member clubs throughout North America. Unlike organizations such as **Trout Unlimited**, which embraces all methods of angling but limits its efforts to coldwater trout and salmon, the Federation of Fly Fishers works to conserve all species that are pursued with a **fly rod**, whether in fresh or salt water. The federation is dedicated to education, and regularly sponsors regional and national conclaves for the exchange of information about fly fishing. The FFF also certifies fly casting instructors who pass a highly structured course.

FERRULE
See Fly Rod.

FIBERGLASS ROD
See Fly Rod.

FIREHOLE RIVER
Located entirely within Yellowstone National Park, the Firehole and nearby Gibbon Rivers form the headwaters of the famous **Madison River**. The Firehole begins as an ordinary mountain stream in remote Madison Lake, but then flows through the famous geyser basins that include Old Faithful and many other fantastic thermal features. No fishing is allowed within a few miles of Old Faithful, but as

the river flows through spectacular meadows filled with smaller thermal features and large herds of wild bison, it picks up colder spring flow from a number of smaller tributaries and becomes good trout habitat, with gentle **riffles**, heavy aquatic weed growth, and long flat water tailor-made for **dry fly** fishing. Most of the **brown** and **rainbow trout** in the Firehole are not large, but are known for their difficult nature and tolerance of high water temperatures. Because of its heat, the Firehole has been called "The World's Strangest Trout Stream," but it is certainly also one of the most interesting trout waters in the world.

FLASHBACK

A Flashback is a style of **nymph** that includes silver, gold, or pearl tinsel stretched across the back of the fly. The flashy material serves to attract fish in fast water, and might also imitate the gas bubbles formed under the exoskeleton of an **emerging** aquatic insect. Most Flashbacks are variations on standard nymph patterns. Some of the most popular flashbacks are the Flashback

Hare's Ear, Flashback **Pheasant Tail**, and Flashback **Scud**. Flashbacks are most useful in fast or dirty water, where trout cannot see their prey well and are attracted by the glitter of the fly.

FLICK, ART (1912–1985)

Art Flick was a tavern owner, fishing guide, and amateur entomologist who wrote the first pocket guide to aquatic insects for fly fishers. Entitled *Art Flick's Streamside Guide*, it was first published in 1947, then was republished in 1969. With the renewed interest in fly fishing, the little book remained a hit and is still in print today. Despite the fact that Flick's book only covered the most common **mayflies** in the Catskill Mountains of **New York**, it simplified aquatic **entomology** for the nontechnical fly fisher and codified the basic Catskill **dry fly** patterns.

FLOATING FLY LINE
See Fly Line.

FLOAT TUBE
See Belly Boat.

FLORIDA

Heading into The Keys for snook, redfish, and speckled trout.

Despite the fact that it has no trout, Florida is a fly fisher's paradise. With a huge coastline, many estuaries, and a semitropical climate, Florida offers great fly fishing 12 months a year, with some species at their prime no matter what month you fish. Besides its rich coastline, Florida also hosts abundant opportunities for freshwater fly fishing, as its many rich lakes, manmade impoundments, and canals offer a year-round growing season for **largemouth bass**, crappie, bluegills, and the introduced peacock bass.

FISHERIES
Probably the most commonly pursued **fly rod** fish in Florida is the **redfish** or red drum. Although they can be found anyplace along Florida's coast, the best fishing for redfish in shallow water is near estuaries on both the Atlantic and Gulf Coasts. Places like Mosquito Lagoon, Indian River, and Banana Creek on the Atlantic Coast and the estuaries of the Gulf Coast from Florida Bay north to the Alabama border offer great sight-casting to redfish in shallow water. Redfish will usually be found along with spotted **sea trout**, although the trout tend to be more plentiful near submerged grass beds.

Although **snook** are also found along the entire coast of Florida, they are more reliable and abundant on the Gulf Coast, particularly on

F

the central Gulf Coast, than on the east coast because cold fronts along the Atlantic can send the snook into a deepwater lethargy. Snook will be found along beaches at dawn and dusk, during the day in deep channels with fast current, and at night in harbors and canals, particularly around lighted docks.

Spanish **mackerel**, king mackerel, and **false albacore** are superb sport on a fly rod and are found close to shore on both coasts, sometimes coming within casting distance of shore. But these species are most reliable from one to ten miles from shore.

Tarpon are one of the glamour species of Florida. The best places to catch the large adults over 75 pounds is from the Florida Keys north along the Gulf Coast to the Apalachicola region. The fish begin their migration north in April and continue along the Gulf Coast as spring progresses. However, all estuaries in Florida will have at least some "baby" tarpon up to 20 pounds all year long. The immature tarpon are wild fun on a fly rod, and they can be found well inland, even into freshwater regions in all but the coldest winter months.

Bonefish are found in quantity only in extreme southern Florida, from Miami south to Key West and into Florida Bay. Florida Keys bonefish are known to be both the biggest and most difficult bonefish in the world, and just catching one of these elusive shallow-water feeders is a cause for celebration. Although they can be caught from shore by the wading angler in a few jealously guarded flats, getting to Florida bonefish usually requires a flats boat, as the majority of Florida bonefish flats are a mucky marl bottom that cannot be waded without sinking up to your waist—or worse.

Permit are found all along Florida's coastline, although they are most common from Miami to Key West and into Florida Bay. The prime place for

Kayaks provide excellent access to snook and redfish in Florida's Everglades.

seeing permit is off Key West, although Florida permit are even more difficult to catch than bonefish, and many fine anglers have been foiled in their attempt to land a shallow-water permit. Offshore, around wrecks, permit can be chummed close to the surface and are relatively easy to catch, but doing it that way is not considered the true way of catching permit on a fly rod.

Peacock bass are a South American freshwater gamefish that were introduced to control the explosive tilapia populations (another introduced fish) in southern Florida, particularly in the Miami area. These hard fighting, aggressive fish now offer an urban fly fishing experience for a spectacular exotic species.

TIME OF YEAR

Most fisheries in Florida are productive throughout the year, but for certain species there are prime times when water temperatures and weather patterns combine to give the best fishing. Redfish and snook can be caught at all times, but are difficult to catch in the shallow water fly fishers prefer during cold fronts in December through March.

Tarpon are difficult to find in winter months and the best time to fish for them is April through early July. Tarpon do not mind warm water and can be caught all summer long, but do not take a fly as aggressively in midsummer (except early and late in the day). Prime bonefish time is April through June, and again in September and October. Permit follow a similar pattern.

Largemouth bass fishing with a fly rod is most productive in March and April, close to the spawning season when they are most aggressive. Peacock bass will take a fly readily all year long, except when cold fronts drive water temperatures below 70 degrees (21°C).

FLOTANT

Because most **dry flies** (except those made from closed-cell foam) are heavier than water, they

require some type of waterproofing compound to repel water and keep them floating longer and better. Prior to the 1960s, most fly flotants were homemade concoctions of paraffin with lighter fluid or carbon tetrachloride to keep the wax in suspension. Most fly flotants today are made with silicone, and it can either be dissolved in a quick-drying solvent, in a paste form, or as a dry powder. They are much safer than the old-style flotants.

Flotants with silicone dissolved in a solvent can be sprayed on, or the fly can be dipped into a jar. The solvent dries after a few **false casts** and the fly is ready to fish. One type, which is applied at least a day before a fishing trip, will last for a full day of fishing, but the quick application types need to be refreshed every hour or so if the same fly is used. These liquid forms are best for delicate **hackled** flies. Silicone pastes are rubbed into the fly, and although they will keep a fly floating longer, they will gum up the hackles of smaller hackled flies and are thus better on bigger, bulkier flies. Silicone powders can be used to pre-treat a dry fly, but they are most often used to dry and refresh a fly that has become waterlogged or covered with fish slime. Many experienced dry fly anglers carry all three types and use them as conditions dictate.

FLUOROCARBON

See Leader, Tippet.

F

FLY BOX

Fly boxes keep flies dry and organized, as a bunch of flies carried in a shirt pocket will create havoc. Fly boxes can be as simple as a discarded cough drop tin or throwaway plastic box, but most anglers opt for something that allows them to find the right fly in a hurry. Thus fly boxes offer some type of compartments or dividers to keep flies in order.

The most common type of fly box is the *compartment box*, a square, rectangular, or round container with a secure lid and a number of compartments to hold like types of flies. These boxes are made from high-impact plastic, metal, or even high-tech carbon fiber for lightweight strength. Metal boxes often have individual spring-loaded tops on each compartment and are beautifully functional but very expensive. The important factor is to make sure the compartments are large enough to hold flies without crushing them out of shape. Those with individual lids on each compartment keep the contents of an entire box from being blown away in a strong wind.

Another very popular type of box is one that offers rows of foam, magnetic, or spring strips so that each fly can be pinned in place with its hook.

These boxes keep flies easy to find and the flies don't get tangled together as they would just placed in a loose mass as they are in compartment boxes. An older style of fly box, technically called a *fly book*, is a sheepskin wallet with fleece inside. These look elegant but they tend to smash flies out of shape, and if a fly is put away wet in a wallet the hook can easily rust.

Big saltwater flies are a special challenge, as few fly boxes will hold a 6-inch **baitfish** imitation. Special oversized boxes are made for these kinds of flies, typically compartment styles with long rows of foam strips. A special type of saltwater box, called a *stretcher box*, carries saltwater flies with **shock tippets** already attached to the fly and a **class tippet** tied to the shock **leader**, so that when a **tarpon** fly with shock tippet has to be replaced to the **butt** section of the leader it can be done quickly with a loop-to-loop connection without tying any difficult knots. These boxes are long and thin, and have posts inside that the tippets can be wrapped around.

FLY LINE

Because a fly has insufficient weight do deliver itself at any distance, weighted fly lines are needed to provide enough mass for casting. Up until the 1850s, fly lines were made from strands of braided horsehair. Then it was discovered that strands of silk could be woven together into a tapered shape and then

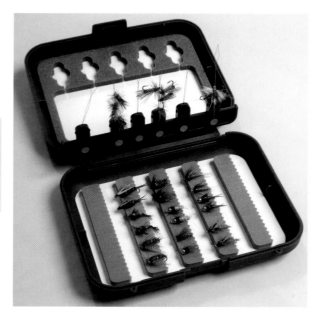

varnished for durability and to get a smooth surface. When treated with tallow, these new lines would float, making fly casting easier and more efficient. After World War II, modern fly lines which incorporated a plastic coating over a core of braided **nylon** were developed, and in the 1960s a process was developed to incorporate microscopic glass balloons into the coating, and the modern **floating fly line** was born. Substituting tungsten powder for the glass balloons also created a fly line that would sink much more quickly than older lines.

Fly Line Sizes

The same fly line that is delicate enough to deliver a tiny **dry fly** to trout sipping in clear water would never be able to drive a big saltwater fly into the wind. And a line with enough mass to deliver a large bass **popper** would land too hard on the surface of a still trout lake, scaring every trout nearby. Therefore, fly lines, whether they float or sink, are classified into sizes based on the weight of the first 30 feet of the line, ranging from 1 to 12, with sizes 1, 2, and 3 for delicate trout fishing and **panfish**, sizes 4, 5, and 6 for basic trout fishing, sizes 7 and 8 for the largest trout flies plus smaller salmon, bass, and saltwater flies, and sizes 9 through 12 for the

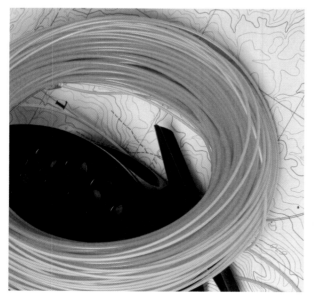

biggest saltwater, bass, and **pike** flies. The American Fishing Tackle Manufacturers Association developed this system in 1961 because an older letter system used with silk lines was based on diameter. Synthetic lines vary in weight depending on the core and coating, and a system based on diameter was no longer practical. **Fly rods** are always designed with a particular line size (or perhaps two) in mind, and since it is the weight of the line that flexes a rod, a fly fisher can buy a standardized line, from any manufacturer anywhere in the world, and be sure that the line balances his or her fly rod.

Fly Line Tapers

In order to cast well and present a fly with accuracy, a fly line must be tapered. Level lines (abbreviated with the letter designation L) don't cast well at all and are mainly used for trolling a fly in lakes. The taper on all fly lines begins with a level tip that is about 6 inches long. Then it gradually increases in diameter for 5 to 8 feet, followed by a "belly," which is where the weight is concentrated, then a rear taper. In a double taper (DT) line, after a gradual increase in diameter for the first 30 feet there is a 60-foot belly followed by a mirror image of the front taper at the rear end. Because double taper lines are a mirror image, once the front end of the line wears out, the line can be reversed.

Weight forward (WF) lines follow an entirely different taper after the first 30 feet or so. The line quickly tapers down at about 35 feet to a narrow-diameter line called *running line*, and because this line is finer in diameter it shoots through the guides easier. Thus longer casts are possible in the hands of an accomplished caster who is able to shoot 30 feet of line through the guides. However, for most normal trout fishing distances, under 40 feet, a double taper and weight forward line perform almost exactly the same. In general, double taper lines are best for fishing distances up to about 50 feet and in tight quarters where roll casts are used often. Weight forward lines are best when casts beyond 50 feet are needed and where wind is a

F

frequent problem. As a result, weight forward lines are the only type used in salt water.

There are various specialized versions of weight forward tapers. A shooting taper (ST) is very heavy in the first 30 feet and then quickly tapers down to a very thin running line, which shoots through the guides easily. Shooting tapers have virtually no delicacy so they are often used for sinking lines and in situations like saltwater fishing in the surf where distance is the most important consideration. (Gamefish feeding in the surf always seem to be just out of casting range.) A triangle taper (TT) is a trademarked taper made by only one manufacturer which has a continuous front taper followed by a quick rear taper. Some anglers feel the triangle taper is more delicate because it keeps the heavier part of the line further from the fly. A long belly weight forward has a longer belly and is useful where longer roll casts and line mending are needed, because it's easier to roll, cast, and reposition a heavier belly than running line.

Fly Line Coatings and Cores

A fly line is also described by its properties once it hits the water. A floating fly line (F) does just that. A sinking line (S) sinks through its entire length, and various densities of sinking coatings are used, ranging from a class 1 (very slow sinking) to a class 5 (very fast sinking). A sinking tip line (F/S) has a sinking head ranging from 6 to 20 feet that transforms seamlessly into a floating line. Intermediate lines (I) have close to neutral buoyancy and will sink slowly if left untreated and will float if dressed with silicone paste. Sink rates of fly lines are determined by the makeup of the coating applied over the core of the line.

Most trout anglers in streams use a floating line 90 percent of the time. Floating lines are obviously the only line to use with dry flies, and when fishing **nymphs** or **streamers** it is often easier just to use a weighted fly and/or weight on the leader to get the fly deeper. Floating lines are easier to cast, easier to pick up off the water (it's quite difficult to pick up for a cast with 30 feet of sinking line underwater), and easier to manipulate on the surface if the line must be **mended**. If a streamer fly is to be fished in fast, deep water the trout angler will sometimes use a sinking tip line so that the fly stays deeper on the retrieve, and the floating portion of the line makes it easy to pick up and mend line. Only when a trout angler is faced with long casts and very deep, fast water is a full-sinking line necessary.

In lakes and in saltwater fly fishing, a fly fisher is severely handicapped without several densities of lines. Fish may be at the surface but they may also be feeding 30 or 40 feet below the surface, and no amount of weight can be added to a fly to get it to sink and retrieve that deep. For instance, a saltwater fly fisher casting from a boat might carry a floating line for fish feeding on the surface, a class 3 sinking line for fishing shoreline rockpiles, and a class 5 sinking line for getting to fish in deep water offshore.

The coatings applied to fly lines have little strength by themselves, nor do they offer any directional stability to a line. This is the purpose of the core. Cores of fly lines are either braided nylon or polyethylene (**Dacron**), or solid nylon **monofilament**. Monofilament cores are stiffer and are better for distance casting, but in water temperatures below 60 degrees they become stiff and kinky and show distinct memory coils; thus these cores are used mostly in lines labeled as "tropical" lines, which also use a harder coating that does not get sticky on the deck of a hot boat. Most trout lines are made on a braided core, which gives a good balance between strength and flexibility.

Some true monofilament lines are made. They are usually clear and may either float or exhibit intermediate buoyancy. However, they are not widely used, perhaps because anglers can't see their lines on the water in tough light conditions.

FLY LINE COLOR

Fly lines are made in many colors, from white to bright red. The brighter lines are easier to see in the air and on the water, and aid in line control and casting. Against a bright sky, it is very difficult to tell the difference between a white line and a red one. Although most floating lines are made in the brighter colors, in some situations where trout or other gamefish are very spooky, a more subdued color like pale olive or gray is used so the line being cast is less obvious to the fish. Duller colors, in shades of green, brown, or gray, are less visible and are more often used for sinking lines, where the line may run quite close to a submerged fish. The most popular color for floating lines is yellow; sinking lines are typically brown or dark green.

FLY LINE RATING SYSTEM

Fly lines are labeled based on three characteristics: their weight, taper, and density. Thus a DT5F line is a size 5 line in a double taper that floats. A WF8F/S line is a size 8 line that has a weight forward taper and has a sinking tip and floating belly. Other characteristics, such as color and core type, can be found on line packaging or by asking the manufacturer.

FLY PATTERN

The term fly pattern is used to describe a recipe for a specific fly. Flies can thus be standardized, and a fly fisher buying a **Royal Wulff** in **New Zealand** can be reasonably certain of getting the same fly he would buy in **Canada**. It is very difficult to patent a fly because it is difficult to prove that a fly utilizes a completely unique method of construction. However, names of flies can be registered as trademarks, so the names of certain patterns are protected by the manufacturer. Fly patterns are usually communicated in a standard format, such as this pattern for a **Hare's Ear Nymph**:

Hook:	Size 10 through 18, 2XL heavy wire nymph hook.
Thread:	Black
Tails:	Guard hair from a European hare, or brown **hackle** fibers, short
Rib:	Oval or flat gold tinsel, or gold wire
Thorax:	Mixed dubbing from the ear of a European hare.
Wing case:	Slip cut from a mallard primary wing quill or other gray feather
Thorax:	Same dubbing as the body, picked out with a dubbing needle.

Typically, the materials in a fly pattern are listed in the order they are tied to the **hook**, and often substitute materials are listed, as in the case of the tails and rib on this pattern.

FLY REEL

A fly reel holds the extra **fly line** that is not in use, and in some cases acts as a brake on a fast-running fish. In small stream trout fishing, where a fish is never strong enough to pull line, the reel merely acts as a storage device when walking from one spot to another. At the other extreme, when fly fishing for **marlin**, strong tension must be kept on a running fish at all times, otherwise it will never tire and will be impossible to land. In the case of marlin fishing, an inferior reel not up to the job can literally explode or get so hot it will smoke.

Prior to the Civil War, most reels used on **fly rods** were the same reels used for **baitfishing** or trolling. A fishing reel was a fishing reel, no matter

F

what lure or bait you had on the end of your line. They were massive and heavy. The first truly practical fly reel was the Billinghurst or *birdcage reel*, which was light in weight, and had a wide diameter spool for quick line **retrieve** without having to resort to the heavy gearing mechanisms used on multiplying reels. Most importantly, the side plates of the reel were ventilated to facilitate the drying of the silk fly lines used then.

After the Billinghurst reel, the next major innovation in fly reels was the Orvis 1874 Patent Reel. Although it was ventilated like the Billinghurst, it had a narrow spool and was mounted below the rod, and is considered the father of American fly reels. In its handsome black walnut case, it sold for $5 in 1875, although Charles Orvis, ever the shrewd Yankee, later substituted a cardboard box to keep his price competitive.

Perhaps the most famous fly reels prior to today's modern reels were those made by Edward Vom Hofe of **New York** City. Vom Hofe, and then his son Edwin, handcrafted fly reels from the 1880s until the 1940s, and his reels were distinguished by their uncompromising quality—hand-cut, countersunk screws, shouldered pillars, unique sliding oil caps, nickel silver frames (actually an alloy of copper, zinc, and nickel) and hard rubber or ebonite (a hard vulcanized rubber) side plates, which were both elegant and lighter in weight than metal.

The most important part of choosing a reel is picking a reel that will hold all the fly line plus sufficient **backing**, anywhere from a few yards to 400 yards. Because line sizes vary in diameter, a 2-weight line takes up far less room on a reel than an 8-weight line, thus a reel used for an 8-weight line is much bigger in diameter than that used for a 2-weight. It's always better to get a reel with slightly larger capacity than you think you need, because a reel can be underfilled and still work properly, but a reel that is overfilled will bind against the frame and won't turn. Although some authorities go overboard in trying to get a reel properly "balanced" to a fly rod, this is not a critical consideration for most people, and as long as a reel is not dramatically bigger or smaller than normal it won't affect an outfit's fishing performance.

REEL MATERIALS

Most reels today are made from aluminum alloys, which are light and strong. Reels can also be made out of titanium (very expensive) or composites (lightweight but plastic-feeling) but aluminum is easy to manufacture to tight tolerances, can be anodized to protect against corrosion, and is relatively inexpensive. Inexpensive aluminum reels are often cast in a mold or stamped, but these reels are not as strong as those machined from solid aluminum, often called *bar stock reels*. Fly reels are usually perforated to lighten them, and all but the least expensive ones are anodized to resist corrosion, especially important in reels used in salt water.

Fly reels are available in many colors, the most common being silver, gold, and black. There is no practical reason to choose one color over another, other than the fact that some anglers prefer black reels because they feel shinier finishes flash in the sun and spook wary fish.

REEL DRAGS

All fly reels must have a drag, also known as a check or brake. If the spool revolved around the spindle without resistance, when stripping line from the reel the spool would overrun the line and tangle. This is the only consideration when fishing for bass, small trout, and **panfish**, because these species seldom pull line from the reel and a mechanical drag is not needed to slow them down. The simplest type of drag is called a *click drag* or *spring-and-pawl* system. Here, a gear on the spool engages one or two triangular metal pawls that are under spring tension. Although the spring tension on the pawls can be regulated by a drag knot, for all practical purposes the range of drag adjustment is so small that drag settings are not that important. Few reels sold today incorporate this kind of drag, however, as disc drags that have a much wider range of adjustment are simple, reliable, and inexpensive.

Disc drags come in as many designs as there are fly reel models. All utilize friction between two smooth surfaces, and these surfaces can be pressed together in increasing tightness to increase the amount of drag needed. For instance, when a big trout is caught in fast water on a light **tippet**, the drag should be set light and smooth so that sudden lunges by the fish don't break the **leader**. If the same reel is used on big **Atlantic salmon**, where runs may be long and the tippet might be as heavy as 16 pounds, the angler would crank the drag down to a tighter setting to help tire a running salmon quicker.

Popular drag surfaces include polished aluminum against plain cork, cork composites, smooth plastic like Delrin or Teflon, and even leather. These materials vary in coefficient of friction, durability, and heat buildup; each reel designer has theories on the best material. Drag surfaces can be circular or conical, centered on the spool or offset to one side, and with a small or large surface area. To an angler, the most important considerations are that the drag surface is smooth so that it won't stutter and break a tippet when a fish is running, and that the drag can be adjusted with an easily handled knob or lever on the outside of the reel.

No matter what type of fly reel drag system is used, the drag is also controlled by some type of

clutch design so that high tension happens when the line is peeling off the reel. When line is being wound by the angler, the disc drag is disengaged so that minimal tension is on the spool and line can easily be wound on the reel.

ARBOR DIAMETER AND RETRIEVES

Fly reels are classified as standard arbor, mid-arbor, or **large arbor**. These are relative terms, but within one manufacturer's line that difference between the three types will be proportional for any size reel. A standard arbor reel is the old traditional style of fly reel, with a very narrow arbor at the center of the spool so that as much fly line and backing as possible can be wound on the reel while still keeping a small profile. Although these reels are small and lightweight, retrieving line is sometimes a chore because the small arbor does not retrieve much line with each crank of the handle. In addition, the fly line is stored at such a severe arc that once pulled off the reel it will retain tight, annoying coils until stretched.

Large arbor reels were developed to solve both the line coiling issue and to improve retrieve speed; a large arbor reel will wind in line as least twice as fast as a standard arbor reel of the same capacity. Winding line quickly is important when a fast-running fish like a salmon or **bonefish** runs toward the angler. With a conventional arbor reel it is often

F

difficult to get control of the fly line fast enough. In addition, it's just easier to wind line on the reel when walking from one spot to another. What a large arbor reel gains in speed it loses in size: A large arbor reel is always bigger than a standard arbor of the same capacity, and some fly fishers just don't like the looks of a more massive reel on their rod. A compromise reel is the mid-arbor design, which offers a faster retrieve than a standard arbor but is not as wide as a true large arbor.

Most fly reels are a direct-drive design, which means that one turn of the reel handle controls one revolution of the spool, regardless of whether the line is coming in or going out. When a strong speedy fish like a **tarpon** or tuna takes line off a reel, the handle spins very fast and trying to grab the handle during a burst of speed can result in bruised knuckles. Some saltwater reels are an anti-reverse design, where the handle turns only when line is being wound and does not spin when line is pulled from the reel, similar to a spinning reel. Although this seems like an advantage, anti-reverse reels have double the number of moving surfaces of a direct drive reel, and must be extremely well made and maintained to perform properly.

In the past, two types of multiplying reels were made: mechanical multipliers where a gear system allow the spool to rotate more than once for each revolution of the handle, and automatic reels, which used a giant coil spring to retrieve line at the push of a button. Both of these reels had unreliable drags and frequent mechanical problems, and few people miss them.

RIGHT OR LEFT HAND?

Because there is an adjustable drag when the line runs in the outgoing direction and a uniformly smooth retrieve direction with minimal resistance, fly reels can be configured to wind on either the right or left hand side of the reel, usually with a simple operation that needs to be done only once (and is often done by the retailer that sells the reel). It makes sense that someone who casts with his or her right hand wants the reel handle on the left side of the reel, the line can be wound without switching the rod from one hand to the other. And that is the case with most anglers today—a righthander cranks with the left hand and a lefthander cranks with the right hand.

However, some anglers like to give their casting hand a break and prefer to cast righthanded and then switch hands when playing a fish, so that a righthander plays a fish with the rod in his or her left hand and reels with the right. There is no right or wrong answer, despite what you might have been told. Pick whichever retrieve feels most comfortable to you.

FLY ROD

HISTORY

Until the nineteenth century, rods were made from whatever strong and limber sticks were at hand. Lines were made from strands of horsehair. And rather than casting, early fly fishers used long rods to "dap" their flies on the surface of the water. Reels were not widely used until the eighteenth century, and if a big fish was hooked, an angler merely threw his rod into the water and waited until the fish tired. Another huge innovation arose in the late eighteenth century—the use of drawn silkworm gut as a more transparent link to the fly,

now known as a **leader**, and braided silk strands for the heavier line that propelled the fly. Instead of tying their line directly to the top of the rod, guides were invented to hold the line to the rod. Now fly casting as we know it today was possible, with line looping back and forth, and additional distance was gained by releasing extra line held in the hand.

Prior to about 1850, rods were made from ash, willow, and many other woods. Greenheart was a tropical wood that made the best rods, but these rods were relatively weak, so they could neither cast very far nor land a big fish without breaking. Then a number of American rod makers experimented with strips of solid bamboo, glued together to form a 4-, 5-, or 6-sided rod. These split **bamboo rods**, also known as cane rods or just plain bamboo rods, were stronger than the older types of wood rods, yet they had enough flexibility to make longer and easier casts. This type of fly rod is still made today by dedicated craftsmen, and was the standard for fly rods until synthetic fibers came into widespread use after World War II.

In the 1940s, fiberglass rods became popular. These synthetic rods were stronger than bamboo and could be easily mass produced. Rods that could tame large **sailfish** or **tarpon** were now within the reach of any angler. However, up until the 1970s bamboo was still considered the best material for casting. With the advent of **graphite** or carbon fiber rods, fly fishers finally had a fly rod that was lighter yet crisper than either bamboo or fiberglass, and rivaled bamboo in its casting qualities. Graphite rods could also be made longer and stronger without sacrificing weight or tensile strength.

PARTS OF A FLY ROD

Fly rods are simple levers with arcane jargon used to describe their parts. The bottom section of a rod, the thicker section to which the reel is attached, is the **butt**. The thinner section where the line exits is called the **tip**. In a 4-piece rod, the second section up from the butt is called the *mid-butt* and the third section up is called the *mid-tip*. The piece that holds the reel to the rod is called a **reel seat**. The piece of cork that acts as the handle is called the **grip** or just *handle*. Just above the grip there is sometimes a small loop of **wire** called the **hook keeper**, which is used to keep a **hook** out of trouble when transporting the rod assembled.

Rod tip

Reel seat

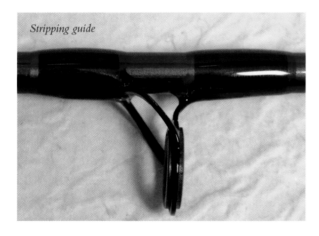

Stripping guide

basic material as the rod itself, but are often a slightly different formula because although by design they have to be larger in diameter than the rod walls, they must not create a stiff spot in the flex of a rod.

Snake guide and ferrule

LINE SIZES

Every fly rod is carefully designed to cast one or perhaps two **fly line** sizes. There is no universal fly rod that can do everything because a rod that will cast a 3-weight and a 9-weight line equally well cannot be made, and the qualities that are required for a 3-weight rod (light weight, lots of flexibility to protect a very light **tippet** and cast a line with extreme delicacy) are not the same as for a 9-weight (ability to cast long distances in the wind and enough power to haul a 30-pound fish from the depths). If any rod approaches the all-around designation, it is probably a 9-foot rod made for a 6-weight line. This rod has enough power to cast into a 15-knot wind, haul in a 15-pound fish, yet still present **dry flies** for trout with reasonable accuracy and delicacy. Yet this rod would probably break when trying to land a 40-pound king salmon and would be overpowering in a narrow mountain trout stream.

Guides are the metal loops that hold the line to the rod. The first one or two guides up from the grip are heavier guides with a ceramic or stainless insert and are called stripping guides. These guides are heavier because there is more stress and abrasion on them than the rest of the guides, which are typically bent loops of polished hard chrome wire called snake guides. The last guide, at the end of the rod is called the *tip top*.

The parts that allow the multiple pieces of a rod to hold together during fishing and are pulled apart at the end of the day to store the rod are called **ferrules**. In bamboo rods these are made from metal. Ferrules on graphite rods are made from the same

When a fly rod is designed by the engineers, it is made for a particular line weight or load. Because fly lines are rated by weight, the rod is carefully balanced to flex properly when making an average cast (30 to 40 feet) with a given line size. With this in mind, it's apparent that if a rod will always be used with 15-foot casts the angler can get by with one line size larger, and if it will be primarily for casting beyond 60 feet one line size lighter might be appropriate.

F

TAPERS AND ACTION

Besides line size, taper and the taper's resulting action are the most critical determinants of how a fly rod will cast. Unfortunately, the process of tapering a fly rod is so complex, and the idea of action is so subjective, that few anglers are able to make sense of the issue. For most of us, it's best to trust the experience of rod designers and our own impressions of how a rod casts (or the advice of friends) to determine the right action.

Fly rod **action** is often described as fast, medium, or slow. Orvis uses the terms tip-flex, mid-flex, or full-flex because it is a more precise way of describing the way a fly rod bends, and can actually be quantified on a numerical scale of 1 to 12. Thus, a fast or tip flex rod bends more in the first 25 percent of the rod's length down from the tip than it does in the rest of the rod. A mid-flex rod bends more into the middle of the rod, and under the same load a full-flex rod will bend well into the butt of the rod. Action is often confused with stiffness, and when picking up a very stiff rod that hardly bends when being cast, an angler might describe that rod as fast. Nothing could be further from the truth. A tip-flex rod is actually quite soft and flexible in the tip section, and a rod that resists bending throughout its length is probably just a poorly designed rod, or one that is rated for a line size that is too light. Fly rods must bend during casting in order to build up enough energy to propel the line without undue effort on the part of the angler.

The way a rod flexes may just appeal to an individual angler's taste, but there are some accepted generalities in fly rod action. A tip-flex rod generally produces casting loops that are tighter and more efficient than wider loops, and thus are better when casting into the wind and when making longer casts. However, tip-flex action is the least forgiving type of action, and if the caster's timing is off, a tip-flex action rod can be difficult to handle. Mid-flex rods throw slightly more open loops and timing is not as

critical, so those with a more casual casting style prefer them. Also, more open loops are advantageous when casting multiple-fly rigs with a strike indicator as there is less chance for tangling, and are better for lifting sinking lines from the water because more of the rod is used to lift the line.

Full-flex action rods are preferred for small stream fishing and delicate trout fishing. The full flex of the rod acts as a shock absorber when playing fish on a light tippet, and is also more comfortable at the short casts often needed for small-stream fishing. In the hands of an average caster, full-flex rods are also more delicate and less likely to slam the line hard on the surface of the water. Full-flex rods are also thought to provide more enjoyment when fighting small fish, as every movement of the fish can be felt in the handle of the rod.

MATERIALS

There are some inexpensive fiberglass rods on the market today, but since these rods are heavier than graphite rods, don't cast as well, and are not that much cheaper than an inexpensive graphite rod, there is little reason to consider them. The only advantage fiberglass rods have is that they are more durable than graphite because of their thicker walls, and thus in a situation where a rod is constantly banged against rocks or trees, a fiberglass rod might last longer.

Bamboo rods are really special purpose rods, used today mainly for small-stream trout fishing. Earlier in the twentieth century, salmon and **steelhead** rods were made of bamboo, but they are awkwardly heavy and slow and really don't offer any advantages

F

over graphite, which can be made much lighter and stronger in heavy line sizes 7 and above. But for short casts, delicate presentation, and the joy of catching fish on a true handmade work of art, bamboo is every bit the equal of graphite. Because bamboo rods are solid as opposed to the hollow tube construction of graphite rods, they are actually stronger if crushed or whacked against a tree trunk, so there is no need to baby a bamboo rod. They can even be made to cast almost as powerfully as a graphite rod—but at the expense of added weight.

Most fly rods today are made from hollow tubes of graphite fiber. Technically, rods are not made from 100% graphite, because the fibers must be held together with either epoxy or thermoplastic resins. Small amounts of fiberglass are also added, particularly in the ferrules for strength, and some rods utilize a small amount of boron fiber in the butt section. Boron is a stiffer and heavier material than graphite, and small amounts are sometimes used to stiffen the butt section of a rod without adding appreciable diameter to the rod.

Graphite fly rod tapers are made by a combination of the stiffness of the material used combined with variations in the wall thickness of the hollow tube. For example, suppose that a rod maker wants to produce a fly rod with a relatively flexible tip for casting, but with a powerful butt section for lifting large fish in deep water. The tip might be made from a graphite that is relatively flexible and with thin walls. To create the more powerful butt section, the rod designer has the option of making the walls of the hollow tube thicker than normal, using a stiffer type of graphite, or adding stiffer boron fibers. All of these options (or a combination of them) will create a stiffer butt section.

In the early days of graphite rods, fly fishers paid a lot of attention to the elasticity of the graphite used to construct a given rod, and manufacturers used this as a marketing tool, claiming that a rod made from a higher modulus of elasticity would be stiffer, thinner, and lighter. However, the stiffer the graphite fibers used, the more brittle the material,

and fly rod manufacturers soon hit a wall—stiffer forms of graphite were available, but the rods broke easily. Today, one manufacturer might use a half-dozen different types of graphite, and might even use three or four different types in a single rod, varying the type of graphite along the length of the rod to get the desired taper. The true determinant in the quality and performance of a modern graphite rod is where the fibers are used, what kind of resin matrix is used to hold them together, and most of all, the taper used to construct the rod.

LENGTH AND NUMBER OF PIECES

The most common fly rod used today is 9 feet. This length gives the angler plenty of casting power, control of the line when it's on the water, and a reasonable length to control a fighting fish. Nearly all saltwater rods are 9 feet long, except for specialized big-game rods designed for fighting huge fish like **marlin** and **tuna**. These rods are typically 8½ feet long because it is actually easier to fight and control a fish with a shorter rod than with a longer one.

Many professional casters feel that the ideal fly rod length for casting accuracy is 8½ feet—it's just how the physical relationships between a fly rod and line work out. And many very popular trout rods are built in this length, and even shorter. Shorter rods, down to about 6 feet in length, are made for small-stream fishing, where casts are very short and streamside brush might not allow enough clearance for a longer rod. These shorter rods won't cast as far as an 8½ footer, and they don't do as well in the wind or in mending line once it's on the water, but conditions on small streams seldom require a strong cast against the wind or a long mend.

Single-handed fly rods are made up to 10 feet long. Although these rods are heavier and make landing fish more difficult, they are superb distance-casting rods and the extra foot enables the fly fisher to control line better once it is on the water. Rods longer than 10 feet long are well suited to wide rivers and long casts, particularly in steelhead and

Atlantic salmon fishing. Two-handed or **Spey rods** are made as long as 16 feet, because these rods are primarily designed for picking up long lengths of line and placing a 90-foot cast back across the river with a single cast, then manipulating the line so that a swinging **wet fly** sweeps across the current exactly as the angler wants it to.

Up until the twenty-first century most fly rods were made in two-piece versions. It was felt that any more ferrules in a rod interrupted the action by creating stiff spots and thus multiple-piece travel rods were at best a compromise. However, ferrule technology in graphite rod construction has gotten so good that the majority of fly rods used today are four-piece versions. A four-piece 9-foot rod fits well in the trunk of a compact car, can be carried onto an airplane, or can be placed inside a small checked duffle bag. Since these short rod cases also fit well in a closet at home, there is really no reason to buy a two-piece rod except for a slightly lower price (ferrules are usually hand-fitted, which translates into a slightly higher retail price.) Travel rods today can be made into 7 or even 8 sections, which allows a rod that when broken down will fit comfortably into a briefcase.

FLY TYING

We'll never know who first attached feathers to a **hook** and used it to lure fish. We do know that as far back as A.D. 200 Macedonians were attaching **hackles** and red wool to a hook, and used these lures to catch speckled fish that we assume were trout. The original reason for tying flies was likely pragmatic—early fishermen observed fish eating insects, and the hooks used in those days were thick and crude, so that a delicate natural insect could not be impaled like other baits. They used whatever delicate, insectlike materials were at hand, and feathers, fur, and wool were the best they could find. Throughout the Middle Ages and into the Renaissance, there are records of these feathered lures becoming more and more sophisticated.

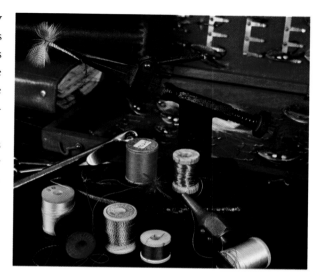

Anglers realized that certain flies worked better than others at different times of year, and as early as the 1500s in Germany, fly tiers were attempting to create different flies to imitate specific insects. We're still making most flies today in a similar fashion.

Fly tying requires no special dexterity or patience. It's true that a complicated **dry fly** or a feathered **Atlantic salmon** fly might require special skill and lots of experience, but the skills needed to tie basic trout and saltwater flies can be mastered in a few evenings. The average fly takes from 5 to 15 minutes to complete. Simple one- or two-step flies can be made in under a minute by a professional tier, and it might take hours to complete a full-dress salmon fly with over 30 different materials.

To construct a fly, a hook is held firmly in place by a special vise that is either attached to a heavy pedestal or clamped to a table. A spool of thread is held in a device called a bobbin, which maintains light tension on the thread via gravity, allowing the tier to release the fly while preparing materials. Materials are lashed to the hook with one continuous piece of thread throughout the process. Sometimes materials like the marabou tail of a **Woolly Bugger** or the hair on a **Clouser Minnow** are just tied in place. Other materials like cotton chenille, tinsel, or hackles are tied in place and then wound around the hook in a spiral, then

F

secured after the winding is complete. Once a fly is completed, the thread is secured with a whip finish or a few half hitches and further secured with a drop of cement for durability.

Flies are made with either natural materials like deer hair, chicken hackles, animal fur, and duck feathers; or from a myriad of synthetic materials including everything from Mylar sheets to rug yarn to silicone tubing to closed-cell foam. Many fly patterns are made from a combination of natural and synthetic materials.

FORCEPS

Forceps are an essential tool for fly fishers. They are used to hold flies while examining them or tying knots, for picking small flies 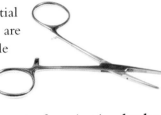 out of fly box compartments, for crimping **barbs** on **hooks** to make flies barbless, for crimping split shot to **leaders**, and for removing hooks from fish. The best forceps for fly tying should lock in place and should have smooth, not serrated jaws at the tip for properly crimping barbs on flies. Some anglers prefer straight jaws while others like curved jaws for getting flies out of fish, but either style works well. Pliers are usually used instead of forceps for the bigger flies used in salt water, but forceps are ideal for smaller saltwater species like **bonefish**.

FORWARD CAST

See Overhead Cast.

FREESTONE

Freestone is the term used by anglers to describe a stream that does not have a dam to regulate its waters and is not greatly influenced by groundwater flow. Thus, most of the water in a freestone stream is derived from rainfall and small rain-fed tributaries.

Of course all streams have some springwater influence or they would go dry in low water periods, but in freestone streams the influence is minimal. Freestone streams are most often found in mountainous areas, where abundant snowmelt keeps them full of water most of the year. They are not as fertile as **tailwaters** or **spring creeks,** so insect life may be diverse but the amount of food is limited. In addition, the great fluctuation of flow in freestone streams keeps them from being as stable as other waters, so the growth rate of fish is slower and trout are typically smaller. Trout in freestone streams are usually not very selective. Fly pattern in these waters is not as important as reading the water to find out where trout may be hiding, and then approaching the fish without disturbing them. Any reasonable fly pattern is usually sufficient because the fish have to grab every morsel that swims by in order to survive. Freestone streams typically fish best in spring, early summer, and fall, when **water temperatures** and flows are at their optimum for trout feeding.

FRYING PAN RIVER

The Frying Pan River is a delightful small **Colorado** trout stream that runs 14 miles from Reudi Reservoir outside of Basalt to the Frying Pan's junction with the Roaring Fork River. Although this very stable **tailwater** river is not large in size, the trout that live here, especially in the first few miles below Reudi dam, are some of the largest stream-dwelling trout in North America. The fish close to the dam primarily feed on **midge larvae** and Mysis shrimp, a small, pale freshwater shrimp that lives in the reservoir above and gets washed through the turbines below the dam. As the river flows further from the dam, its **riffles** and pools offer the more traditional **mayfly**, **stonefly**, and **caddis hatches**, including a tremendous **Green Drake** mayfly in June and July, a relatively large (size 12) mayfly that brings large trout to the surface. The Frying Pan is open year-round and winter fishing with **nymphs** can be very productive.

Green Drake irresistible

GAFF

A gaff is a sharp pointed hook used to land fish that will not be released. The gaff is placed in the water next to a tired fish and is jabbed quickly upward into the body of the fish. The gaff is obviously reserved for fish that will be kept for the table and has no place in catch-and-release fisheries. Even a lip gaff, which causes less bodily damage than a regular gaff, is not recommended where fish will be released. Instead, devices such as the Lipper or Boga grip are used; these devices snap rounded prongs of metal around a fish's jaws, allowing the fish to be brought to hand for a photograph or fly removal, and cause little injury to a fish that will be released quickly.

GEL SPUN

See Backing.

GEORGIA

OVERVIEW

Although northern anglers may not think of Georgia as a good place to own a **fly rod**, Georgia offers the fly fisher a host of diverse opportunities, from wild trout streams in the mountains of northern Georgia to a **tailwater** trout fishery that runs right through Atlanta. Most of the Georgia coast is undeveloped and unspoiled, and saltwater species that will take a fly are numerous. And of course, nearly every body of water in Georgia supports **largemouth bass** and bluegills.

FISHERIES

Trout fishing is extremely popular in Georgia; there are 4,100 miles of flowing waters in northern part of the state classified as trout waters by the Georgia Department of Natural Resources. The extreme southern range of **brook trout** is in the mountains of north Georgia, and although high water temperatures from development and competition from the non-native **brown** and **rainbow trout** have

Because of Georgia's warm climate, trout fishing is year-round.

pushed the brookies up into colder headwater creeks, they can still be found by an angler who is willing to hike and explore.

Because of its proximity to Atlanta, the lower Chattahoochee River, below Lake Sidney Lanier, is the most famous (and most heavily fished) trout stream in Georgia. The river flows year-round at about 54 degrees, so it offers trout fishing even on the hottest summer days. Because of its constant temperature it's also a great winter fishery. Like many tailwaters, the Chattahoochee's hatches are mainly small olive **mayflies** and **midges**, but since the river's trout are stocked the fishing is not difficult and larger flies, especially those that imitate the river's abundant stonefly **nymphs**, will catch browns and rainbows on a regular basis. Further north the Chattahoochee is also a trout stream, and the river in the Chattahoochee Wildlife Management Area offers fine trout fishing in a less urban setting. Many of the river's tributaries in this area support wild trout, including brook trout in some of the smaller streams.

The Chattooga River, best known as the river where the movie *Deliverance* was filmed, is a free-flowing river shared by South Carolina and Georgia. This is a big, brawling water, but the Chattooga's brown trout can be surprisingly selective.

There are also a number of smaller tributaries within Warwoman Wildlife Management Area and Ellicot Rock Wilderness Area that support wild trout in a more intimate setting.

The Conasauga River, in the Cohutta Wilderness area in northwest Georgia, is the most remote trout fishery in the state. Much of this water is accessible only by hiking, but worth the effort since most of the river's brown and rainbow trout are wild—and there are wild brook trout in its tributaries.

The Noontootla River, which flows into the Toccoa River and then Blue Ridge Lake south of the Georgia-Tennessee border, is considered by many the finest trout stream in Georgia. Because this river is catch-and-release and the banks are quite brushy, it does not get as much angling pressure as its reputation would indicate. The river offers mostly rainbow trout with some large browns mixed in, and many of its tributaries support wild brook trout populations.

Bass fishing in Georgia with a fly rod is best in the smaller lakes and ponds throughout the state. The bigger lakes attract more fishing pressure and boat traffic, and because the larger bodies of water are famous for their tournaments, the smaller lakes are often unknown and lightly fished. Georgia is a

G

great place to catch all five species of freshwater bass—largemouth bass everywhere, **smallmouth bass** in rivers in the northern part of the state, Suwannee bass in the extreme south, and spotted and redeye bass in the Chattahoochee and Savanna river systems. Wherever bass are found you'll discover **panfish** as well, and bluegills and redbreast **sunfish** are two of the best fly rod panfish in Georgia.

Green sunfish

Saltwater fly fishing can be found along the entire Georgia coast, and although Georgia has a small coastline, its many estuaries and marshes plus large tides provide perfect flats and marshes for sight fishing in shallow water. The most abundant fly rod targets on the **Florida** Coast are spotted sea trout and **redfish** (red drum in Georgia), but a short distance offshore will get the fly fisher close to schools of Spanish **mackerel** and perhaps a **tarpon** during the summer.

SEASONS

Because of Georgia's warm climate, trout fishing is year-round, but best in the spring and fall. Summer water temperatures, except in the Chattahoochee tailwater and in high mountain creeks, can exceed the comfort level for trout. Bass fishing in shallow water is best in February through June, when the bass will be in shallow water and interested in surface food. Saltwater fly fishing is practiced year-round, but the best fishing is from March through November. A saltwater fly fishing trip should be planned around a full or new moon, because the tides are much bigger at these times and sight fishing in shallow flats and grass beds is more productive.

GLO-BUG

Glo-Bugs are simple flies that imitate the eggs of trout, salmon, or suckers. They are made by lashing a large amount of special yarn to the middle of a **hook**, raising the yarn upright under tension, and snipping the yarn in one quick motion with sharp scissors. The yarn then falls around the hook in a sphere-shaped ball, looking very much like a pom-pom. Glo-Bugs are usually tied in red, pink, and orange to imitate salmon eggs, although white and blue are often used to simulate the color of loose eggs that have been in the river for a long time and are starting to decay. Charteuse is also very popular because it is highly visible in stained water and may mimic the greenish cast of sucker spawn. Glo-Bugs are almost always fished close to the bottom, **dead drift**, with weight on the **leader**. Although they are deadly flies and extremely popular in **Alaska** and in the Great Lakes tributaries for **steelhead**, many anglers in the steelhead's native range in northwest North America frown upon them as being too close to bait fishing.

GODDARD, JOHN

John Goddard is a British fly fisher, fly tier, author and photographer. The author of 10 fly fishing books including the landmark *The Trout and the Fly* (1980, co-authored with Brian Clark), he is also the originator of the famous Goddard Caddis, an imitation of adult **caddisflies** that is made almost entirely of spun deer hair. An accomplished saltwater fly fisher as well, he helped develop and popularize the Seychelles as a **bonefish** destination.

GOLDEN TROUT

The beautifully colored golden trout, *Oncorhynchus aquabonita,* is very closely related to the **rainbow trout**—in fact, some taxonomists consider it a subspecies of rainbow. The fish is native to a very limited range in the **California** Sierras above 10,000

G

feet, specifically the South Fork Kern River, Golden Trout Creek, and Volcano Creek. It has a brilliant golden belly, a bright red lateral line along its flanks, and a number of bluish-purple oval "parr" marks along its side. Golden trout in their native range seldom grow larger than ten inches, but fish introduced into high altitude lakes of the Wind River Range in **Wyoming** grow much larger, up to several pounds in weight. Golden trout have also been stocked in high altitude lakes in western **Montana** and **Utah**'s Uinta Mountains. Standard **dry flies** and **nymphs** will take these trout easily, as catching them is nowhere near as difficult as hiking into their habitat.

The true golden trout should not be confused with an albino rainbow trout also called a "golden trout" by public relations people. That fish is a flabby hatchery monstrosity that is stocked in some streams because it is easy to see and thus gets a lot of attention by anglers who follow hatchery trucks. Fortunately, these trout are easily spotted by other predators as well as anglers, so they seldom last more than a few weeks in nature.

GORDON, THEODORE
(1854–1915)

Theodore Gordon was a virtual hermit for most of his life; he left a career in finance because of poor health and lived the last part of his life in the Catskill Mountains, tying flies commercially and writing for both British and American sporting magazines. Gordon is often called the "father of **dry fly** fishing" which he was certainly not, though he was an important figure in the field. Anglers had been fishing dry flies in Europe and North America for decades before Gordon wrote about them, and in fact Gordon learned about dry flies from samples sent to him from Britain by **Frederick Halford**. Gordon was a fine writer and much of the advice he wrote 100 years ago about trout fishing is still valid today. Gordon also initiated the Catskill

style of dry fly, and the **Quill Gordon** fly that anglers fish today is little changed from his original pattern.

G

GRAPHITE ROD

See Fly Rod.

GRASSHOPPER

Grasshoppers are a major trout food in both the northern and southern hemispheres, and many fly patterns have been developed to imitate them. Grasshoppers can fall or fly into the water, and they are more abundant on sunny, windy days when the insects are active and more likely to wind up in the water. Typically grasshoppers do not become active until the sun warms the fields they inhabit, and trout seem to know this, so grasshopper fishing is a late morning through evening event.

Most anglers fish grasshoppers close to grassy banks, but since many of the bigger grasshoppers are strong fliers it also makes sense to try grasshopper flies in the middle of a river channel. Grasshoppers are effective fished **dead drift**, but an occasional twitch or two during a presentation will sometimes interest a trout that has not quite committed to the fly. Trout will often follow a grasshopper for quite a distance before eating it, so the fly should be fished to the end of the drift, even if it seems to float out of productive water. Grasshopper flies can also be fished under the surface. Natural grasshoppers are not good floaters and trout may actually take more of them under the surface than in the surface film. A **dry fly** can just be allowed to sink, or the angler can give it some help by adding a small amount of **split shot** or other weight about a foot above the fly on the **tippet**.

Grasshopper flies can be simple constructions like the basic Letort Hopper, which is an excellent fly to fish both wet and dry, or more complicated constructions like Dave's Hopper, with jointed legs and realistic wings. Foam hopper imitations are also very popular, with the advantage of being unsinkable. The foam flies are probably less effective on very selective fish, but their low maintenance

makes up for the occasional refusal by the trout. Many flies designed to be simple **attractors** also work well when trout are eating grasshoppers, like the PMX, Parachute PMX, Stimulator, and Chernobyl Ant. Grasshoppers vary in size and color by river and season, so the wise angler will carry hoppers in several different styles in sizes 6 through 12, in both olive and tan shades.

GRAYLING

The grayling is a beautiful northern salmonid, in the same family as trout and salmon, which is distinguished by its iridescent colors and its extremely large dorsal fin. Two species are most often pursued by fly fishers. The arctic grayling, *Thymallus arcticus*, is found throughout western **Canada** and **Alaska**, although small populations live in the upper Missouri river watershed, especially the Bighole River, and in the upper Gibbon River in **Yellowstone** National Park. These southern fish are known as **Montana** grayling, but they are the same species as the northern grayling. Graying were once native to tributaries

G

of the Great Lakes, but pollution, overfishing, and excessive logging eliminated these populations over 100 years ago. The European grayling, *Thymallus thymallus*, thrives much closer to civilization and is common in trout rivers from **England** east to the Ural Mountains.

Unlike trout, grayling are a schooling or shoaling fish. Where you catch one there will be others close by. They prefer deeper pools and runs to **riffles**, and will seldom be found in current that will hold trout. Grayling also rise to a **dry fly** in a manner unlike trout. Rather than hovering under the surface and inhaling flies, grayling lie close to the bottom and shoot up through the water column to catch an insect on the surface. Thus, their rises are splashier than those of a trout, and they often miss the fly. Although grayling are easier to catch on a subsurface fly, at times they rise eagerly to a dry where they show a decided preference for dark patterns like the Black Gnat.

The fly fisher specializing in grayling will fast become a serious **nymph** expert. Grayling are selective but very active subsurface feeders, and feed heavily on **mayfly**, **stonefly**, **caddisfly**, and **midge** larvae, as well as small freshwater crustaceans like **sow bugs** and **scuds**. Larger grayling will also prey on small **baitfish**, so if you are looking for a trophy grayling (one over two pounds) streamer patterns are a better choice. In Alaska, like nearly everything else, grayling are also fond of salmon eggs; egg imitations work well on them when salmon are in the rivers.

GREAT BRITAIN

See England, Scotland, Wales, and Ireland.

GREEN DRAKE

The Green Drake is the name of a number of common artificial flies in both Europe and North America, but it is also the fisherman's name for a number of important **mayfly hatches** on both sides of the Atlantic. In the United States west of the Mississippi, the name Green Drake refers to two mayflies: *Ephemerella grandis*, the large Green Drake, and *Ephemerella flavilinea*, the small Green Drake or "Flav." The large species is imitated by a size 10 or 12 and the smaller one by a size 14 **hook**. These flies hatch from June through August, depending on the river system, and both the large and small varieties are loved by fly fishers because they hatch in great numbers and take a long time to dry their wings, so the vulnerable just-hatched flies are favored by trout. Both

G

of these mayflies have an olive body tinged with tan or brown and gray wings.

The Green Drake of the eastern United States, *Ephemera guttulata*, is a monstrous fly (at least in mayfly terms) and is a full size 8. The cream-bodied **duns** with speckled wings tinged with green hatch throughout the day in late May and early June, especially on cloudy days. Trout feed sporadically on the duns all day long, although on bright sunny days the big mayflies may be ignored. However, when the egg-laying **spinners** return to **riffles** to lay their eggs just before dark, the entire river will be alive with feeding fish, from the largest trout to the smallest minnow. Even **shad** and channel catfish have been known to eat the spinners off the surface. Green Drake spinners are known to fishermen as "Coffin Flies," and are a ghostly white with black speckles in the wings.

The Green Drake of Europe (*Ephemera danica*), also known as just The Mayfly in England, also hatches in late May and June. Unlike their North American namesakes, the duns are favored highly by the trout and the best dry fly fishing of the season will occur during the few weeks of their emergence. These flies have a similar appearance to North American Green Drakes, but are slightly smaller; most effective imitations are a size 12.

GREEN RIVER

There are hundreds of rivers in North America with this name, but to fly fishers the Green River that begins in **Wyoming** and flows south through Flaming Gorge Reservoir and into **Utah** is the most important one. In Wyoming, in the vicinity of Pinedale, the Green is a medium-sized trout stream that offers decent but seldom spectacular fishing for wild **brown**, **cutthroat**, and **rainbow trout**. However, by the time the Green flows out of Flaming Gorge Reservoir, its flow and temperature is stabilized and the water has picked up a heavy load of nutrients.

Utah's Green River is a world-class fishery. For over 30 miles until the river hits the Colorado border (where it becomes too warm and silt-laden for trout), the river changes character from canyon water close to the dam to more open flat-land scenery in the lower 20 miles. Fish close to the dam feed most heavily on **midge larvae** and **caddisflies**, but in the lower stretches various species of **mayflies**, especially small **Blue-Winged Olives**, become more abundant. The lower Green is superb water for **grasshopper** fishing, and in certain years the riverbanks host an invasion of big cicadas.

When cicadas are abundant, large trout can be taken on huge dry flies as big as size 4 or 6.

GRIP
See Fly Rod.

GUIDE
See Fly Rod.

Harry Mark

H

HACKLE

Hackle refers to both a part of a fly and a material used to tie flies. In most cases, the hackle on a fly is the fibers that encircle the **hook** just behind the eye. This is the standard configuration on a fly, but hackle can also be wound in a spiral along the entire body of a fly, in which case it is called *palmered hackle.* The stiff, fuzzy hackle at the front of a **dry fly** is in the standard configuration, whereas the hackle that encircles the body of a **Woolly Bugger** or Woolly Worm is palmered hackle.

On a dry fly, the hackle helps float the fly by keeping the hook pinioned in the surface film. The hackle also imitates the wings and the legs of the natural insect. Dry fly hackle is made from the neck feathers of a rooster, and glossy hackles from the neck or saddle of a rooster. A good quality cape (the full set of hackles on the skin) can cost a fly tier more than $50. An expensive cape will tie hundreds of flies.

Wet flies and **nymphs** sometimes utilize hackle as well. Because the angler wants a wet fly to sink quickly and breathe with underwater currents in order to look alive, hackle used in wet flies is either soft, webby fibers from a chicken or feathers from different kinds of game birds. Partridge, woodcock, pheasant, and snipe are just some of the wild bird feathers used. **Streamers** and saltwater flies also use hackle. Sometimes long, thin chicken hackles called *saddle hackles* are tied to the hook to imitate the body and fins of a **baitfish**, and these same feathers can be wound around the hook palmer-style to create a fuzzy body.

HALFORD, FREDERICK (1844–1913)

Frederick Halford was the Victorian high priest of **dry fly** fishing, and we owe both the snobbish attitude of the dry fly purist and much of modern dry fly techniques to this fine writer and thinker. Halford practiced his craft on the chalk streams of southern **England**, notably the Rivers Test and the Itchen, and although he was not the not the first angler to purposely fish for trout with a floating fly, he codified much of the dry fly tradition we practice today, notably stalking a rising fish, **false casting** the line for accuracy and to dry the fly, and fishing **upstream** to minimize the effect of drag.

Although Halford was a brilliant thinker, he sincerely believed that fishing a dry fly this way was a superior method of fishing, and all other methods were less sophisticated. His first two books, *Floating Flies and How to Dress Them* (1886) and *Dry-Fly Fishing in Theory and Practice* (1889) are as valid and helpful today on the smooth, rich chalk streams of England and similar spring creeks throughout the world as they were well over a hundred years ago. Halford is credited with influencing famous American fly tier and writer **Theodore Gordon**, and also carried on a lifelong debate with **G.E.M. Skues**, who was equally convinced of the superiority of the artificial **nymph**.

HAND TWIST RETRIEVE

See Retrieve.

HARE'S EAR NYMPH

The Hare's Ear Nymph is one of the most popular and effective flies ever designed. Fly tiers had been using mixed fur from the ears and face of the European hare since Medieval times, but it was not until the turn of the twentieth century that tiers began using this material for artificial **nymphs**. The mixed colors and textures of hare's ear fur create an impression of life and movement under-

water, and few materials, natural or synthetic, can match its lifelike, impressionistic qualities.

The basic hare's ear nymph consists of a brown fiber tail, abdomen, and thorax of hare's ear fur, a gold tinsel rib along the abdomen of the fly, and a wing case of duck wing primary fibers. Many variations of this fly exist, including the **bead head** variety, with a brass or tungsten bead at the head of the fly, and the **flashback** version, with a piece of iridescent pearl tinsel lashed along the dorsal side of the fly. This fly is used as large as size 8 and as small as size 20, and is usually weighted, either with a metal bead or heavy wire wound underneath the body before the rest of the fly is tied.

HAT

A hat is an essential piece of fly fishing gear. The brim of a hat keeps sun off the eyes of the angler, giving better vision and less eye strain. It also keeps flare off the **sunglasses**, enabling better resolution. The brim also keeps rain and sun off the face and neck of the fly fisher, making extremes in weather much more tolerable. And, finally, a hat can give protection against the occasional errant cast, keeping a fly from embedding itself in an angler's head.

Any type of hat is better than nothing, but the style of hat chosen determines comfort and protection. Baseball hats and simple visors protect the face and are light and comfortable. Caps with very

long bills, called swordfisher style, are popular in salt water fishing because the longer brim protects the face even better on the open ocean, where the sun can be intense. Caps can also be found that have a long flap in the back, to protect the angler's neck from sunburn. Cowboy hats are popular with stream fisherman because the circular brim protects both the face and neck from sun and rain, but they are not as useful in saltwater fly fishing because the wind catches the large brim and blows them overboard.

HATCH

A hatch is when a group of insect **larvae** or **pupae** rise from the bottom of a river or lake at about the same time, split their exoskeletons, and emerge on the surface as winged adults. Some types of insects, particularly **midges**, hatch almost year-round. However, most species of insects hatch once a year, at a particular time of the season and often at a specific time of day. For instance, the **mayfly** imitated by the Hendrickson **dry fly**, *Ephemerella subvaria*, hatches daily between 3:00 and 5:00 P.M. on eastern and Midwestern rivers for a three-week period from late April through mid-May. The giant *Pteronarcys* **stonefly** of western rivers may hatch for only a few days in June in a given stretch of river, and the hatching time of the insects often moves upstream every day as water temperatures in cooler headwaters increase.

Because most insect larvae are hidden from trout, buried in silt or under rocks for most of the year, when they begin to hatch, drifting in the current as they rise to the surface, trout begin to feed aggressively and are thus easier to catch on a fly. Trout eat insects from a hatch under the surface as they drift (known as **nymph** fishing), in the surface film as they are splitting their exoskeletons (**emerger** fishing), and as the winged insects ride the surface, drying their wings, preparing to fly away (dry fly fishing). It appears that the long-term trigger for hatches is photoperiod (so a species of insects all

hatches together at about the same time), but water temperature is also a short-term trigger: Water that is too cold or too warm in any given day may depress the numbers of insects hatching, and on days when the water temperature is optimum for a given species of insects, hordes of them will hatch at once.

Rivers with rich aquatic life may show almost constant insect hatches during the spring and summer, and many species of mayflies, **caddisflies**, stoneflies, and midges could be hatching at the same time. At these times, trout will often feed selectively, choosing one type of insect over another. In more infertile rivers, hatches are less frequent and on many days not enough insects hatch at once to bring trout to the surface,

HEWITT, EDWARD RINGWOOD (1866–1953)

Edward Ringwood Hewitt was a wealthy inventor and fishing writer who lived in New York City and on the Neversink River in the Catskill Mountains. He was a tournament caster and influenced **bamboo**

H

rod design in the first half of the twentieth century, and was also an early proponent of **nymph** fishing in North America, Unfortunately, he was also quite opinionated and his theories of hard, stiff nymph fly have fallen out of favor, as opposed to the soft, fuzzy designs used today. However, he may have been the first to use lead on a **leader** combined with a **strike** indicator, one of the most popular methods of fly fishing for trout today.

Hewitt was also years ahead of his time in leader design (he favored longer 12- to 14-foot leaders as opposed to the much shorter leaders used in his day), and developed innovative flies like the Bivisible and Neversink Skater, made entirely of **hackle**. Hewitt was also innovative in his use of in-stream structures to improve trout habitat, and long before biologists proved his theories, he postulated that log structures and trees were far superior to rock dams in providing good habitat for trout.

HEX MAYFLY

The giant **mayfly** known as the Hex has the scientific name *Hexagenia limbata*, but is erroneously called the **Green Drake** in New England and the **Michigan** Caddis in the Midwest. The adult insect is not green (although it has tinges of olive) nor is it a **caddisfly**, so fly fishers call it the Hex for short to eliminate regional confusion. The Hex is the largest mayfly in North America, and both **nymphs** and adults measure about 2½ inches long, including the tails. Corresponding imitations are usually tied on a size 6 **hook**. Because it is so large, when the Hex hatches it brings the largest trout in a river to the surface, fish that might ordinarily ignore hatching insects. In fact, the insects are so prized by fish that **bass**, **sunfish**, **carp**, and even catfish will rise to them. The **hatch** lasts for about 10 days, and depending on location it can emerge anytime from late June to mid-August. The most common period to see these insects hatch is in early July.

Hex **nymphs** live in rivers and lakes with sand or silt bottoms and don't occur in every trout stream. They are most common on Midwestern trout streams, in the Great Lakes, and in large New England lakes. Hex mayflies are not as common in the western United States but are locally abundant on waters such as **California**'s Fall River. The adults almost always hatch in the evening, just at dark, and continue hatching into the night. Most of this fishing is by sound rather than sight, but fortunately the rise of a big trout to a Hex mayfly makes quite a noisy splash.

HIP BOOTS

See Waders.

HISTORY, FLY FISHING

We'll never know who first attached feathers to a **hook** and used it to lure fish. We do know that as far back as A.D. 200, Macedonians were attaching **hackles** and red wool to a hook, and used these lures to catch speckled fish that we assume were trout. The original reason was likely pragmatic— early fishermen observed fish eating insects, and the hooks used in those days were thick and crude, so that a delicate natural insect could not be impaled like other baits. They used whatever delicate, insect-like materials were at hand, and feathers, fur, and wool were the best they could find. Thousands of years later, we're still making many flies in a similar fashion. Throughout the Middle Ages and into the Renaissance, there are records of these feathered lures becoming more and more sophisticated. Anglers realized that certain flies worked better than others at different times of year, and as early as the 1500s in Germany, fly tiers were attempting to create different flies to imitate specific insects.

Early fly fishing was not like we see it today. Rods were made from whatever strong and limber sticks were at hand. Lines were made from strands of horsehair. And rather than casting, early fly fishers used long rods to "dap" their flies on the surface of the water. Reels were not widely used until the eighteenth century, and if a big fish was hooked, an angler merely threw his rod into the water and waited until the fish tired. Another huge innovation arose in the late eighteenth century— the use of drawn silkworm gut as a more transparent link to the fly, now known as a **leader**, and braided silk strands for the heavier line that propelled the fly. Instead of tying lines directly to the top of the rod, guides were invented to hold the line to the rod. That made fly casting possible, with line looping back and forth, and additional distance gained by releasing extra line held in the hand.

The nineteenth century ushered in fly casting as we know it today. In England, Alfred Ronalds attempted to classify and imitate all the insects trout

fed upon in the British Isles. Although American fly fishers were mostly using English fly patterns, Yankee ingenuity soon made history in **fly rod** construction. Prior to about 1850, rods were made from ash, willow, and many other woods. Greenheart was a tropical wood that made the best rods, but these rods were relatively weak, so they could neither cast very far nor land a big fish without breaking. Then a number of American rod makers experimented with strips of solid bamboo, glued together to form a 4-, 5-, or 6-sided rod. These split **bamboo rods**, also known as cane rods, were stronger than the older types of wood rods, yet they had enough flexibility to make longer and easier casts. This type of fly rod is still made today by dedicated craftsmen, and was the standard for fly rods until synthetic fibers came into widespread use after World War II.

Another innovation was the eyed hook. Hooks prior to the 1850s were crude pieces of bent wire, and it was difficult to make an eye loop on the end, so pieces of silkworm gut were permanently attached to the hook when the fly was tied and that piece was tied to the leader. These hooks were heavy and would sink quickly, so flies that floated on the surface were not practical. However, the eyed hook made it possible to create hooks of wire light enough to float when enough materials were put on the hook. Concurrent with this, silk fly lines that were oil impregnated and varnished were developed. These lines lasted longer, and they would float when treated with grease, so the road to fishing with a floating fly was opened.

Not content to tinker with just tackle, fish culturists began to mess with the environment. **Brown trout** from Europe were transplanted as far away as **New Zealand** and **Argentina**, bringing salmonid species to the southern hemisphere for the first time. Rainbow trout from **California** were introduced to the eastern United States and around the world. **Carp** were brought from Europe and Asia to the new World, and **largemouth bass** from **Florida** were introduced to Europe and even as far away as Japan.

H

In England, fly fishing bloomed in the Victorian era. **Frederick Halford** codified and refined **dry fly** fishing, and **G.E.M. Skues** did the same for fishing with the artificial **nymph**. **Theodore Gordon** was a prolific American correspondent and magazine writer at the turn of the twentieth century, and after communicating with Halford, he developed fly patterns inspired by the English flies but made from local American birds and animal fur, designed to imitate the different insects that trout preyed upon in American rivers. **George LaBranche**, just a little later in the twentieth century, scoffed at the idea of imitating specific insects and placed more emphasis on how the fly floated and how it was presented. Thus began the debate that continues today—should a fly fisher concentrate more on an exact insect imitation, or should he strive to present his fly in a natural manner? Most anglers hedge their bets and try to do both.

One of the first American anglers to fish seriously with nymphs, **wet flies** designed to imitate specific immature insects, was **Edward Ringwood Hewitt**. He was a brilliant and eccentric character, and held over 50 patents on inventions that ranged from improvements on gasoline engines to color photography processes. But his first love was fly fishing on his beloved Neversink River in the Catskills, and he wrote many important books on fly fishing. He once said that he could catch every trout in a river on his nymph patterns. Luckily for the trout populations that was a major exaggeration.

The early twentieth century showed great progress in the sophistication of fly fishing. American fly tiers crafted elegant flies that both imitated **baitfish** and showcased the fly tiers art. In the 1930s, **Lee Wulff**, perhaps the most famous and influential fly fisher of the twentieth century, invented the fishing vest and the Wulff series of flies, explored the salmon rivers of Labrador and Newfoundland—and perhaps most notably, began the first serious drive to release fish with his statement "Game fish are too valuable to be caught only once."

Fish had been caught on flies in salt water for hundreds of years, but most of this was done for sea bass in Europe and **striped bass** and **bluefish** on the East Coast of North America. Most rods and reels weren't up to the task of playing a **tarpon** or even a large **bonefish**, so most fly fishers just thought it could not be done. However, after World War II pioneering fly fishers like **Joe Brooks** and Lee Wulff teamed up with experienced guides in the **Florida** Keys to prove that not only could bonefish and tarpon be caught on flies, they could be landed with the stronger rods and smoother reels now available. It was not long before Wulff was catching **marlin** and **sailfish** on a fly, and today nearly every species of fish that can be caught on conventional tackle has been fooled with a fly.

Until the late 1940s, most fly fishing was practiced by rich old men, smoking pipes and wearing tweeds. But with the advent of inexpensive **fiberglass fly rods** instead of the temperamental and expensive bamboo rods, **nylon** leaders instead of drawn silkworm gut for leaders, plus increased leisure time and the widespread use of automobiles, fly fishing began to catch a more populist flavor.

Fly fishing remained a relatively arcane pastime through the 1960s. Much progress was made in developing new flies to imitate specific insects, and with the advent of modern rods and reels, fly fishing in salt water for strong gamefish like tarpon and bonefish was finally within the reach of fly fishers, but it was still difficult to learn how to use a fly rod. There were no fly fishing schools, and you'd be lucky to find a book on fly fishing in your local library.

Then, in the early 1970s, a publisher, English professor, and passionate fly fisher named Nick Lyons began to bring some of the classic fly fishing titles back in print, and worked hard to get new fly fishing writers into print. Fly fishing blossomed, with many innovations in fly design, the introduction of the **graphite rod**, and advances in lines and leaders that made them more durable and easier to care for. With the launch of the movie *A River Runs Through It*, huge audiences were exposed to the romance and beauty of fly fishing. With the increased demand for knowledge came scores of fly fishing schools, videotapes and DVDs on fly fishing, hundreds of new books—and competition in the fly fishing industry brought prices for tackle down to the point where anyone could afford a fly fishing outfit.

HOOK

Hooks designed for fly fishing are more varied than those used for any other kind of fishing, because the hook affects how well a fly will float or sink. The style used also determines the proportions of a finished fly. The loop at the front of the hook is called the *eye*, and is where the **tippet** is tied. The straight part of the hook is called the *shank*. Where the hook begins to curve is known as the bend, and the sharp end that sticks into a fish's jaw is the point. Just above the point a small cut is made into the wire to form a barb, which helps keep the hook in place. Some hooks are made without a barb to enable quick release of a fish, and anglers will also pinch the barb with a pair of pliers or forceps to make a barbed hook barbless.

Hooks begin with a length of steel **wire**, which varies in thickness from quite fine for **dry flies** to very heavy in order to hold a **tarpon** or **sailfish** without bending or breaking. The wire is then cut

to length, one end is sharpened to a point, the wire is bent to create the shape of the hook, and finally the eye is formed. The finished shape then goes through a tempering process where the wire is strengthened, and is finished to prevent rust and corrosion. Freshwater hooks are covered with a lacquer called *bronzing* that keeps the hook from rusting, but saltwater hooks are often either made from stainless steel or plated to give them further protection against the corrosive effects of saltwater.

The point of the hook is obviously a critical area of design. Less expensive and older styles of hook points are made by forging the bend of the hook flat and then cutting the point by slicing along both sides of the wire. Better quality hook points are made by "chemical sharpening," where the point of the hook is formed with a circular grinder, followed by a bath in corrosive chemicals that reduce and sharpen the diameter of the point.

Hook sizes are determined by the vertical distance between the point and the shank of the hook, known as the *gap* or *gape*. The larger the number, the smaller the hook; the smallest hook made is a size 32, which is about $\frac{3}{16}$ of an inch long. From size 32, hooks increase in size in even numbers (although odd-numbered hooks were sometimes made in the past, nearly all hooks today follow an even-numbered system) down to a size 2, then the next bigger size is a 1, followed by 1/0, 2/0, 3/0, 4/0, and 5/0. Most trout flies are in the size 6 through 22 range, saltwater flies are typically tied on size 3/0 through 6, and bass flies are size 1/0 through 10. Size 24 through 30 hooks are rarely used except for extreme cases when trout are feeding on tiny midges because these tiny sizes don't hook and hold fish well—and are tough to see. Hooks bigger than a 3/0 are seldom used in saltwater fishing. The very large hooks have wire so heavy that it is difficult to sink the hook without a lot of force, and if a fly tier wants to create a giant fly, he or she will just use more material.

Within a given hook size, shank length, wire diameter, and the shape of the bend can vary. A 2X long hook in size 10 has the same gape as a normal size 10 hook with a shank length that is the same as that on a size 8. A 4X long hook in size 10 has the same shank length as a size 6 hook. A 2X fine hook in size 10 has the same wire diameter as a size 12 standard hook. Despite this often confusing and arcane system of measuring hooks, exact measurements and interpretations vary with manufacturers. Because most gamefish key in on a particular length fly, the fly fisher should pay more attention to the length of a finished fly than the exact size hook it is tied on.

HOOK HONE

A hook hone is a critical yet often overlooked tool. The point on a fly can get dull when dropped on a rock with a careless **back cast**, and **hook** points with even a slight coat of rust will lose their penetration efficiency. Since flies are expensive, it makes more sense to sharpen a dull hook with a hone than to replace the fly. Hook hones are made from ceramic, fine Arkansas stone, or diamond dust applied to a surface. Standard knife sharpeners are too wide for all but the largest saltwater hooks, so a hook hone designed for fishing hooks should be used. Fine-toothed files are also used on heavy saltwater hooks.

Hooks are sharpened by drawing the point of the hook against the sharpening surface. The sharpest points are obtained by stroking the bottom and both

sides of the hook point until the point looks like the sharp end of a needle. A hook is sharp enough when it digs into a thumbnail when drawn across its surface. The finished point should be sharp but not too long, because a long point is thinner and weaker than a short, sharp point. This is especially critical when sharpening hooks larger than size 4.

HOOK KEEPER
See Fly Rod.

HOOKING FISH

Flies are not as soft as the natural prey that gamefish eat, nor do they have the right taste and smell. Thus it's critical that when a fish that **strikes** a fly the line is tightened immediately, enough to drive the point of the **hook** into a fish's jaw. For smaller fish like trout and **panfish**, merely raising the rod tip quickly until the line tightens is enough to securely hook a fish. It's difficult to suggest exactly how much to raise the tip, because on a short cast with a tight line the rod tip may only have to move 2 inches, whereas on a 60-foot cast with a lot of slack in the line the rod may have to be brought almost to the vertical or beyond. It's important not to strike too hard, because often a fish is moving away from the angler at the same time the strike is made, and enough force can be generated by the strike to break off a 1-pound fish on a 6-pound **tippet**.

Another method of setting the hook, used in streamer fishing for trout and for saltwater fishing, is the strip strike. It's most often used when fishing a fly that is fished subsurface with a swimming motion, where the angler strips line to keep the fly moving. When a strike is felt or if the angler feels a fish has taken the fly, a hard, long strip is made with the rod tip kept low and pointing at the fly. In this way, the fish can be hooked if the fly is in its mouth, but if the fish has not taken the fly or has rejected it, the fly just continues to move away as if it were frightened prey instead of leaping from the water as it would if the hook was set by raising the rod tip. By using the strip strike, an angler might get another chance at the fish instead of frightening it.

When fishing for larger species like **tarpon**, **sailfish**, big **striped bass**, and **pike**, raising the rod tip may be sufficient but usually another strategy is better. For instance, when striking a large tarpon, with its hard, bony jaw, a fly fisher can seldom generate enough force to drive the point home by raising the rod tip or by using just a strip strike. Here, the best strategy is to move the rod in a quick horizontal motion away from the fish and down, using the lower, stiffer butt section of the rod rather than the more flexible tip to set the hook. This is usually combined with a long hard strip strike to generate even more force, because sometimes the rod cannot be moved far enough to drive the hook into the fish's jaw.

Some species of fish take a long time to inhale a fly. Although they seem to have taken it, they may still be moving to the fly and a premature hook set may result in a missed fish. Large **cutthroat trout** and **Atlantic salmon** are two species that exhibit this behavior, and when fishing for them it's wise to hesitate briefly before setting the hook. Small **brook trout** are the other extreme—sometimes they reject a fly so rapidly that it seems as though even lightning reflexes are not good enough. Fish seldom miss a fly when they really want it. Missed fish are most often due to a strike that is too fast or too slow, or may be due to a fish that has moved for a fly but has decided to reject it at the last minute and has merely splashed at the fly with its mouth closed. Missed strikes can also be due to a hook point that is dull or bent.

HOUSATONIC RIVER

The Housatonic River is one of the best and most scenic trout rivers in the eastern United States. The river begins near the town of Pittsfield, **Massachusetts** and flows south through Connecticut into the Atlantic Ocean. Although the river contains stocked and wild trout from its headwaters down into Connecticut, the best stretch of water is a 10-mile Trout Management Area centered around West Cornwall, Connecticut. Here, the river consists of large pools connected by areas of fast, rocky runs and **riffles**. **Hatches** are abundant and some of the best are the Hendrickson **mayfly** in late April and early May, **caddisflies** from mid-May through June, and the **Green Drake** mayfly in late May and early June. Because the river here is regulated by a shallow reservoir, the water gets too warm for good trout activity in the heat of the summer, but cooler waters in fall produce excellent hatches of small olive mayflies with rising trout responding to them.

Although the Housatonic is almost entirely supported by hatchery trout, the stocked **brown** and **rainbow trout** grow quickly on its abundant food supply: Fish up to 20 inches are not uncommon. Below the Trout Management Area the river gets too warm to support trout, but there is excellent fly fishing for **smallmouth bass** and **carp** in its large pools. The mouth of the Housatonic, where it meets Long Island Sound, is also a productive spot for **striped bass** and **bluefish**.

Irresistible

ICELAND

Overview

Iceland is a barren, volcanic, windswept land almost devoid of trees, yet it has a stark beauty. It is best known for its **Atlantic salmon** fishing, and is one of the most reliable places in the world to connect with this fickle gamefish. All of Iceland's salmon fishing is in private hands, typically farmers, and the landowners take great pride and care in maintaining this resource, from building fish ladders to help salmon make their way, to establishing hatcheries to supplement natural salmon reproduction.

Iceland also offers productive fishing for resident **brown trout**, sea-run brown trout, and **arctic char**. Most of the salmon rivers support trout and char, but other rivers, above impassable falls that prevent the migration of salmon, have populations of pure brown trout. One important consideration when traveling to Iceland for fly fishing is that all tackle and waders must be disinfected by a certified veterinarian prior to arrival in the country, to pre-vent spores or eggs of alien organisms or fish diseases from entering the country. Tackle can be disinfected at the airport in Iceland, but this can involve delays.

Fisheries

Nearly every river in Iceland supports a run of Atlantic salmon. With a population of only 275,000 people, fishing pressure is sparse, but still some rivers are much better producers of salmon than others, and the fish in certain rivers are bigger. The best salmon rivers in Iceland, both for quantity of fish and size, include the Blanda, East Ranga, Hafralonsa, Laxa I Adaldal, Vatndalsa, and Laxa I Kjos. Many of Iceland's salmon rivers are small and manageable with a single-handed 9-foot rod that handles a 6-, 7-, or 8-weight line. However, bigger rivers like the Laxa I Adaldal may require a double-handed rod, especially on days when the wind blows hard. Icelandic salmon prefer small, sparse flies, and common sizes are 10, 12, and 14.

Brown trout fishing in Iceland is not as well-

Iceland offers productive fishing for resident brown trout, sea-run brown trout, and arctic char.

known but it is superb. Resident brown trout, sea-run brown trout, and arctic char can all be taken in the same pool on the same fly. Icelandic trout are all wild and the average size is quite large, because the rivers are very rich with minerals from the geothermal influence in the waters—in fact, in some rivers geysers will erupt regularly along the banks as you are fishing. Although the placid surface of most Icelandic rivers is perfect for fishing **dry flies**, **nymphs** and **streamers** are more productive.

SEASONS
The Icelandic fishing season is short, due to the short summers at this high latitude. Trout season begins in April and ends in October, with the most productive fishing in June, July, and August. Salmon season runs June through September, and the best time to fish varies by river, so it's best to check the previous season's salmon records before planning a trip.

IDAHO

OVERVIEW
Idaho offers some of the best trout fishing in North America, and outside of the more famous rivers like the Henry's Fork, South Fork of the Snake, and Silver Creek, Idaho trout streams are typically less crowded than those of other states. Because agriculture is king in Idaho, many rivers there are **tailwaters**, which means that although

runoff in flood stage might not be as severe as in free-flowing rivers, these rivers can also exhibit heavy flows in midsummer, when agricultural demands create high flows below irrigation reservoirs. Of course agriculture also means hordes of **grasshoppers** from July through September, and fly fishers like to cast big hopper patterns as much as trout like to eat them.

The native **cutthroat trout** is the most important species in Idaho. Known for daytime feeding habits and relatively easy to catch (except in heavily fished rivers like the South Fork of the Snake), the cutthroat is often found with the introduced **rainbow trout**. (Because the species are closely related, you'll often catch hybrids of these two species.) **Brown trout** are also common in some of Idaho's larger rivers, especially in their lower reaches, although not as common as in other states. And **brook trout** can be found in many of the smaller, colder rivers and lakes in the mountains.

FISHERIES
Silver Creek, near Sun Valley, has been famous since the 1930s, when local inns attracted guests like Hemingway and Gary Cooper with its promise of great duck hunting and trout fishing. Primarily a rainbow trout fishery, Silver Creek's clear waters, smooth flow, and abundant insects make for large fish that are notoriously difficult to catch. Don't go there looking for a high volume day, but appreciate the scenery and the

opportunity to try to fool one of these difficult rainbows. If you're after easier fish in the Sun Valley area, you might try the Big Wood River, where the water is faster and the fish are easier.

The Henry's Fork of the Snake River is even more famous than Silver Creek, although its rich, insect-filled waters are more fickle than other rivers in Idaho, and environmental issues with low winter flows from reservoirs can depress the river's rainbow trout population. The Henry's Fork is part spring creek, part tailwater. It originates in Henry's Lake on the **Montana** border and then flows into Island Park Reservoir. Between Island Park Reservoir and Ashton is where most of the famous and productive water of the Henry's Fork is found. Along the way, many natural springs enter the river to stabilize its flow and temperature.

The river alternates between stretches of canyon water like the Box Canyon and Cardiac Canyon, where big **stoneflies** and **caddisflies** are the rule, to the placid meadow stretches near Ashton and in the famous Harriman Ranch stretch, where many famous and innovative fly patterns have been

Excellent fly-fishing rivers in Idaho include the Lochsa River, Clearwater River, Selway River, and Kelly Creek in the northern panhandle.

developed. The smooth, rich, weedy waters of these meadow stretches are veritable insect factories, often with many species of **mayflies**, caddisflies, **midges**, and **damselflies** hatching at the same time.

The third famous river in Idaho is the South Fork of the Snake River, from Swan Valley downstream to Byington. This large tailwater river is famous for its large and abundant cutthroat trout, as well as some rainbows and browns. South Fork fish can be fussy at the height of an insect **hatch**, but they are far easier to catch than the rainbows of Henry's Fork or Silver Creek. Although the South Fork does not host the abundant diversity of life that these other rivers do, it does have a superb hatch of giant **Salmonfly** stoneflies and profuse summer hatches of small **Pale Morning Dun** and tiny olive mayflies, plus the ubiquitous grasshoppers later in the summer.

Other excellent fly fishing rivers in Idaho include the Lochsa River, Clearwater River, Selway River, and Kelly Creek in the northern panhandle. These rivers are mainly cutthroat trout waters (although the Clearwater has a great run of **steelhead** that come all the way up the Columbia River system and arrive in late August through November). In the central part of the state, the upper Salmon River offers good spring and fall steelhead fishing, with decent trout fishing for smaller cutthroats and rainbows during the summer. But the main attraction here are the hundreds of lakes and small streams in the Frank Church River of No Return Wilderness Area, many of which hold populations of trout that hardly ever see a fly. In the Henry's Fork area, a few smaller streams that offer smaller but easier-to-catch trout include the Fall River, Warm River, and Teton River.

The lower, warmer reaches of many trout rivers in Idaho offer some excellent **smallmouth bass** fishing on a **fly rod**. In particular, the Snake River on the Washington-Idaho border downstream through the Hell's Canyon area gives up fly rod smallmouths in the five-pound range. Spring and fall fishing is best, particularly in the fall, when the water is lower and the fish are feeding in preparation for winter.

SEASONS

The general trout season in Idaho is from Memorial Day through the end of November, although some rivers with special sections, in particular the Big Wood River, are open all year long and offer excellent midge and **nymph** fishing on bright winter days. In June and early July, fishing can be difficult due to snow runoff, except on smaller streams, tailwaters, or spring-fed rivers like the upper Teton. By late June, if rivers are clear the giant salmonflies hatch and fishing can be wild and exciting with big **dry flies**. During the summer as long as water temperatures stay above 65 degrees there is excellent fishing with smaller mayflies, caddisflies, and stoneflies, as well as grasshoppers in late summer and early fall. Fall on Idaho rivers can be spectacular, with fewer anglers on the river, lower flows, and cooler temperatures. Later in the fall, cold rain and snow can make for uncomfortable conditions—but usually the trout feed better on dreary days.

IMAGO
See Mayfly.

INDICATORS
Indicators, also known as **strike** indicators, are small floating devices attached to the leader that aid the angler in determining when fish take a subsurface fly, most often a **nymph**. They are merely bobbers reduced to a scale small enough to be cast with a **fly rod**, and although some fly fishers scorn them, strike indicators make nymph fishing much easier for the novice angler, and have opened up the world of **dead drift** nymphing to many anglers who would otherwise have given up on nymph fishing. Strike indicators provide much more than a hint of an otherwise unseen strike. They help the fly fisher determine about where the fly is drifting, and they also help keep the fly in a natural drift, as if the indicator on the surface begins to drag across the current, it's obvious that the fly underneath it is

not drifting naturally, and the line can be **mended** to get a natural drift back on course.

Most anglers place a strike indicator on the **leader** above the fly at a distance that is between 1½ and 2 times the water depth. Because the fly does not hang straight down (it's usually at more of a 45-degree angle), this ensures that the fly drifts close to the bottom where trout lie in the current. During a **hatch**, when insects are drifting in the middle of the water column and rising to the surface, a strike indicator may be set closer to the fly to allow it to drift further from the bottom.

Strike indicators are made from closed-cell foam, cork, Styrofoam, yarn, and floating putty. The best kinds are the ones that can be removed from the leader and moved, because during a few hours of fishing an angler might move from a shallow **riffle** to a deep pool, and the indicator must be moved for best performance. The foam or cork types are threaded on the leader and held in place with a toothpick or rubber grommet, which can be easily moved. These are the most durable and the best floating of all. Yarn, treated with silicone fly **flotant** and held in place with a slip knot, is more subtle and lands softer, and these are preferred in quiet water where trout may be spooked by the splash of a bigger indicator. Floating putty indicators are molded to the leader, usually at a knot for added security. They are best for the angler who is switching back and forth between **dry flies** and nymphs because they can be removed from the leader in seconds, but they do not stay on the leader as well as other types.

Yet another way to detect strikes and follow the drift of a nymph is to use a dry fly attached to the leader and a nymph as a **dropper**. The dry fly must be large and float very well, so the best dries to use in this arrangement are foam dry flies or those with a lot of bushy **hackle**. Although more difficult to cast than a slim indicator, a big dry fly doubles the chances of a strike and tells the angler whether the fish are more interested in surface or subsurface food.

INTERMEDIATE FLY LINE
See Fly Line.

THE INTERNATIONAL GAME FISH ASSOCIATION (IGFA)
See World Records.

IRELAND
Overview
With its cool temperate climate, warmed by the Gulf Stream yet in northern latitudes with plentiful rainfall, Ireland has a vast number of scenic rivers and lochs (loughs in Ireland) that offer productive fishing for **Atlantic salmon**, sea-run **brown trout**, resident brown trout, and private and public lake fisheries for stocked **rainbow** and brown trout. **Pike** may also be caught on a fly in loughs and in larger, slower rivers.

Fisheries
Like Atlantic salmon fishing anywhere, salmon fishing in Ireland is fickle and entirely dependent on local rainfall and the strength of a particular year's salmon run. Ireland is not known for its giant salmon, but many rivers have productive runs of grilse in the spring with runs of bigger fish February through April and then again in July through September. Many of Ireland's rivers are "spate" rivers, which means salmon run them only when swollen with a recent rainfall; in periods of drought these rivers don't have enough flow to entice salmon up from the sea. The most productive salmon rivers in Ireland include the Blackwater (County Waterford), Drowes (Donegal), Mourne (Tyrone), Bush (Antrim), Caragh (Kerry), and the famous Owenmore River fishery near Ballynahinch Castle.

Lough fishing enjoys an old and grand tradition in Ireland.

I

Ireland has a long tradition of developing classic Atlantic salmon flies. Most of the popular flies used today are shrimp patterns like the Siler Shrimp, Apache, and Ally's Shrimp, but sparse traditional patterns like the Stoat's Tail, Thunder & Lightning, Blue Charm, and Hairy Mary are often used as well. During the early season, for big water and high flows, flies in sizes 4, 6, and 8 are used on 14- to 16-foot double-handed rods. During the lower flows of late spring and summer most anglers switch for single-handed 9-foot rods for an 8- or 9-weight line.

Lough fishing enjoys an old and grand tradition in Ireland. Although **stillwater** techniques effective in other parts of the world will catch fish, the best method is to fish a long (10- to 11-foot) single-handed rod with three flies on the **leader**. The top or "bob" fly is usually a bushy pattern that is fished on the surface and the other two flies are dragged just under the surface. **Dry fly** fishing is also productive. In April, dark **mayflies,** typically with olive bodies, begin to **hatch,** followed in May and June by **caddisflies** (known here as sedges) and black gnats (**midges**) appear. In September, **wet fly** and **nymph** fishing is good but most of the insect hatches have diminished.

Because most Irish loughs have boggy or rocky shores, wading or bank fishing is difficult and it's really necessary to hire a gillie (guide) or rent a boat. Most of the better Irish loughes, like Melvin, Corrib, Mask, Conn, Allen, and Arrow are large, windswept bodies of water. The fish will be concentrated in certain areas and without the help of a knowledgeable gillie, fishing this big water could be an exercise in frustration. In addition, maneuvering the boat so the flies drift perfectly with the wave lines is not easy for a trout fisherman used to river fishing.

Ireland has many fine trout rivers, with a combination of rich limestone waters and less productive peat-stained "blackwater" rivers. All Irish river trout are wild brown trout, and although most are not of gigantic size (a good one would

be 16 inches) they are beautiful, spirited, and often quite selective. All trout rivers are private but getting access for a moderate fee through hotels or gillies is quite easy. Early season is mostly nymph fishing, with dry fly fishing better as spring and summer progress and waters get low and clear. Perhaps the best trout river in Ireland is the Suir, a large limestone stream in Tipperary with prolific hatches, and its tributary the Tar is also highly regarded. The River Nire in this area is a freestone stream that has good fishing but fewer hatches. In Kildare County, the River Boyne is another excellent limestone stream with great hatches, and its tributary, the Kells Blackwater, is known for its sea trout fishing.

SEASONS

Salmon season in Ireland begins in January but the best spring salmon fishing is from February through April. Early spring is good for small grilse and medium-sized salmon. Midsummer salmon fishing can be very spotty unless rivers get a good amount of rain, but by late July fresh fish enter from the sea on the way to spawning grounds in late fall.

Lough fishing for trout begins in April and the fishing is best in April and May, when optimum water temperatures and productive fly hatches coincide. Lough fishing in midsummer can be difficult, but the fishing picks up again in September when water temperatures cool. Trout fishing in rivers, on the other hand, is slow in early spring but picks up in midsummer, when water levels drop, insects hatch, and the fish feed actively on the surface. Trout fishing can be productive around midday in spring, but is best in the evening during the summer months. In the fall, the best fishing time reverts to the middle of the day.

ISONYCHIA

Isonychia is a genus of **mayflies,** often known to fly fishers as "Isos," that live in trout streams throughout

North America. These mayflies are large (size 10 and 12, between ½ inch and one inch in total length) and abundant, thus they attract the attention of both trout and fly fishers. *Isonychia* **larvae**, unlike most mayflies, are very fast swimmers and are often confused with tiny minnows when seen in the shallows. Because they do not hide under rocks all the time, they are more available to trout even when not **hatching** so are a regular source of food. The larvae are well imitated by **nymphs** made with peacock herl like the Prince Nymph and Zug Bug, although specific imitations like the Wiggle Iso may sometimes work better. Because the nymphs move under their own power, this is one mayfly nymph that can be fished with fast strips instead of **dead drift**.

Nymphs hatch into adults throughout the summer and fall in most rivers, with June, August, and September producing the best hatches. Unusual for mayflies, this insect does not hatch in mid-current but swims to the shallows and crawls onto rocks just above the waterline to hatch. However, the big, clumsy **duns** do fall back into the water or get blown there by the wind, so trout also feed on them when available. The egg-laying **spinners** also return to the water in a day or so, and trout feed on them heavily. For some reason, **rainbow trout** seem particularly fond of Isonychia adults, perhaps because they hatch in the fast water that rainbows prefer. Best imitations of the adult insects, both dun and spinner, include the Rusty Comparadun, Dun Variant, and Oh-So Iso. Both nymphs and dry flies should be carried in sizes 10 and 12.

Jack's fighting crab

J

JENNINGS, PRESTON (1898–1962)

Preston Jennings was the first American angler to catalog important trout-stream insects in their proper scientific names, so anglers throughout the country could begin to communicate on the timing of **hatches** and suitable imitations. Prior to his *A Book of Trout Flies* in 1935, American fly fishers communicated in common names like "Whirling Blue Dun," and an angler from another river would not even know if the fly in question was a **mayfly** or a **caddisfly**, much less its genus or species. British fly hatches had been cataloged over 100 years before Jennings's book, so it was a welcome reference for American trout streams. Jennings was also fascinated by the nature of fish vision and the optical properties of water, and developed a series of trout and salmon flies called the "Optic" series that based the color scheme of the flies on the colors of the spectrum.

JETTY

A jetty is a structure placed along the shore or at the mouth of a harbor to break the waves and protect

boats or beaches from the ravages of wind and waves. Jetties harbor schools of **baitfish** and crustaceans, and thus are likely places to find feeding gamefish. Baitfish and gamefish are typically more common in the lee or downwind side of a jetty; where a pair of jetties marks the entrance of a harbor, the fish will more often be found on the outside walls of the jetty on the outgoing tide and inside the harbor on the incoming tide. Jetties are often slick with algae and the rocks may be slanted and sharp, so when fishing from the jetty itself it helps to wear cleated boots for safety. The jumbled rocks of jetties also create a trap for loose fly line, so another important piece of gear when fishing from a jetty is a stripping basket, to keep coiled fly line from tangling among the rocks and debris.

Killer Bee

KAYAK

Kayaks are superb fly fishing crafts because they are swift and silent, and are more reliable in wind and strong tides than **canoes** or **belly boats**. Kayaks can be launched anywhere, unlike power boats, and a fly fisher is able to get much closer to feeding fish in a kayak. Although any kind of kayak can be used for fly fishing, most anglers choose the "sit-on-top" variety because they have more room for storage and quick access to gear, can be made so stable that the fly fisher can cast from one standing up, and can also pole through very shallow water in search of fish. Essential in any kayak used for fishing is a rod holder, so that a fully strung rod can be safely put aside while paddling from one location to another. A 9-foot kayak is best for smaller lakes and rivers because it is highly maneuverable, but for salt water, where wind and tides make it difficult to stay on course, a 12- or 14-foot kayak is a better and safer craft.

KELSON, GEORGE (1835–1920)

George Kelson was a prominent salmon fisher and fly tier in Victorian England, and caught over 3,000 salmon on the fly in his lifetime. His monumental work, *The Salmon Fly*, published in 1895, is still considered by salmon fly tiers to be the ultimate reference on the proper recipes for the complicated featherwing salmon flies of this era. Kelson was instrumental in the design of "Farlow's Patent Lever" reel, which had a drag system comparable in sophistication to today's disc **drag reels**.

KNIGHT, JOHN ALDEN (1891–1966)

John Alden Knight was a fishing writer of the 1930s and 1940s, most famous for his development of the "Solunar Tables." While fishing in **Florida** in the 1920s he interviewed some market hunters and fisherman regarding popular folk wisdom about the relationship of the sun and moon position to feeding activities of freshwater fish, similar to tidal effects in salt water. These people who made their living chasing fish and game had determined that besides sunset and sunrise, there are two major feeding periods in each day, when the moon is either directly overhead or directly underfoot. After considerable research, Knight also discovered what he thought were also two less significant but productive minor feeding periods each day. The Solunar Tables are still published today.

KREH, LEFTY (1925–)

Bernard "Lefty" Kreh was one of the most famous fly fishers of the twentieth century. Actually right-handed, he earned his nickname because he was able to fly cast equally well with either hand. Lefty Kreh learned to fly fish from **Joe Brooks** in 1947. Although already an accomplished hunter and fisherman, he soon became passionate about fly fishing, especially saltwater fly fishing. He began his saltwater fly fishing career in Chesapeake Bay fishing for **striped bass**, where he developed the Lefty's

Deceiver, a saltwater fly so famous that it graced a U.S. postage stamp. Kreh soon moved into the world of **Florida** Keys fly fishing, and was a pioneer in developing the **bonefish** and **tarpon** fisheries in Florida. He has written over 20 books on fly fishing and thousands of newspaper and magazine articles, and has consulted for many tackle manufacturers.

KRIEGER, MEL (1928–2008)

Mel Krieger was a San Francisco–based tournament fly caster and internationally recognized fly casting teacher. Through his books, classes, and videos, he taught thousands of people to cast using a method based on a combination of tournament casting principles and common sense. He was instrumental in helping to develop the **Federation of Fly Fishers'** Fly Fishing Instructor Certification Program.

Lime Wulff

LABRANCHE, GEORGE (1875–1961)

George LaBranche was a contemporary and friend of **Edward Ringwood Hewitt**, and like Hewitt owned water on the Neversink River in the Catskill Mountains of **New York** State. He was a tournament caster and early saltwater fly fishing pioneer, but is most famous for his two books *The Dry Fly and Fast Water* (1914) and *The Salmon and the Dry Fly* (1924). LaBranche was an ardent proponent of "fishing the water" with a **dry fly** instead of trying to present an exact imitation of an insect to the fish. His books, especially *The Dry Fly and Fast Water*, are as useful today as they were in the early twentieth century, especially for the fly fisher who prefers mountain or wilderness trout streams.

LAKE FISHING

Lake fishing, or stillwater fishing, presents its own set of challenges. Although the difficulties of conflicting currents and **line drag** don't occur in still water, fish can get much deeper in lakes and are thus sometimes beyond the realm of practical trout fishing. The smooth water of a lake surface also makes fish, especially trout, more wary and more particular about the flies they eat. Getting around in a deep lake is not as easy as wading a shallow stream, and often requires the help of some type of water craft.

GETTING TO THE FISH

Fly fishing can be done from shore. If fish are feeding in the shallows, the edge of a shallow lake or pond can be waded as long as the water is shallow enough and not so mucky that it traps your feet. If the edge of a lake is covered with trees or brush that prevent a **back cast**, it's an easy matter to wade into the shallows and cast parallel to the shore. If you are faced with a wall of brush and the water is too deep to wade, you can always resort to a **roll cast** or some variation of a **Spey cast**, but these casts disturb the water more than an **overhead cast** and seldom place the fly accurately very far from shore. Of course, fly fishing can be done from docks as well, and sometimes a strategically placed dock is a great way to get your fly further into a lake.

Most lake fishing is best done with some type of watercraft. **Belly boats** are an easy way to work the shallows, as long as you don't have heavy weed growth to plow through or the wind does not blow hard, as these craft are very hard to paddle against the wind. For longer trips, and to get through mats of lily pads or other aquatic vegetation, a **canoe** is a time-honored way of fly fishing in a lake or pond. Quiet and relatively swift, a canoe does not require a boat-launching area

and can get the fly fisher to places that a motorboat can't reach. Because you can't paddle and fish at the same time (unless you just want to troll a fly behind your canoe), it's best to fish with another person in a bigger canoe, so that one person can concentrate on fishing and the other maneuvers the boat into position. **Kayaks** are also excellent fishing craft for the same reasons; since kayaks can handle the wind and can cover distances better than canoes, many fly fishers prefer them for bigger lakes.

You can fly fish from any kind of motorized craft, but some are better than others. A good fly fishing motorboat should have a shallow draft to get you into tight spots and the shallows where most feeding takes place. Motorized boats also make it difficult to sneak up on feeding fish, unless they can be brought into the final fishing position with a push-pole, paddle, or electric motor. Thus the best motorized boats for fly fishing are simple bass boats, flats boats, or johnboats. The simpler the better for fly fishing, because any gear that sticks up from the deck or gunwales will clutch a fly line and create casting obstacles.

FINDING FISH

The fly fisher used to fishing in a river, with its complicated structure and currents, may at first be mystified when presented with a 20-acre surface that at first glance appears devoid of features. However, fish are not everywhere in lakes, and are usually concentrated in small areas. The most obvious and productive place in a lake is near shore. Most **baitfish**, **crayfish**, **scuds**, and insects are shallow-water dwellers, and if **water temperatures** are within an optimal range, gamefish will be in the shallows as well. But not all shallows are created equal. Weeds, submerged brush, piles of large rocks, points of land, docks, and bays all provide refuges for food organisms. So the

first thing to look for is some kind of structure along the shore.

Streams entering lakes provide current for certain kinds of insects, as well as warmer water in winter and cooler water in summer. Some species of gamefish like trout and many types of baitfish also enter streams to spawn, so any moving water entering a lake will create a likely place to find fish. In a similar manner, the outlet of a lake also offers the necessary current and some species of fish will spawn in outlets as well.

If the fish are over deeper water in the center of a lake, which is common during the summer, you can also look for structure. A point of land that sticks out into a lake does not end at the shoreline, and chances are the point extends well out into the lake, creating a structure that will hold both gamefish and their prey. Springs entering the bed of a lake also concentrate fish, particularly trout. The best spring holes are known historically to local fishermen just from experience, but a thermometer carried on a long string can help you sound various places in a lake to find cooler summer temperatures. Of course, a depth finder is a great way to find concentrations of fish, either by spotting the fish themselves or by spotting structures on the bottom.

On a calm surface one of the best ways to find fish in a lake is to cruise and look for movement on the surface. Fish rising to insects in a lake don't splash, especially when feeding on tiny **midges**. You may have to get quite close to see the rings made by fish sipping tiny insects. When gamefish are chasing schools of baitfish, however, it's a different story. This commotion can often be seen a half-mile away, and sometimes its possible to hear the splashes as trout, bass, or landlocked **striped bass** herd baitfish on the surface.

Techniques for Catching Trout

The most enjoyable way to catch trout in a lake or pond is when they are feeding on the surface. However, trout rising to insects in still water don't behave the same way they do in streams, and are also more

difficult to catch. The most important difference is that trout feed on the surface by cruising. In a river they stay in one place and let the food come to them; in lakes they have to range to capture their food. A good plan of attack is to watch a trout rise at least twice, as then you at least have an idea as to which way the fish is cruising. They often feed in a line for quite a while, then turn around and cruise back in the same direction, especially if the quantity of food they encounter diminishes. The best tactic is to cast well ahead of a feeding fish with a **dry fly** or **emerger** and wait for the fish to come to the fly. If the fish rises in an unexpected direction, you can carefully pick up your line and make another cast on the new trajectory.

Casting for brook trout on Sullivan county lake, Pennsylvania.

The most conservative approach is to just cast your dry fly and let it sit, hoping a trout will stumble into it. However, there are times when a subtle twitch, made by stripping a small amount of line, will make a trout notice your offering. And sometimes, as a last resort, a fly twitching across the surface in a steady manner will interest an aggressive fish.

Although fly fishers always hope to find trout feeding on big, juicy **mayflies**, **damselflies**, or **caddisflies** that are easy to imitate with a high-floating fly, one of the most important surface foods in lakes is **hatching** midges. And even though the fish appear to be eating midges on the surface, they often feed on midge **pupae** just below the surface, so a small emerger or midge pupa, either cast and left to sink slowly or stripped back with a steady, patient retrieve is a wiser move than starting out with a small dry fly. **Leaders** for fishing dry flies in lakes and ponds should be long—a 12-foot leader is the minimum length, and often a 15-foot or even 20-foot leader is a better choice for presenting the fly to wary stillwater trout.

Nymphs are the second choice of most still-water fly fishers. The most exciting situation is where trout are feeding on scuds or insect **larvae** in clear, shallow water and its possible to sight-cast to the fish. Here, a feeding fish is carefully stalked and the fly is cast about five feet in front of the fish and allowed to sink. When the trout approaches the fly, one small strip may get the fish to **strike**, but if the trout does not inhale the fly then a steady retrieve may work. You will usually feel the strike, but it's often apparent that a trout has taken your fly when you see its mouth open or you see the fish shaking its head from side to side.

Nymphs will also work to invisible fish in deeper water. Find a place that you suspect holds trout and cast the nymph, retrieving with short, steady strips to make your fly look like a damselfly or mayfly nymph scooting through the water. This can be done with a floating **fly line** in shallow water, but any fly fisher who frequents lakes or ponds will eventually want to get a **sinking fly line**. In shallow ponds an intermediate line may be all that's needed, but when fishing lakes that are more than six feet deep the need for a full-sinking line will come up quicker than you think. Not only do sinking lines get the fly deeper, they keep the fly swimming deeper instead of pulling it toward the surface as a floating line would do.

Streamers are often the most successful way to fish lakes and ponds when no feeding fish

are seen. A streamer can be worked quicker than a nymph (because baitfish swim faster than insects a fast retrieve is realistic). Leeches are one of the most common trout foods in lakes and ponds, so a dark brown or black leech imitation is often a first choice, but baitfish, crayfish, and damselfly nymphs also swim with a brisk motion, so a streamer can cover a wide variety of potential trout prey. A sinking line is the best way to fish streamers. When one location is suspected, such as off the end of a point or stream mouth, a streamer can be fished using the count-down method, where the fly is cast and the line is allowed to sink for two seconds, followed by three or four seconds for the second cast, allowing the fly to fish deeper on each succeeding cast until a fish is caught or the fly snags on the bottom. In the middle of a lake, where the fly fisher has no idea where fish might be, the fly can be cast methodically in the 360 degree circle (called the clock method) until a fish is caught, and this method can be combined with the countdown method to cover even more water.

Techniques for Catching Bass, Pike, and Panfish

Like trout, the most enjoyable way to catch bass and **panfish** is in the shallows with a floating **popper.** This technique is most effective during the summer in early morning and evening when bass range out of deep water and into the shallows searching for food. During the spawning period for bass in March through June, depending on location, bass will take a floating popper throughout the day, when they are aggressively defending their nests. A quick scan of the shallows will show the saucer-shaped nests or **redds** where fish have cleaned the bottom to lay their eggs, and if fish are in the vicinity of the redds a popper cast over the top is bound to provoke a strike. At other times of the year, when bass are feeding in the shallows during periods of low light, the most effective way to fish a popper is to cast it close to weeds or submerged logs and let the fly sit completely still until all the rings have dissipated, then make a single strip enough to move the fly, wait again until all movement has stopped, and strip again. Bass will sometimes eyeball a motionless fly for over a minute before taking it, or will follow a fly for ten feet before deciding to strike. **Sunfish** and other panfish are not as cagey and will usually strike a small popper right after it hits the water, or just after it moves.

Bass and **pike** can also be caught on streamer flies that imitate baitfish, swimming frogs, leeches, or crayfish. In spring when the fish are shallow, cast the fly over a likely place and retrieve with steady pulls. It's best to use weedless flies as the best presentation is when the fly swims through brush piles, lily pads, or cattails where prey would be hiding. **Largemouth bass** prefer a slow and steady retrieve, **smallmouths** like their flies moving a little quicker, and pike (and their relatives pickerel and **muskellunge**) like the fastest moving fly of all. During a bright summer day or during cold weather when bass and panfish appear to be deep, the best bet is a streamer fly fished on a sinking line. Here, the same broadcast methods used for trout are the best approach.

The red-breasted sunfish, a common panfish in warmwater lakes.

LAKE TROUT

Lake trout, *Salvelinus namaycush*, also known as gray trout or togue, are actually char and are more closely related to **brook trout** or **arctic char** than to **rainbow** or **cutthroat trout.** Their native range is deep, cold lakes from Alaska to Labrador and south to the Great Lakes and upper Mississippi drainage. They grow quite large on a diet almost exclusively comprised of **baitfish**, and specimens of over 20 pounds are not uncommon. Lake trout are paler than most other trout, and can be identified by a grayish green color with a dense pattern of small pale spots.

Lake trout are most often found in depths of over 100 feet in lakes, but in the spring and fall they can be found in shallow water, within the reach of a fly fisher. Lake trout will also ascend rivers to chase baitfish, and in Labrador they can be found in moving water throughout the summer, where they are regularly caught on **streamer** flies. In lakes, lake trout are almost always caught on **sinking fly lines** off rocky points or over shoals in the spring and fall. Lake trout are not strong fighters in lakes, although a big specimen in the fast current of a big river will test a light **fly rod** to its limits.

L

LANDING FISH
See Playing Fish.

LARGE ARBOR REELS
See Fly Reel.

LARVA

Aquatic insect larvae are the most important trout foods. Aquatic larvae are also known as naiads or **nymphs**, and the term nymph is also used to describe, in generic terms, the flies that imitate them. The winged terrestrial adult of a given species of aquatic insect is only available to trout for a few days or weeks during a yearly cycle, but once **hatched** from eggs on the stream bottom, the larvae are present beneath the surface year-round. Common species of aquatic larvae include the **mayfly**, **caddisfly**, **stonefly**, **midge**, **damselfly**, **cranefly**, and **dragonfly**, and all of them have specific flies tied to imitate them (as well as generic flies that may imitate a number of different types, like the **Hare's Ear Nymph** and **Prince Nymph**). Although midges, craneflies, and caddisflies transform into a **pupa** stage for a short time before hatching, mayflies, stoneflies, dragonflies, and damselflies exhibit incomplete metamorphosis, and hatch into adults directly from the larva stage.

Just because larvae are under the water's surface for so long does not mean that trout are able to eat them at will. Caddisflies attach sticks or stones to their skins and glue themselves to rocks. Mayflies and stoneflies are flattened and hold tenaciously to the underside of rocks. Craneflies and midges bury themselves in the mud. Because trout more often feed on objects drifting in the water rather than grubbing on the bottom like pigs in a sty, they eat more larvae when the bottom is disturbed during a flood or when the insects begin to drift in the current prior to hatching into winged adults. Additionally, aquatic insects periodically release their grip on the bottom of a stream and drift in the

Caddis larva

current after dark, a re-colonization phenomenon known as "periodic drift." For this reason, imitations of aquatic larvae work best during a rise of water, just before a hatch, or early in the morning when larvae that have drifted through the night begin to find new locations.

LEADER

Fly fishing is impossible without a relatively flexible, transparent or translucent link between the fly and **fly line**, because fly lines are very thick in relation to the fly and are usually opaque. It would be a very hungry or vicious fish that would eat an artificial fly tied directly to a fly line—**bluefish** and **sharks** are two species that might, but because of their razor-sharp teeth even these species require a piece of wire between the fly and line.

A leader can be as simple as a 3-foot piece of 20-pound monofilament fishing line tied to the end of a fly line. Fish like **largemouth bass** in weedy lakes or **striped bass** in the surf, where delicacy is not an issue and flies are large, may require nothing else. However, many fish, from **bonefish** in ocean flats to trout in small streams, require some element of stealth and delicacy between the line and the fly. Most game fish, when "lined" with the fly line, where the fly lands right on top of them, immediately run for cover and stop feeding.

Most leaders are **tapered**, with the thickest section (the butt) joined to the line, either with a **loop connection** or permanently knotted to the fly line with a **nail knot**. The greater diameter closest to the fly line and the gradually decreasing diameter as it approaches the fly ensures that the energy from the unfurling casting loop is dissipated by the greater air resistance at the finer diameter **tippet**. In a well-constructed leader (and with a well-executed cast), the fly lands where you point the tip of the rod, but with a minimum of disturbance.

LEADER TYPES

From Medieval times until the late eighteenth century, leaders (and lines) were made from twisted horsehair. Horsehair is neither transparent nor particularly strong, and it's brittle so we can imagine that early fly fishers lost a lot of fish and had to change their leader often. Around 1800, drawn silkworm gut was introduced. The silkworm digestive tract, when drawn through a gauge of a particular diameter, formed a flexible, translucent thread that made a fly on the water look a lot more realistic. To get a taper, sections were knotted together in decreasing diameters. These *gut* leaders were used until **nylon** was introduced after World War II. Nylon leaders were a revelation because they were stronger, more flexible, more translucent, and didn't need to be soaked before use (silkworm gut is brittle until it is soaked in water for several hours).

Nylon remains the most popular leader material today, and there have been many advances in nylon leader material since its early days. Improvements have made today's nylon leaders stronger in diameter and more resistant to degradation by ultraviolet light. In the 1990s, **fluorocarbon** (or PVDF) was introduced. This material, first used in the packaging industry, is denser than nylon so it sinks quicker, and its specific gravity is closer to that of water, so it is nearly invisible in water. Fluorocarbon is also completely impervious to ultraviolet light, absorbs little water (water absorption makes knots weaker), and is more abrasion resistant than nylon. Fluorocarbon, however, is much more expensive than nylon and is more difficult to knot, so it is used for leaders in more specialized situations, especially in saltwater leaders where its qualities are most beneficial. Most leaders are made from **monofilament**, which is a solid piece of material that is uniform in consistency in cross section—although some materials have coatings added to them to protect them from UV or to enhance abrasion resistance.

Leaders can be knotted or knotless. Knotted leaders are made by tying together individual sections of leader material, in gradually decreasing diameter, to obtain the proper taper. Knotless leaders are made by machine. Nylon or fluorocarbon is extruded and then heated, stretched, and cooled (sometimes several times) to obtain the correct taper. Machines to make tapered leaders are expensive and complicated to run, but they can produce a precise taper for many different types of fishing. Knotless leaders land softer, they don't have knots that can potentially weaken the leader if not tied properly, and knots can catch on weeds or other debris in the water.

L

Knotted leaders are cheaper to make and more interesting if you like to design your own leaders. Most anglers today use knotless leaders, and when the tippet gets too short or too heavy, they add a new piece of tippet material. One knot in a leader is less obtrusive than a dozen.

Although the tippet section of all leaders is made from nylon or fluorocarbon monofilament, some leaders use a different type of butt section. Braided leaders are made from many tiny nylon filaments braided around a hollow core, and the taper is obtained by gradually decreasing the number of filaments as you get closer to the tippet. A standard piece of monofilament is then either looped or knotted to the end of the braid. Furled leaders are similar, but instead of being hollow they are made from a solid braid of heavier-diameter monofilament strands. Both of these leaders are more flexible than monofilament and their proponents argue that they transmit casting energy from a fly line more efficiently and thus cast better in the wind. Being more flexible, they also offer some assistance in reducing **drag** on the fly when placing the leader across conflicting currents. Braided and furled leaders are also supple right out of the package, and don't need to have the coils removed from them by pulling and stretching the leader prior to use.

LEADER LENGTH

The length of the leader is an important consideration. Problems arise is casting the fly when the leader gets too long and fine. With a leader over 15 inches long, the casting energy imparted by the fly line is diminished too much and accurate casting becomes difficult. Additionally, as a leader gets longer it becomes more air resistant, and leaders longer than 9 feet long are difficult for most casters to straighten in the wind. Luckily, most fish can be presented a fly with a 9-foot leader or even shorter without frightening them.

At the short end of the spectrum, leaders fished with sinking lines in fast or discolored water can be as short as 24 inches long and don't even have to be tapered. Sinking lines don't offer much delicacy, because the idea is to get the fly well below the surface of the water, usually far away from the fish, so this line merely sneaks up on the fish from under the surface. (Even in clear water fish can't see very far below the surface because of the diffusion of light rays by diffraction and small particles in the water.) A standard leader used with a sinking line is about 6 feet long—this keeps the fly far enough from the heavy line, but is easy to cast with a relatively awkward sinking line. In addition, because nylon has a specific gravity close to water and any oil or dirt on the leader will make a nylon leader float, too long of a leader will buoy the fly close to the surface, defeating the purpose of the sinking line.

Other places where short leaders, between 6 and 8 feet long, are used include fishing for species that are not "leader-shy," typically predators like **sharks**, freshwater bass, **bluefish**, **pike**, and the group of small freshwater fish known as **panfish**. Although trout are known to be very leader-shy, shorter leaders can be used when fishing for them with sinking lines in fast current, and in small streams, where the fly may only drift a few feet and casts are very short.

The standard leader for most species that are relatively shy when feeding is 9 feet long. This length is almost as easy to cast as a 7½-foot leader, but the extra foot and a half seems to be key in keeping the fly line far enough away from the fish. Trout, **bonefish**, striped bass, **permit**, **tarpon**, and members of the **tuna** family are all fish that typically require a 9-foot leader for proper presentation.

Leaders between 12 and 18 feet long are used when nervous fish are found in clear, shallow water. A trout feeding in the shallow tail of a pool is more aware of its surroundings than one feeding in a fast **riffle**, and thus a longer leader might be required. Striped bass, bonefish, tarpon, and other saltwater species out in the open on shallow flats can also be particularly nervous about being exposed to predators without deep water nearby to hide their movements, and a fly line landing 9 feet away can be cause for alarm. When fishing in shallow water with a 9-foot leader, if fish bolt for cover when a cast lands near them, it's a clear sign that a longer leader is needed.

Leaders longer than 12 feet long are used in some extreme situations but you'd have a tough time finding one in your local fly shop. When a leader this long is required, most anglers give up and search for some fish that are less spooky. But if you are willing to put up with the difficulties even a small gust of wind will give you and you are a good enough caster to manage a 15-foot leader, you may enjoy the challenge. The best way to modify a 12-foot leader to make it longer is to add another foot or two of heavy leader material to the butt section of your leader (typically .021" to .028" in diameter) and then add another 2 feet to your tippet.

SPECIALTY SALTWATER LEADERS

Most freshwater leaders are relatively simple—just a precisely tapered strand or strands of monofilament from the fly line to the fly. However, for fish with very sharp teeth like sharks, **barracuda**, **bluefish**, and **pike** and **muskellunge** in fresh water, you'll need to protect your tippet from cut-offs with a wire shock leader, sometimes known as a *trace*. In most cases, this is simply a piece of **wire** attached to the regular tippet with an **Albright Knot**, and then looped to the fly with a Haywire Twist **loop knot**.

For species that have abrasive mouths and gill plates without razor-sharp teeth, like tarpon, **snook**, and tunas, most fly fishers use a monofilament **shock tippet** instead of wire, as these species seem to be more reluctant to bite a fly attached to a piece of dark wire than they are to a fly tied to a piece of heavy but relatively transparent monofilament. Also, big fish like a 150-pound tarpon can take upward of an hour to land, and with the tippet rubbing against a tarpon's sandpaper mouth and sharp gill plates, a thick piece of abrasion resistant material is needed to maintain the connection.

A shock tippet is a piece of monofilament, usually fluorocarbon because of its greater abrasion resistance, attached to the regular or **class tippet** with an Albright or Huffnagle Knot. This material is typically 40- to 100-pound-test material, even thicker than the butt section of the leader. Because it does not allow the fly to swing freely and thus look more lifelike in the water, it is always attached to the fly with a loop knot especially designed for heavy material, like the Homer Rhode Loop Knot.

Leaders with shock tippets seem to be counterintuitive. What sense does it make to attach a piece of 80-pound material to the fly end of the leader when the butt section may only be 30 or 40

L

Northern pike need wire leaders.

pounds? Why not just make a leader out of 80-pound material and dispense with the rest of it? First of all, it's nearly impossible to knot a piece of 80- or 100-pound material to a fly line because this monofilament is too stiff and heavy to form a nail knot. In addition, when fishing for the record books, the maximum tippet size allowed by the IGFA (**International Game Fish Association**) is 12 inches, and a 12-inch leader is too short to fool most game fish. Besides, the heaviest tippet size that can be used for records is 20-pound, so a shock tippet by itself automatically disqualifies you unless it's incorporated into a special shock leader that includes at least 15 inches of the tippet size for which you are applying (records are awarded for 2-, 4-, 6-, 8-, 12-, 16-, and 20-pound tippets).

LETORT SPRING RUN

The Letort Spring Run is a small, clear, vegetation-rich stream that runs through Carlisle, **Pennsylvania**. Despite its size, this river has always supported a good population of large **brown trout**, and its difficult fish were the laboratory of many famous fly fishers, including **Vincent Marinaro**, Ed Shenck, Charles Fox, and **Ernest Schwiebert**. The Letort Cricket, Letort Hopper, Jassid, and **beetle** imitations were developed and refined in the middle of the twentieth century. Much of the early development of flies to imitate crustaceans like **scuds** and cress bugs was also done on this river. Today, fishing in the Letort has suffered from suburban development but it still supports a wild brown trout population, and many fly fishers feel obligated to try its time-honored waters.

LIGHT CAHILL

The Light Cahill is both the name of a popular Catskill **dry fly** pattern and also the fly fisher's common name for the species of **mayfly** it imitates. The fly pattern matches the cream-colored,

size 14 mayflies of the genus *Stenonema* that **hatch** on Eastern trout streams in June, so over time the name of the fly was given to the insect. The original Cahill fly, a much darker pattern with a gray body, was developed in the 1880s by Dan Cahill, and a light version was attributed to **Theodore Gordon**. Later, a Catskill fly tier named William Chandler lightened the fly even further, giving us the cream-toned fly so popular today. The Light Cahill is tied with cream or light ginger hackle and tails, a wing of wood duck flank feather fibers, and a body of cream-colored fur from the belly of a red fox.

LITTLE TUNNY

See False Albacore.

LOOP KNOTS

USES FOR LOOP KNOTS

Loops have valuable utility in fly fishing, and learning how to tie them is essential. Unless a **leader** is attached directly to a **fly line** with a **nail knot**, a permanent loop is incorporated into the end of a fly line, and a looped leader is the attached to the line with a loop-loop connection. This makes it easy to change leader types or lengths without tying knots.

In saltwater **leaders** with a **class tippet** and **shock tippet**, a combination class tippet and shock tippet (sometimes with the fly attached) is stored in a special **fly box** ready to fish. This arrangement has a loop on the end of the class tippet, and a permanent looped butt section is already attached to the fly line, so when the angler wishes to change flies a simple loop-loop connection can be made instead of tying the fly to the shock tippet, tying a class tippet with **Bimini twists** in both ends, and tying a knot between the class tippet and the butt section. What could be a 30-minute project thus turns into a 30-second switch.

Loops can also be used to tie a fly onto the **tippet**. A fly swinging free on a loop swims better and is more realistic than a fly tied directly to the tippet. This is especially important when a fly is attached to a stiff piece of 80-pound **monofilament** shock tippet or stiff **wire**.

PERFECTION LOOP

The Perfection Loop is the most common loop used on the butt section of leaders. It is a strong, neat knot, and the loop lies perfectly in line with the standing part of the leader, which is perhaps its most important attribute.

- Form a loop by bringing the tag end behind the standing part of the leader.
- Form a second, smaller loop in front of the first loop. Roll the tag end around the front of the first loop, then behind it to form this second loop. Push it flat against the first loop, keeping the tag end at right angles to the standing part of the leader.
- Fold the tag end 180 degrees to the opposite side, passing it between the two loops.
- Reach behind the first loop and pull the second loop through it. Make sure the tag end stays in place. Tighten the knot by pulling on the top of the second loop and the standing part of the leader.

SURGEON'S LOOP

The Surgeon's or Double Overhand Loop is much simpler to tie than the Perfection Loop but it is not as neat and the loop when finished is cocked off to one side of the leader. It is best in smaller diameters of monofilament but can be used anytime a loop needs to be made quickly, as it is nearly impossible to tie this knot incorrectly. It is most commonly used to double a piece of class tippet that has been doubled with a Bimini Twist because a Perfection Loop would be very difficult to tie in doubled material.

- Make a loop in the end of the leader material. Then tie an overhand knot in this looped portion.
- Bring the single loop through the loop just formed in the overhand knot a second time. Tighten the loop by pulling on the single loop, holding the standing part of the leader and the tag end together.

NON-SLIP MONO LOOP

The Non-Slip Mono Loop is a very strong knot used to attach a fly to a tippet. It works best in smaller diameters, under about .023". It keeps the fly swinging free of the tippet so the fly swims in a more lifelike manner.

- Tie an overhand knot in the tippet but do not tighten it.
- Pass the tag end of the tippet through the eye of the fly in either direction, then back through the overhand loop in the tippet. Make sure it enters the loop on the same side of the loop that it exited.
- Bring the tag end above the overhand knot in the tippet. Wind it five times around the standing part of the leader, away from the overhand knot, then bring it back through the overhand knot, on the same side of the knot again.
- Tighten by first pulling on the tag end until the loop tightens. Then pull the fly and the standing part of the leader to fully tighten.

HOMER RHODE LOOP

This knot is used to attach a fly to a very heavy piece of monofilament shock tippet. Other loop knots are too bulky, but this knot should only be used in heavy materials as it is not as strong as a Non-Slip Mono Loop in smaller diameters.

- Make an overhand knot in the tippet but do not tighten it.
- Pass the tag end of the tippet through the eye of the fly in either direction, then back through the overhand loop in the tippet. Make sure it enters the loop on the same side of the loop that it exited.
- Tighten the overhand knot loosely against the eye of the hook by pulling on the fly with one hand and both pieces of leader with the other.
- With the tag end of the leader, tie another overhand knot around the standing part of the leader. Tighten this knot.
- Pull on the fly and the standing part of the leader. The two overhand knots will jam against each other, forming a loop in front of the fly.

HAYWIRE TWIST

The Haywire Twist is the only knot that will tie a loop in a piece of single-strand wire. It can be used to make a loop to which the leader will be attached, or a fly can be placed inside the loop to attach it to the wire.

- Place the wire through the eye of the fly and wind the tag end of the wire around the standing part at a 45-degree angle, making five turns.
- Next bend the tag end of the wire 90 degrees to the standing part and take three tight coils around it.
- Put a bend on the tag end of the wire making a little crank handle with it, and twist this little handle until the wire breaks next to the knot. This is safer than cutting the wire, which produces a dangerous razor-sharp edge.

LOUISIANA

OVERVIEW

Just because Louisiana does not have any trout does not mean an angler can't have lots of fun with a **fly rod**. This hot, wet state offers a myriad of inland lakes, rivers, and bayous full of **largemouth bass** and **panfish**, and a wrinkled coastline full of protected bays and marshes in the Mississippi Delta that give the saltwater fly fisher a lifetime of opportunities for catching **redfish**, **sea trout**, cobia, Spanish **mackerel**, and **false albacore**.

FISHERIES

The most important sport fish in Louisiana is the redfish, and Louisiana probably offers the best place to catch a big redfish (over 20 pounds) on a fly in the world. In late fall, big bull redfish enter the shallows along the coast. But smaller redfish of 10 to 12 pounds stay in the shallows all year long in Louisiana, and even during winter cold fronts, these fish only retreat to holes that are, at the most, 12 feet deep, and will return to the shallows as soon as the sun warms the flats. Redfish can be spotted by the wakes they make when feeding in the shallows, or by the sight of their tails or fins above the surface. A **Clouser Minnow** or crab fly cast to them and stripped slowly past a feeding fish will result in a hard **strike**, and redfish then fight with a strong battle and powerful runs, especially in very shallow water. Redfish can be found along the entire coast, but the most productive spots are the vast marshes south of Slidell, Lake Ponchatrain, Grand Isle west of the Mississippi, and the Mississippi Delta south of Venice. Big redfish will also be found year-round further offshore in the Gulf, especially near oil rigs, where a surface **popper** will often draw vicious strikes,

Sea trout are abundant in Louisiana in the same places you find redfish, but they will typically be found in slightly deeper holes. The best depth for sea trout is between 8 and 12 feet. Just a bit further offshore the fly fisher can chase schools of Spanish mackerel crashing into **baitfish**, and around oil rigs big cobia will take a **streamer** or popper. False

Gulf of Mexico, New Orleans

albacore are an abundant gamefish in Louisiana waters, typically a few miles offshore in the Gulf, and these fish will be found slashing through schools of baitfish as well. The most popular spot for catching false albacore is offshore of the Venice area.

Freshwater fishing with a fly rod is not popular but should not be ignored, as there are many possibilities for great sport. In the rivers of southern Louisiana, chasing the rare Kentucky bass with poppers and streamers, especially from a small kayak, is great fun, and the fly fisher will also encounter largemouth bass and bluegills in the small rivers and bayous. Large lakes and reservoirs like Toledo Bend, Lake D'Arbone, Lake St. John, and Lake Concordia can be effectively fly fished for largemouth bass and bluegills in the shallows around lily pads with poppers and streamers. In addition, these lakes hold dense populations of crappie (known in Louisiana as **white perch** or sacalait), which are great fun on small white streamers fished on **sinking tip lines**.

SEASON

The time for big redfish in the shallows of the Mississippi Delta is November through January. At other times of year, the bigger fish will be found offshore in the Gulf around islands or oil rigs. But the smaller redfish and sea trout will be in shallow water throughout the year, although during the dead of winter it may be necessary to fish holes for the trout. The best time for freshwater bass is from March through May, when the fish are in the warmer shallows spawning. Bass can be caught during the summer at dawn and at night, but in the smaller creeks, where water temperatures stay cool, they will feed in shallow water during the day. Bluegill action is the hottest from March through the summer, and some Louisiana streams even have **mayfly hatches** that bring vast numbers of these panfish to the surface. Crappie fishing is best in February and again in the fall, when the fish are concentrated in huge schools and easy to find.

March brocon

MACKEREL

Mackerel are small members of the **tuna** family, and are great fish on a **fly rod**. They feed voraciously and hit hard, and make swift runs that pull a surprising amount of line when a larger one is **hooked**. They are typically caught with a fly when trying for more glamorous saltwater species, but often turn a potentially slow day into a lively experience. Because most mackerel have small mouths and teeth, they prefer smaller baitfish, which makes them the perfect fly rod fish. Best flies are small flashy saltwater streamers with a thin profile like epoxy minnows, sparse **Deceivers**, or any other fly that is predominantly thin, silver or white, and flashy. The best presentation is to cast the fly ahead of a feeding school with a **sinking line** and **retrieve** with fast, steady strips.

The Atlantic mackerel, found on the Atlantic Coast north of the Chesapeake, travel in huge schools that often froth the water when feeding on small **baitfish**. They are easy to catch on almost any small saltwater streamer. Another popular species that is sometimes found as far north as New England is the Spanish mackerel. Unlike Atlantics, Spanish can be maddeningly difficult to catch, compounded by the fact that their sharp teeth will sever most **monofilament** lines, but the fish tend to shy away from **wire shock tippets**. The best option for

Atlantic Mackerel

catching Spanish is to use a small epoxy minnow and a single-strand wire shock tippet. King mackerel, the largest members of this family, also require a wire **tippet** and are most often caught in nearshore waters from the Carolinas south and throughout the Gulf of Mexico. Kings will take a larger fly than the other mackerels and will often be seen clearing the water when chasing baitfish, which makes them exciting to catch with a fly.

MADISON RIVER

The Madison River flows mostly through **Montana**, although its headwaters are in **Yellowstone** National Park, which is technically part of **Wyoming**. This river is one of the world's finest trout streams, and combines a rich ecosystem full of aquatic insects and crustaceans, a healthy population of wild **brown** and **rainbow trout** and mountain **whitefish**, spectacular scenery, and over 100 miles of public access.

The Madison River begins at Madison Junction in Yellowstone Park, where the **Firehole** and Gibbon Rivers meet. For the next 25 miles, the river flows through a broad meadow and is mostly long runs and deep, weedy pools. Because of the warm nutrient flow from the Firehole (where a number of thermal features including Old Faithful flow), the river here is very rich. Water temperatures are warmer than optimal for trout in midsummer; although trout fishing is good here, it is better in spring and fall than in summer. It is great **dry fly** water: Despite being alongside a major Yellowstone Park highway, it is lightly fished.

Just outside of West Yellowstone, Montana, the river is impounded by Hebgen Lake. This large reservoir has a good population of large brown and rainbow trout, best fished by **belly boat** in the morning before the inevitable afternoon breezes pick up. **Streamer** and **nymph** fishing are excellent, and the occasional fly **hatches** make dry fly fishing spectacular if the lake is calm. Large spawning trout from Hebgen Lake also enter the Madison in Yellowstone Park, rainbows in the spring and browns in the fall.

Below Hebgen Lake, the river flows for two miles before entering the smaller Quake Lake, formed by the 1959 earthquake. Water flows at a constant temperature of about 40 degrees so it stays cool all summer. Fishing here is good, especially in the spring, but the best fishing in the Madison begins below the outlet of Quake Lake at Slide Inn. From here to Ennis Lake, the river flows for 50 miles through a broad valley flanked by spectacular mountain ranges. Although there are no big pools in this entire stretch of water, trout will be found in every seam between fast and slow current, close to

the banks, and in side channels. The river can be floated or fished by **wading**. In some stretches no fishing is allowed from boats, which gives the wading angler a fighting chance at the best water. Best fishing is with large dark nymphs that imitate the large salmonfly **stonefly**, dry flies and nymphs that imitate **caddisflies**, and large dry flies that imitate **salmonflies** in June and July and **grasshoppers** in late July through early September. Streamer fishing for large brown trout is always good, especially on cloudy days.

Below shallow Ennis Lake the water often gets too warm for good trout fishing, but it gets enough oxygen in the tumbling Beartrap canyon to keep fishing productive most of the summer. This canyon can only be accessed by a rugged hike through rattlesnake, tick, and poison ivy country or by floating in a whitewater raft with one of the few experienced local guides licensed to float the canyon's class 5 rapids. However, the brown and rainbow trout here are quite large, and by concentrating on nymphs and streamers the fly fisher can have a shot at a very large trout. Below Beartrap canyon, until the Madison meets the Jefferson and Gallatin Rivers to form the Missouri River at Three Forks, the river is a marginal trout stream in spring and fishes poorly during the summer, except for the large **carp** that can be found in the slower pools.

MAINE

OVERVIEW

Unlike many other states, where fly fishing is often looked upon as an elitist method only used by snobs or tourists, Maine has a long tradition of grassroots fly fishing. Because fishing with a **fly rod** for trout and salmon has historical precedence and popular support in Maine, there is an extensive list of ponds and rivers that by law can only be fished with a fly rod and conventional fly. In addition, Maine has an equally long list of waters reserved for catch-and-release angling.

Maine is the best place in the United States to

catch a wild **brook trout** in its native habitat; in fact, each year the state publishes a list of brook trout waters that have never been stocked. It is also one of the best places to catch a trophy brook trout (over four pounds). It is possible to catch bigger brook trout in places they were introduced, like the Rocky Mountains or South America, but outside of northern Canada, no other place offers such a vast resource for this native **char**. Maine is also the best place in the United States to catch wild landlocked **Atlantic salmon**.

Much of Maine is a vast wilderness with easy public access, either on public land or on paper company land that is open to the public for fishing. It is still possible to hike or **canoe** for 20 miles to a wilderness brook trout lake that has never been stocked.

FISHERIES

If time and physical condition are not deterrents, the best way to see the Maine wilderness and catch native brook trout is in northeastern Maine, specifically in the Allagash Wilderness Waterway and Baxter State Park, as well as the extensive paper company land in the area. The Allagash River is the most remote large river in Maine, and can only be traveled by canoe. The main species are brook trout and landlocked salmon, and the river is one of the best places in Maine to catch a large brook trout. In addition to trout and salmon, Allagash Lake is a place where catching a 10-pound **lake trout** on a fly is possible, especially in the spring when these big trout are in shallow water. However, nearly every river and pond in this region has brook trout and most support salmon as well.

Moving southeast, the next major area of interest

to fly fishers is the West Branch of the Penobscot River. The upper West Branch, between Seboomooc and Chesuncook Lakes, is a wilderness river accessible only by logging roads, but the state maintains campsites along the river. Its wild brook trout and landlocked salmon see very few anglers, so the fishing is relatively easy. In contrast, the lower West Branch, below Ripogenus Dam on Chesuncook Lake, is relatively easy to access by car, and even though it has one of the best populations of wild landlocked salmon in the state, this big tumbling river does not always give up its fish easily. When rising or feeding on **nymphs**, the salmon in the Lower West Branch can be as selective as **brown trout**—but the dense population of fish and big water ensures that there are plenty of opportunities for the persistent fly fisher.

The Moosehead Lake region offers a wealth of trout rivers, ponds, and lakes. The lake itself supports brook trout, landlocked salmon, and **smallmouth bass** (especially in Lily Bay), but it's the smaller ponds and rivers that are most attractive to the fly fisher, as Moosehead itself is so big that it can be tough to find fish without trolling. There are over 40 excellent brook trout ponds within an hour's drive of Greenville, where the fly fisher can concentrate on large numbers of smaller fish in some waters or smaller numbers of trophy fish in the more remote ponds. The East and West Outlets of the Kennebec River are excellent fisheries for landlocked salmon, particularly on their fall spawning runs, and also offer decent brook trout fishing. Another river in this area, the Roach, flows into Moosehead Lake at Spencer Bay and has over 6 miles of high-quality, catch-and-release fishing for brook trout and landlocked salmon.

As the Kennebec River flows south through numerous impoundments, it becomes less of a brook trout and landlocked salmon fishery, with these species replaced by introduced brown and **rainbow trout**, which are more tolerant of higher water temperatures. Below Wyman Dam in Bingham the river supports one of the few natu-

Fishing the Dead River for landlocked salmon and brook trout.

rally reproducing populations of rainbow trout in the state, and further downstream below Shawmut Dam is a 600-yard stretch of water that can be waded and gives the fly fisher the opportunity to fish for large brown and rainbow trout sipping tiny insects from the surface film. In between these pockets of excellent trout fishing, the entire lower Kennebec is perhaps the best smallmouth bass fishery in Maine. For the angler who wants to catch a trophy brook trout on a fly, Pierce Pond is one of the best places in the state to catch a large one. Landlocked salmon are also common in Pierce Pond and the surrounding area.

The Rangeley Region is where much of Maine fly fishing traditions such as trolling with flies and the use of large streamer patterns to imitate the smelt **baitfish** originated. As a result, many of the waters are restricted to fly fishing only, and many have restrictive catch limits as well. These regulations have ensured that brook trout fishing in Maine improves every year. Foremost in this region is the remote Rapid River, the outlet of Richardson Lake. Brook trout of over four pounds are taken on a fly each year, and landlocked salmon fishing is also excellent, particularly in spring and fall. Other productive rivers in this area include the Cupsutic, notable for its abundant although small brook trout, and the Kennebago River, which is a very productive river for large brook trout and landlocked salmon. The mighty Androscoggin River, once nearly an open sewer because of paper mill effluent, is rebounding, with brown and rainbow trout close to the **New Hampshire** border, plus excellent smallmouth bass fishing below Rumford.

Although eastern Maine does not offer the same quality of trout and salmon fishing as northern and eastern Maine, one standout river is Grand Lake Stream, just over three miles of excellent habitat for brook trout and landlocked salmon, with good public access. Grand Lake Stream is also one of the best places in Maine to catch smallmouth bass on a fly. Extreme southwestern Maine also provides fewer opportunities for trout and salmon fishing, with the exception of the Sebago Lake region, where excellent landlocked salmon fishing can be found in the lake itself and in its tributaries.

The rugged coast of Maine, with countless tiny islands and many large estuaries, is prime habitat for **striped bass** during their summer run. Most striper fishing in Maine is done either along rocky shores, where waves crashing against rocks pin baitfish against the shoreline, or in more placid large river estuaries, where stripers can be found feeding on baitfish, crabs, and shrimp. Stripers cruise the entire Maine coast, but the best places are where large rivers enter the Atlantic, particularly at the mouth of the Kennebec and Penobscot Rivers, plus Casco Bay near Portland. Although not often targeted by fly fishers, Atlantic **mackerel** take a fly well, give a spirited fight on a trout outfit, and are found in most harbors. For the adventurous fly fisher, bluefin **tuna** come very close to shore in some years and the smaller ones, under 100 pounds, can be caught on a fly.

SEASON

Fly fishing season in Maine begins at "ice-out" time, when surface and near-shore temperatures in lakes are more comfortable for trout and salmon than their deeper summer habitat. Fish also follow the annual run of smelt into tributary rivers and streams. Ice-out typically occurs in early May in most lakes in Maine. At this time of year, both **streamer** flies imitating smelt, plus nymphs that look like **stonefly**, **dragonfly**, and **damselfly larvae** are productive, either on a sinking or **sinking-tip fly line**. Stream

fishing in Maine in May is also mostly subsurface fishing with nymphs and streamers, as hatches in this part of the world happen later than most other regions of the country.

Mayfly and **caddisfly hatches** get heavy in June and early July, and this is the best time for dry fly fishing in Maine for trout and salmon. Smallmouth bass are also aggressive in June around their spawning time, and will readily take a **streamer** or **popper**. Of special note to Maine fly fishers is the annual emergence of the *Hexagenia* (**Hex**) mayfly, often known locally as the **Green Drake**. This giant (size 6–8) mayfly hatches at dark on lakes and larger rivers, and trout, salmon, and bass make gluttons of themselves and offer the most exciting dry fly fishing of the season.

Summers in Maine can get surprisingly warm. Some of the wilderness rivers, or those below large bottom-release dams, stay cold enough to offer good fly fishing throughout the summer. But in many rivers and most lakes, summer fishing is a matter of finding spring holes or cold tributaries where trout and salmon will congregate. Sinking lines again are the key, especially in lakes. When fall arrives, both brook trout and landlocked salmon begin their spawning migrations from lakes into rivers and streams. Fishing with nymphs and streamers can be fantastic when fish are found at this time of year, but timing is critical because fish can move miles in a single day.

Striper fishing in Maine is a summer opportunity. Like most places in the northeast, smaller "schoolie" stripers arrive first, usually in late May, followed by the bigger fish in June. Because coastal water temperatures in Maine are colder than in more southern states, striped bass stay shallow and will feed during the day more often than in other places where warm summer water temperatures move them into deeper offshore waters. Stripers leave Maine in September, and although fishing then can be spotty, it can also be wild if the fly fisher happens to stumble upon a school of large stripers heading south, feeding heavily prior to winter.

MARBURY, MARY ORVIS (1856–1914)

Mary Orvis Marbury was the daughter of Charles Orvis, founder of The Orvis Company. Throughout her life, she ran the fly tying department at Orvis, supervising a half-dozen fly tiers to make sure the flies were up to Orvis standards. In 1892 her book, *Favorite Flies and Their Histories*, with plates of 290 fly patterns in full color, was published. It was the first work to standardize American fly patterns, which prior to her time were not consistent from one state to another (or even one river to another) so that how the Queen of the Water fly pattern looked to an angler in **Maine** might have no relation to the same-named fly in **Pennsylvania**. Mary did not write all of the text; instead she and her father solicited recommendations from 200 fly fishers in 38 states, forming a definitive encyclopedia of American flies for trout, bass, and salmon.

M

MARINARO, VINCENT
(1911–1986)

Vincent Marinaro was an attorney who spent his life fishing and studying the rich trout streams that flow through the limestone belt of south-central **Pennsylvania**, most notably **Letort Spring Run**. He was a persistent researcher and scholar as well as a fine writer, and his primary contribution to fly fishing was the development of **dry flies** to imitate land-bred insects or terrestrials (along with Ed Schenk, Charles Fox, and **Ernest Schwiebert**) and to develop flies and techniques to catch trout feeding on tiny insects, especially in the summer. His most important book, *A Modern Dry-Fly Code* (1950), sold few copies but is still revered by fly fishers as being one of the most important books on technical trout fishing. His second book, *In the Ring of the Rise* (1976), concentrated on trout feeding behavior and was more commercially successful.

MARLIN

Catching a marlin on a fly is one of the most exciting and physical exploits you can do with a **fly rod**. Everything must be just right. First, a concentration of the smaller marlin (under 250 pounds) that can be handled on a fly rod must be found, often after days of long-range running on the open ocean. The fish must be lured close to the boat with hookless teaser lures or bait, optimally within 30 feet of the stern. The teaser is then yanked free of the water and the fly is cast along the edge of the boat wake. (To qualify for a fly rod world record the boat must also be thrown into neutral before the fish takes the fly.) A strong **mend** should be thrown into the **fly line**, so the fly swims sideways instead of toward the boat, and for proper hookup the marlin should take the fly moving away from the boat, so the hook sets properly in the corner of the jaw. Fights are long and spectacular, with the fish "greyhounding" across the surface and then sounding into deep water. Often 600 yards of **backing** will be needed on a giant **fly reel**, and the boat may have to chase the fish for many miles. The fight can last for hours and an angler must be in top physical condition.

Leaders are typically composed of a **class tippet** with 16- or 20-pound-test **monofilament** and a 100-pound **shock tippet**. **Sinking fly lines** are most often used to keep the fly below the surface, and fly rods should be the stiffest made, from 12-weight to 16-weight. Fly reels must also be the best available, capable of holding the line plus 600 yards of backing, a very smooth and strong **drag**, and the ability to dissipate the intense heat caused by the drag system putting pressure on a fish running at greater than 20 miles per hour for hundreds of yards. Most anglers use tandem-hooked **streamer** flies from 8 to 14 inches long in bright colors.

Marlin are found in warm ocean currents throughout the world. Prime spots to catch striped marlin on a fly are Magdalena Bay in Baja **California**, Cocos Island south of Costa Rica, and the Galapagos Islands. White marlin have been caught on a fly off the coast of Cape Hatteras, La Guaira

M

Bank off the coast of Venezuela. Small black marlin are commonly found off Australia's Great Barrier Reef. Blue marlin of fly rod size are also found off the coast of Australia and Venezuela.

MARYLAND

OVERVIEW

Fly fishing in Maryland, especially trout fishing with a fly, is a relatively recent phenomenon. Although Maryland has some small mountain trout streams in the western part of the state, through extensive cooperation between the Maryland Department of Natural Resources and private organizations like **Trout Unlimited**, Maryland has created a number of larger trout rivers below cold-water dam releases where trout had not lived in historical times. And of course with the rich Chesapeake Bay estuary system, Maryland has some of the best fly fishing for trophy **striped bass**, as well as brackish water **largemouth bass**, in the country.

FISHERIES

Maryland boasts one of the best suburban trout streams in the country. The Big Gunpowder Falls River, just off Interstate 83 north of the Baltimore Beltway, was turned into a trout fishery in 1983 when coldwater releases from Prettyboy Dam were regulated to form a year-round trout fishery. The result was so successful that **brown** and **rainbow trout** are naturally reproducing in the river and have not been stocked since 1990. The Gunpowder is an intimate, productive river with good **hatches**, even in the midsummer Maryland heat, but its fish are never easy due to nearly constant fishing pressure.

Big Hunting Creek was one of the first Maryland streams to be stocked with trout. Located in Catoctin Mountain National Park and Cunningham Falls State Park near Thurmont, its tumbling mountain pools make trout easier to catch than in the more placid lowland rivers. There are

brown trout in its lower reaches and brook trout above Cunningham Falls Reservoir.

Further west, in Maryland's relatively undeveloped panhandle, are a number of excellent trout streams, **tailwater** rivers flowing through lush hardwood forest and rhododendron-lined banks. The Savage River above Savage River Reservoir and its tributaries provide true wild **brook trout** fishing, in small streams where these little fish love to inhale dry flies. This is walk-in fishing that as a result is seldom crowded. The Savage River below the reservoir also has some brook trout, but browns and rainbows predominate in a little stream that is scenic and easy to access and wade—although its fish are not pushovers. The Savage runs into the North Branch of the Potomac River, which was once nearly sterile due to acid mine drainage. Extensive work to lower the acidity of this river was combined with extensive trout stocking and management. As a result the river has good populations of brown and rainbow trout, along with good numbers of **cutthroat trout**—one of the few places in the eastern United States where cutthroats can be taken with a fly. The North Branch is best floated with a raft to see the best water, but there are also extensive trails on old railroad beds along its length.

Smallmouth bass fishing in rivers is one of the best fly fishing opportunities in Maryland. The

M

entire length of the Potomac has excellent small-mouth bass fishing, and both subsurface **streamers** and popping bugs are effective. Other places for great smallmouth fishing with a **fly rod** include the Susquehanna River below Conowingo, where **carp**, channel catfish, and **shad** can also be taken on a fly; and the Pepacton River near Baltimore. Largemouth bass are a great target for the fly fisher in Maryland's many brackish rivers that flow into the Chesapeake. The best way to catch these tidal largemouths is with a large popping bug at dawn or just before dark.

Most of the East Coast's striped bass spawn in Chesapeake Bay rivers; during the spring spawning run striped bass of all sizes will be found in the bay and its tributaries. However, when stripers are in big water it can be tough to find and catch them with a fly rod. Luckily, the 8-mile-long Susquehanna Flats, where the Susquehanna flows into Chesapeake Bay, offer striped bass in shallow water that are perfect targets for a well-placed streamer or **Clouser Minnow**. This area can be wild fishing for stripers 30 pounds and even bigger, but the season is short and a windy day can stir the water into a silty mess, making fly fishing difficult.

Season

Trout fishing in Maryland can be productive with **midge** dries and **nymphs** throughout the winter, especially on the Big Gunpowder Falls, but **mayfly** and **caddisfly** hatches, which really get the trout feeding on the surface, begin in earnest in April and last through June. Although caddisflies and some mayflies hatch all summer long, Maryland's hot summers depress the trout fishing due to high **water temperatures**—except for rivers that receive cold bottom-release flows from dams, most notably the North Branch of the Potomac and Big Gunpowder Falls Rivers.

Smallmouth bass fishing in rivers begins in April when fish begin spawning, and is best from April through June with a fly rod. During the summer, smallmouths will go deep during the day, and

although they can be caught with streamers and **crayfish** patterns on sinking lines, better fly fishing for both smallmouths and largemouths is at dawn and dusk.

The catch-and-release striped bass season on the Susquehanna Flats is in April, when the big fish are getting ready to spawn and chasing herring in the shallow water. During the summer, smaller juvenile striped bass will still be found in shallow water, but the bigger fish will be further offshore, closer to the mouth of the Chesapeake. With a boat, great fly fishing for stripers can be found during the summer on streamers and poppers out in the open water, with the added bonus of **bluefish** and Spanish **mackerel**.

Spanish mackerel

MASSACHUSETTS

Overview

Although Massachusetts does offer a few trout streams, and a couple of them are quite productive, the best fly fishing in the state is in salt water. With a coastline that ranges from rocky shores in the north to the massive sand and gravel shorelines of Cape Cod and the outlying islands of Martha's Vineyard and Nantucket, Massachusetts offers world-class saltwater fly fishing, especially for **striped bass**.

Fisheries

The best and largest trout stream in Massachusetts is the Deerfield. This **tailwater** river leaves **Vermont**'s Harriman Reservoir in the northwest corner of the state and flows across the state into the Connecticut River. The best trout fishing is in the western half of the river, but it is stocked throughout its length. The Deerfield is big enough

Big stripers abound offshore at Monomoy point.

to be floated with a drift boat, and the trout here are not particularly difficult to catch. Another river in the same area is the Westfield, which is heavily stocked with trout and offers very scenic fishing in Chesterfield Gorge. The Swift River, a tailwater outlet of massive Quabbin Reservoir near Belchertown, has a year-round catch-and-release section for very fussy trout. It's not a large river, but it has surprisingly large trout that sip **midges** and **mayflies** even in the heat of summer. The Miller's River along Route 2 in central Massachusetts, once heavily polluted, has made a strong comeback and offers big pools and attractive pocket water. There are many small streams in western Massachusetts in the Berkshire hills that support wild **brook** and **brown trout**, but trout fishing gets poor as you move east because of warmer **water temperatures** and more acidic conditions. Cape Cod also has numerous freshwater kettle lakes, spring-fed bodies of water left by the glaciers that offer both

trout and bass fishing, but are largely ignored because of the more famous saltwater species.

Striped bass and **bluefish** will be found anywhere along the Massachusetts coast. Because these species often feed in very shallow water, they can be caught from a power boat, **canoe**, **kayak**, or by **wading** the shorelines. Even Boston Harbor has dense populations of striped bass and bluefish, and fly fishing for these species can be done right beneath the skyline of downtown Boston. At the mouth of the Merrimack River in northeastern Massachusetts, and also near the Parker River, and in Plum Island Sound, striped bass fishing is superb in late May and June, when stripers chase spawning herring into freshwater rivers. Sight-fishing is possible on the famous Joppa Flats, along the causeway to Plum Island. Between here and Boston the coast is classic "rock fishing," with striped bass and bluefish feeding in the foam lines where the surf crashes against the rugged shoreline. South of

Boston, Plymouth Bay has sheltered waters that produce superb striped bass fishing, even sight-fishing on beautiful sand flats, and this area is far less crowded than the more famous beaches of Cape Cod and the outlying islands.

Cape Cod is one of the most productive places for striped bass and bluefish for the fly fisher because of its extensive shallow bays and sand flats. The Cape Cod Canal, which separates Cape Cod from the mainland, can be fished with a **fly rod**, but because of rocky, steep shorelines and swift current, fly fishers have their best luck in the shallow flats at either end of the Canal. Cape Cod Bay, with tidal flats that stretch for more than a mile at low tide, is an excellent place for wading or fishing from a kayak, but waders should beware as the tide comes in quickly and can come in around a wader, so it's best to carry a compass or GPS in case fog rolls in, and to have a quick escape route planned back to shore. The flats in the vicinity of Brewster are well-known and productive, but the entire shoreline of Cape Cod Bay, all the way to its tip at Provincetown, can be waded to various degrees and stripers will be seen all along its length.

The south shore of Cape Cod, on Nantucket Sound, is equally good, although wading opportunities are not as abundant, except in the area of Chatham, where the extensive white sand flats of Pleasant Bay, Nauset Inlet, and Monomoy Island attract big striped bass and bluefish that prowl these flats in crystal clear water in search of crabs, shrimp, and **baitfish**. But with a boat, the entire length of the western side abounds in estuaries and offshore rock piles that attract striped bass and bluefish of all sizes. In addition, some years **bonito** and **false albacore** run these beaches, the extreme north end of their late summer feeding spree. For those looking for a little more excitement, the open ocean surf north of Chatham can be fished with a fly, as the prevailing winds are from the west, which keeps the surf down and the wind at a caster's back.

Life on the large islands of Martha's Vineyard and Nantucket has always been centered around fishing, and fly fishing has become very popular. Besides striped bass and bluefish, they have abundant runs of false albacore, bonito, and even Spanish **mackerel** in late summer and early fall. Because Nantucket extends further into the Gulf Stream, these typically offshore species are more abundant there. Both islands have fly fishing that ranges from swift currents on rock **jetties** to shallow inshore flats to crashing surf on outer beaches.

Although bluefin **tuna** are never easy to find, there are opportunities to catch one off a fly in Massachusetts, and of course stripers, bluefish, and false albacore can be chased if the bluefins don't show up. Best places to find school bluefin tuna (the small ones, which are the only size possible on a fly rod) include Massachusetts Bay north of Boston, Cape Cod Bay, the open ocean off the eastern shore of cape Cod, and the waters south of Nantucket and Martha's Vineyard.

SEASON

Trout fishing in most Massachusetts rivers is best in late April through June, as many of the rivers in this state (other than the Swift River tailwater) get too warm for decent trout fishing during the summer. Striped bass and bluefish begin to arrive in early May, typically smaller fish first, with schools of the bigger fish of 10 pounds and more by the end of the month. June is one of the best months for striped bass, as the water is cool enough for the fish to stay near the shoreline. Striped bass and bluefish feed heavily all summer long, although they will be found further offshore except for beaches on the outer beaches, where summer water temperatures stay in the mid-60s. By July, bonito will invade Martha's Vineyard and Nantucket, followed in August by false albacore. These species stay in Massachusetts waters until late October, but by the time they begin to leave big schools of bluefish and striped bass begin their southern migration, feeding heavily on the abundant baitfish along the coast.

MAYFLY

IDENTIFICATION AND LIFE CYCLE

Mayflies are some of the most important insects in trout streams, and although in some waters they may be overshadowed in abundance by other aquatic insects, a mayfly **hatch** always brings joy to the heart of a fly fisher because trout seem to be easier to catch when feeding on these insects. Mayflies typically ride the water for quite a distance after hatching from the **nymph** stage, unlike **caddisflies** and **midges**, which often spring from the water quickly, or **stoneflies**, which almost always hatch by crawling out of the water onto rocks rather than riding the current. Thus mayflies provide the best opportunity for **dry fly** fishing.

Mayflies are aquatic insects of the order *Ephemeroptera*. They live in cool, highly oxygenated water in rivers and lakes throughout the temperate regions of the world, and because they need clean water to survive, they are often used as an indicator of the health of a body of water. Their life cycle is almost exactly 12 months. Eggs are laid by adults, which soon hatch into tiny **larvae**, known also as nymphs or naiads. The nymphs live on the underside of stones, in gravel or sand, or in aquatic vegetation, growing and shedding their exoskeleton a number of times. Almost exactly a year after the eggs are laid, the nymphs release their hold on the bottom and rise to the surface. Once at the surface, the nymph exoskeleton splits and a winged insect emerges. This winged insect is actually a sub-adult called a **subimago** or **dun** and must go through

one final molt within the next 24 hours before becoming sexually mature.

Duns flutter their wings to dry them and then rise in a stately manner and fly to nearby trees and brush, where they molt one more time to become an imago or **spinner**. The spinners form large mating flights over the water and mate in midair. The females then drop their eggs into the water from above, dip into the water to dislodge them, or crawl underwater to deposit them. The exact strategy depends on the species. Both males and females then fall spent to the surface of the water, where they are carried away by the current, sink, and die.

Mayfly duns and spinners can be identified in the air by their cross or T-shape, with the wings forming the arms of the T and the abdomen the base. Duns fly slowly and are relatively clumsy, their wings are translucent, and their bodies are opaque and robust. Spinners are quick fliers that dart above the surface of the water, often hovering for a moment followed by a rhythmic dipping motion. The wings of spinners are usually completely clear or are clear with dark speckles, the bodies are long and thin, and the tails are much longer than those of the dun, usually twice the length of the abdomen. Mayfly nymphs have a distinct abdomen and thorax and visible legs and tails. Some are flat, others more rounded in cross-section, but all have tiny gills along each section of the abdomen. The only aquatic insect that looks like a mayfly nymph is a stonefly nymph, but stoneflies always have feathery gills under the thorax and never along the abdomen.

Mayflies can hatch at any time of year, but few

species hatch in winter. Hatches are most common April through September, with May through July the peak time of emergence. (Mayflies also occur in the Southern Hemisphere, where they hatch most often in December through March). Each species of mayfly hatches at the same time each year, and the hatch of any given species will last from anywhere from a few days to several weeks. There are often overlapping hatches of mayflies during the spring and summer months, and on very rich trout streams it is not unusual to see several species hatching at once. Because trout often prefer one species over another, it's important to try to observe which species the trout are eating before tying on a fly, because a mayfly imitation of the wrong size or color may be ignored.

FISHING MAYFLY IMITATIONS

Trout and other gamefish like **smallmouth bass**, **panfish**, and even channel catfish eat mayflies in every stage of their life cycle. Mayfly nymphs are eaten by trout below the surface when they rise to the surface during hatches, when a rise of water dislodges them from their perches on the bottom, or when they migrate from evening through early morning in a phenomenon called diurnal drift. Most of this drift happens after dark when trout can't see them, but nymph fishing is often very productive early in the morning, when the nymphs are finishing their migration but there is enough light for trout to spot them. Even though mayfly nymphs are always present below the surface during the day, trout seldom root around on the bottom for them, preferring an easy capture when the nymphs are hatching. Thus knowing what mayfly has been hatching in the last few days will help the fly fisher determine which pattern to try.

Mayfly nymphs are relatively helpless when drifting. Most species show a feeble wiggle when in the middle of the water column, so nymph imitations should be fished **dead drift**, perhaps with an occasional lift of the rod to simulate an insect rising to the surface. However, a few species of mayfly

nymphs are quick and agile swimmers, especially those in the genus *Isonychia*, so it never hurts to experiment with a more active **retrieve**. The time when a mayfly nymph reaches the surface and begins to emerge from its exoskeleton is its most vulnerable period and trout recognize this. This stage, not quite a nymph and not quite an adult, is known as an **emerger**; many fly patterns have been developed to imitate this fleeting but important stage. Emergers should always be fished completely dead drift, with no **drag** on the **leader** or other motion imparted by the angler.

Once the dun has emerged and rides the surface, drying its wings, is when the classic winged **dry fly** comes into play. Some mayflies ride the surface for over 100 yards, fluttering, twitching, and bouncing until they finally get airborne. Others leave the water after only a brief ride on the surface. How long a dun stays on the surface depends on the species and the air temperature—on cold, damp days mayflies will stay on the water longer than on dry, sunny days. The fly fisher can sometimes tell if a fish is eating duns or emergers by the rise form. Rises to the more active duns are likely to be splashy or even violent, while rises to the emergers are more sedate, where just the head and dorsal fin of the fish break the surface without splashing. To be sure, watch an individual fish. If it appears to rise to an unseen insect, it is probably eating emergers, and if a fluttering dun disappears into a rise, guesswork is eliminated.

Identifying a "spinner fall" or spinner mating flight is trickier than a hatch of duns. Spinners often stage in the air high above a **riffle**, and unless the angler looks up and into the sun, they can be hard to see. The entire cloud of spinners will usually fall to the surface quickly, often right at dark (although it can happen at any time of day) and the first thing the confused angler will notice is trout feeding all over the surface when no insects are seen. But a careful look at the surface will show scores of mayfly spinners, wings outstretched and prone, lying flush in the film. As with emergers, these dying insects can't get away and trout know it. And the heavy concentration of so many insects at the same time will often bring the largest trout in the river to the surface. Thus although spinners do not get the same recognition as duns and have nowhere near the same number of fly patterns devoted to them, having a reasonable imitation of these spent mayflies in a fly box can make the difference between a productive evening and a frustrating one.

IMITATING SPECIFIC MAYFLIES

Mayflies are sometimes identified by fly fishers by the fly that imitates them (Hendricksons and **Light Cahills**), by their scientific name (*Isonychias* and *Hexagenias*), or by a shortened form of their scientific name (*Hexagenias* are often called "**Hexes**" and *Tricorythodes* are called "**Tricos**"). There is neither rhyme nor reason to this convention and it's just one of those idiosyncrasies fly fishers have to live with. There are 2,500 known species of mayflies in the world (with over 600 of them in North America), so to try to match each species of mayfly with a fly pattern would be ludicrous. Many of them look identical and for any given trout stream in the world, less than a half-dozen dun and emerger patterns, the same amount of spinners, and several nymphs in a range of about four sizes will cover any hatch you'll encounter throughout the season.

The most common mayflies you'll hear about include **Blue-Winged Olives**, **Pale Morning Duns**, Little Blue Quills, Little Red Quills, **Pale Evening Duns**, **Green Drakes**, Hexagenias, Isonychias, March Browns, Light Cahills, Hendricksons, and Tricos. To imitate the duns and emergers of all these mayflies you would need only the following dry flies (the exact pattern can vary as long as a rough approximation of the color and the correct size are used):

- Gray wings and olive body, sizes 12–24
- Cream body with gray wings, sizes 14–22
- Cream body with speckled brown wings, sizes 8–14
- Rusty red body with dark gray wings, sizes 12–18

To imitate the spinners of all those mayflies, you'd need just a few patterns as well:

- Rusty brown body with light gray wings, size 12–18
- Olive body with light gray wings, size 14–18
- Cream body with cream wing with light speckles, size 8–14
- Black body with light gray wings, size 18–24

Of course there is the rare occasion, like picky fish on the South Fork of the Snake in **Idaho** that will only take a size 18 fly with an orange body and cream-gray wing during August. But for nearly any trout stream in the world, if you have dry fly patterns that fall into each of the eight groups above in the correct sizes you can get a decent match to any mayfly hatch you encounter.

MCCLANE, AL. (1922–1991)

Albert Jules McClane was fishing editor of *Field & Stream* magazine for over 40 years, and it is doubtful that any other twentieth century fishing writer produced so much helpful and entertaining educational material for the fly fisher. Among his 20 books was the massive *McClane's Standard Fishing Encyclopedia* (1965), with 1,057 pages and over 100 different contributors. McClane was a well-rounded angler, equally expert at chasing **Montana** trout or Bahamas **bonefish** with a **fly rod**, two of his special favorites. Trained at the Ritz in Paris, he was also a chef specializing in fish cookery. McClane fished with royalty, world leaders, and movie stars, but was equally adept at teaching the basics of fly casting to novices through his books and magazine articles.

MEND

Fly lines, **leaders**, and flies all drift at different speeds in a current because they all present different degrees of resistance. And when a fly line is cast for 30 feet or more in moving water, it's almost certain that it will fall across areas of different current speed. Some flies, especially **dry flies** and **nymphs**, are best fished with a **dead drift**, where the fly drifts the same as a piece of debris in the current, with no motion contrary to it. Here, the essence of presentation is to manipulate the line and leader so that they drift at the same pace as the fly. **Steelhead** and **Atlantic salmon** flies are fished by swinging them in the current, but the exact speed at which they drift should be controlled and not dictated by current speed. And even in ocean fishing for species like **marlin** and **sailfish**, the fly should move sideways to the caster. In all of these cases a technique called a mend is an essential skill.

Mending is quite simple. The fly line is lifted from the water with enough motion to move the line between the angler and the fly but not the fly itself (figure 1). With a roll of the wrist for short casts or the entire arm for longer casts, the fly line is flipped into a curved shape to counteract the effects of currents (figure 2). In a typical situation, a trout is feeding in the slow water next to the bank and the angler is in the middle of the river, where the current is swift. A cast with a dry fly made above the trout would immediately skim the

1)

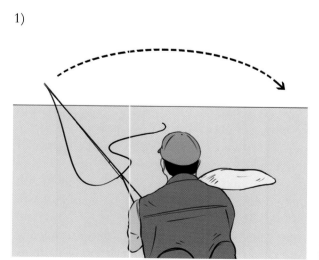

2)

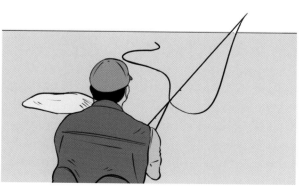

fly back toward the center of the river because the fast current puts a strong bow into the line. By moving the fly line in the center of the river with a brisk **upstream** flip after the line hits the water, the fly will have a chance to float for a longer distance before **drag** sets in.

Mends can also be made in a **downstream** direction. Sometimes a trout feeds in fast water in the center of the river and the cast will be made across slower water, making the fly line lag behind the fly pulling it back upstream. Here, the line is flipped in a downstream direction to keep pace with the fly. Mends can be made multiple times through a drift, especially on long casts and often with sinking flies, to help sink the fly deeper and slow its drift in the current. An extremely useful mend, and one that won't ensue the risk of moving the fly, is an aerial mend. Here, just before the cast is finished the angler makes an exaggerated reach with arm extended in the direction the mend is intended. The result is a curve cast with the mend already in the proper place, with no disturbance of the water.

MICHIGAN

OVERVIEW

Surrounded by four out of the five Great Lakes (Michigan, Huron, Superior, and Erie), Michigan has a wealth of fly fishing opportunities. Although practical fly fishing in these big lakes is restricted to shallow waters along the shoreline, the rivers that drain from central Michigan to all points of the compass are the main draw for the fly fisher. Michigan has more than 11,000 inland lakes and 36,000 miles of streams, and is famous for its inland trout fishing. The many rivers draining into the Great Lakes offer seasonal runs of **steelhead**, **Pacific salmon**, lake-run **brown trout**, and **Atlantic salmon**. But fly fishers should not ignore the possibility of exciting fishing for warm water species like **smallmouth** and **largemouth bass**, **pike**, **walleye**, **carp**, and **panfish**.

FISHERIES

Michigan's premier fishery for resident (non-lake-run) trout is the **Au Sable River** in the central part of the Lower Peninsula. This river, the birthplace of **Trout Unlimited**, has healthy populations of wild **brook**, brown, and **rainbow trout**, and it also has a vigilant local conservation organization, the **Anglers of the Au Sable**, to make sure it stays that way. The Boardman River, near Traverse City, is also an excellent river, with good **hatches**, cold water, and wild brook and brown trout. In contrast to the Au Sable, its fish are easier to catch, and **attractor dry flies** are a popular way

Attractor dry flies are effective on the Boardman River.

to fool its abundant trout. South of the Boardman is the Little Manistee, which has brook trout in its headwaters and large brown trout in its lower reaches close to the lake. Although its resident trout are not as abundant as in other rivers, it does have a run of large lake-run browns and steelhead. Again moving south, the Pere Marquette River has similar fishing—Pacific salmon in the fall, steelhead from November through April, and resident browns and rainbows throughout the year. Next in a southward migration is the Muskegon River, a massive **tailwater** that offers a rich insect population, especially **caddisflies**, below Croton Dam. It has year-round trout fishing for large brown and rainbow trout, as well as fall and winter fishing for salmon and big steelhead.

Michigan's Upper Peninsula also hosts some fine trout streams. The massive St. Mary's River, which drains Lake Superior into Lake Huron, is a mile-wide river that is famous for its landlocked Atlantic salmon run, as well as steelhead, Pacific salmon, and resident rainbow trout. This is a river that requires a boat and an experienced guide. Two of the larger rivers (with large trout) in the Upper Peninsula include the Fox and Escanaba. If easier but smaller trout are your choice, a great high-volume trout stream is the Yellow Dog.

Michigan is surrounded by rivers that host runs of large, migratory, lake-run steelhead, Pacific salmon, and brown trout. The Grand River, right in the middle of Grand Rapids, is a place to catch these species as well as lake trout on a fly. Moving up the coast of Lake Michigan, the best rivers to catch a steelhead or salmon run include the Muskegon, White, Pere Marquette, Little Manistee, Big Manistee, Betsie, and Platte. Lake Superior tributaries that have runs include the St. Mary's, Big Two-Hearted, Big Huron, Chocolay, and Ontonagon. Lake Huron tributaries that produce salmon and steelhead runs are the Rifle, Au Sable, and Ocqueoc.

Smallmouth bass fishing often gets overlooked in Michigan by fly fishers, but this species offers some of the best fly fishing in the state. The shores of all the Great Lakes have opportunities for small-mouths, but one of the finest places in the world for them is Grand Traverse Bay, with its extensive network of shallow, very clear water that at times can look like a **bonefish** flat. Steelhead, brown trout, pike, and carp can also be stalked in this shallow water. Lake St. Clair, at the headwaters of the Detroit River, is a wonderfully fertile lake that, on calm days, gives the fly fisher the opportunity to catch smallmouth and largemouth bass, carp, pike, and **muskellunge**. Hubbard Lake in the northeastern part of the Lower Peninsula is also a **fly rod** destination for anglers pursuing pike and smallmouth bass. Smallmouth fishing is also excellent in the lower reaches of Michigan's trout rivers, especially the Manistee, Muskegon, Au Sable, and Boardman.

SEASON

Michigan does not have a time when you can't catch fish with a fly rod. In the middle of winter, steelhead will take a fly in rivers like the Muskegon and Pere Marquette (although fishing for them is more productive in November and April). March ushers both steelhead spawning, which makes them more aggressive, and the beginning of **mayfly** hatches on inland trout streams. By May, most steelhead have dropped down into the Great Lakes, but important mayfly hatches like the Hendrickson mayfly bring trout to the surface. In June, hatches of caddisflies and mayflies are in full swing, especially the giant night-hatching *Hexagenia*, which brings even the biggest trout in a river to dry flies. May and June are the best times for bass fishing with a fly rod, although the cooler waters of most rivers ensure that smallmouths chase flies all day long. In May through July, Atlantic salmon enter the St. Mary's River and offer thrilling runs and leaps when hooked on a fly in that river's massive rapids. Midsummer on trout streams brings hatches of tiny mayflies like the **Trico**, and **terrestrial** insects like deer flies, flying **ants**, and **beetles** keep trout active during the day as well. In September, Pacific salmon and lake-run brown trout begin entering rivers, and fishing for them remains good until November, when steelhead run in earnest and the cycle begins again.

MIDGE

Midge adult

Although to some fly fishers a midge can mean any small **dry fly**, to most it means a small, nonbiting two-winged insect of the order Diptera and family Chironomidae. Fly fishers refer to these insects variously as dipterans, chironomids, or buzzers (primarily in Europe). There are over 5,000 described species in the world and fly fishers don't attempt to distinguish between them. (Worry only about color and size.) Midges occur in almost all types of water, both moving water and **still water**. Because their environmental tolerance for pollutants and low oxygen levels is quite high, high populations of midges as opposed to other aquatic insects can indicate an ecosystem in trouble.

Although midges live in all trout waters, they are most common in lakes, ponds, and slower-moving rivers. In fact, in many **tailwater** rivers, midges are the primary trout food, accounting for close to 80 percent of a trout's diet. The **larvae** and **pupae** are easy meals and a single trout can eat thousands in one day. Fly fishers who ignore these tiny flies, particularly on lakes, western tailwaters, and weedy spring-fed rivers risk fishless days throughout the season. This is especially true for winter fly fishers, as midges are often the only aquatic insects **hatching** on a winter day and thus the only food in the current.

LIFE CYCLE

Midge larvae are simple, legless worms that live in silt and mud. They can be bright red (called a bloodworm by fishermen), tan, brown, and even bright green. Larvae get dislodged by currents, animals, and wading fishermen; a single footstep can introduce thousands of them into the current. Prior to hatching into adults, the larvae pupate and then rise to the surface with tiny gas bubbles produced within the body of the insect. Pupae are usually drab brown or black, with a humped shape and distinctive wing pads at the thorax and a slender abdomen. Tiny feathery gills at the head also help to identify them, and placing a piece of mesh in the surface film when they are hatching will help to identify the size present. While pupae are drifting and especially when they reach the surface film and struggle to **emerge** as adults, they are most vulnerable to feeding trout and either a pupa imitation fished deep or an emerger just below the surface film will catch trout. In fact, as long as the angler is willing to fish these tiny flies, the fishing is quite easy.

Once midges hatch, the winged adults skitter across the surface before flying. At this time, small trout may slash at the adults but bigger trout seem to prefer the easier drifting pupae. After a few days the adults return to the river to mate and lay eggs in massive swarms, usually in the evening, and at this time trout of all sizes pay more attention to the adults. The best fishing is when one or more males attach themselves to a female and fall to the water. These balls of midges, called cluster midges, will bring big trout to the surface and often individual fish will select only the double or triple clumps of flies and ignore drifting singles. This is a great advantage to the fly fisher as it allows a bigger fly to be used.

Midge larva

FISHING TECHNIQUES

Midge larvae should be fished close to the bottom, and it usually takes some weight on the **leader** and a **strike indicator** to do this properly. It's common to fish two flies, perhaps two different colors of midge larvae **nymphs**, a larva and a pupa, or a midge larva combined with a larger **mayfly** or **caddisfly** nymph when the angler is not certain what type of larva the fish are feeding on. In all cases, the angler should strive to get a completely **dead drift**, as midge larvae do not swim at all and

any movement contrary to the flow of current will alert the fish. Midge larvae can be fished at any time of day and at any time of year, as there are always midge larvae present.

Pupae may also be fished deep like larvae, as they begin their hatching close to the bottom. However, because the pupae rise to the surface, they can also be fished in the middle of the water column and at the surface. Sometimes a midge pupa fly with a tiny bead incorporated into the pattern is fished below a strike indicator, or when fish are seen making small boils at the surface a pupa can be fished just below the surface or in the surface film. A deadly technique is to fish a sinking midge pupa attached with a dropper to a floating emerger, using the floating fly as a strike indicator.

Once the adults hatch a high-floating dry fly can be effective, especially if the fish make splashing rises and adults are skating across the surface. A dry fly can either be fished dead drift or skated across the surface using a leader treated with paste fly dressing. When the adults return on their mating flight, dead drift is again the best practice but sometimes a moving fly is effective, especially on lakes and ponds. If careful observation shows trout selecting only clumps of midges instead of singles, then a fly two to three times the size of the individual adults will often attract a fish that has ignored the standard dry fly.

FLY PATTERNS

Trout are commonly not selective about fly patterns when eating midges as long as the size is the same as the naturals; however the correct size is critical unless the fish are eating clumpers. Color seems to be more critical when fishing larvae and a trout that is eating green midge larvae will often ignore a red imitation. Colors of pupa imitations are not as important as most are a dull tan or brown. Most adults are either gray, tan, or cream, and as long as the color is relatively close, trout should accept a well-presented pattern. Best larva imitations include the Bloodworm, Red Hot, and

Brassie. Popular pupa imitations are the Zebra Midge, Bead-Head Brassie, Crystal Midge, CDC Midge Pupa, and Disco Midge. Best adults are the venerable Griffith's Gnat, Black Midge, and Matt's Midge. When clumpers are on the water, there is nothing better than a size 16 or 18 Griffith's Gnat.

Midges can be tinier than the smallest fly hook, and on certain tailwater rivers like the Farmington in Connecticut, fish in the summer can be seen feeding on midges that are impossible to imitate. However, the most common sizes are size 18 through 24, and on lakes midges can grow as big as a size 14. It's a good idea to have wide variety of sizes as you can never be certain what size will be hatching when you reach the river.

MINNESOTA

Overview

Minnesota is a state better known for walleye trolling and **smallmouth bass** fishing, and both of these species as well as **panfish**, **pike**, **muskellunge** are taken on a **fly rod**. This state is a maze of waterways, from the Mississippi River to Lake Superior to the endless lakes of the Boundary Waters **Canoe** Area. There are over 14,000 lakes of over 10 acres in Minnesota and 63,000 miles of rivers and streams where you can chase warmwater species with a fly rod. However, Minnesota also offers some excellent small-stream fishing for trout, as well as lake-run **steelhead** and **Pacific salmon** from streams that run into Lake Superior, and Minnesota offers 3,300 miles of trout water on 651 designated trout streams.

Fisheries

The best trout fishing in Minnesota is in the southeastern and northeastern sections of the state. These areas are quite different in stream character, **hatches**, and fishing methods. The Arrowhead region above the north shore of Lake Superior contains about 250 of these streams, and this wild and scenic area is most noted for its **brook trout** fishing, as well as lake-run steelhead and Pacific salmon upstream from Lake Superior to the first impassable falls or dam. These relatively infertile streams grow trout that aren't terribly picky about what they eat, and basic **Prince Nymphs**, **Elk Hair Caddis** dries, and Pass Lake and **Muddler Minnow** streamers will work well.

The Knife River is the primary steelhead spawning river on the North Shore, and accounts for nearly 70 percent of the steelhead in this area. Its upper reaches are also home to resident brook, **brown**, and **rainbow trout**. The Temperance River, with its headwaters in the Boundary Waters Canoe Area, is a wide river with a good population of brown trout in its main stem and brook trout in

M

its tributaries. The Cascade River has a similar makeup of fish species, with a spectacular canyon in Cascade River State Park. Other good trout streams in the area include the Baptism River, Beaver River, and Junco Creek.

West of the Boundary Waters Canoe Area are a number of productive trout streams. The best is the Straight River, located west of Park Rapids. The Straight is one of the best brown trout streams in Minnesota, and its spring-fed waters flow slow and deep over a bottom composed mostly of silt and sand, which produces hatches of big Brown Drake and **Hex mayflies** in June and July. Other good trout streams in north central Minnesota include Stony Brook and the Dark River.

The southwestern corner of Minnesota is home to what is known as Minnesota's "secret" trout streams. With underlying limestone bedrock, which increases the productivity of these spring-fed streams and thus abundant insect and crustacean populations (leading to big trout), these small streams become more famous each year. At one time most of these streams were marginal due to poor land-use practices, but habitat restorations by the Minnesota Department of Natural Resources with assistance from **Trout Unlimited** has added hundreds of miles of streams to the list of trout waters in this region. Wild brook trout are found in headwaters and smaller tributaries and rainbow trout are stocked in some streams, but the majority of the fish here are wild brown trout, with concentrations of fish up to 300 pounds per acre—which is about as good as it gets anywhere.

The South Fork of the Root River and Trout Run Creek, which runs into the North Branch of the Root River, are two of the best streams in this area. The South Branch is a big river for this part of the state and has an excellent hatch of **Trico** mayflies in August, but Trout Run Creek hosts an incredible population of wild brook and brown trout, with densities as high as 5,000 fish per mile. The Whitewater River and its North, Middle, and South Forks gives up large brown trout to the fly

every year and fishes well even in the dead of winter. Beaver Creek is another excellent stream, especially the East Beaver, a spring-fed stream that runs entirely within Beaver Creek Valley State Park.

Minnesota has so much great fishing for the warm-water species—**largemouth bass**, smallmouth bass, northern pike, **walleye**, and panfish— that it's difficult to pin down which lakes and rivers are best. For largemouth bass fishing, you may not need to go any farther from the Twin Cities than Lake Minnetonka, with its many shallow bays and inlets. Massive Mille Lacs Lake north of the Twin Cities is also an excellent place to catch largemouths on the fly, as well as northern pike, walleye, black crappie, and smallmouth bass. Next to trout, though, fly fishers seem to prefer smallmouth bass in rivers, and Minnesota offers superb river fishing for them. Best bets are the Mississippi, upper St. Croix River, Snake River, lower Root River, Rum River, St. Louis River, and the Zumbro River. You'll also find muskellunge and walleye in these rivers.

SEASON

Because of colder temperatures and high spring runoff, trout fishing in the northern Minnesota streams is best from late May through late August. Steelhead and salmon will be found off the mouths of rivers or in streams that drain into Lake Superior from September through November, and steelhead will stay in these northern rivers through April. The southwestern spring-fed streams fish well all year long. Trout can be taken on **nymphs** and streamers, or even **dry flies** in the middle of winter, but the action really heats up with the abundant mayfly and caddisfly hatches from May through August.

Perhaps the most exciting fly hatch on Minnesota rivers and lakes is the giant *Hexagenia limbata* mayfly. This June through July mayfly, the largest mayfly in North America, hatches in late evening on not only trout streams and lakes but also on warm-water lakes and rivers. It's possible to catch trout, bass, panfish, and even walleye on a dry fly when these big bugs are around, and during the hatch a fly fisher can often do better than a spin fisher, even for walleyes.

The best time for northern pike fishing with a fly is when they are in shallow water in April and then again in early fall. Muskellunge prefer warmer water temperatures, so fly-fishing for them is better in June. May and June are also the times when bass are in the shallows spawning, which makes them perfect targets for a fly rod.

MONOFILAMENT

See Leader, Tippet.

MONTANA

OVERVIEW

Montana is considered by some to have the best trout fishing in North America, if not the world. A combination of high mountains that store the snowmelt that keeps trout streams cool throughout hot, dry summers, reservoirs that store water and enrich it with accumulated nutrients, a stream access law that allows public fishing on nearly every river in the state, and an enlightened fisheries management policy that stresses wild trout over hatchery fish all combine to provide a rich and diverse fly fishing resource.

In contrast to states like **Wyoming** and **Colorado**, where the landowner owns the bottom of a river and can technically prevent a drift boat from anchoring or an angler from wading within his or her property, in Montana an angler is allowed to use all rivers and streams up to the high-water mark. This does not include, however, the right to cross private land that is visibly posted without permission. Lands are typically posted by the placement of orange fenceposts or signs along a boundary, and to cross these lands, unless you stay in a river channel, you need permission from the landowner. Happily, Montana has a wealth of state-owned fishing access sites along most major rivers.

Montana also has an abundance of highly trained, professional guides and most of them specialize in fly fishing for trout. Standards in Montana are high, and the visiting angler can be confident of getting a superior guide through a reputable fly shop or outfitter. For the angler capable of handling a **drift boat**, there are also many places where they can be rented and shuttles arranged for a moderate fee.

Montana has a stream access law that allows public fishing on nearly every river in the state.

M

FISHERIES

The best fly fishing in Montana is on the western side of the state, where mountain ranges and abundant precipitation (plus many reservoirs that create excellent **tailwater** fisheries) create the ideal habitat for trout. In the northwest corner of the state, the Kootenai is a large tailwater river that has some great fishing for mostly medium-sized wild **rainbow trout**. Because of its size, the river is best fished from a drift boat, but it gets less fishing pressure that any other large river in Montana, and the fish are relatively easy to catch on **attractor** flies. A similar experience can be enjoyed on the Flathead River and its Middle, North, and South Forks, as the Flathead is the most remote large trout river in Montana, with the South Fork in particular, as it begins in the vast Bob Marshall Wilderness Area. Besides the typical rainbow and **cutthroat trout**, the Flathead system also has **grayling** and supports the threatened **bull trout**, which should be immediately released if hooked as it is illegal to even purposely fish for these.

Moving further south toward Missoula, the Clark Fork is a massive river (the largest by water volume in Montana) that is very productive but not as well known as other large rivers in the state. Its rich waters harbor great insect life and healthy populations of rainbows, cutthroats, rainbow cutthroat hybrids, and **brown trout**. In the lower Clark Fork, downstream of Missoula, trout are not everywhere and seem to concentrate in pockets so a guide is a good idea. Above Missoula and in the Clark Fork's famous tributaries the Bitterroot, Blackfoot, and Rock Creek, wading is more productive and trout population densities are higher. The Bitterroot is a small river with high concentrations of browns and rainbows but it can be a moody river, productive one day and difficult the next. Rock Creek is more friendly, with **riffles** and **pocket water** that run through national forest land, with plenty of opportunities for wildlife viewing. It's mostly **brook trout** and cutthroats in its headwaters, with bigger rainbows and browns

The Yellowstone River is the longest freeflowing river in the lower 48 states.

closer to its confluence with the Clark Fork. The Blackfoot, once nearly devoid of life from mining waste, has come back to life due to efforts by local conservation organizations and **Trout Unlimited**, and has 60 miles of excellent trout fishing and good insect hatches.

The **Yellowstone River** is the longest freeflowing (undammed) river in the lower 48 states. As a result, the main stem of this river is often high and dirty with snow runoff well into July, but when it finally clears the Yellowstone offers some of the best **dry fly** fishing for large trout anywhere in Montana. The river is one of the finest places to catch wild Yellowstone cutthroats, especially in its headwaters in Yellowstone Park (technically Wyoming). The river then runs through the lightly fished Grand Canyon of the Yellowstone before leaving the Park near the town of Gardiner and entering Montana proper. The river now offers fishing for large brown and rainbow trout, and of course mountain whitefish, for nearly 100 miles until it slows and warms near Columbus. This giant river

Some of the best fishing in Montana is March through early May, prior to runoff and before the summer vacation crowds.

has numerous access points for the wading angler, but so much water needs to be covered to find trout that a float trip is a far more popular way to fish.

A better bet for the wading angler is some of the Yellowstone's smaller tributaries. The Gardiner, near the town on the border of Yellowstone Park that bears its name, is a small pocket water stream full of mostly rainbow and brown trout eager to take any reasonably presented dry fly or **nymph**. Further downstream in the Paradise Valley toward Livingston are three spring creeks open to the public for a fee. The ranches that surround Armstrong Spring Creek, Depuy Spring Creek (actually the lower end of Armstrong Spring Creek), and Nelson's Spring Creek limit the number of anglers each day for a quality experience. Rising fish can be found on these streams 12 months a year, and fishing to the educated trout in these crystal-clear, weed-filled streams is a pilgrimage that all fly fishers should try at least once. Downstream of Livingston, both the Stillwater and Boulder Rivers

near Big Timber give up their fish much easier in their boulder-strewn riffles and runs, and contain healthy populations of brook, brown, rainbow, and cutthroat trout.

The **Bighorn River**, a major tributary of the lower Yellowstone, is the easternmost trout stream of note in Montana. Unlike most rivers in Montana, it flows through arid high desert and would not be a trout stream without the icy waters flowing out of Yellowtail Dam. Heavily fished, it has one of the highest trout populations per mile of any stream in Montana, but it does not have the same rugged scenery as rivers in the eastern part of the state.

The Missouri River drainage includes some of the world's best and most famous trout streams. The main stem of the Missouri, between Three Forks (where the Madison, Jefferson, and Gallatin meet) and Canyon Ferry Lake is relatively warm and slow, and although big trout lurk in its deeper pools, the trout are not abundant. A similar fishery is downstream between Hauser and Holter Lakes. The 50 miles of water downstream of Holter Lake are what most fly fishers think of when speaking of the Missouri. This is wide, smooth, relatively shallow water with rich weed growth and abundant aquatic insects. **Hatches** are frequent but trout are never easy here because of heavy fishing pressure.

The Jefferson River itself suffers from massive agricultural water withdrawals in summer and becomes very warm and shallow. It's not a bad fishery in spring and fall, but a lot of water should be covered with **streamer** flies in order to find its big but sparsely distributed trout. However, the Jefferson's tributaries include the famous Beaverhead, Bighole, and Ruby Rivers, all first-class trout streams. The Beaverhead is narrow, fast, and brushy and best fished from a drift boat. It has a very dense population of rainbow and brown trout and good hatches throughout the spring and summer. The Bighole winds through a scenic valley filled with giant hay meadows and its riffle-and-pool makeup is much more friendly to the wading angler. Although it also warms considerably in the summer, it holds up better than the Jefferson, and after its big hatch of **Salmonfly stoneflies** in June fishing pressure is light. There are **grayling** in its headwaters but most of the river is a mixture of browns and rainbows. The Ruby is a smaller, alder-lined stream with a dense population of surprisingly large brown and rainbow trout.

The **Madison River** is the most famous river in Montana. From its headwaters in Yellowstone Park through the Hebgen Lake impoundment trout are numerous, but the best part of the Madison is between Quake Lake and Ennis Lake, with a combination of float and wade fishing areas. Below Ennis Lake it flows through Beartrap Canyon with its rattlesnakes and class V whitewater, so a knowledgeable guide is needed there. Downstream of Beartrap Canyon to Three Forks the river gets warmer and is best fished early and late in the season.

The Gallatin River is a lovely tumbling mountain stream that begins in Yellowstone Park. Fishing in its meadow water within the Park is productive, but the best fishing is in the vicinity of Big Sky, where majestic canyons and long riffles provide great trout habitat and breathtaking scenery. This is the water where the movie *A River Runs Through It* was filmed. Downstream of Bozeman, the river widens and trout habitat degrades, but its spring-fed tributary, the East Gallatin, is a wonderful little stream with an abundance of small and large trout and rising fish almost any time of year.

Bass, both **largemouth** and **smallmouth**, are common in Montana but are ignored by most fly fishers because of Montana's trout fishing. Bass are common in the lower, warmer reaches of the bigger trout streams including the Lower Flathead, Yellowstone, Bighorn, and Missouri Rivers. Smallmouth bass are abundant and grow quite large in Canyon Ferry Lake, Holter Lake, Flathead Lake, and Fort Peck and Tongue River Reservoirs. Northern **pike** are found in all of these waters, as well as **panfish** like bluegills, pumpkinseed **sunfish**, yellow perch, and **white bass**.

SEASON

Montana's larger rivers are subject to snow melt runoff, and as a result some of them become unfishable for about three weeks any time from May through July, depending on the altitude, snow pack, and spring weather. However, flows close to dams on tailwater rivers usually run clear unless the reservoirs behind them are overflowing with snowmelt, and spring creeks, both those in the Paradise valley and others such as Big Spring Creek near Lewistown and Poindexter Slough, a tributary of the Beaverhead, will be clear and in good shape any time of year. In fact, the spring creeks fish well all winter long. On a warm winter day, the lucky fly fisher can even have dry fly fishing to midges in January.

Some of the best and most uncrowded fishing in Montana is in March through early May, prior to runoff and before the summer vacation crowds. February and March bring an inch-long olive stonefly known as the Skwala, which is especially abundant on the Bitterroot River. In late March the tremendous **Blue-Winged Olive** mayfly hatches begin, and in late April the famous Mother's Day **caddis** hatch begins.

In June, if runoff cooperates, the giant Salmonfly stonefly hatch begins and then ends within a few days on any given stretch of a river. It's difficult to plan a trip around this hatch, but if you are ever on a river when it happens and you see five-pound trout inhaling dry flies as big as a size 4, you'll know why many anglers take the risk. From early summer through August, the **Pale Morning Dun** mayfly hatches on a fairly regular basis. It is a reliable hatch but trout by this time of season are fussy and the fishing is seldom easy. Various species of caddis hatch all summer long, usually in late morning and evening. Some rivers get too warm for reliable daytime fishing, but trout will eat nymphs early in the morning and various dry flies in the evening. Once **grasshoppers** get active in late July, the rest of the summer and early fall revolve around fishing grasshopper and **beetle** flies, unless the tiny **Trico** mayfly hatches in the morning, when great sport can be had with diminutive dry flies and pods of rising trout.

Trico and grasshopper fishing can last into September, but once the first big rains and snow squalls begin, most fly fishers turn to streamer fishing. This is when big brown trout are on the move to their fall spawning grounds, and when rainbows and cutthroats fatten themselves on minnows prior to winter's colder water temperatures. Trout can be caught all winter on nymphs and streamers in most rivers, but some of the best fishing in winter is for mountain **whitefish**, a close relative of trout that, while not as pretty, put up a strong battle and are delicious to eat. With liberal catch limits and abundant populations they are great for the fly fisher who occasionally likes to keep fish for the table.

Fishing for smallmouth bass, carp, pike, and panfish is best in Montana June through September, although pike are sometimes quite active during their spawning season in March through May, where they will often be found in flooded shorelines. Smallmouth bass are easiest to catch on a fly during their spawning season as well, which can be from May through June.

MOON PHASE

It is well known that animals have periods of strong activity at dawn and dusk, particularly feeding activity. However, animals also seem to have peaks of activity when the moon's gravitational forces are at a maximum. This effect is strongest twice a day, when the moon is directly overhead or directly underfoot. There are also supposedly minor periods of activity when the moon rises and sets. **John Alden Knight** formulated his famous Solunar Tables on these major and minor periods. Because fish, even freshwater fish, are all descended from oceanic ancestors, it makes sense that they may still respond to these tidal forces even where there are no **tides**.

The moon phase has strong effects on ocean tides, which are important in determining the feeding behavior of saltwater species. But freshwater fish also seem to be influenced by the phase of the moon. For instance, many freshwater fish feed poorly during the day during a full moon. Exactly why is poorly understood, but it is thought that fish that normally feed during the day feed heavily at night on a full moon. Migratory species like salmon and **steelhead**, whether they are migrating in landlocked freshwater rivers or into

M

rivers that feed the sea, are also much more likely to move long distances during a full moon.

MUDDLER MINNOW

From its development in 1936 until the **Woolly Bugger** became popular in the 1980s, the Muddler Minnow was responsible for catching more large trout than any other fly. Don Gapen was fishing on the Nipigon River in northern Ontario when he noticed native Americans using **sculpins**, (or "muddlers" as they are known in **Canada**) as bait for large **brook trout**, and he tied the fly using mottled turkey feathers for the wing and tail, gold tinsel for the body, gray squirrel tail for the under wing, and a head made of spun and clipped deer hair. The deer hair head gives the fly a wide profile and probably sets up vibrations in the water that help fish find it, even in dirty water.

The Muddler Minnow can be fished on a sinking line as a **streamer**, dry as a **grasshopper** imitation, sunk as a **stonefly nymph**, and has even been used in salt water for everything from **striped bass** to **sharks**. Sculpins also live in salt water, but it may just be the unique shape and action of this fly that gives it such strong attraction to fish. The Muddler has spawned many variations. Brass and tungsten beads or cones have been added to the head of the fly to make it sink faster. The wing is sometimes made from fluffy marabou feathers to give the fly a wiggling action in the water. And Muddlers have been tied in every color of the spectrum, from white to yellow to black, replacing the natural drab brown-gray shade of the original.

MUSKELLUNGE

Muskellunge, large members of the **pike** and pickerel family native to the Great Lakes, south-central **Canada**, and upper Midwest, have become a popular target for fly fishers seeking a new challenge. They have been introduced into many places in the U.S. and Canada, and are now found far outside their native range. These fish are never easy to lure (even among bait and lure anglers they are known as "the fish of 10,000 casts"), but in certain waters, especially large rivers, they can be taken with some regularity on large **streamer flies** and **poppers**. Muskies begin to enter shallow water when temperatures climb into the sixties (above 16°C), and will stay near shallow water for most of the summer—although during the day they will stay deep when the weather gets hot or the sun is bright.

Muskie fishing with a **fly rod** is a sport for the angler who likes to cast a big rod, all day long. Rods should be either 9- or 10-weight, **leaders** should be short and stiff (3 feet of 30-pound **nylon** is probably perfect), and between the leader and fly should be 8 to 10 inches of **wire** because muskies have an impressive array of sharp teeth. **Fly lines** should be intermediate sinking or slow sinking varieties. Look for them along the edges of shallow water where it drops into deep water, or close to submerged logs and rocks where they can lie in ambush for their prey. Muskies prefer a very fast, erratic **retrieve** (anglers who troll for them keep the boat moving at 10 miles an hour), and it's wise to use a two-handed strip with the fly held under the arm, plus a **stripping basket** to keep control of the line. Muskies are not picky about their fly patterns, but flies should be big and bulky—from 6 to 10 inches long.

Best fly fishing for muskies is in May and June, and again in September and October when the fish are in shallow water. Popular places to catch them on a fly include northern **Wisconsin**, **Pennsylvania**'s Allegheny River, Canada's Ottawa River, **Michigan**'s Lake St. Clair, northwestern Ontario, Piedmont Lake in **Ohio**, and Cave Run Lake in Kentucky.

Nymph

NAIL KNOT

The Nail Knot is one of the most useful knots in fly fishing, and can be used to attach both a **leader** and **backing** to a **fly line**. It is not only very strong; it is also a slim knot that runs through the guides of a **fly rod** without catching on them. The nail knot was discovered in Argentina in the 1960s by **Joe Brooks**, who watched local fishing guides **whip** a leader to a fly line with a horseshoe nail. (Although the nail knot *can* be tied with a nail, it's easier to tie with a thin plastic or metal tube, or with one of the many nail knot tools on the market today.)

When tying a leader to a fly line with a nail knot, the leader is knotted directly to the front end of the fly line. To make the strongest connection (although a slightly bulkier one), double the end of the fly line over itself and then tie three closely spaced nail knots over both pieces of line to form a strong, totally secure loop at the end of the line. This fly line loop is standard procedure in line weights 10 and above, where large **tarpon** or **sailfish** may be the target species and the strongest

connection possible is desired. The back end of a fly line can be doubled over as well, and if a large **Bimini Twist** loop is tied into the backing, a new fly line that that is still on the plastic spool that came with it can be attached to backing already on a reel with a loop-to-loop connection.

To attach a leader or backing to a fly line without a special tool, it's best to use a narrow diameter plastic or metal tube, such as the hollow plastic sticks used to stir coffee. A metal inflation adapter for a football or basketball also has the correct diameter tube. Here are the steps in tying a leader to a fly line with a tube:

- Lay the tube alongside the fly line, about an inch from the end of the line. Place the butt end of the leader in line with the tube and fly line, leaving the last four inches of the heavy part of the leader extending beyond the tube, in the opposite direction from the end of the fly line (figure 1).

- Pinch the tube, leader, and fly line together with one hand. With the other hand, wind the butt of the leader back over itself, the tube, and the fly line. It should wind toward the end of the fly line in tight, adjacent wraps (figure 2).

■ After five wraps, slip the end of the leader through the tube so that it goes under the wraps you have just made. Keep pinching the wraps tightly to the fly line (figure 3).

■ Slip the tube out from under the wraps while pulling both ends of the leader away from each other. This should be done quickly so that the coils made over the fly line don't overlap (figure 4).

■ Tighten the knot by wrapping the standing part of the leader around one hand and pulling on the tag end of the leader with a pair of pliers or **forceps** (figure 5). Enough pressure should be put on the leader so that it snubs into the coating of the fly line. Finally, pull the fly line and leader in opposite directions with your hands to make sure the knot is secure. Trim the tag ends of the line and leader. The finished knot is sometimes lightly coated with waterproof rubber cement or super glue to make it smoother, but it isn't really necessary for strength.

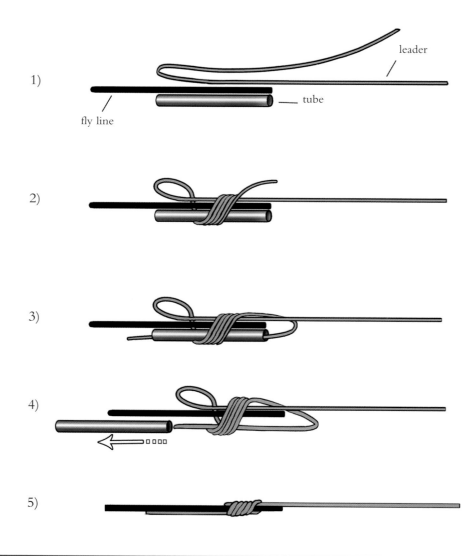

1)   leader /   fly line /   tube

2)

3)

4)

5)

NET

Fly fishers use everything from large aluminum boat nets for big game fish like salmon, **steelhead**, and **striped bass** to tiny handcrafted wooden nets for small stream trout. A net makes landing a fish much quicker than trying to tire it out until it can be handled, and a fish can be kept in the water while removing a fly or taking a photograph, which cuts down on handling time and increases the survival rate of released fish. For catch-and-release fishing, the best net bags are those made from wide strips of rubber. Cotton and **nylon** nets are more abrasive and can remove the protective slime layer on a fish's skin, increasing the chance of a fungal infection on a released fish. If nylon net bags are used, the type with fine, soft mesh is easiest on the fish.

A large net can be cumbersome, but a net that is too small can be a disaster. Choose a net opening where the long dimension is about two-thirds the size of the largest fish you expect to catch—in other words, a net with a 16-inch diameter will handle a 24-inch fish. Short-handled nets are fine for wading anglers but from a boat, a long-handled net is more practical. Guides also like long-handled nets as they can net an angler's fish from farther away, preventing a last-minute bolt for freedom when a tired fish sees the angler.

Swiping at a fish with a net often results in a broken **leader**. The best way to land a fish is to place the net in the water well before the fish gets close to the angler. This way, a fish can be led over the top of the net and it can be quickly swept under the fish before it realizes what is happening.

NEW HAMPSHIRE

OVERVIEW

Although overshadowed by neighboring **Maine**'s great wilderness areas and abundant trout and salmon fishing, New Hampshire also offers good fishing with a **fly rod**, from **brook trout** fishing in the White Mountains to bass fishing in its larger lakes. And despite New Hampshire's short 17-mile coastline, it is prime habitat for summer **striped bass** fishing. Most of New Hampshire's trout fishing is located in the northern half of the state, as development and flatter terrain in the southern half keeps most rivers warmer than optimum for trout in summer. However, stocking, restrictive harvests, and habitat improvements in southern New Hampshire rivers has brought trout fishing back to some waters that were formerly polluted by mills, particularly the Piscataquog, Souhegan, and Contoocook Rivers.

FISHERIES

New Hampshire's premier trout river is the upper Connecticut River, which forms the border between Vermont and New Hampshire. In its headwater, between the three Connecticut Lakes (First, Second, and Third) the river provides small-stream fishing for wild brook trout. Between the First and Second Connecticut Lakes, a bottom-release dam keeps the water cold all summer and thus brook trout fishing is good even in August. Below First Connecticut Lake until the river enters Lake Francis to the south, the river is also a **tailwater** fishery, and besides brook trout, the river here has a substantial population of landlocked **Atlantic salmon** that run out of Lake Francis in spring and fall. Below Lake Francis a stretch of big, wide water that alternates between long **riffles**, fast

runs, and slow, deep pools runs for 30 miles. The river here is large enough for **drift boats** and several experienced guides run trips on this trophy trout water, which holds brook trout, **rainbow trout**, large **brown trout**, and some landlocked Atlantic salmon. It is seldom crowded and midsummer fishing can be excellent because of the cold water temperatures. **Dry fly** fishing is productive, although large **nymphs** and **streamers** are often more effective.

Although there are pockets of trout in riffles and at the mouths of cold tributaries along the remaining stretch of the Connecticut River south to the Massachusetts border, the remaining 200 miles of river to the south is mostly slower, deeper water. **Smallmouth bass** fishing is excellent throughout its length, especially on streamers and large deer hair **poppers**. In slower water and in the many backwaters, fly fishing for northern **pike** and **largemouth bass** is also productive, and below Bellows Falls and Vernon dams, runs of **American shad** have been reestablished; fly fishing for them in June gets better each year.

The other large trout and salmon river in northern New Hampshire is the Androscoggin. A large river big enough for drift boats, the Androscoggin is divided into two distinct sections. The upper section, from the outlet of Lake Umbagog in Errol for about 10 miles downstream, is a free-flowing river with wild pocket water and long deep pools. Large brown and rainbow trout are common, and the famous Alder Fly **hatch** (an aquatic insect that looks like a large dark **caddisfly** but is actually in a separate order of insects) in July is famous throughout New England.

The two best trout rivers in east central New Hampshire are the Saco and Ellis Rivers, near North Conway. The Ellis has extensive pools and pocket water and is best with dry flies and nymphs, while the Saco has wide pools that are most productive when fished during the evening with a dry fly. Further south, the Contoocook has excellent fly hatches all summer long, and this pretty river is especially productive in the vicinity of West Henniker.

New Hampshire has established a special fishery

for brood stock Atlantic salmon in the Merrimack and Pemigewasset rivers. These are large salmon raised to provide young salmon for regular stocking programs, and once they have reached a large size their egg production is not as vigorous, so the brood stock is placed into these two rivers in spring and fall. Although not the same as fishing for wild Atlantic salmon, it's a chance to catch a large, hard-fighting fish on a fly.

New Hampshire also has many lakes and ponds loaded with trout, salmon, and bass. Nearly every lake in the state has largemouth and smallmouth bass, and most of the larger lakes are stocked with landlocked salmon and rainbow trout. The best trout ponds in the state include Willard, Dublin, Stonehouse, Sky, Profile, Echo, and Clarksville. The New Hampshire Fish and Game Department manages and stocks 15 lakes with landlocked salmon: Big Dan Hole Pond, First and Second Connecticut Lakes, Conway Lake, Lake Francis, Merrymeeting Lake, Newfound Lake, Ossipee Lake, Big and Little Squam Lakes, Sunapee Lake, Lake Winnipesaukee, Winnisquam Lake, and Nubanusit Lake.

The best striped bass fishing on New Hampshire's short coastline is in the Piscataqua River and its estuary. This is a giant river best fished with a boat, but the wading angler can find striped bass throughout the estuary and in salt marshes, as well as along beaches in the Rye Beach and Hampton Beach areas.

Season

Fishing season does not begin early in New Hampshire. The first fishing of the season (for trout and landlocked salmon) is in lakes just after ice-out, which is typically in April or early May, depending on the altitude of the pond and spring weather. Dry fly fishing in northern rivers like the Androscoggin and upper Connecticut, is typically slow until June, with early July the best time for strong **mayfly** and caddisfly hatches. In central and southern New Hampshire, good fishing begins earlier, in May, but high summer water temperatures

makes these rivers a poor choice in midsummer. In September, rivers across the state cool down and landlocked salmon begin entering rivers for their spawning run, so fall fishing can be almost as good as late spring. Striped bass fishing on the coast begins in May with the arrival of small "schoolie" bass, followed in early June by large stripers, which remain in the area until September, when they migrate south to the Chesapeake.

NEW JERSEY

Overview

Although to an outsider, New Jersey does not seem like a state for great **fly rod** fishing, this little state, although heavily industrialized and populated in the northeast, has excellent fly rod opportunities in both fresh and salt water. New Jersey has over 500 miles of streams that support trout year-round, and many other stretches of water that stay cold enough to support trout through early summer. New Jersey has an extensive trout-stocking program along with over 120 streams that support wild, naturally reproducing **brook trout**, plus 79 streams that support wild **brown trout** and 18 streams that support wild **rainbow trout**. Most lakes in New Jersey also support good populations of **largemouth bass** and **panfish**, and saltwater fly fishing along the coast of New Jersey is some of the best on the East Coast. **Striped bass**, **bluefish**, **weakfish**, **false albacore**, and **bonito** are abundant at certain times of year, and for the offshore fly rodder, small bluefin **tuna** appear during the summer to test the strength of even the strongest fly fisher's arm muscles.

Fisheries

The southernmost notable trout stream in New Jersey is Toms River, **upstream** of the town of the same name. In its headwaters the stream is narrow and brushy, but further **downstream**, through the famous New Jersey Pine Barrens, it widens and becomes less accessible, providing solitude and good fishing, including stocked trout plus some wild brook

trout. **Mayflies** are not abundant here, although **caddisfly** and **midge hatches** are plentiful.

In the north central part of the state, the North and South Branches of the Raritan River have some of the best insect hatches in the state, with a mixture of mayflies, caddisflies, **stoneflies**, and midges throughout the spring and summer months. The small North Branch is more of a seasonal trout stream, with its hatchery fish disappearing with the heat of summer. The South Branch has much better trout fishing for both wild and stocked fish. Some of the best fly fishing is in the boulder-strewn pocket water of Ken Lockwood Gorge, which the state has designated as a Year-Round Trout Conservation Area, where only one trout bigger than 15 inches may be kept. Just north of the heavily industrialized greater Newark area is the Ramapo River, and although it winds through suburban and industrialized areas south of Suffern and is one of the closest trout streams to New York City, its slow pools have decent hatches of **Pale Evening Dun** and **Blue-Winged Olive** mayflies, along with bigger **Isonychia** mayflies in the **riffles**.

The northwestern corner of New Jersey is a rockier area where most of the state's small wild trout streams are found. There are also some bigger trout streams like the Musconetcong and Pequest, which host most of the major fly hatches found in the northeast and have an interesting and diverse combination of big pools, riffles, and **pocket water**. Further north is the Big Flatbrook River, perhaps the best trout stream in New Jersey. With clear, clean, cold water, this river flows through 15 miles of heavily wooded country and has a great deal of public access. This river has especially good hatches of **Hendrickson**, Pale Evening Dun, **Light Cahill,** and **Trico** mayflies, with abundant caddis hatches as well.

New Jersey's saltwater fly fishing is excellent because of the state's location in the middle of the migration paths of striped bass, bluefish, false albacore, and bonito. Weakfish are also common in New Jersey's inshore waters, although these fish are more prone to boom and bust cycles and thus not always an easy target with a fly rod. One of the best aspects of saltwater fly fishing in New Jersey is its extensive series of jetties along the coast, which trap **baitfish** as well as giving the shorebound fly fisher an opportunity to get into deeper water without requiring a boat. The mouth of the Toms River in Barnegat Bay is an excellent place for wading the shallows, although at the right time of year, any beach in New Jersey will have some type of gamefish that will eagerly take a **Clouser Minnow** or **popper**. Other great places for fly rod fishing on New Jersey's coast include Sandy Hook, the Shark River Inlet, Manasquan Inlet, Island Beach State Park, and Barnegat Inlet.

Season

New Jersey has year-round trout fishing. During the winter months, the best fishing is restricted to the warmest days with small **nymphs** and **streamers**, but in early April mayfly hatches begin in earnest. The best **dry fly** fishing is in May and June. Some New Jersey rivers become too warm for decent trout fishing in July and August, but the colder streams in the northwest corner of the state fish well throughout the summer with **terrestrials** and when the tiny Trico mayflies hatch in late July and August. In saltwater, good numbers of striped bass show up in May, although smaller fish may arrive in April. Striped bass and bluefish are abundant throughout the summer, although in midsummer the fish will be found in deeper offshore

N

waters except at dawn and dusk. False albacore and bonito stalk baitfish off New Jersey's inlets from August through October, along with migrating striped bass and bluefish. Striped bass and bluefish can be caught on a fly until December in years with warm fall weather.

NEW MEXICO

OVERVIEW

When most people think of New Mexico they envision cactus, bleached cattle skulls, and Los Alamos—yet for knowledgeable fly fishers, northern and western New Mexico is a paradise, with uncrowded rivers (except for the famous San Juan), rich high altitude lakes, and wild **brown** and **rainbow trout**, as well as the rare Gila trout, an endangered relative of the **cutthroat trout** that survives in the Gila Wilderness area in the mountainous southwest corner of the state.

FISHERIES

New Mexico's most famous trout river is the San Juan, and for two dozen miles the river flows through high desert below Navajo Dam in the northwest corner of the state. Although solitude is hard to find on the San Juan, the river offers one of the best populations of wild trout in the southern Rockies. Even in the middle of winter, fly fishers from around the world flock to this river to catch its large rainbow and brown trout. Although there is estimated to be 15,000 trout per mile on the San Juan, its trout are not pushovers. Much of the time the fish feed on tiny **mayflies** and **midges**, and a size 22 or 24 **dry fly** or **nymph** is standard on the San Juan. However, close to the dam, and when high flows wash gobs of aquatic earthworms from vegetation along the banks, trout gorge on this bigger fare and are much easier to fool. In May and June, larger mayflies and **caddisflies hatch** as well.

In the rugged, high altitude north central part of the state some of its best small trout rivers are found. The famous Rio Grande in this part of the

Most of the rivers in the high mountain areas of New Mexico fish best midsummer, when the water is warmer and bigger terrestrials abound.

world is hardly the muddy trench it is along the southern U.S border. Here, wild rainbow, brown, and cutthroat trout abound in its cool, fast water. Although the river fishes well when conditions are right it can often be too high and muddy for easy fly fishing. In that case, the fly fisher is better off trying some of its smaller tributaries like the Red River, famous for its run of large spawning trout that run out of the Rio Grande in the fall, or little **tailwater** rivers like the Cimarron, Costilla, or the Culebra. Most of the mayfly hatches on these rivers are small **Blue-Winged Olives** and **Pale Morning Duns**, but even more important are terrestrial insects like **grasshoppers** and **beetles**. New Mexico rivers also seem to have an unusually high occurrence of moths that fly into the water, and a large, pale **Elk Hair Caddis dry fly** is a must on these mountain rivers.

Fly fishing in southwest New Mexico is not as strong, but it does offer a good variety, from the

N

rich meadow waters of the Rio Pensaco, one of the only true spring creeks in the southwest, to the tiny mountain rivers in the Gila Wilderness Area. Although it is illegal to fish for the endangered Gila trout, many of the high mountain creeks in the wilderness area have good populations of wild brown, rainbow, and cutthroat trout. Also worth exploring in this area are the Pinos Altos Range, Black Range, San Francisco River system, Mogollon Creek System, and the Blue River.

Not to be overlooked in New Mexico are its numerous lakes. The best trout lakes include Stone Lake, and McAllister Lake, as well as the Shuree Ponds in the northern part of the state, east of Costilla. Ramah Lake about 130 miles from Albuquerque offers both trout and **largemouth bass**, and Navajo Reservoir has great fly fishing for **smallmouth bass** along its shoreline.

SEASON

The San Juan River can be fished with a fly year-round, although most winter fishing is with tiny midge dries and nymphs. Hatches of bigger mayflies, caddisflies, and **stoneflies** on the San Juan are better in spring through fall. Most of the rivers in the high mountain areas of north central New Mexico and southwestern New Mexico fish best in midsummer, when the water is warmer and bigger terrestrial insects like hoppers and moths as well as aquatic caddisflies and mayflies abound. However, the Red River fishes best from fall through winter because it receives a large run of spawning brown, rainbow, and cutthroat from the Rio Grande.

NEW YORK

OVERVIEW

New York has some of the most diverse fly fishing opportunities in the world. From **striped bass** fishing in New York Harbor at the base of the Statue of Liberty to world-class **dry fly** fishing in the Catskills to **Pacific salmon** and **steelhead** fishing on Great Lakes tributaries to pond fishing for **brook**

trout on a remote Adirondack lake, an angler can spend a lifetime in New York State and not scratch the surface of its fly fishing. Unlike many regions, some of the good fishing is even close to major metropolitan and transportation centers, so the traveling fly fisher can easily reach some of its best fishing with only a short drive from an airport.

FISHERIES

The best trout fishing in New York State is in the Catskill Mountains, about two hours by car from New York City. This is the place where a great majority of the traditional eastern fly patterns and fishing techniques were developed; besides the great trout fishing, the area is a historical shrine to fly fishers interested in the history of the sport. The most famous stream is the Beaverkill, a large free-stone river with almost total public access in its lower reaches. Much of the Beaverkill is restricted by catch-and-release regulations, which protect its mixture of wild and hatchery fish. The Beaverkill runs through a valley between low mountains, and its **hatches** are legendary. The best fishing on the lower Beaverkill is from the town of Roscoe downstream to Cook's Falls, where warm summer temperatures restrict the abundance of trout. The Beaverkill's main tributaries, the Little Beaverkill and Willowemoc, also offer excellent fishing in smaller, less crowded pools, and although the upper

Landing a brown trout on the West Branch of the Delaware River.

Casting toward the shade on the Beaverkill.

reaches of both streams are mostly in private hands, both offer some public water, especially on the lower section of the Willowemoc upstream of the town of Roscoe.

The East and West Branches of the Delaware River, plus the main stem of the Delaware from the town of Hancock downstream to Callicoon offer some of the best fishing for wild **brown** and **rainbow trout** in the northeast. These big rivers are all **tailwaters** and thus stay cool throughout the summer, and despite issues with sufficient water releases from Pepacton Reservoir on the East Branch and Cannonsville Reservoir on the West Branch, most years the rivers run cold and clear throughout the summer. The main Delaware and the lower East Branch do suffer from warm **water temperatures** in midsummer in years when releases from the dams are not adequate, but the West Branch fishes well throughout the season. The West Branch also has more profuse and predictable fly hatches, but it does attract bigger crowds. These rivers are big enough for **drift boats** and excellent

guides are available, although perhaps the best fishing is stalking big rising trout while wading the still pools of these wide rivers.

On the eastern side of the Catskills, Esopus Creek is also famous for its abundant population of wild rainbow trout, but it also supports large brown trout in the bigger pools. Much of the river is fast pocket water, and hatches of **Isonychia** mayflies are especially common. Above the town of Phoenicia, a large pipe known as "The Portal" channels water underground from Schoharie Reservoir into the Esopus. Although The Portal helps keep the Esopus cold during the summer, it often dumps extensive silt into the river, making fly fishing difficult. The Neversink River is another river important to the Catskill trout fishing legacy because it was the home river of **Theodore Gordon** and **George LaBranche**. However, the water fished by Gordon and LaBranche was inundated when Neversink Reservoir was completed in 1955. Most of the Neversink above the reservoir is on private, posted land, but the water below Neversink Dam stays cold and

N

stable because of the dam releases. Although the fishing is not as good as in the Beaverkill and Delaware, the water is scenic, especially where it flows through Neversink Gorge. Schoharie Creek in the northern Catskills is a marginal trout stream, with nice pools and stocked trout, although warm water temperatures make fishing for trout after June 15 difficult. However, the Schoharie is an excellent **smallmouth bass** and **walleye** fishery, and both of these species take a fly readily in its lower reaches.

A misty morning on the AuSable River.

Although the Adirondack Mountains of New York are wild and rugged, trout fishing is not as widespread as one might imagine. Their granite bedrock makes the lakes and rivers especially sensitive to acid rain, although reductions in acidic precipitation in the twenty-first century and an extensive liming program by the state have improved the fishing. The best trout river in the Adirondacks is the West Branch of the **AuSable River** near Lake Placid. Beautiful **pocket water** alternating with flat pools, abundant and diverse insect hatches, and spectacular scenery make this river the best destination for fly fishers in the Adirondacks. Although not as productive as the West Branch of the Ausable, other good trout streams in the Adirondacks include the Saranac River, upper Hudson River, Bouquet River, West Canada Creek, and Fish Creek. The lower Bouquet, AuSable, and Saranac

Rivers also have fall runs of landlocked salmon from Lake Champlain, although these runs can be spotty. Lake George, Schroon Lake, and Eighth Lake also have landlocked salmon. Despite the acid rain problem, the Adirondacks still offer good wilderness brook trout fishing in places that look much like they did when Winslow Homer painted them. The best places to find these ponds are the St. Regis **Canoe Area**, Pharaoh Lake Wilderness Area, and West **Canada** Lake Wilderness.

Fall, winter, and early spring fly fishing for migratory salmonids is excellent in New York State. The biggest fish come from Lake Ontario tributaries like Oak Orchard Creek, Oswego River, and the Salmon River. These rivers host runs of Pacific salmon, brown trout, steelhead, and even limited runs of landlocked **Atlantic salmon** in the Salmon River. Although fly fishing can be accomplished in the Niagara and Genesee rivers, both of these can be treacherous wading. However, there are few tributaries of Lake Ontario that don't have runs of fish in the fall, and there are scores of smaller streams worth exploring. The tributaries of Lake Erie are smaller and easier to wade. Although the average size of the steelhead are smaller than those from Lake Ontario, fish are more plentiful and over a dozen steelhead can be hooked in a day of fishing when conditions are right. The best Lake Erie steelhead rivers are Cattaraugus Creek and Chautauqua Creek, but there are over 40 rivers and creeks that drain into Lake Erie from New York State, and all have runs of steelhead to some degree. New York's Finger Lakes, in the center of the state, also have steelhead runs. Naples Creek at the south end of Canandaigua Lake, Cayuga Inlet, and Catherine Creek, which runs into Seneca Lake, are the most productive.

There are a number of high-quality trout streams even closer to New York City than the Catskills. North of the city, the East Branch of the Croton River between Diverting and East Branch Reservoirs has excellent fishing for stocked and holdover brown and rainbow trout.

N

It has an especially good **Pale Evening Dun** hatch in late May and June, but this river is a tailwater fishery and thus has good insect hatches throughout the summer. East of the city, there are several fine trout streams on Long Island. The Connetquot is a true spring creek with a special section within the state park of the same name. It is stocked with large brook, brown, and rainbow trout and can be fished year-round. Other spring-fed trout streams on Long Island include Carmans River in Southaven County Park, and the Nissequogue River in Caleb Smith State Park.

New York has plentiful opportunities for **largemouth** and smallmouth **bass** on a **fly rod**. Best places to catch them on shallow water on a fly rod include the shorelines of Lake Erie and Lake Ontario, the Niagara River, Oneida Lake, Lake Champlain, Lake George, Hudson River, and the Thousand Islands region of the St. Lawrence River.

New York has extremely productive saltwater fly fishing. The Hudson River is one of the most productive spawning grounds for striped bass on the East Coast. Stripers can be caught on a fly rod from Albany south to New York Harbor, although much of this fishing is deep-water fishing with sinking lines and is best done from a boat. The north shore of Long Island offers many extensive bays and shallows where stripers can be caught by wading, especially in the extreme western end of the sound and also in Great Peconic Bay. There are more fly fishing opportunities on the south shore of Long Island, with more variety and better access, although heavy surf can make fly fishing difficult. Montauk Point is a natural migration point for striped bass, **bluefish**, **false albacore**, and **bonito**, but it gets too crowded at peak times for easy fly fishing. Best fishing there is from a boat. However, spots like Shinnecock Inlet, Moriches Inlet, Fire Island Inlet, Jones Inlet, and Breezy Point often have enough room for the fly fisher, as well as the many **jetties** along the shoreline.

SEASON

Catskill trout rivers begin to see insect activity and good fly fishing in April, but the best fishing is in May and early June, and then again in September. Midsummer trout fishing is excellent on the East and West Branches of the Delaware; in cold, wet summers it can also be good on other Catskill rivers. Adirondack rivers follow two to three weeks behind Catskill rivers, and often get warm quickly in June because of exposed streambeds. When waters cool off in the fall they fish well again. Pacific salmon and brown trout begin to ascend Great Lakes tributaries in late August but the salmon die after spawning in October and brown trout drop back into the lakes in November. Steelhead enter most Great Lakes tributaries in October and November and most spend the winter in rivers, so fishing can be good all winter long if the frigid temperatures can be tolerated by the angler, as ice in the guides and slush in the river can make fly fishing miserable. Steelhead fishing picks up again in March when the fish begin spawning, and can remain excellent until late April, when the fish

N

drop back into the lakes. Bass fishing with a fly rod is best in late May and early June, when the fish are in shallow water spawning, but in rivers small-mouth bass fishing can be excellent all summer long, especially at dawn and dusk.

The Hudson River hosts striped bass year-round, and stripers can be caught in New York Harbor all year. However, the best fishing is in May and June and then again in November and December. Stripers from the Hudson begin showing up in Long Island Sound in April, and in May and June striped bass can be caught from nearly every beach on Long Island Sound. In May, striped bass and bluefish from the Chesapeake begin showing up on the south shore of Long Island and although some remain through the summer, the fishing here really peaks in October and November, when fish feed on the shoreline's abundant **baitfish** populations on their fall migration.

NEW ZEALAND

OVERVIEW

New Zealand is a rugged, mountainous country with abundant rainfall. Thus every type of trout stream, from brawling mountain rivers to **spring creeks** are available. The country is composed of the North and South Islands. Because 65 percent of the country's population lives on the North Island, many anglers prefer the South Island for its less developed and more pristine landscape. But the North Island also has many fine fisheries.

The trout fishing in New Zealand is unlike fishing anywhere else in the world. **Brown trout** from Scotland and **rainbow trout** from California were introduced there in the late nineteenth century, and since then have thrived in mountain rivers without much additional stocking. The average size of the brown and rainbow trout is large, around four pounds, but fish upward of ten pounds are taken on **dry flies** every year. However, the fishing is not easy. Although New Zealand trout are not terribly selective and readily take dry flies and **nymphs**, they are extremely wary, and the number of trout per

mile on most New Zealand rivers is quite low. Most fishing is done by stalking the banks, looking for fish feeding on nymphs or surface insects, followed by a careful stalk and delicate presentation with a minimum of **false casts**. Guides in New Zealand often spot fish for the angler from a carefully concealed position on a high bank, so the relationship between guide and angler is paramount. Because a lot of country must be traveled between fish, a guide is almost essential and a means of getting around to remote rivers is necessary. Thus New Zealand fishing requires a lot of hiking and travel in four-wheel-drive vehicles or helicopters. To enjoy this world-class fishing for large trout an angler should be in reasonably good physical condition.

New Zealand trout streams and lakes contain **mayflies**, **caddisflies**, **stoneflies**, and **midges** in similar colors and sizes to those in other parts of the world. Thus standard dry fly, nymph, and **streamer** patterns used in Argentina or the Rocky Mountains will work fine. However, New Zealand typically has large **hatches** of **cicadas**, so a complete **fly box** for New Zealand should include some large foam dry flies like the Chernobyl Ant in sizes 6 and 8.

An important aspect of New Zealand fly fishing is that as an isolated island country its waters are susceptible to introduced pests, especially microorganisms that can enter the country as spores on the **wading boots** of traveling anglers. Visitors to New Zealand should either purchase new **waders** or wading boots prior to a trip or have their existing waders disinfected by a certified veterinarian before leaving for New Zealand. However, the major ports of entry also have disinfecting stations that are typically quick and efficient.

FISHERIES

Fishing on the North Island is centered on two regions in the center of the island: Lake Taupo and the Rotorua region. The Tongariro River, which runs into giant Lake Taupo, is one of the most famous trout rivers in the world. The river has a

N

Brown trout from Scotland and rainbow trout from California were introduced to New Zealand in the late nineteenth century, and have thrived in mountain rivers without much additional stocking.

large population of resident rainbow and brown trout, plus one of the largest runs of lake-run rainbows in the world. The rainbows run out of Lake Taupo from June through November (New Zealand's winter) but trout fishing in this river remains excellent all summer long. The Tauranga-Taupo is another tributary to Lake Taupo famous for its rainbow trout. Northwest of Rotorua is a concentration of smaller rivers and spring creeks know for their large but difficult brown trout, and top rivers here include the Waihou and Waimakariri Rivers. North of this area near Thames is a concentration of smaller, very scenic mountain streams such as the Waitawheta and Ohinemuri rivers. These rivers fish particularly well with dry flies and nymphs during New Zealand's summer.

The South Island is more noted for its large brown trout than rainbows, and great trout rivers are found throughout the island. At the extreme north is the Nelson and Marlborough area, with a combination of very remote rivers plus some that are more easily accessible. The Motueka River is one of the best rivers on the South Island. Because it is easily accessible in its lower reaches the trout are not easy. Nelson Lakes National Park also offers great rivers including the Travers, D'Urville, and Sabine Rivers. The Buller is an expansive river with braided channels that provide many fishing opportunities, and its many tributaries like the Owen, Mangles, and Mauria are excellent in their own right.

The West Coast is a frontier land with the heavy rainfall typical of coastal mountain ranges. For this reason, rivers can be high and discolored at times, but generally the smaller rivers and spring creeks clear quickly and are fishable most of the season. The Karamea River and its tributaries are within Kahurangi National Park, and although it is a wilderness river system accessible by long hikes or

N

helicopter, it is one of the top brown trout streams on the South Island. The Lake Brunner area is full of smaller streams and spring creeks. Other notable rivers include the Mokihinui, Grey, Arnold, and the LaFontaine Stream, an excellent spring creek.

The Canterbury area is a much drier region and can suffer from extreme winds during the summer. There are some sheltered rivers in the Christchurch area like the Waimakariri and Selwyn, and their upper reaches produce some especially large trout. The Hanmer Springs area is also a popular fishing destination with the Waiau and its tributaries the best bet in this area.

The Central South Island is a huge area with a number of large hydroelectric projects, so much of the fishing is in **tailwater** rivers, with resulting fast growth rates and large brown and rainbow trout. The best river in this area is the Ahuriri, and the shallows where this river flows into Lake Benmore are noted for large cruising brown trout. Other notable rivers in this area are the lower Waitaki, Ashburton, and Rangitata river systems.

The Otago Region is a popular tourist destination with magnificent mountains and streams known for their clarity. The best fishing in this area is in the western mountains, where rainfall is higher and the weather is cooler. The giant Clutha River is known for its large and dense trout population. The Matukituki often flows colored with glacial silt, but the fish here respond well to big dry flies. The Routeburn is known for its large trout and was designated as a catch-and-release river to protect them.

The Southland Region is known as the brown trout capital of New Zealand for good reason. The Mataura River is known throughout the world, with expanses of pocket water punctuated by channels and large backwaters. Brown and rainbow trout over six pounds are common, and this river is known for its profuse hatches. The Oreti River is an accessible river with the best fishing in its middle reaches, where the channels braid and multiply the available trout habitat. The Fiordland region in the West has hundreds of wonderful trout rivers and lakes, and some of the rivers in the massive Fiordland National Park are trophy rivers that are so inaccessible they have never been fished, especially those on the western slopes.

SEASON

The spring season in New Zealand is October, and although the weather may be cool and rivers high, fish have not been disturbed for months and are the easiest to catch. Early summer, November and December, sees long days, better hatches, and is the best time to fish the high mountain streams. Midsummer in January and February is the time most visiting anglers travel to New Zealand, but the fish can be tougher and effective flies tend to be smaller. Careful stalking or a visit to inaccessible mountain streams is the best tactic. Late summer in March and April brings low water but cool evenings although days are warm. Great dry fly fishing, and the chance for a trophy brown trout on the surface, are the hallmark of late summer. May brings the onset of colder weather and perhaps the best fishing at this time of year is on the North Island for the run of spawning rainbows out of Lake Taupo.

NIGHT FISHING

Although the thought of casting a fly into the dark is not appealing to many fly fishers, it's a way to catch some fish that are difficult to take on a fly in bright light. Large **brown trout**, **striped bass**, **snook**, **tarpon**, and **largemouth bass** are often nocturnal feeders, especially during the heat of summer. And the famous *Hexagenia* (**Hex**) mayfly never **hatches** until dark, forcing dedicated trout anglers to stay on the river well after dark.

Fishing at night requires using your senses of hearing and touch much more than your eyes. It's actually a good way to improve your fly casting, because it's necessary to feel the line bending the rod during casting when there are no visual cues, and the improved timing on your cast can actually benefit daytime fishing. Unless there is a bright

N

moon (and night fishing is typically better during a new moon or on cloudy nights, although no one knows why) or a lighted dock or bridge nearby, fish are located by sound. Large brown trout make quite a slurping sound when feeding on the surface at night, and striped bass and snook make a sharp popping noise. Cast your fly right to the sound as best you can and either let the fly drift in the current or **retrieve** it slowly. There is a temptation to retrieve too quickly at night but it's always best to barely keep a tight line to the fly. Most **strikes** at night are subtle; if any resistance is felt a firm strip-strike is the best option, so that if the fish has missed the fly it does not get frightened by the fly suddenly becoming airborne.

Needless to say, before attempting any night fishing, the area should be scouted in full daylight. Look for holes, drop-offs, and snags that might trip you up, and bear in mind the tides may be different at night if you are fishing in the ocean. Casts should be kept short to keep the line under control, and a very heavy leader, over 10 pounds in strength, should be used, even when trout fishing. Fish don't see the leader as well at night and the fish must be played as quickly as possible to keep it out of hidden obstructions.

NORTH CAROLINA

OVERVIEW

North Carolina fly fishing opportunities are mostly in the far western points of the state in terrain above 1,800 feet, an area that contains more trout streams than in any other part of the southern Appalachians, and in the coastal areas where fly fishing has become popular for saltwater species. In between the two extremes, there are plenty of opportunities for fly fishing for **smallmouth bass** in rivers and **largemouth bass** and **panfish** in lakes. But for fly fishers, typically the smaller the bass lake the better, so these waters remain unheralded, known and appreciated only by local anglers.

Western North Carolina's trout waters are cov-

ered by a dizzying confusion of regulations. There are wild trout waters that are not stocked, some of which can be fished with bait as well, some of which are catch-and-release only, and others where one or two trout can be kept. There are hatchery waters with more liberal regulations, some of which are designated "delayed harvest," where fish can be kept in spring and summer but not fall and winter. Most public streams are posted with symbols that indicate the type of regulation that applies—but if you fish with flies and don't keep any fish, then just beware of straying on private lands. This is not a minor concern, as many of North Carolina's small trout streams are privately owned and jealously guarded. But the state contains vast areas of public water in the Smoky Mountains National Park, along the Blue Ridge Parkway, in state game lands, and on the Cherokee Indian Reservation (where a special tribal permit must be purchased).

FISHERIES

One of America's top trout streams, the Nantahala River in extreme western North Carolina hosts a dense population of large **brown** and **rainbow trout**. However, this popular **tailwater** river is also very popular with **kayakers** and inner tubers, and because access from the road is easy, parts of the river are often crowded. The main river is best fished in the fall after the crowds leave, or it might pay to explore small streams like Forney, Deep, and Hazel Creeks. Another option is to fish the smaller

N

headwaters of the Nantahala above the lake of the same name, where the trout are much smaller but are all wild fish. North of the Nantahala is Slick-rock Creek. Known for its brightly colored wild brown trout, this river is the place for solitude because it has no road acess. Located within the Joyce Kilmer-Slickrock Wilderness Area, this river is also lightly fished because few are willing to take the hike in. Big Snowbird Creek is another remote river in this area. Although the lower part of the river, where it flows into Santeelab Lake, is easy to drive to and has a good population of stocked trout, the upper reaches of this river, after a six-mile hike, offer some of the best wild **brook trout** fishing in southern Appalachia.

South of Asheville are a number of prime trout rivers. The South Mills River is a wild trout river that holds big browns and rainbows and produces heavy **caddisfly hatches** during the summer. The Tuckasegee River is a big river for this part of the world, and is known for its very large brown trout. Many of its tributaries support trout as well, especially Deep Creek, which is a fine brown trout stream in its own right. The Davidson River is another excellent wild trout stream in this area, and is famous for its hatch of large **Green Drake mayflies** in May, which bring the Davidson's large brown trout to the surface. A major tributary, Looking Glass Creek, is full of wild rainbows; its trout are easier to fool than the wise old fish in the Davidson. Further south, the Green River and its tributaries offer some wild trout fishing in their headwaters and stocked fish further downstream.

Northeast of Ashville are a number of fine trout streams. Wilson Creek has deep pools and large brown trout in its lower reaches. As you move upstream the river harbors more wild trout. The upper river is reached only by hiking, but has a good population of wild browns and rainbows and is lightly fished. Lost Cove Creek and North Harper Creek are two tributaries of Wilson Creek that also require a hike in, but both are famous for their large brown trout. The Linville River has a gentle flow in its upper reaches and is considered one of the richest streams in North Carolina. It has a very dense population of both wild and stocked trout. Further downstream, the river changes character and plunges through Linville Gorge Wilderness Area, with huge pools, raging currents—and some of the largest brown trout in North Carolina. Although the water in the gorge has plenty of room for fly casting, it's a long walk in and the terrain is rugged.

Fly fishing for popular saltwater species extends quite far inland when you consider the Roanoke River striper fishery. Each spring, vast pods of big **striped bass** travel over 100 miles from Currituck Sound to spawn and chase spawning herring and **shad** in the rapids below Weldon Dam. The fish can be caught on **streamer** flies and **poppers**, but this is a vast river and must be fished from a boat. On the coast itself, opportunities for fly fishing are not as abundant, except under certain conditions. Although the waters off the Outer Banks teem with striped bass, **bluefish**, **redfish**, Spanish **mackerel**, and **weakfish**, beaches here are long and sloping, so the shorebound fly caster is usually out of range of feeding fish. Fly fishers are much better off fishing the inside waters of Pamlico Sound, where by wading or with a small boat the fly fisher can reach these species without braving the heavy surf. Because the Outer Banks are so close to the Gulf Stream, a boat that can go 15 miles offshore safely can get the fly fisher into such exotic species as **barracuda**, amberjack, **sailfish**, bluefish, and even bluefin **tuna**. One fishery that has become very popular with fly fishers is the **false albacore** fishery at Cape Lookout in the fall months. Centered around Harker's Island, fly fishers from around the world gather to chase huge concentrations of these small tunas that take a streamer fly or popper and take a line well into the **backing**.

SEASON

North Carolina's spring starts earlier than trout streams further north, and by March and April spring fly hatches are in full swing. Small **Blue**

Wing Olive mayflies and **midges** begin first, with caddisflies and Green Drake mayflies following in May—although not all North Carolina rivers support these big flies. Summer trout fishing in North Carolina can get difficult in the lower reaches of bigger rivers because of water temperatures that approach the lethal range for trout, but tailwater rivers and creeks high in the mountains stay cool enough for good trout fishing. Fall brings a return to cooler waters, fewer anglers, and fish feeding heavily on **terrestrial** insects. Fishing in the dead of winter can be decent on North Carolina rivers, especially in tailwater rivers below dams.

Saltwater fishing in North Carolina begins with the April run of striped bass in the Roanoke River, which peaks in May and usually ends in June when the fish return to salt water. Large redfish (or *red drum* as they are called in North Carolina) move into Pamlico Sound in May, followed by bluefish, cobia, and Spanish mackerel. Weakfish and **sea trout** move into holes and flats in the Sound from September through November. And the great run of false albacore at Cape Lookout is from mid-September to late November, but the peak time is mid-October to mid-November.

NORWAY

OVERVIEW

Norway is best known for its expensive but high quality **Atlantic salmon** fishing. Its salmon are some of the largest in the world, as over thousands of years these fish have evolved to handle the heavy current and raging waterfalls typical of Norwegian rivers. Salmon of average size could not negotiate these raging torrents, and the larger body mass and muscles of Norwegian salmon have evolved to handle these far northern rivers. Most fishing in Norway is on private land, and while access to the best salmon rivers can cost up to $15,000 per week, less famous salmon rivers and trout streams can be accessed for a modest fee. Most of the rivers are regulated by local forestry associations, and a

Norway's salmon rivers, their tributaries, and nearby lakes hold good populations of resident brown trout.

license to fish salmon rivers and trout streams can usually be obtained from them inexpensively.

FISHERIES

The best fishing for the famous giant salmon in Norway is found from the extreme north down to the Trondheim area. The Alta, north of the Arctic Circle, has been fished by European royalty for well over 100 years and its salmon of up to 60 pounds are well out of the reach of most travelers. The Lakselv, also north of the Arctic Circle, is a much less pricey river and is famous for its late-season (August) fishing, when both large salmon and sea-run **brown trout** are in the river. The Beiar River, also in the arctic region, is known as one of the most beautiful rivers in Norway and its deep green currents flow cold all summer long. Just south of the Arctic Circle, the Abjora River flows through a very remote area and is famous for its long pools and canyon water. The mighty Namsen River, north of Trondheim, has been world-famous for its very large salmon since British noblemen discovered it in 1830, but also gives up a vast number of smaller salmon each year. Because it flows through lower agricultural land, this river is best fished in June and July as the water often gets too low in August.

The huge Trondheim Basin host three major salmon rivers: the Gaula, Verdal, and Stjørdal. The Gaula and Stjørdal are known as two of the finest salmon rivers in Europe, and although the Verdal does not get as much attention the local anglers feel it is just as productive. The rivers are all known for

N

their large salmon, and with their more gentle flows and wide pools and easier access they are also some of the most popular. Not as famous are Norway's southern rivers, including the Otra and Mandal. But since this tiny country has more than 450 salmon rivers it's hard to go very far without seeing one.

All salmon rivers, their tributaries, and nearby lakes hold good populations of resident brown trout. In addition, salmon rivers host runs of sea-run brown trout. **Arctic char** are very common, especially in the northern rivers, and great sport can be had when a shoal of them is found moving upstream from the sea. In addition, many Norwegian lakes have large northern **pike**, which at these latitudes tend to stay in shallow water and thus take a fly very well.

A single-handed **fly rod** with a length of nine feet that takes a 6- or 7-weight **fly line** is fine for most trout and **char** fishing and is sufficient for smaller salmon rivers with smaller fish. However, the standard rod on these giant rivers is a two-handed rod from 12 to 14 feet long, calling for a 10-, 11-, or even 12-weight line. Not only is a rod this big necessary for taming the large salmon, it's mandatory for the very long casts needed to reach salmon lies in these monstrous rivers.

SEASON

Salmon season in Norway runs from May 15 until September 30, although the best fishing is in mid-summer. The big salmon tend to arrive first, in June, followed by strong runs of grilse (smaller salmon) in July. August sees another run of big salmon, especially in the far northern rivers. **Sea trout** and arctic char begin ascending rivers from estuaries in late July and early August, and fishing for them can be excellent until the end of September. Fishing for resident brown trout is excellent from May through October.

NYLON

See Leader, Tippet.

NYMPH

Although the term nymph can mean the **larva** of a **mayfly**, **caddisfly**, **stonefly**, or **midge**, it is also used to describe the class of flies that imitates these larvae. A nymph artificial can also refer to a fly that imitates crustaceans such as **scuds**, **sow bugs**, or **crayfish**. In general, any sinking fly designed to imitate an invertebrate, whether a specific imitation or a more general imitation that looks like a number of different creatures, is called a nymph. Nymphs and **wet flies** are often used interchangeably, and the only real difference between the two is that a wet fly is an older style of **sinking fly** that usually has a wing or full **hackle**. Wet flies are usually fished by swinging them in the current; while nymphs are sometimes fished swung on a tight line they are usually fished **dead drift**, with no added motion added by the angler or the **fly line** bellying in the current.

TYPES OF NYMPHS

Many of the most popular nymphs do not imitate a specific insect, but suggest some type of insect larva or crustacean. Sometimes called prospecting nymphs, these flies rely upon materials that move with every nuance of current and look alive to the fish. For instance, the **Hare's Ear Nymph** is made from spiky fur from a European hare, ribbed with a piece of gold tinsel. The tiny fibers might suggest the legs of an insect larva or crustacean, the gills of a mayfly nymph, the flat shape of a large mayfly or stonefly larva, or the halo of gas bubbles surrounding an emerging caddis **pupa**. The gold tinsel suggests the segmentation common to the abdomen of most invertebrates. The Pheasant Tail Nymph is a slimmer artificial that better suggests the slim profile of a small swimming mayfly, a tiny brown stonefly larva, or a midge larva. Examples of other popular and effective prospecting nymphs include the Prince, Copper John, and Zug Bug.

Many nymphs mimic more specific insects. Joe Humphreys' Sulfur Nymph imitates the larva of the **Pale Evening Dun** mayfly. Greg Senyo's

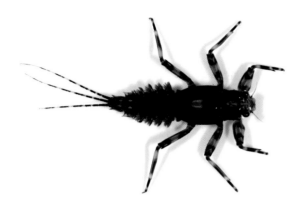

Wiggle Iso squirms like the swimming *Isonychia* mayfly nymph. Gary LaFontaine's Deep Pupa is a specific imitation of a drifting caddis pupa. The Flashback Scud looks like a swimming scud. Most of these kinds of nymphs don't work quite as well as the more general prospecting nymphs when fish are feeding on a host of different insects, but when trout are feeding selectively on a certain kind of insect or crustacean they can be far more effective.

Stonefly nymphs are typically large and robust and imitate the flat shape and robust legs, wing cases, and tails of these larvae. They are most popular in the western United States and on South American rivers, where stoneflies are the bread and butter of trout diets for most of the year. Unlike flies tied to imitate mayflies and caddisflies, where the most common sizes are size 10 to 18, stonefly nymphs are usually tied on bigger hooks, from size 4 through size 10. At the other end of the scale, midge nymphs are tiny and are made on hooks size 16 through 26. Midge nymphs imitate either the larva or the pupa of midges, and are slim and simple to simulate the skinny, legless larvae of these diminutive but important insects.

Nymphs can be made weighted or unweighted. The unweighted types can be fished deeper by adding split shot or other weight to the **tippet**, but they are mostly used when trout are feeding on **emerging** larvae close to the surface and are visibly boiling just under the surface. But the most popular nymphs are the weighted variety. Nymphs used to be weighted by winding lead **wire** on the shank of the **hook** before tying the fly, but with the advent of both voluntary and mandatory bans on the use of lead weights in fishing, lead has been replaced by brass or tungsten beads. These beads are slipped onto the hook before tying the fly, and the beads can be silver, copper, brass, or black. The shinier colors are best in faster water because their sparkle can catch the eye of a trout. Black beads are more subtle and are best in slower currents, where trout get a closer look at the fly, and the duller beads can also be more effective where trout have been caught and released frequently on flies with brighter beads. For moderate current and shallow water brass beads are best, but in deep, fast current the heavier tungsten beads work better. Flies tied with beads are called **bead head** flies.

HOW TO PICK THE RIGHT NYMPH

If trout have been observed feeding on scuds in a weed-filled stream or the air is filled with a particular size and color of caddisfly, nymph selection can be easy. However, in most cases nymphs are fished when trout are not visibly feeding. The best bet is to fish a nymph that has been suggested by a guide or local angler, but on an unfamiliar river, that's not always possible. Turning over rocks or rooting through submerged vegetation is one way to discover what sizes and shapes of nymphs are common; trout typically feed on objects that look like their regular diet and seldom prey upon items that look foreign.

Just looking at the water can often clue the angler in to a reasonable nymph selection. Streams with big flat rocks and fast water will be filled with large, flat stonefly and mayfly nymphs because these bigger, flatter larvae survive better on the underside of flat rocks than the slimmer mayfly nymphs and midge larvae. Thus a big Copper John or Hare's Ear nymph may be a good choice. Streams with lots of submerged vegetation and a silty bottom will have few big, flat nymphs but will be loaded with tiny swimming mayfly nymphs, midge larvae, and scuds. In

N

this case, a Pheasant Tail Nymph, a Flashback Scud, or a Zebra Midge Nymph will be more effective. **Tailwater** rivers invariably have more caddisfly and midge larvae than stonefly or mayfly larvae, because both caddis and midges are filter feeders and thrive in the nutrient-rich waters below dams.

NYMPH-FISHING TECHNIQUES

The easiest way to fish a nymph is to cast it across the current and let the fly line swing the fly across the current, either on a floating or sinking tip fly line, depending on water depth. The line should be **mended** once when the fly lands and perhaps several times as the fly swings to slow down its swing and to get the fly deeper. However, this technique works only on unsophisticated fish in mountain rivers and in other waters when insects are hatching and fish are seen feeding close to the surface. In most cases, fish will turn away from a fly swinging in the current and will only eat a fly on a dead drift.

The easiest way to fish a nymph with a dead drift is to place a **strike indicator** on the **leader**, with the distance between the fly and the indicator equal to twice the depth of the water. Weight can be added to the leader about a foot above the fly in very fast or deep water. The easiest way to get a dead drift is to cast directly upstream. Little

mending is needed and all that is required is to retrieve line as the indicator floats down to the angler's position. However, this method is extremely tiring: Line must be gathered constantly, and it's often impossible to wade directly below the suspected location of the fish. Thus, the nymph and indicator are often cast quartering **upstream**, and a dead drift is assured by any number of techniques. One is to make a **reach cast**, which puts an upstream arc into the line. Another is to mend the line upstream as the fly drifts. Yet a third, called "high-sticking," is to raise the tip of the rod high to keep most of the fly line off the water, thus keeping a direct connection between the fly rod and the indicator and eliminating the drag of the fly line on the cast. Sometimes all three of these techniques are used on the same drift, with a reach cast beginning the presentation, a mend after a short drift, and then high-sticking as the fly gets closer to the angler.

Indicators and weight on the leader make casting difficult. Some anglers prefer to fish without indicators and instead watch the tip of a floating line of the butt section of the leader while the fly drifts, looking for the slightest hesitation and striking when a hit is suspected. This can be done by fishing straight upstream or **across-stream**, and when fishing across it's best to use the high-sticking method. A variation on this is the "Polish" or "Czech nymphing" technique, where very heavily weighted flies are used and the tip of the rod is in constant contact with the fly.

Two flies are often used at once in nymph fishing. The upper fly is typically larger and more heavily weighted than the lower fly. The easiest way to fish tandem flies is to tie a 6-inch piece of tippet to the bend of the upper hook and attach the lower fly to the extra piece. This gives the angler a great way to determine which fly the fish prefer.

Orange Glow Wiggler

OGLESBY, ARTHUR (1923–2001)

Arthur Oglesby was a BBC broadcaster and one of the most influential **Atlantic salmon** anglers of the twentieth century. He wrote or co-authored nine fly fishing books, the most notable being *Fly Fishing for Salmon and Sea-Trout*. He was instrumental in forming the Association of Professional Game Angling Instructors, and was a widely respected teacher of **Spey casting** and Atlantic salmon angling. He was especially famous for catching two salmon over 40 pounds on **Norway**'s Vosso River.

OHIO

OVERVIEW

Although Ohio once hosted abundant populations of native **brook trout**, land-use practices over the centuries have eliminated them. The native trout of Ohio now occurs as reproducing populations only in a few experimental streams, although brook trout are stocked in some put-and-take streams. Introduced **rainbow** and **brown trout** are more

likely to be found in Ohio's inland rivers, but the most exciting fly fishing in Ohio is found in tributaries to Lake Erie, where **steelhead**, lake-run brown trout, and **Pacific salmon** (mainly king salmon) have been introduced. These large fish spend the summer in the central depths of Lake Erie (once known as "The Dead Sea," but pollution controls instituted through the Clean Water Act have brought it back to a healthy state). Because Erie has more productive shallow water than the other Great Lakes, it is more productive and fish grow quickly on its abundant **baitfish**, insects, and crustaceans.

One fish native to Ohio, the **smallmouth bass**, still thrives. It is perhaps the second most popular (after the various trout species) **fly rod** fish. Smallmouth bass are found in nearly every river in Ohio and lakes with clear water and rocky shorelines. **Largemouth bass** and **pike** are common in slower, warmer waters, and the introduced **carp**, once considered a trash fish, has become a favorite target with the fly rod in Ohio.

Fall steelhead fishing on a tributary of Lake Erie.

FISHERIES

With its mainly flat land and intensive farming, Ohio is a not a premier trout-fishing state. Although trout are stocked in many lakes and rivers, they don't live long and those that aren't removed quickly by anglers die from warm **water temperatures** during the summer. However, Ohio does have two decent trout streams: The Mad River near Bellafontaine in eastern Ohio is kept cold because of abundant springs in its watershed, and the Clear Fork south of Mansfield is a **tailwater** that stays cold from the bottom releases from the depths of Clear Fork Reservoir and Pleasant Hill Lake. Both streams are small but very productive, because fertilizer from surrounding farm runoff encourages algae growth, which in turn supports dense insect populations. Both rivers are brown trout fisheries, and the Mad River in particular gives up some very large brown trout each year to **streamer** flies fished at night.

Although steelhead, brown trout, and king salmon can be caught in almost any tributary to Lake Erie under the right circumstances, the state limits its stocking program of 400,000 steelhead fry per year to four rivers: Rocky River, Chagrin River, Grand River, and Conneaut Creek. However, other rivers have runs of stray fish and can be quite productive, including the Vermilion, Ashtabula, Arcola and Cuyahoga rivers. Steelhead are the main attraction for fly fishers because brown trout and king salmon runs last only about a month, where the more aggressive steelhead are found in Lake Erie tributaries from September until May. And because of the relatively shallow nature of most of Ohio's steelhead rivers and the high concentration of fish, these rivers are some of the most productive (in terms of number of fish hooked per hour) of any steelhead rivers in the United States.

The shore of Lake Erie is one of the most productive smallmouth fisheries in the country, and fish will be found from May through October in 5 to 20 feet of water. The best places are where rivers enter the lake, like Sandusky Bay and the mouth of the Grand and Chagrin Rivers. However, fly fishing for smallmouths in a big lake is often productive only at dawn and dusk. A better suggestion for the fly fisher, especially for midday fishing, is to float or wade one of Ohio's interior smallmouth rivers like Big Darby Creek, Kokosing River, Stillwater River, Ohio Brush Creek, Grand River, Little Beaver Creek, Hocking River, Licking River, or Sandusky River.

Carp can be caught with a fly in almost any river or lake in Ohio. The biggest ones are found in shallow bays along the Lake Erie shoreline, particularly Sandusky Bay. The clear water along the shoreline lets the fly fisher sight-fish with **nymphs** and streamers. Another very popular carp-fishing location, where they seem especially susceptible to flies, is Alum Creek Reservoir near Columbus.

The Ohio River on the southern boundary of the state is a very productive fishery, with smallmouth bass and **striped bass/white bass** hybrids ("whipers") the top species for fly fishing, although catfish, saugers, and even skipjack **shad** can be caught on streamer flies. Best places to fly fish in the Ohio are the mouths of tributary streams and around shallow gravel bars.

Season

Ohio's inland trout streams fish best in spring and fall. In April and May, **mayfly** and **caddisfly hatches** bring trout to the surface, and although trout can be caught all summer long on **terrestrials** and hatches of small mayflies like the **Trico**, inner tubes and swimmers make the prospect of daytime trout fishing unappealing during the summer. A better plan is to float a smallmouth bass river in a **canoe** or **kayak**. Best fishing for smallmouths is late May through early July, and these willing gamefish can be caught all day long in rivers. Carp fishing is most productive in June and July, when carp are prowling the shallows for insects and crustaceans and will respond to a fly.

Migratory salmonids enter Lake Erie tributary streams as early as September, with brown trout and king salmon arriving first. Steelhead may enter rivers with browns and salmon, but strong runs of steelhead begin in November and will continue through March. Any time a rain or snow melt raises the water level in these tributary streams during the winter, a fresh run of fish will arrive from the lake. Steelhead may stay in rivers until May before dropping back to the lake, especially if water levels in the rivers stay at April levels.

OREGON

Overview

Oregon is most noted for its **steelhead** fishing, although the state has many thousands of miles of resident, nonmigratory trout streams and lakes. Most rivers from central and northern Oregon flow north into the mighty Columbia River system, while the steelhead rivers of the southwestern corner of the state like the Umpqua and Rogue flow directly into the Pacific. Fishing conditions in Oregon run a wide gamut, from short, fast coastal rivers in the northwest rainforest to the arid lakes of Oregon's southeast desert.

Fly fishers in Oregon who want to get to better waters should be prepared for a long hike or a long float. Only 10 rivers in Oregon have been declared navigable, with access for wading anglers to the high water line. On all other rivers, unless part of state or federal land, the landowner owns the bottom of the river; although anglers can float through rivers on private land, they cannot anchor or get out of the boat without landowner permission. This situation is especially critical on the beautiful Wood and Williamson Rivers in the Klamath Lakes area, where there are few public access points. Many of the public river access points on Oregon rivers involve a long walk from the road and a good map, as many watersheds are a patchwork of public and private lands. While permission can sometimes be obtained to cross private lands, this sometimes entails preliminary research and phone calls.

Fisheries

The northwest coast of Oregon is home to short, fast coastal steelhead rivers and great small-stream fishing for resident and sea-run **cutthroat trout**. The Nehalem, Kilchis, and Salmonberry Rivers all have good but quick runs of winter steelhead. Timing is important in these rivers as steelhead will enter them during a rise of water and will then be difficult to find once they disperse in a river. The Siletz is one of the larger rivers that offers good fishing for both sea-run cutthroats and summer steelhead. Inland, the great Willamette river system has great fishing for resident **rainbow** and cutthroat trout, plus steelhead runs. One of its most productive tributaries is the McKenzie River near Eugene. This river has a good population of

O

large rainbow and cutthroat trout and the fish respond well to the river's abundant **mayfly**, **stonefly**, and **caddisfly hatches**, although because the insect population is so rich the fish have the reputation of being difficult to catch. Other Willamette tributaries with good trout and steelhead fishing include the North Santiam, South Santiam, and Clackamas.

Southwestern Oregon is home to two of the world's most famous steelhead rivers, both popular with famed author Zane Grey in the 1920s: The North Umpqua and the Rogue. The North Umpqua is famous for its abundant winter and summer-run steelhead, tricky wading, and tight casting. In many places, the river is narrow and deep, with steep dropoffs alongside giant boulders and ledge rock. Often only one large rock in a pool offers a casting platform, and because of swift flows, deep channels, and slippery rocks, wise

anglers here wear metal cleats over their **wading shoes** and carry a **wading staff**. Still, the river always seems to hold steelhead and the summer-run fish seem to be especially willing to take a **dry fly**. The Rogue is a massive river system that has a run of mostly small steelhead called "half-pounders" (that typically weigh more than a half-pound). These little steelhead are fish that have spent only a brief time in salt water before returning to the river, although some of the bigger ones have been to the ocean for two springs. Although they only range in size from 12 to 20 inches, they feed more aggressively than larger steelhead and often stack up in a pool, so that it's possible to catch a half-dozen fish in the same place. Although less common, the Rogue also has repeat-spawning steelhead that can range in size from 6 to 10 pounds.

Southern Oregon trout fishing is best in the

O

Klamath Lakes region, where abundant flows of groundwater keep rivers cool and clear throughout the summer. The Williamson River, really a giant spring creek that flows into Klamath Lake, Oregon's largest natural lake, is known for its big mayfly hatches but unfortunately the big rainbows that run out of Klamath Lake into the river usually ignore the floating insects, and better fishing can be had with large **nymphs** and **streamer** flies under the surface. The Willamson also has spotty public access and is best floated with a guide who knows the area. The Sprague River, a tributary of the Williamson, has easier access and better dry fly fishing, although the fish are smaller and less numerous. The Klamath River itself, a famous steelhead river further downstream in California, has excellent fishing for large rainbow trout below Boyle Dam. The Wood River is another beautiful spring-fed river in this area, but not only is almost all of the river on private lands, boat launches are difficult unless you are willing to launch a **canoe**, **kayak**, or pontoon boat at a bridge access. Still, the Wood has great insect hatches, good **grasshopper** fishing in late summer, and dense populations of wild **brown** and rainbow trout, so it is worth the effort. This area also has some of the best stillwater trout fishing in Oregon, particularly in Agency and Klamath Lakes. These shallow but productive lakes host an array of aquatic insects, crustaceans, and **baitfish**, and wild rainbow trout grow quickly to

10 pounds in weight. Streamers and large nymphs are the best bet for the larger fish.

Central Oregon is best known for its expansive **Deschutes** river system. However, central Oregon has some smaller rivers with easier access than the Deschutes and also is home to some of the best still-water trout fishing in the state. The Metolius is a spring-fed river that flows through mostly public land and its rainbow trout respond well to numerous stonefly and caddisfly hatches in the summer, and also has a good **Blue-Winged Olive** mayfly hatch during the winter. The Crooked River is known for its perennially murky water but eager rainbow trout that rise well to a dry fly. Giant but shallow Crane Prairie Reservoir is famous for its fast-growing rainbow trout and heavy summer **damselfly** hatches, but the recently introduced **largemouth bass** are also popular with fly anglers. And Hosmer Lake, high in the Cascade Mountains, is one of the few places in the western United States where a fly fisher can catch landlocked **Atlantic salmon** and large **brook trout.** Large mayflies and caddisflies can bring these fish to the surface. The fish also feed heavily on everything from tiny midges to large leeches so a fly fisher should be prepared with a large selection of patterns.

The rugged and mountainous northeastern corner of Oregon offer more solitude than any other place in Oregon. The Grande Ronde is the best steelhead river in the area, with good access in its upper reaches and hatchery steelhead from four to eight pounds. Although the John Day River, the longest river in Oregon, does have a summer run of steelhead, warm summer **water temperatures** make fishing sketchy. However, the lower John Day is a fantastic **smallmouth bass** fishery, and this introduced eastern species grows large and provides great sport for the fly fisher. In fact, the best fly fishing in this area may not even be trout and steel-head fishing in the mountains, but on the backwaters of the Columbia River and the lower reaches of its tributaries, which are all excellent smallmouth habitat.

O

SEASON

Summer-run steelhead begin entering rivers in July, but since many steelhead rivers warm quickly in the midsummer heat, steelhead fishing is better at dawn and dusk, when water temperatures are cooler and the fish more active. September and October are the best months for summer-run steelhead, when fish respond well to a swung **wet fly** or streamer, or a dry fly skated across the surface. In November and December, early winter-run fish or late summer-run fish, although bigger, require **sinking lines** and weighted flies as the fish lie deeper and the current is often faster. February through April is best for winter-run fish because they are approaching their spring spawning season and are more aggressive. Although the fishing for winter-run fish is less productive and more difficult, these steelhead run much larger, and fish up to 20 pounds can be caught on the fly.

Trout fishing in Oregon is year-round, but December through February are tough, unless a warming spell brings fish to the surface for **midge**, stonefly, or Blue-Winged Olive mayfly hatches. The best months for active fish on fly hatches are May through June and then again in September and October. Stillwater fisheries are especially tough in July and August, when warm water temperatures and profuse aquatic weed growth make fly fishing difficult.

ORVIS KNOT

The Orvis Knot is a strong knot used to tie the **tippet** to a fly, and works well for tiny flies and light tippets as well as for tying heavier (up to 20-pound) tippets to big saltwater and **bass flies**. It is quick and easy to tie, retains nearly 100 percent of the tippet's strength, and is less bulky than the traditional **clinch knot**.

■ Pass the tippet through the eye of the **hook** and form a figure-eight in front of the fly by passing the end of the tippet over the standing part on the far side (figure 1), around the

standing part again just in front of the first loop, and back through the first loop formed from the far side. It helps to tie this knot if the second loop is bigger than the first loop (figure 2).

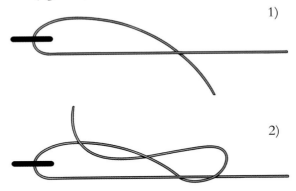

1)

2)

■ Wind the tag end around the inside of the second loop twice (figure 3).

3)

■ Tighten the knot by pulling first on the fly and the tag end, which tightens the second loop against the standing part. Then release the tag end and pull on the standing part and the fly to fully tighten the knot. Trim the tag end close to the fly (figure 4).

4)

OVERHEAD CAST

HOW THE OVERHEAD CAST WORKS

The overhead cast, also known as the forward cast or pick-up-and-lay-down cast or just the "basic cast" is the most common and efficient way to cast a fly, provided the caster has as much room behind as in front. Like all fly casts, the overhead casts use the weight of the line to deliver the fly, and the **fly** rod builds up energy during the cast, much like a coiled spring, to deliver the **fly line** loop properly. The cast is composed of two parts: the **back cast** and the forward cast (which is a confusing term because sometimes the entire cast is called a "forward cast," thus the term overhead cast), with a deliberate stop in between these two motions. Both forward and back casts, when done properly, accelerate the rod quickly to a distinct stop.

BASIC MOTIONS

Begin an overhead cast with the rod held at waist level in a comfortable position with elbow bent. The rod should be parallel to the water (figure 1). The cast begins by moving the tip of the rod straight up (figure 2), which begins to move the fly line across the surface. Continue raising the rod, gradually accelerating until most of the line is off the water, and then make a quick acceleration to a dead stop (figure 3). This quick acceleration is called the power stroke. At the point of the stop, your casting hand should be about even with your ear, and if you superimposed a clock parallel to the angle of your cast, the tip of the rod should stop at somewhere between 1:00 and 2:00 o'clock (figure 4). The entire motion should be smooth and continuous, and it's important to initiate the cast with the strong muscles in your forearm, not your wrist. Your wrist muscles merely add the acceleration at the end of the cast, much as you use mostly forearm to hammer a nail, adding the wrist at the last minute for the final acceleration.

When accomplished properly, the forward cast drives the line over the tip of the rod in a tight loop (figure 3), and the line behind you straightens parallel to the ground (figure 4). Most problems on the back cast are caused by using too much wrist (called "breaking the wrist"), which drives the tip of the rod past the 2:00 o'clock position. When this happens, the back cast is not straight, most of the power built up in the flexing of the rod is lost, and on the forward cast a sloppy, open loop is formed, which dumps the fly line in front of you like a pile of limp spaghetti.

A good back cast gives maximum flex to the rod and makes the forward cast almost effortless. The moment the line straightens behind the tip, the rod should move forward to initiate the forward cast (figure 5). Throughout the cast, you should feel constant tension on the tip of the rod: Any break in this tension robs you of power, which is why it is so important to bring the tip of the rod to a dead stop at the correct position. There is no way to estimate how long the rod should be at that dead stop before moving forward, because the timing changes depending on how long a line is being cast. With 15 feet of line the pause is virtually nonexistent, but with 50 feet of line the rod should pause for a full second without moving. When practicing, it is perfectly legitimate (and recommended) to turn your head to determine when to begin the forward cast (figures 3 & 4). With practice, this timing becomes intuitive.

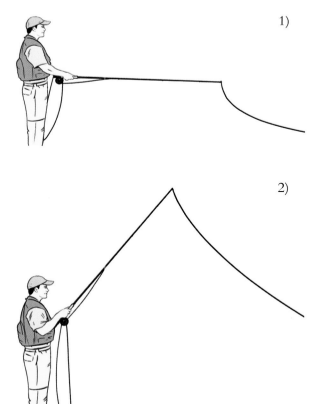

1)

2)

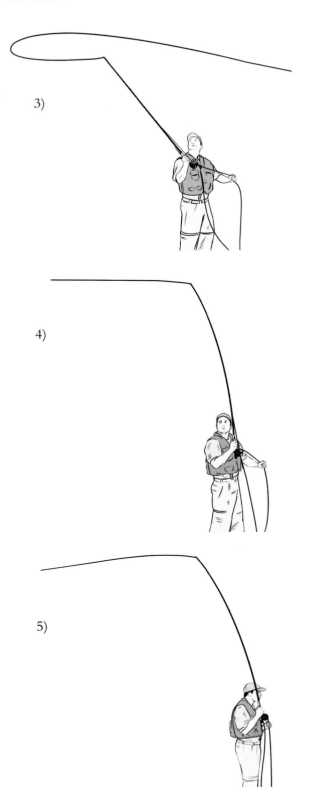

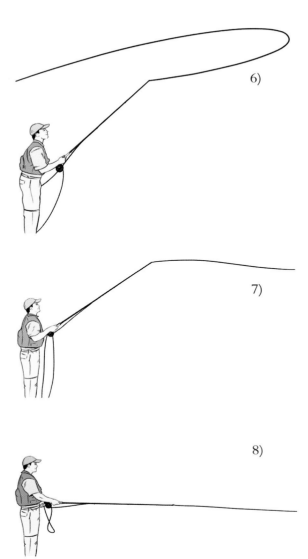

THE CASTING LOOP

When executed properly in an overhead cast, the line describes a U-shaped loop, with the open end facing forward on the back cast and the open end facing backward on the forward cast, as the tip of the U slices through the air, unrolling at the final moment to deliver the fly and **leader**. The smaller the arc on the loop (a "tight loop"), the more efficient the cast because the line traveling in both directions is more aerodynamically shaped and offers less air resistance. Loop shape is especially critical on long casts or when casting against the wind, as more energy is needed to drive the fly line.

The way to get a tight loop is to increase the speed of the power stroke and shorten up the entire casting arc without increasing the speed of the overall casting motion. Too casual a power stroke results in a sloppy, open loop. And the power has to be applied in just the right place. One way to grasp this concept is to imagine a marshmallow stuck on the tip of the fly rod. Your goal is to flick the marshmallow up into the air on the back cast and out over the water on the forward cast. Applying the power stroke too early in the cast or too late can cause what is called a "tailing loop," where the loop curls over on itself. Catching the fly on the leader or on the tip of the rod is a good indication of a tailing loop.

GAINING DISTANCE

Once a basic 30-foot cast has been mastered and timing improved, distance can be gained by modifying the casting technique and timing. Because more line must be moved, it's necessary to bend the rod through a longer casting arc, otherwise all the power has to be applied over a short arc and motions become jerky. It is important to begin the cast with the rod tip close to the water, and the entire cast should go through a longer arc by raising the arm slightly. More wrist will be used on a longer cast, but it's still critical that the wrist does not break and drop the back cast below the tip of the rod on the back cast.

When making longer casts, there is a tendency to underpower the back cast and then try to throw the line forward with a mighty heave. Equal effort should be placed on both back and forward casts. The rod should never lunge on the forward cast. Ending up with your arm stuck straight out in front of you after a long cast, instead of comfortably at your side, is a good indication that you are lunging.

Longer casts can never be made without

releasing additional line. This is called *shooting line.* By holding additional loose line in your non-casting hand and then releasing it as the loop of the forward cast begins to unfurl, the forward energy of the casting loop will pull the additional line from your hand. Line should be released just after the power stroke on the forward cast. If the line is released too early it takes all the energy out of the casting loop, and if it is released too late there is not enough momentum left in the cast to pull all of the line through the **guides**.

O

FALSE CASTING

False casting is making several overhead casts in succession without dropping the line to the water. It serves to whip the moisture out of a dry fly between casts, change the direction of the cast from one place to another, to work out additional line by shooting some on each false cast, and can be used to estimate accuracy before the fly is finally delivered. Remember not to false cast too many times in a row—most anglers spend far too much time with the line in the air than on the water, and the more times you make a cast without pausing the greater the chance you will introduce a problem into the motion. And when casting over spooky fish, a constant waving of the rod and line over its head may frighten your quarry.

False casting should be done with short lines. Any additional distance should be obtained by shooting line. To false cast, begin with a normal back and forward cast, but as soon as the loop unfurls in front of you, begin another back cast. Don't follow through with the rod and don't let the line hit the water. The entire casting motion goes through a much shorter arc. When you are ready to deliver the fly to the water, just follow through by lowering the rod, parallel to the water and the final loop will unfurl just above the water and drop to the surface.

There are a number of variations on the overhead cast:

SIDE CAST

The standard overhead cast can be turned 45 degrees or up to 90 degrees on its side. All of the casting motions are the same, except that the rod travels at an angle instead of vertically. Because there is little ground clearance when casting the rod at a full 90 degree angle to the vertical, it's even more critical to make sure the back cast does not drop; by keeping side casts short it will be easier to keep the line under control. Side casts are when it's windy, because the wind is always less closer to the ground, and because the casting loop unfurls on a low horizontal plane this cast is critical when trying to fire a fly beneath overhanging branches.

TOWER CAST

Also known as the steeple cast, anglers use this cast when backed up against a cliff or streamside brush but would prefer not to use a **roll cast**, which is usually not as accurate as an overhead cast. With this cast, the casting arm is raised as high as possible over your head on the back cast, and the line is directed straight up rather than back behind you. Because of the high angle of the back cast, this cast tends to slam the fly line into the water if the casting arm follows through to waist level on the forward cast, so the casting arm should remain above your head on both back cast and forward cast.

CURVE CASTS

Sometimes it is necessary to cast a deliberate curve into a fly line. If a fish is feeding in front of a rock and you are directly behind the rock being able to cast a controlled curve into your line is a great advantage. Curve casts are also helpful in getting a **dead drift** in tricky currents. For a righthanded caster, there are two ways to make a cast that curves to the right. The easiest way is to make a side cast and just before completing the forward cast, pull back slightly on the rod. This makes the casting loop kick back into an inverted and upside-down J shape, making a nice curve. Another way is to turn the wrist of the casting hand sideways at the end of the forward cast, so that your palm is facing you. A curve to the left is much harder for a righthander as it requires a cross-body cast in conjunction with these motions. Lefthanded casters need to reverse the process. In most situations, a reach cast is easier and more reliable than a curve cast.

CROSS-BODY CAST

When a right-handed caster is faced with obstructions behind or off to the right side, a cross-body cast can be used. This uses the same motions as an overhead cast, but the casting angle of the rod starts slightly offset to the right for the back cast, and the back cast is then directed over the left shoulder so that the rod passes in front of the caster. The forward cast is then directed off to the right side of the caster. This is a tricky cast to accomplish and should be used only with 30 feet of line or less.

REACH CAST

The reach cast puts a curve into the fly line but the reach is accomplished immediately before the line straightens on the water. It is sometimes known as an aerial mend, because the caster merely puts a **mend** into the fly line just before it touches the water. Most anglers feel this method is easier and less prone to errors than a curve cast. To make the fly line curve to the right (with the closed end of the curve to the caster's right side), make a forward cast as normal but just before the casting loop fully unfurls, push the rod tip out and to the right by straightening the casting arm and reaching out to the right. The more exaggerated the reach, the bigger the curve. To make a lefthanded curve, push the rod off to the left, in front of the body.

A long upstream reach cast helps this angler avoid drag in a fast riffle.

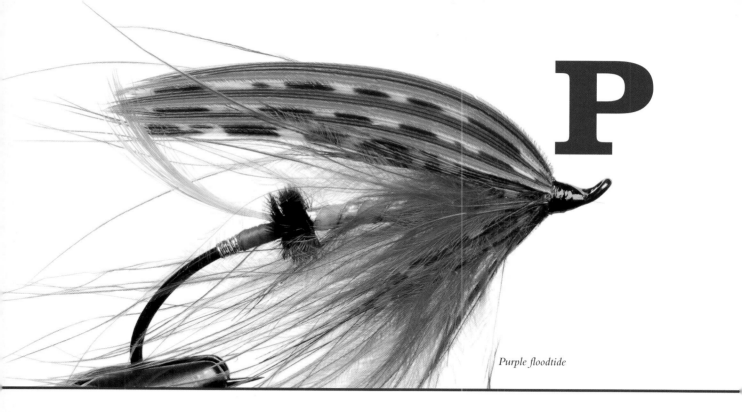

P

Purple floodtide

PALE EVENING DUN, PALE MORNING DUN

Pale Morning Duns (often called PMDs) and Pale Evening Duns (also known as sulphurs) are **mayflies** of similar appearance and behavior, typically small (between size 16 and 20), with cream or pale gray wings and yellow bodies, often with a tinge of olive or orange. Pale Morning Duns are more common in the western United States, where the most recognized species are *Ephemerella inermis* and *E. infrequens*, and Pale Evening Duns are more common in the eastern United States, where the most abundant species is *Ephemerella dorothea*. However, many eastern **tailwater** rivers and **spring creeks** have **hatches** of pale yellow mayflies in the late morning, and western rivers also have a Pale Evening Dun (*Heptagenia* species), so small yellowish-colored mayflies may be found anywhere in North America both during the day and just before dark.

Pale Morning Duns begin hatching in late May and may continue to hatch until August or even September. Streams at high altitudes are most likely to have hatches of these insects later in the season. Hatches of duns can begin as early as 9:00 A.M. and last until mid-afternoon, but typically they begin hatching about 11:00 A.M. and the hatch lasts for about two hours. Pale Morning Duns are one of the best hatches of the season where they are found. Due to the abundance of flies during the hatch and the small size of the insects, trout become quite selective and require a close imitation and careful presentation. Best patterns are **emerger** or **parachute** flies that ride low in the surface film.

Trout are equally difficult when feeding on Pale Evening Duns, and this difficulty is compounded by the insect's habit of hatching just at dark, when both fly and rise forms are difficult to see. However, fishing a Pale Evening Dun hatch is worth the effort, because the biggest trout in a pool, the ones that seldom rise to surface food, will often join the smaller trout in rising. Pale Evening Duns begin hatching on eastern rivers in late May and last on some rivers until late June, where on western rivers they may hatch from June through September. As with PMDs, emerger patterns are quite effective, but many anglers choose parachute flies for this hatch because the fly is more visible in waning light.

PANFISH

Panfish is a term reserved for small warm-water fish that are not commonly considered gamefish. This group includes the various species of **sunfish**, rock bass, **white bass**, **white perch**, yellow perch, and crappie. In the southern United States, panfish, especially various species of sunfish, are often col-

lectively known as bream or "brim." Although none of these fish will get a fly fisher into the **backing** or even pull much line off the reel, they will eagerly inhale a fly and are more readily available than most gamefish. A day chasing sunfish or white perch on a light (1-weight to 4-weight) **fly rod** will be action-packed and is a great way to enjoy fly fishing close to urban areas, on a farm pond, or when trying to teach a youngster the basics of fly fishing.

Most panfish will be found close to shore, spawning, when **water temperatures** get above 50 degrees (10°C), which can be any time from March in **Florida** through June in northern **Maine**. Sunfish, rock bass, and crappie are particularly easy to find because they construct spawning nests or **redds** in shallow water, moving mud and silt aside to form light-colored patches of clean gravel that are extremely easy to spot. Yellow perch and white perch are broadcast spawners that lay eggs over open water, but can also be found in spring over shallow sand and gravel bars. Sunfish and rock bass will stay in shallow water throughout

the summer and thus are easy to catch throughout the day, even in the heat of an August day. Yellow perch, white perch, and white bass stay in deeper water during the summer, but any species of panfish can be found feeding close to the surface in early morning and evening.

The most commonly pursued sunfish are the bluegill, recognized by the long blue-black projection on its gill plate; the pumpkinseed, recognized by its colorful blue and orange bars and red-tipped gill plate; and longear sunfish or "shellcracker," which looks similar to a pumpkinseed but lacks the striking orange and blue bands along its head. All of these sunfish eagerly take **nymphs**, **wet flies**, and small **streamers** in sizes 10 and 12, but the most entertaining way to catch them is on tiny **poppers** or sponge rubber bugs. Although sunfish will quickly investigate a popper cast in their vicinity, getting them to take the fly is not always as easy as it looks. The best bet is to keep the fly perfectly motionless. Often the fish will stare at the popper for what seems like an eternity before finally grabbing it. If they begin to swim away, often a small twitch or a very slow **retrieve** will change their mind. Poppers used to catch panfish must be very small because their mouths are tiny, and sizes 10 through 14 are best.

Rock bass, yellow perch, white perch, and crappie will take a larger, faster moving surface bug, but these species feed more on minnows and small crayfish than on insects, so the best approach for these species is a small white streamer in sizes 8 through 12. Color does not seem to be important in panfish streamers, but a white fly with a little silver flash in it like a Black-Nose Dace bucktail or White Marabou streamer are usually all that is required. Daytime fishing for these species may require a **sink-tip fly line** to get down to their level, but they can be caught near the surface on a floating line early in the season, and throughout the summer at first light and just before dark.

PARACHUTE FLY

A parachute fly is a type of **dry fly** rather than a specific pattern, and most standard dry flies can be modified into a parachute style. Parachute flies are tied by winding **hackle** parallel to the long axis of the **hook** shank rather than perpendicular to it, so when the fly rides in the surface film the all of the hackle spreads out like a parachute to aid in flotation. Parachutes land softly and the body of the fly rides low in the surface film rather than above it, which is very effective when **mayfly spinners** are on the water, or when any kind of insect is just **emerging**. Parachute flies are often tied with a white wing post, which makes them highly visible in fast water or in low light.

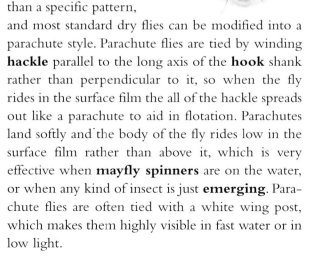

Popular parachute flies that imitate mayflies or **caddisflies** include the Parachute Adams, Parachute **Blue-Winged Olive**, Parachute Pheasant Tail, and **Hare's Ear** Parachute. Because **terrestrial** flies always ride low in the surface film, parachute versions of **ants**, **grasshoppers**, and **beetles** are also extremely effective.

P

PENNSYLVANIA

OVERVIEW

With its mild winters, warm summers, and rich limestone geology, Pennsylvania is one of the most popular trout-fishing states in the Union. Limestone springs in central and southern Pennsylvania keep many of its rich streams cold enough for trout survival, and in the northern mountains dense forests and cooler temperatures help mitigate warm summer temperatures. Pennsylvania has an extremely large and dedicated fly-fishing population; in fact there are more fly shops in Pennsylvania than any other state. Because of the large number of fishing licenses sold, the Pennsylvania Fish Commission is well funded and able to stock fish and maintain habitat better than most other states.

Although trout is king in the Keystone State, there are many other great game fish to chase with a **fly rod**. It has arguably the best **smallmouth bass** fishing in the world, with a short but very productive Lake Erie shoreline, and many of its larger rivers are shallow and rocky—perfect smallmouth habitat. Pennsylvania also has some of the best Lake Erie **steelhead** rivers within its borders. **Muskellunge** are native to northwestern Pennsylvania, but both purebred muskies and tiger muskies (a cross between northern **pike** and muskellunge that is more aggressive and easier to catch) have been stocked in suitable waters throughout the state. Pennsylvania also has an extensive stocking program for **striped bass** in inland lakes, and natural runs of striped bass in the Delaware River.

FISHERIES

The best trout fishing in Pennsylvania is located in the eastern half of the state, where low mountains, hills, and limestone bedrock provide the cold springs that keep trout streams cool. Pennsylvania's most famous streams are the **spring creeks** of Cumberland County in the south central part of the state. Letort Spring run is the most famous, known throughout the world because it was here that **Vincent Marinaro**, Charles Fox, and **Ernest Schwiebert** (among many others) experimented with and documented fishing with tiny **mayfly** and **terrestrial** imitations. This small watercress-lined stream, while currently threatened by suburban sprawl, still grows large wild **brown trout** that feed on tiny **Blue-Winged Olive** and **Pale**

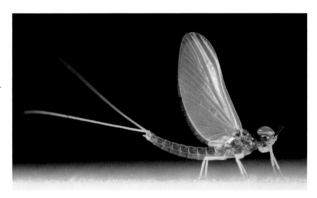

Evening Dun mayflies in spring and early summer, along with **midges** and terrestrials later in the summer. The wily trout of the Letort feed on **scuds** throughout the year, even in the dead of winter, and a carefully placed **nymph** is often the best way to fool one. Falling Springs run is another tiny but famous spring creek in Cumberland County, which offers great fishing for wild brown trout and the easier-to-fool wild **rainbow trout**. Its **Trico** hatch in August is heavy and brings many trout to the surface. Big Spring Creek near Newville has equally good fishing and great hatches, both in its narrow **upstream** "ditch" section where it can be fished from the bank, as well as the lower reaches of this stream, with a wider

P

streambed and fewer trout—but less fishing pressure. Although it has a rocky bottom instead of the weedy, silt bottom of most other spring creeks in the area, Yellow Breeches Creek is a popular trout stream, heavily stocked with hatchery fish but with the corresponding crowds that hatchery fish draw.

To the north and west of Cumberland County are two streams known for their large brown trout and prolific fly hatches: Spruce Creek and the Little Juniata River. Similar in character, Spruce Creek is entirely in private hands with the exception of a very short stretch owned by Penn State. Fee fishing is available in certain stretches where crowds won't be found, but the Little Juniata has equally good fishing in a bigger river with more casting room. The river has a dense **crayfish** population which feed its big brown trout, so although nymph and **dry fly** fishing are popular during the day, so is **night fishing** with large **streamers**.

Centre County right in the middle of Pennsylvania has two of Pennsylvania's most famous trout streams: Penn's Creek and Spring Creek. Penn's Creek begins in limestone springs in Penn's Cave. The upper six miles of river are in private hands, but there is good public access near the town of Coburn and some of the best hatches and biggest fish come from this area. For anglers looking for wild brown trout, wilderness settings, and great hatches, there is a long stretch of river that is inaccessible except for an old railroad bed. The four miles of river in this stretch are catch-and-release only with year-round trout fishing. Penn's Creek is most famous for its **Green Drake** mayfly hatch (known locally as the **Shad** Fly), and when these giant mayflies are on the water around Memorial Day, the river is crowded. (Many dedicated trout anglers take their vacations to coincide with this hatch.) However, Penn's Creek has great fishing throughout spring, summer, and fall, and most of the famous eastern mayfly and **caddisfly** hatches are found in its waters. Equally famous is Spring Creek, home of the famous Fisherman's Paradise stretch where large and numerous trout can be seen

Fall fly fishing in the Poconos.

Drift boating down the Delaware River provides access to trout, bass, and shad.

P

moody and gives up its hefty wild brown and rainbow trout less often, but it is one of the most scenic trout rivers in the eastern United States. Both rivers can be waded but many anglers prefer to see more water by hiring a guide and **drift boat** or by floating the rivers in a **canoe**, **kayak**, or pontoon boat. Access on both rivers is spotty with much posted land, and to get to the best fishing it is sometimes necessary to park at a state fishing access point and walk in. Also in eastern Pennsylvania, the Brodheads is a typical small eastern trout stream, home to the famous Brodheads Forest and Stream Club where Buffalo Bill and Annie Oakley cast upon its waters, along with many of the most famous anglers of the nineteenth and twentieth centuries. From the club boundary **downstream** to the Delaware River is public water that fishes well throughout the spring and summer.

North central Pennsylvania is home to a number of mountain streams that offer great fishing from spring through early summer. Pine Creek is a large rocky river that is more famous for its white water rafting, but its remote Grand Canyon area is well stocked with trout and early season hatches are thick. Kettle Creek has wild trout in its upper reaches. The lower water downstream of Ole Bull State park is well stocked but still suffers from heavy fishing pressure. Both Pine Creek and Kettle Creek become too warm for good trout fishing during the summer, but for superb wild trout fishing both rivers have excellent tributaries that do stay cold, and because they require a walk and have special regulations do not get as much pressure as the stocked waters. Slate Run and Cedar Run are the best Pine Creek tributaries, and Slate Run in particular supports some large but wary brown trout in a heavily forested canyon. Cross Fork, a tributary of Kettle Creek is the stream most serious fly fishers prefer, and has good hatches and wild **brook** and brown trout. South of these mountain streams is Fishing Creek, a rich stream that has water that remains cool enough to support trout throughout the year and has wonderful mayfly and caddisfly hatches. Access

from its banks (no wading is allowed) and regulars try for its very selective and wary trout. Less crowded stretches of this premier river can be found upstream of the Paradise on State Penitentiary property and below the Paradise, where the river runs through backyards but access is easy with a polite inquiry from landowners.

Without a doubt, the best trout stream in northeastern Pennsylvania is the Delaware River, both its main stem from Hancock, New York, downstream to Callicoon, New York (the Delaware forms the border between New York and Pennsylvania from Hale Eddy downstream). The West Branch is a rich **tailwater** with **riffles** and smooth runs that offers an incredible soup of aquatic insects and brown trout that average about 16 inches long. The main stem of the river or "The Big D" is a wider, slower, and sometimes warmer piece of trout water that is is good on this stream and fly fishing on this stream is excellent from April through November. Just be careful—Pennsylvania has five streams named Fishing Creek but this one, in southern Clinton County, is by far the best of them.

Fly fishing for **steelhead**, although limited to streams in the extreme northwestern part of the state where rivers flow into Lake Erie, is excellent and very productive. Near the city of Erie, the best steelhead streams are the Conneaut, Elk, Walnut, and Twenty Mile. Although these streams are too warm for trout during the summer and are home to **panfish**, **carp**, and smallmouth bass most of the year, from fall through early spring they host spawning runs of steelhead from hatchery fish stocked in Lake Erie.

Lake Erie is perhaps the best smallmouth bass fishery in the world, and Pennsylvania's short piece of it encompasses one of the best places to catch big smallmouth bass on a fly rod, Presque Isle Bay. Because this bay is shallower than the rest of the Lake Erie shoreline, smallmouth bass are more accessible on the fly rod and its big bass respond well to both **poppers** and streamer flies, especially from April through early June. The Susquehanna River is perhaps the best smallmouth fishery for fly rod fishing throughout the summer. It has an excellent population of fish, and its extremely wide but shallow riverbed is easily accessible by wading or by small water craft like canoes, kayaks, and johnboats. Although the Susquehanna supports smallmouths throughout its 400-mile journey through Pennsylvania, the best fishing is both upstream and downstream of the city of Harrisburg, where smallmouths can be caught on anything from mayfly imitations to **baitfish** imitations like the famous **Clouser Minnow** (it was developed for this river's smallmouths) to poppers. The river has an abundant crayfish population, perhaps a smallmouth's favorite food, so streamers and large nymphs that imitate this crustacean are a staple in any serious fly fisher's box. When fishing the Susquehanna for smallmouths, it's not unusual to

come upon a school of large carp as well, and these brutes will take the same nymphs and streamers as a smallmouth—but they require a more careful approach. Although not as productive as the Susquehanna, the Alleghany River, Juniata River, and Delaware River are also excellent places to fish for smallmouths with a fly.

Striped bass migrating up from the Atlantic Ocean can be found in the Delaware River in the spring well upstream into the trout waters near Callicoon, but the best place to find them is in the vicinity of Easton, Pennsylvania. Large poppers and streamer flies cast into the mouths of streams running into the Delaware are the best places to catch one on a fly, particularly at dawn and after dark when the fish feed heavily on migrating schools of shad and herring. In May, striper anglers will also

encounter huge schools of shad, which can be taken on small streamers and nymphs if they are in the right mood. The state also stocks striped bass and striped bass/**white bass** hybrids in deep reservoirs. The best places to catch one on a fly are Raystown Lake and Lake Wallenpaupack, especially in spring and fall when the fish cruise near the surface.

Chasing muskies with a fly has gotten popular in Pennsylvania and there are many places to do it. One of the best is the lower Alleghany River, but muskies can also be caught on a fly in one of the lakes where they are stocked, including Lake Somerset, Lake Wilhelm, and Woodcock Creek Lake. Largemouth bass and panfish will be found in any shallow, weedy lake in Pennsylvania, and although they are overshadowed by the more popular smallmouth bass, they provide great sport on a fly rod during the heat of summer when other fish aren't cooperating.

SEASON

Most Pennsylvania trout streams are open year-round, and fishing in the spring creeks can be productive on warm winter days, especially with midge imitations and nymphs that imitate scuds. March and April usher in the early season mayflies, the Blue-Winged Olives and Quill Gordons, followed in May by the Hendricksons and March Browns. By Memorial Day, the famous **Green Drakes** will be hatching, although trout will sometimes pass up the bigger insects and feed on the more numerous Pale Evening Duns and caddisflies. Because most of Pennsylvania's better trout streams are fed by cold springs, summer fishing can be excellent. Fish will feed on **ants**, **beetles**,

grasshoppers, and other **terrestrial** insects throughout the summer, and in late July the famous Trico hatch begins, which some fly fishers consider the best hatch of the season in Pennsylvania. Other summer hatches include a morning-hatching Blue-Winged Olive as well as **Light Cahills** and Cream Variants, both large pale mayflies that hatch just before dark. Fall fishing can be excellent with nymphs and streamers, and for those who don't mind fishing very tiny flies, there is a small pale olive mayfly in size 24 that hatches into November, offering dry fly fishing until the snow falls.

Although smallmouth bass fishing is good throughout the spring and fall, it is best during the special early catch-and-release only season in mid-April though mid-June. Smallmouths in rivers will feed well throughout the summer and well into the fall, but fish in lakes tend to go deep and out of reach of all but the most persistent fly fishers during the summer. Striped bass and shad are best from April through early June when they are fresh from the ocean, although they can be caught at night through fall. The best time to catch a muskie on a fly in Pennsylvania is in late June and then again in early fall.

PERFECTION LOOP

The Perfection Loop is a clean, very strong knot used to form a loop in a **leader**. It is more difficult to tie than a **Surgeon's Loop**, but is less bulky and the standing part of the finished knot lies perfectly in line with the loop, which makes a the leader land straighter when cast.

- Pinch the leader material in your hand about 4 inches from the end. Bring the end of the leader around behind the standing part and pinch the loop formed in your thumb and forefinger (figure 1).
- Bring the tag end around and in front of the loop and back to the side it began, forming a second loop in front of the first

loop. Pinch this loop against the first so that both loops are held by your thumb and forefinger (figure 2).

■ Fold the tag end to the opposite side of the loops, passing it between the first and second loop. Continue pinching both loops and now the tag end with the thumb and forefinger (figure 3).

■ Reach from behind the first loop and pull the second loop completely through (figures 4 & 5). Tighten the knot by pulling on the second loop and standing part of the leader. When tied properly, the tag end will be protruding at 90 degrees to the final loop and standing part of the leader. Trim the tag end close to the knot (figure 6).

P

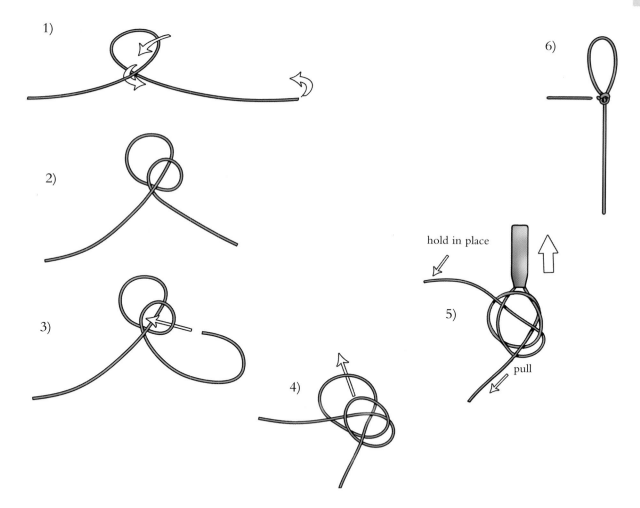

1)

2)

3)

4)

5)

hold in place

pull

6)

PERMIT

The permit is a fish of both shallow and deep tropical waters, and when caught by sight-fishing is one of the most elusive trophies in fly fishing. Permit can be caught easily in deep water on **streamer** flies by chumming with **baitfish** and shrimp over reefs or wrecks, but for most fly anglers the most exciting way to catch a permit is over a shallow flat when the fish are rooting on the bottom for crabs, their primary food.

Tactics used to catch permit are similar to those used for **bonefish**, except the fish are usually found in slightly deeper water and the flies are larger and more heavily weighted. The common 9-foot 8-weight bonefish outfit is often replaced with a 9-foot, 10-weight rod because an 8-weight has trouble pushing the bigger flies, especially in the wind. Permit are most often seen at the beginning of an incoming tide on the deep edge of a flat or reef. They are easier to spot than bonefish in shallow water, because their black dorsal fin and sickle-shaped tail stand out quite well, and when a permit decides to tip down and take a crab in shallow water its tail waves in the air and is often visible for 100 yards, especially on a calm day.

Presentations to permit are made either when the fish are just cruising, looking for food, or are visibly feeding on the bottom. Lone permit are sometimes spotted, but more typically a school of between 4 and 20 fish will swim together, and the more fish in a school, the better as competition between fish may make them more aggressive to the fly. The fly should be cast well ahead of a school of cruising permit, because it is most effective when lying on the bottom. The typical reaction of permit is to completely ignore the fly and swim away—which is why they are such an elusive trophy. The second most common circumstance is for a permit to swim over and look at the fly—and then ignore it and swim away. The only option available to the angler in this case is to move the fly slightly, perhaps an inch or so, in the hope that a permit may react to the slight movement and pounce on the fly. Stripping the fly quickly invariably results in fish that spook or just turn away from the fly.

Permit that are busily tailing on a flat require a different approach. Here, the fly should be cast as close to a tailing fish as possible. When tailing, permit are concentrating on a piece of bottom just a few inches in diameter; a fly just a foot to one side may be completely ignored. Crabs swim to the bottom when disturbed, so the hope here is that the permit will think the sinking fly is a crab it has just disturbed. The soft "plop" of a permit fly hitting the water may actually attract the fish, but if the sound is not exactly right it can spook the fish instead of attracting it.

Effective permit flies are those that mimic the quarter to half-dollar-sized crabs that permit eat. The most effective fly ever developed is the Del Brown Permit fly or Merkin, a simple yarn fly with rubber legs. Many other crab patterns will also work, particularly the Borksi Chernobyl Crab, Jack's Fighting Crab, and Enrico's Palmeta Crab. Permit flies should be heavily weighted to get to the bottom quickly, so most of these patterns incorporate metal eyes to increase the sink rate. Simon Becker, a noted Florida Keys guide, developed a floating crab imitation that suspends from the bottom while a weight is placed on the leader. It goes against conventional wisdom but is quite effective in his waters. Permit are also fond of mantis shrimp, and imitations of these large green shrimp can be deadly, especially in Belize.

Landing a permit is almost as difficult as getting one to take a fly. Permit are extremely strong, fast swimmers, and use their flat shape to great advantage. The initial run of a large permit may strip almost 200 yards from a fly reel. After the first run, the angler will be able to **retrieve** some line, but the permit will then make a number of subsequent but shorter runs, followed by a last run when it gets close to the boat or to the wading angler. Once it is close enough, a permit can be landed by grasping the base of its sickle-shaped tail firmly; the fish should be kept in the water to remove the fly and take pictures so that it returns to the water with a minimum of handling.

Two of the best places in the world to catch a large permit in shallow water are Biscayne Bay south of Miami and in the waters off the **Florida** Keys. Smaller and more numerous schools of permit are found in the islands off the coast of Belize, one of the most reliable places in the world to catch one. Permit are also found on the west coast of Florida and in the **Bahamas**.

PHEASANT TAIL NYMPH

The Pheasant Tail Nymph is one of the most effective trout flies ever created. It was first tied in the 1950s by British river keeper **Frank Sawyer**, who wanted a simple, quick-sinking fly that would imitate various species of slim **mayfly nymphs** that trout fed upon. The original fly was tied from just two materials—the rusty fibers from the tail of a cock ringneck pheasant and copper **wire**. Later modifications by other tiers added a thorax of peacock herl feathers and legs of partridge **hackle**, but the original slim version is still equally popular.

The fly is usually tied in sizes 14 through 20, with 16 and 18 the most common **hook** sizes. The Pheasant Tail is one of the best imitations of the *Baetis* mayfly, one of the most common species of mayfly in the world, but is it really a general imitation that mimics small mayflies, **caddis pupae**, small **stoneflies**, and **midge** pupae. Effective variations include the addition of a brass or tungsten bead at the head of the fly to make it sparkle and sink quickly, in which case the fly is called a Bead-Head Pheasant Tail, and the Flashback Variation, where a strip of pearlescent tinsel is added to the fly

to create added visibility to the fish without increasing the sink rate of the fly.

PICKEREL

The pickerel, *Esox niger*, also called the chain pickerel, is a small member of the **pike** family that takes a fly very well. Although it can grow to three feet long, most fish caught on a fly rod are between 14 and 20 inches. It is found throughout the eastern United States, but is most common in the New England and Mid-Atlantic States. Typical habitat is in shallow, weedy lakes; pickerel will seldom be found very far from heavy weed growth. Pickerel can sometimes be moody, but they feed 12 months a year and will eat almost anything that moves, so they are a fun quarry with a **fly rod** when other species are not cooperating.

Pickerel will take either surface **poppers** or **streamers**, and the exact pattern is not important as long as the fly moves quickly. Sometimes a pickerel will take a motionless popper, but more are caught by **retrieving** the surface lure at a steady pace. Streamers should be fished even faster and practically ripped through the water, not only because pickerel like it that way, but because the streaking wake of a pickerel chasing a fly through shallow water is quite exciting. Weedless flies are more practical for pickerel because the fish seldom move far from their thick ambush points and seldom feed in open water.

Redfin pickerel

P

Chain pickerel

Any kind of fly rod, from a 5-weight to an 8-weight, makes a suitable rod for pickerel although these small fish are more fun with lighter tackle. **Leaders** should be short and stout: Although pickerel have a mouthful of sharp teeth a **wire** bite guard is not needed if the end of the leader is 15- to 20-pound test.

PIKE, NORTHERN

The northern pike, *Esox lucius*, is a large, toothy freshwater fish that provides exciting sport on a fly rod. Circumpolar in distribution, the fish is native to the Great Lakes through Nebraska and north into **Canada** and **Alaska**, and is also found in Europe at the same latitudes. It has also been introduced into New England and the southern and western United States. Northern pike grow to over 40 pounds, but catching one over 20 pounds on a **fly rod** is rare. Their most common prey is whatever small fish is most abundant, but pike will also eat **crayfish**, frogs, mice, leeches, and even young muskrats and waterfowl.

Despite their diet and ferocity, pike are not always easy to catch. In the lower 48 states, pike are most cooperative after their spring spawning season, which can be from late April through June. After **water temperatures** rise above 65 degrees, pike feed less often and although they stay in water of less than 20 feet throughout the summer, it may be difficult to find one that is in a feeding mood. On the other hand, in northern Canada and Alaska, where water temperatures seldom rise above 65

degrees, pike feed heavily throughout the summer and all day long. Thus the best fly rod pike fishing is found in the north country—especially in Labrador, Manitoba, Saskatchewan, Northwest Territories, and Alaska.

Pike are strong fighters and the flies used to catch them should be from three to six inches long, so a heavy fly rod is needed to **play** the fish and to drive the bulky flies needed to fool them. An 8-weight rod is considered the minimum size and many anglers use a rod as big as a 10-weight. Floating and intermediate **fly lines** are the best options, but if the fish lie deep sometimes a **sinking line** is needed. The **fly reel** should hold the line plus 100 yards of **backing**, as although pike aren't capable of a sustained fight, they are excellent sprinters and a big one may pull a lot of line on its initial run. **Leaders** should be short and stout, six feet long with a 15- to 20-pound test tippet. A **wire shock tippet** is essential as a big pike can bite through 30-pound-test **tippet**. Pliers or large **forceps** should be close at hand when pike fishing, as it is dangerous to remove a fly from a pike's mouth with bare hands.

Pike will strike **poppers** or floating deer hair **bass flies**, and seeing a large pike slash a floating fly in shallow water is one of the most heart-pounding events in fly fishing. As in bass fishing, let the popper lie motionless at first because a pike might think the fly is a crippled frog, mouse, or baitfish. But unlike bass fishing, once you begin to move the fly strips should be quite rapid and aggressive, and pike are capable of great bursts of speed and cannot resist prey that looks like it is trying to escape.

The most reliable flies are large streamer flies or saltwater flies in hook sizes 1/0 or 2/0. Any color can be effective on pike at times, but the most productive colors seem to be black, red, white, and chartreuse, or any combination of these. If a pike is suspected to be lying in a location, the best tactic is to cast as long a line as possible, parallel to the shore if possible, because pike typically lie close to shore facing open water, waiting for prey. By

casting parallel to the shoreline, the fly passes all the possible ambush points so the likelihood of getting a strike is better. If pike are seen lying in shallow water, as they often are in clear northern lakes, cast well beyond the fish and parallel to its position, so the pike sees the fly moving away, as a baitfish will never swim toward a lurking pike. Pike streamer should be retrieved with long, steady strips, and usually a fast retrieve will draw the most strikes.

PLAYING FISH

Playing a fish involves bringing a fish to **net** or hand without breaking the **tippet** or having the fly pull out of a fish's mouth. For catch-and-release fishing, another important consideration is to bring the fish to hand as quickly as possible so the released fish still has enough energy to recover. In the past, it was thought quite "sporting" to catch a large fish on a light tippet and light rod and to play it to exhaustion, but today most fly fishers like to use as heavy a tippet as possible and prefer to fight a fish with a strategy that allows a quick release. In

fact, in fishing for **tarpon**, where the most exciting part of the event is the initial strike and the first jumps (followed by a long, slogging battle that can tire both the angler and the fish), some fly fishers will use a barbless hook and purposely break off the fish early in the fight. This is especially common in waters where **sharks** are common, as a shark can make quick work of an exhausted tarpon that has just been released.

Playing a small trout or **panfish** can be as simple as just stripping in line and quickly releasing the fish. Neither of these fish is strong enough to pull any line from the reel or break a tippet, so playing them requires no special skill or strategy.

Playing large trout, salmon, **steelhead**, and most saltwater species requires varying degrees of strategy, depending on the size and energy of the fish. A common question is: "How do I know when to play a fish from the reel?" In other words, when do you switch from just stripping in a fish to letting it pull line from the reel? This question is usually answered by the fish, as when a **bonefish** or steelhead is strong enough to pull line from your reel, it will pull any slack you have in your hands in a flash and will begin pulling line from the reel. It's usually best not to try to snub a fish that has made a sudden run as even a four-pound fish can break a heavy tippet if you try to stop its first run. The only situation where you'd want to take a different approach is when a fish like a salmon is headed for a fast rapid below which is an impassable falls. In this case, two options are available: One is to tighten down on the reel drag or snub the fish by holding the line or applying pressure to the rim of the reel spool and hoping that the fish turns before breaking the tippet. The other is to suddenly strip as much slack line as possible from the reel, hoping the fish senses a release in pressure and swims back **upstream**, thinking it is free.

One of the most important points in the initial part of the game is to clear any excess slack line through the **guides** as the fish is running. If line gets tangled on a boat cleat or around a reel handle when a fish is running, the usual outcome is a broken tippet and a lost fly. Thus it's important to make sure, while fishing, that excess line does not catch on any projections on the deck of a boat, or any weeds or brush at the feet of a wading angler. Another smart move is to do what bonefish guides call "the crucifix," which is to bring your casting hand and line stripping hand as far apart as possible during the initial run of a fish, until all the slack line has cleared the guides. By doing this, it's less likely that the fly line will wrap around the reel handle or the butt of the rod.

In open water with no logs, sharp rocks, coral, or other obstructions in the way, its best to let the fish run until it slows or stops—this might be 5 feet with a 12-inch trout or 400 yards with a **tuna** or **sailfish**. Once the fish has slowed, regain as much line as possible by pumping the rod to just below the vertical on the upstroke and reeling line on the downstroke. Most fish will make multiple runs, so be prepared at any time for a sudden surge and lower the rod and keep your hand away from the reel handle as the fish runs again. With very strong fish like tarpon, sailfish, or sharks, it's important to fight the fish as aggressively as possible with no letup in pressure, as a fish that is rested can outlast an angler, and the quicker its spirit is broken and it realizes it cannot win, the shorter the battle. Fish that jump require a "bow." If a fish jumps and lands on a tight line, it's very easy to break the tippet. Thus, when a salmon, steelhead, or tarpon jumps, quickly lower the rod and point it at the fish as far as you can reach to increase the slack in the line. In a river, when a fish runs **downstream**, the best approach if terrain allows is to run down the bank until your position is downstream of the fish, because a fish will run against opposing pressure and thus will fight against the current, which tires it quicker.

Once the fight is at close quarters, the fish should be "led" in one direction or another. Fighting a fish with a rod straight overhead does not allow you to control a fish as well as playing the fish at an angle, where you can put more pressure on it. If the fish wants to run to the left, hold your rod low and to the right and apply as much pressure as you can. Once you turn a fish's head, change your angle to the opposite direction so that you are constantly putting pressure on the fish. If a fish is running straight for a log, fighting it with a rod straight in front of you will assure that the fish continues to bolt for that log, as it will move against opposing pressure. It's much better to apply pressure to one side or another so that by pulling against the pressure the fish moves away from the obstruction.

For most fish up to 20 pounds or so, like **striped bass**, bonefish, large trout, steelhead, and salmon, once the angler can get the fish's head above water the fish is beaten and they can often be slid over the net quite easily. When fighting a very large fish with a heavy tippet, it's always advisable to play the fish low and to one side, as that allows the angler to use the **butt** of the rod, where all the lifting power is located. Especially with tarpon, the "down and dirty" angle keeps pulling the fish to the bottom and keeps it off balance, where it has to fight harder than if its head is upright.

Most fish are lost and rods are broken at close quarters. A fly rod is not meant to be bent at a 180 degree angle, and by lifting the rod straight back or straight overhead even a very strong rod can be broken on a small fish. Pressure must always be kept to one side, whether in a boat or wading in a river, and with a tired fish it will go wherever its head is pointed. When netting a fish, the net should be submerged and the fish should be led over the top of the net, which is lifted quickly once the body of the fish is above the net. In a river with a big fish where no one is available to help net a fish, the angler should look for a piece of slow, shallow water where the fish can be led in order to beach it, as once a fish is in water so shallow it has to lie on its side it can be easily approached and released. In a boat, a tired fish should be led with side pressure so that it is close to another person, who will either grab the fish or the leader. Once someone has control of the fish, immediately release all pressure on the rod to prevent it from breaking because a fish close to the boat puts a rod at a dangerously extreme angle.

POCKET WATER

Pocket water is moving water with a high gradient and large rocks, anywhere from bowling-ball-sized to house-sized. It is characterized by lots of turbulence and conflicting currents, white foamy spots interspersed with **riffles** and smooth spots that indicate slower and deeper water, and lots of dissolved oxygen. Because of the relatively high dissolved oxygen content, pocket water is a refuge for trout and **smallmouth bass** during midsummer, when slower **pools** do not hold enough dissolved oxygen to support them.

Pocket water is easier to fish than slower water because fish cannot see the angler as well, and the turbulence hides the disturbance of a sloppy cast. However, because of the many conflicting currents, pocket water can make presenting the fly with a **drag**-free float tough, as the swirling water pulls the line and **leader** in opposing directions. The best way to fish pocket water is with very short casts, sometimes keeping all the **fly line** off the water and only allowing the fly and leader to touch it. Keeping the tip of the **fly rod** high, at about a 45-degree angle from the horizontal, helps keep most of the line off the water. Because visibility is difficult in the foamy water, **dry flies** should utilize highly visible wings, and **Wulff**-style flies and **parachute** patterns are popular. **Nymphs** are easiest to fish using a **strike indicator**, which shows when a fish has taken the submerged fly and also allows the angler to track where the fly is drifting. Large **mayflies** and **caddisflies** are plentiful in pocket water, but **stoneflies** are especially abundant because their flattened shape and high oxygen requirements are best met in pocket water. Imitations of stonefly dries and **nymphs** can be deadly in pocket water when the cast-off-shucks of the nymphs are seen on streamside rocks, a sure indication they have been hatching.

When fishing pocket water, it's important to remember that as many trout will be found in front of rocks and along their sides as behind the rocks. The fast current digs a trench along all edges of a rock, and it is often easier for a trout to feed in front of a rock or along its edges than it is to lie behind a rock, where the current may be weaker but not as much food drifts. In shallow pocket water, look for the smooth places without foam that indicate the deeper pockets where trout may be hiding.

POND FISHING

See Lake Fishing.

POOL

A pool is any place in a stream where fast water dumps into deeper water, forming a deep bowl where trout or other stream fish will congregate. Pools can be the size of a bathroom sink on small

mountain streams, or they can be over a mile long in large rivers. Pools are formed by a sudden drop in elevation, the result of a stream running against a high bank, or just a pile of rocks that slows the flow of water. Without interference by man or flash floods, most rivers form a sinuous progression of pools and **riffles** due to the constant erosion and deposition of streambed materials.

In most pools, the easiest place to fish is the head, where fast water begins to slow. The rough water at the head of the pool hides the approach of the angler and casting mistakes, and usually a shelf forms, with fast water above that brings drifting food, but with a slower current close to the bottom that allows fish to hold in the current without wasting energy. The productivity of the middle of a pool depends on the degree of structure, both on the bottom and along the banks. If the middle of a pool is mostly sand or fine gravel, it won't support many fish. However, if the middle of a pool is strewn with larger rocks or submerged logs, it will provide more protection from predators and from the current and will hold more fish. If the middle of a pool is deeper along one side, with the main current flowing close to the bank, it will also hold more fish. The greater the number of downed trees, rocks, or points of land projecting out into the pool, the more fish the bank will hold. The tail of a pool is the most difficult part of a pool to fish because the shallow water allows fish to see the angler's approach easily. However, tails of pools concentrate flow and food, and often the largest trout in a pool will feed in the tail, especially during heavy hatches of aquatic insects.

All pools have hotspots where fish will congregate. Trout will be found where there is protection from predators close at hand as well as a main thread of current to supply drifting food. Migrating fish like **steelhead** and salmon will typically occupy places close to the main flow of current, but exactly where they will lie during their migration is often known to knowledgeable anglers and guides. (A spot that looks perfect may not hold fish because of some unknown aspect of the hydraulics that only the fish understand.) Both trout and migratory species may prefer the same lies for decades, until a catastrophic flood changes the stream bed.

POPPER

Poppers are floating flies that utilize foam, cork, and buoyant plastic or hollow hair from the belly of a deer to keep them on the surface. They are larger and more colorful than the **dry flies** used for trout. Unlike dry flies, the intention is to move the fly across the surface making a disturbance that will attract a game fish. Poppers are most commonly used in fresh water for **largemouth bass**, **smallmouth bass**, **pike**, and **panfish**. In salt water, larger versions are deadly on **striped bass**, **bluefish**, **sailfish**, **sharks**, **redfish**, and **snook**. Most poppers have a concave "face" in front of the fly, which produces a gurgling noise when the fly is moved through the water. However, a style of popper called a slider has a pointed head that makes fewer disturbances on the water, and is especially useful when fish shy away from a noisy conventional popper or fish are feeding on crippled **baitfish** on the surface.

Poppers may look and sound like a frog or crippled baitfish swimming along the surface. They may sound like another fish is feeding on the surface, making the fish react to what is perceived as a feeding frenzy. Poppers may just attract a hungry fish with a nonspecific commotion that seems to indicate something alive struggling on the surface.

The way a popper is retrieved can be varied by the angler depending on conditions. Freshwater bass and striped bass on a calm day may actually take a popper that has been cast and allowed to remain motionless for several minutes. The rubber legs, **hackle** feathers, or bucktail used to adorn the tail of the popper may create enough movement to make the fish **strike**. Sometimes a gentle line strip that makes the popper gurgle once will induce a strike. Often, a slow but steady **retrieve** with short pauses in between each pull of the line is effective, especially for smallmouth bass in rivers. At the other end of the scale, bluefish and **barracuda** prefer a popper that moves as fast as the angler can strip, and if the fly pauses even for a second the fish will likely turn away.

Poppers made out of cork, foam, and hard plastic like urethane are the most durable. The body of these flies is painted with enamel and often coated with a thin coat of epoxy for durability. Tails are tied onto the rear of the **hook** and are usually made from hackle feathers, bucktail, or flashy synthetic materials. Rubber legs are often added to the tail and threaded through the body for added movement. The most popular colors are black, chartreuse, red-and-white, yellow, and blue-and-white, although any color or combination of colors has been used. For freshwater bass fishing, the popper will often be painted in the colors of a frog, with a white or yellow body, green back, and yellow or black spots. Poppers can also be made from spun and trimmed hair from the belly of a deer, elk, or caribou. This hollow hair contains air chambers that help float the fly, and the softer body of the fly may look more realistic and may also make the fish hold onto the fly longer. Different colors of hair can be used when spinning the fly, and very beautiful and artistic shapes and colors can be created. Deer hair poppers (or bugs as they are commonly called) eventually absorb water and don't float as well, and they are not as durable as hard-bodied poppers so they are seldom used in salt water, where the sharp teeth

of most saltwater fish will destroy one in short order. Poppers range in size from tiny ½ inch panfish versions to eight inches or larger (including the tail) for sailfish. The most common sizes for freshwater and striped bass are from two to four inches long.

POWER STROKE
See Overhead Cast.

PUPA

Insects with complete metamorphosis have a pupa stage in between the **larva** and winged adult. Among the most common aquatic insects that trout eat, only **caddisflies** and **midges** go through complete metamorphosis and have a pupal form. Although this stage is short in duration, usually from two to three weeks, pupae are consumed more than any other life stage of these insects because the pupa that rises to the surface is available to drift-feeding trout.

Pupae are comma-shaped with a thin abdomen and bulbous thorax, where the unformed wings of the adult are stored. Most are relatively dull in color, ranging from almost black to various shades of brown, olive, and gray to cream-colored. The larva transforms into a pupa while still on the bottom of a river—in the case of many species of caddisflies when the larva is still in its stick or stone case. Just prior to hatching, gas bubbles

P

form inside the exoskeleton of the pupa, which gives it the buoyancy to rise to the surface. Some pupae rocket to the surface quickly, while others drift for hundreds of feet and may rise up and down in the water column several times, giving trout a good opportunity to capture one. A few species of caddisfly pupae swim very quickly just under the surface prior to **hatching**, but most caddisflies and all midge pupae drift helplessly while struggling to emerge as an adult. The rise form of a trout may betray the type of pupa it is eating—ones that skitter across the current or pop to the surface quickly produce explosive rises from the trout, while trout feeding on emerging pupae drifting in the film will be quiet and sedate.

Imitations of pupae are generally divided into drifting pupae, which are typically fished deep in the water column and imitated by a weighted nymph, to pupae at the moment of changing into a winged adult, which are imitated with a **dry fly** or **emerger**. When fishing a deep pupa imitation, the fly should be fished **dead drift** close to the bottom with an occasional quick lift to the surface to mimic a pupa rising through the water column. Emerging pupae should be fished completely dead drift.

PVDF
See Leader, Tippet.

Quill Gordon

QUARTERING
See Across-Stream.

QUILL GORDON
The Quill Gordon is the quintessential Catskill **dry fly**. Developed by **Theodore Gordon** at the turn of the twentieth century, it was the first dry fly ever tied in the distinctly American style, with upright wings of duck flank feather and long, stiff **hackles** for flotation. In contrast, the dry flies used in America prior to this fly were English patterns with less hackle and more delicate construction, as they were developed for the more placid English meadow streams in contrast to the tumbling mountain rivers more common in North America. The Quill Gordon is still a popular dry fly today. The tails are made from stiff hackle fibers from a blue dun (natural gray) chicken hackle. The body is wound from a peacock tail quill that has been stripped of its flue. The wings are made from the speckled flank feather of a wood duck, and the hackle is hackle wound from the same colored hackle as the tail. The fly is most often used in sizes 12 through 16.

Although it is likely that Gordon designed the fly to imitate a number of **mayfly** species, the fly resembles the *Epeorus plueralis* mayfly so closely that most fly fishers call this mayfly a "Quill Gordon." Thus the insect has gained the moniker of the fly that imitates it. The actual Quill Gordon mayfly is common only to very cold, pristine trout waters and is the first large mayfly of the season to hatch, anywhere from late March in North Carolina to mid-April in the Adirondacks. However, the Quill Gordon artificial catches trout throughout the season, any time thin grayish mayflies are on the water. Because of its thin segmented body, the Quill Gordon fly is also an excellent imitation of mayfly **spinners**.

Rogers fancy

R

RAINBOW TROUT

The rainbow trout, *Oncorhynchus mykiss*, is native to streams of the Pacific Coast of North America from the Tropic of Cancer in Mexico to the Arctic Circle in **Alaska**. Across the Bering Sea, it is also native to rivers of the Okhotsk Sea on the Kamchatka Peninsula and in the Commander Islands. Because the rainbow trout is the easiest of all trout species to transport and grow in hatcheries, it was transplanted throughout North America and to temperate rivers throughout the world, from **Argentina** and **Chile** to **New Zealand**, throughout Europe, and even into the mountains of Kenya. Today, there are populations of rainbow trout on every continent except Antarctica, and in every state except **Florida**, **Louisiana**, and Mississippi.

The taxonomy of rainbow trout has been confusing over the centuries. Originally thought of as a single species, by the middle of the twentieth century taxonomists had identified what they thought were 15 different species of rainbows. But by the

1990s, genetic studies suggested only a single species, and the trout that was originally called *Salmo gairdneri* (*Salmo* being the genus of **Atlantic salmon** and European **brown trout**) was changed to *Oncorhynchus mykiss* to reflect the fish's closer kinship to **Pacific salmon**. To compound matters even further, rainbow trout will hybridize with the closely related **cutthroat trout** and relatively rare species of trout like the Apache trout and Gila trout of the southwest, along with the **golden trout** of California. Although ichthyologists now lump rainbows into the more colorful redband variety and the duller-colored coastal variety, hatcheries have mixed the strains in the past 100 years so that stocked fish are a true amalgamation of various races and strains. **Steelhead trout** are merely rainbows that, if given access to the ocean, have a genetic predilection to becoming anadromous and use the rich waters of the ocean to grow very large on a diet of marine **baitfish** and crustaceans, returning to freshwater to spawn.

Rainbow trout are identified by their abundant

black spots on the back, dorsal fin, and tail. All races show a red stripe along the sides to some degree— it may be very faint pink or bright red. The belly ranges from pale yellow to white, and the back can be silvery, bluish-gray, or olive. The redband variety is more colorful overall and has distinctly white-tipped dorsal, pelvic, and anal fins, plus blotchy purple parr marks (oval-shaped marks that are commonly found only on young trout and salmon or parr), and the cheeks are rose colored with a dark spot behind the eye. The coastal varieties are duller overall, without the distinct parr marks, white-tipped dorsal fin, and cheek blotch.

Where rainbow trout are found, they prefer faster **riffles** and **runs** to **pools**, although they will also be found in slower pools and in **spring creeks** if the food supply is abundant. It is said that rainbows prefer more oxygenated water, but recent studies suggest that rainbows feed more frequently than other species of trout and are more efficient at converting even tiny **midge larvae** to body weight, thus they are found in the fastest current where food is delivered in the highest quantity. It is this aspect that endears rainbows to the fly fisher, because where brown trout seem to feed only when food is abundant, especially at dawn and dusk, rainbow trout continue to feed throughout the day. Even large rainbow

trout eat tiny insects, thus are more commonly taken on the fly.

The best places to catch large rainbow trout in their native range are the streams of the Bristol Bay region of Alaska and in the inland streams of Kamchatka. Nearly pure strains of the redband trout are probably found only in the headwaters of the McCloud River in **California**, as most of the rivers in the lower 48 states where native rainbows once existed have been genetically diluted by a century of stocking. Although rainbow trout fishing is superb in **Montana**, **Wyoming**, and **Colorado**, it's often surprising for anglers to find out that rainbow trout are not native to most rivers of the Rocky Mountains except for the upper Kootenai River drainage in the extreme northwest corner of Montana. In the southern hemisphere, the best rainbow trout fishing is found on the North Island of New Zealand, and in the rivers of Patagonia in Chile and Argentina.

The optimum temperature for rainbow trout is from 56 degrees to 70 degrees Fahrenheit, although some local populations have evolved to feed in much lower and higher temperatures. In this temperature range, rainbows feed heavily and when hooked, put up a spirited battle that often includes spectacular leaps similar to their cousins the steelhead.

REACH CAST

See Overhead Cast.

RED QUILL

As in many trout fly patterns, the term Red Quill refers to both an artificial fly and the insect it imitates. The artificial fly was first tied by **Art Flick** in the 1930s, and uses dark blue dun chicken **hackle** for tails and hackle, barred wood duck flank for wings, and a body made from the stem of a Rhode Island Red rooster hackle. Usually tied in sizes 12 through 16, the fly imitates both the **dun** and **spinner** stage of many different **mayfly** species, particularly those with a rusty red body and gray wings. Mayflies known as "Red Quills" include the male dun and spinner of the *Ephemerella subvaria* mayfly, the *Paraleptophlebia adoptiva* mayfly, and the spinner of the Western **Green Drake**, *Drunella grandis*.

REDD

A redd is a nest made by female fish, most often used in reference to trout and salmon. Females dig into gravel on the bottom of a stream by thrusting their bodies sideways, making repeated wiggling motions, and then fanning the gravel with their tails. By clearing the bottom in this manner, the female ensures that eggs are laid into spaces between pieces of fine gravel, free of silt that might suffocate the eggs. Redds can be identified as circular or oval-shaped spots of clean gravel, most often in the tail of a **pool**. Redds can be the size of a saucer in the case of **brook trout** to ten feet in diameter for large salmon. In some fisheries (like wild trout or **steelhead** rivers) fishing near redds is considered poor etiquette, but often fish like **rainbow trout**, steelhead, and **Arctic char** take up a position downstream of redds of Pacific salmon, and in places like Alaska where salmon eggs are the main source of food for other fish, imitating this source of food may be the only way to catch fish.

REDFISH

The redfish, *Sciaenops ocellatus*, is a very popular saltwater gamefish that takes a fly very well. Also known as the red drum, puppy drum, or channel bass, it is found along the Gulf Coast from **Texas** through **Florida**, and its range also extends along the Atlantic Coast to **North Carolina**. Smaller redfish, from 2 to 20 pounds, are found in shallow water throughout the year, and larger fish, up to 40 pounds or more, are typically found offshore in deeper water, except when they move into shallow water in late summer and fall for spawning. Redfish feed on small **baitfish**, crabs, and shrimp, making them ideal fish for the fly rod.

Redfish feed over shallow grass beds, oyster bars, and mud flats. Although they feed on the same kind of food as **bonefish**, redfish are often found in deeper, murkier water than bonefish, and their eyesight is not as acute. Where a bonefish may spot a moving fly from 10 feet away, it's often necessary to place the fly within a foot or two of a redfish's nose. Thus, flies used for redfish are bigger and brighter: **Clouser Minnows**, **Deceivers**, Sea Ducers, and similar **streamers** from two to four inches long are some of the most popular flies. **Crab flies** from half-dollar to silver dollar size are also very effective for redfish. Redfish may also respond to small **poppers** at times, although a popper should be fished with gentle twitches rather than aggressive pops.

Although redfish can be caught blind-fishing with a **sinking fly line** and streamer pattern over a

deep channel, most fly fishers prefer to cast to visible fish in shallow water. If the sun is high, redfish can be seen cruising the shallows, where their pinkish-red tones give them away. When bottom food is abundant, redfish will stop and "tail" over choice spots, and if the water is shallow enough their tails will wave above the surface, making them easy to spot from a hundred yards away on a calm day. If the fish themselves are not visible, anglers look for wakes in calm water or muddy spots in the water where a school of redfish has disturbed the bottom.

When redfish are seen cruising, it's best to place the fly from 6 to 10 feet ahead of the fish's expected direction so that it sinks close to the bottom, **retrieving** the fly with short strips and a distinct pause in between each strip as the fish swims by. When redfish are tailing, or if a patch of muddy water in an otherwise clear area is spotted, the fly should be cast as close as possible to the fish (or right into the cloud of mud). With a crab fly, a single twitch is usually enough to get a redfish to inhale the fly.

The perfect **fly rod** for smaller redfish in shallow water is a 9-foot rod that calls for an 8-weight fly line. This rod will cast the larger flies with ease, and is more than heavy enough to subdue even a large redfish. For very windy days, or when targeting spawning redfish of 20 pounds or more, a 9-weight rod may be a batter choice. Redfish are not spectacular fighters, so a **fly reel** that holds 200 yards of **backing** will be more than enough. Most redfish are caught with a floating fly line, but for deeper channels a full-sinking or **sink-tip line** may be helpful. A 9-foot leader with a 12-pound **tippet** is about the only leader needed for redfish.

Although redfish can be caught throughout their range with a fly rod, certain places are known for their concentrations of fish in shallow water. The Laguna Madre region in south Texas is one of the best places to catch redfish on a fly rod. In Louisiana the vast islands of Chandeler Sound are a vast wilderness where redfish abound, including some big offshore fish that come into shallow water in late summer. In Florida, Apalachicola Bay, Charlotte Bay, and Florida Bay offer the best fly-fishing opportunities on the west coast, and the Mosquito Lagoon on the east coast has the most extensive flats and best opportunities to catch a redfish on a fly. Along the **Georgia** coast, St. Simon's Island, Sea Island, and Jekyll Island offer good shallow water fishing, especially in spring and fall. In South Carolina, the extensive bays and flats of Cape Romain National Wildlife Refuge are especially productive. Although the North Carolina coast has smaller redfish in shallow water year-round, huge fish up to 40 pounds congregate to spawn each August and September around the mouths of the Pamlico and Neuse Rivers.

REEL SEAT
See Fly Rod.

RELEASING FISH

The best way to release a fish unharmed is to **play** the fish quickly and remove the fly without touching the fish. This means using the heaviest **tippet** possible to fool the fish (using very light tippets is not "more sporting"), playing the fish cleverly, using a **net**, and having a pair of **forceps** or pliers ready so the fly can be twisted free of the fish without lifting it from the water. Pinching the barb of the **hook** flat before using can make hook removal much easier.

During the fight, fish use up glycogen and build up lactic acid in their white muscles, which are used for burst swimming when escaping from predators. Expelling the lactic acid and replacing glycogen in the muscles can take some time, but the quicker a fish is brought to net, the quicker it can revive. It may be necessary to hold the fish upright in gentle current, or move the fish slowly back and forth in still water until the fish gains enough strength to escape from your gentle grasp under its own power. The best place to revive a fish is in a gentle current free of silt, in order to transfer as much dissolved oxygen as possible past through the gills. For a large fish caught in warm water, where dissolved oxygen concentration is low and glycogen replacement is slow, it may take up to five minutes to revive a fish properly.

Using a net with soft cotton, rubber, or nylon mesh greatly facilitates a safe release. A fish should be kept in the water and supported by the net while the hook is removed. If the fish is handled at all, hands should be wet before touching the fish, as dry hands can remove a protective mucus layer on a fish's skin that protects it from bacterial and fungal diseases. Removing a fish from the water not only deprives its gills of oxygen, a fish's anatomy is not built to support its internal organs out of water. If a photograph of a trophy fish with an angler is desired, the photographer should pre-focus the lens and be prepared while the angler supports the fish's body and lifts it just above the water for a brief instant.

When fishing for **bonefish**, where nets are not often employed, a fish can be kept in the water and immobilized by gently stroking the forehead of the fish while removing the fly without a struggle. Then the fish should be revived by gently moving it back and forth in clean water, away from silt-laden water the angler might have stirred up by wading.

Members of the **tuna** family need a great deal of oxygen passing through their gills and standard release techniques are not effective. The best way to release a tuna, **bonito**, or **false albacore** is to

gently lift the fish from the water, supporting its belly as much as possible, and then throwing the fish headfirst into the water with as much force as possible. This seems to supercharge the amount of oxygen that gets to the gills.

RETRIEVE

Fly fishers only use the reel to gather line when moving from one spot to another, or to **play** a fast-running fish. Otherwise, line is manipulated by using one or more retrieves. Line that is retrieved is either held in loose coils, dropped on the surface of the water or deck of a boat, or kept from tangling with a **stripping basket**.

SINGLE-HANDED STRIP

The single-handed strip is the retrieve used most often by fly fishers. After the cast is made, the line is brought over to the rod hand and placed over the index or middle finger. The line hand then reaches behind the rod hand and pulls line, while the finger of the rod hand keeps tension on the line. If a fish **strikes**, the rod is raised and the finger of the rod hand pinches the line to keep tension on it. Alternatively, when using a strip strike, the finger of the rod hand puts slightly more tension on the line, but the **hook** is set by pulling quickly and firmly straight back with the line hand.

When fishing with a **dry fly** or **nymph**, where the fly is cast **upstream**, the angler watches how fast the current drifts and strips line only enough to keep up with the current, so there is always a tight line between the rod tip and the fly. When actively moving a **streamer** or saltwater fly, the line hand controls the speed of the fly. To make the fly dart through the water, line is stripped about eight inches at a time. The longer the pause between strips, the more the fly sinks in between each strip. Shorter

strips are best for smaller flies, because smaller **baitfish** and crustaceans don't have the power to move more than a few inches at a time. For large baitfish imitations, the angler might make 20-inch strips with little pause in between. A slow, steady movement of the fly can be obtained by making a slow strip as far as the line hand can reach, then quickly reaching back to the rod hand to begin the next slow strip.

In all cases, the rod tip should point at the fly. Moving the rod tip off to one side to move the fly makes it difficult to control the line, makes it difficult to set the hook, and makes subsequent strips almost impossible. When wading, unless the water is filled with weeds or the current is very fast, most fly fishers just strip the line onto the water, where it will be handy for the next cast. When fishing from the bank, it might be necessary to pinch coils of line between the thumb and forefinger of the line hand so that loose line does not tangle in streamside brush. When fishing from a boat, line that is stripped should be placed carefully on the deck, away from cleats and other gear that can tangle the line, making casting easier and preventing a snag when a hard-running fish pulls line quickly. If a boat is jammed with fixtures that cannot be removed, line can be stripped onto a piece of netting or into a bucket to keep it from blowing around and getting caught in snags.

HAND-TWIST RETRIEVE

The hand-twist retrieve is the one that old-time **wet fly** fishers learned first because it crawls line slowly upstream at a speed and cadence that seems to appeal to fish. It is a good retrieve to use any time a slow, steady movement of the fly is desirable, and is especially effective when **night fishing**, because fish feeding at night will seldom strike a fast-moving fly. The hand-twist retrieve has the advantage of storing neat coils in the palm of the line hand, but is difficult to use in fast current or when a fly must be moved quickly, as it cannot gather line rapidly.

To perform a hand-twist retrieve, the line does not have to be hooked over a finger of the rod hand. With the line hand grasping the fly line between thumb and forefinger, reach up along the line, palm down, twisting the hand sideways, until the pinky of the line hand catches the line. The palm then rotates up, pulling about four inches of line back toward the angler. This line is then palmed while the thumb and forefinger reach up to grab the next length of line. The process is repeated until the hand is full of line coils or the fly has reached the end of the retrieve. When making the next cast, the coils are kept in the palm until the forward **power stroke**, and the palm is then opened, allowing the coils of line to unwind and shoot through the **guides**. The process is easier than it sounds and can be learned in just a few minutes.

TWO-HANDED STRIP

When angling for fish like **barracuda**, **tuna**, and **bluefish** that prefer a very fast retrieve, the best way to strip line is with a two-handed retrieve. To make this retrieve, the rod is tucked under the arm of the casting hand and line is stripped with both hands, using the same motion as climbing a rope. Because this retrieve gathers a lot of line quickly, it is often used in conjunction with a stripping basket so that the loose line does not tangle at the angler's feet. Although not used for a slow retrieve as often, the same motion, performed in slow motion, can make a fly swim through the water at a steady rate without pausing. It's often a good idea to try the two-handed strip just for a change of pace when fish don't seem to respond to a single-handed strip.

RHODE ISLAND

OVERVIEW

Although Rhode Island does have some stocked trout rivers in the southern part of the state and many ponds that have stocked trout or bass and **pike**, the main attraction of the little state is its 400-mile shoreline. Saltwater fly fishing from boats, **jetties**, or beaches is some of the most productive in New England, and the fishing holds up well throughout the summer. Unlike **Massachusetts** and Connecticut, where shallow sounds cause warm summer water temperatures, Rhode Island's coastline does not have a barrier to the open ocean, so cold North Atlantic waters keep gamefish active throughout the summer. The ponds and bays along the coast of Rhode Island also produce vast quantities of **baitfish**, which attract saltwater gamefish throughout the season.

FISHERIES

The Wood River in Arcadia Wildlife Management Area is Rhode Island's best trout stream. The main river is stocked annually with large trout, and wild **brook trout** still exist in some of its tributaries. The river's placid currents are easy to wade, and its tea-colored water serves up **hatches** of most of the major **mayflies** of the east, including the giant **Hex** mayfly—the river's best hatch and one that brings its large **brown trout** to the surface. Other trout streams in Rhode Island include the Pawcatuck, Moosup, and Fall Rivers, all located in the southern part of the state. The Pawtucket River also hosts an annual run of sea-run brown trout, supported by a fry stocking program of over 20,000 young fish each year.

For such a small state, Rhode Island has a diverse saltwater fishery. At various times of the year, the inshore fly fisher can catch **striped bass**, **bluefish**, **weakfish**, **false albacore**, **bonito**, bluefin **tuna**,

and skipjack tuna. From Newport north to the Massachusetts border, the coastline is rocky with many opportunities to fish from shore. Just outside of Newport are various parkways where the fly fisher can drive and wade carefully along the slippery rocks for the abundant striped bass and bluefish. Narragansett Bay has good populations of both species as well: Fishing in the Bay for striped bass is best in spring during the day and at night throughout the summer.

South of Newport, the Point Judith area is known for its superb fly fishing from shore and from a boat. At the mouth of Point Judith Pond are two long jetties, the West Wall and East Wall, with deep water on both sides and the ability to find an easy place to cast in almost any wind direction. Both jetties provide a place for shore fly casters to get into false albacore. West of Point Judith are breach ways at the outlet of Quonochontaug Pond and Weepaug Pond. These are narrow channels bordered by rock jetties that spew hordes of baitfish into the ocean on outgoing tides, and draw striped bass, bluefish, and false albacore into the ponds on incoming tides. Both the jetties at the outlets of these ponds and the ponds themselves provide incredible opportunities for the shorebound fly fisher, with equally good fishing from a boat in the offshore areas.

The area around Watch Hill and Napatree point are also excellent for fly fishers, but shore fishing is more limited in these places. The rip just off Watch Hill features striped bass throughout the summer in large numbers, as well as bonito, false albacore, and small bluefin tuna later in the summer. Twelve miles offshore lies Block Island, one of the finest places on the East Coast for striped bass and false albacore. Good fishing will be found all around the island, but the shorebound fly fisher will probably have the best luck in the entrance to Great Salt Pond by the Coast Guard Station. This area offers the best concentration of baitfish on the island, and is especially productive for bluefish, striped bass, and false albacore.

SEASON

Trout fishing in Rhode Island heats up in April, when the Black Quill mayflies hatch on the Wood River and other Rhode Island trout waters. The Hex hatch begins in June and lasts into early July, and is the best time to catch large trout in Rhode Island. Rhode Island trout streams get relatively warm in summer and offer inconsistent fishing, but once waters cool off in the fall the activity picks up again. Saltwater fishing begins in late April and May, when migrating striped bass enter the shallow bays and harbors along the coast. Bluefish arrive in late May, and are active throughout the summer and sometimes into November. Bonito come inshore chasing the abundant baitfish in late July through early September, and false albacore arrive a few weeks later and may stay until early November. Small bluefin tuna, often accompanied by skipjack tuna and bonito, first start to show off Rhode Island in late July and stay until late October, although these species are not as dependable as the other fish and may not show up in great numbers every year.

RIFFLE

Riffles are the pastureland of trout streams. At the bottoms of deep pools scant light penetrates to encourage the growth of algae and diatoms, the main food source of many insect **larvae**. Those insect larvae that don't eat these foods filter particles of leaves and other organic debris from the water, and only the fast current of riffles supplies enough food to support them. Most adult aquatic insects lay their eggs in riffles. And tiny **baitfish** find security from bigger fish in the shallow water and broken surface of a riffle. All other things being equal, a trout stream with an equal amount of riffles and pools will support more and bigger trout than a river that consists mostly of deep pools.

As long as the water is over two feet deep and a sanctuary of deeper water, rocks, or logs is nearby, trout will live and feed in riffles. A small deep slot in a riffle the size of a bathtub might hold several adult trout, while a large, deep riffle might hold hundreds of them. For instance, the Madison River in Montana between Quake Lake and Ennis is almost 50 miles of straight riffle without a single classic pool, yet this piece of river holds tens of thousands of trout of all sizes and is one of the finest trout streams in the world because of its abundant food supply.

Riffles are the pastureland of trout streams.

In trout streams that offer a combination of riffles and pools, most anglers immediately head for the pools because they know trout will be found there, and often the biggest ones. Yet pools are more difficult to fish, and the fish living in pools see crowds of anglers throughout the season. Trout in riffles are not disturbed as much and thus may be easier to fool, plus the broken water of a riffle makes presenting the fly without disturbing the trout easier. In riffles, look for smooth, dark spots that indicate deeper and faster water than the rest of the riffle. If these spots run along a bank, the likelihood of finding trout there is increased, because rocks, logs, and points of land along the bank all provide the trout with added protection from predators and relief from the fast current.

RIFFLING HITCH

The riffling hitch is a half hitch taken over the head of a salmon fly to make it skitter across the current, just under the surface. Also called the Portland hitch because it was first used by local fly fishers for **Atlantic salmon** on Newfoundland's Portland Creek, it is a deadly method on salmon and summer **steelhead** rivers where the fish seem to be attracted to wakes on the surface. The hitch is also sometimes used on trout flies, especially when trout chase adult **caddis** skittering across the surface.

To make a Portland hitch, a half hitch is made in the **tippet** just in front of the fly, and the hitch is tightened down over the head of the fly. In order to wake properly, the hitch must extend from the correct side of the fly. The easiest way to remember which side to put the hitch on is to look at the fly from the side and point the eye of the fly upstream. The hitch should come from the side of the fly facing you.

ROLL CAST

The roll cast is a simple cast, typically used in tight spots because the line only travels a few feet behind the angler. Commonly used in small trout streams, it can also be helpful when **wading** along a deep, brushy bank on large rivers or from a boat when a standard forward cast might place the fly in a radio antenna or in the anatomy of a guide or fellow angler. Because it is not as easy to shoot line with a roll cast, because it won't cast as long a line, and because for most anglers it is not as accurate as the standard **overhead cast**, the roll cast is typically used only when necessary.

To perform a roll cast, bring the rod tip slowly off slightly to your outside and behind you until an arc of line forms behind the rod (figures 1). The rod should be moved to the rear so slowly that the line does not pick up off the water or travel more than two feet behind the caster (figure 2). Once the arc of line is formed (figure 3), the cast is the same as

R

the traditional overhead cast, with a quick acceleration into a **power stroke** followed by a dead stop. A loop will form just in front of the rod, which then rolls out over the water, straightens, and drops (figures 4 & 5).

A roll cast will not develop the same line speed as an overhead cast, so it is not as efficient a cast when faced with a headwind. It is also not very useful for drying the water off a **dry fly** because the fly does not leave the water for very long.

The roll cast can be used as a prelude to an overhead cast, in which case it is called a roll cast pickup. Make a single roll cast, and just as the loop unfurls but before it touches the water, begin a

3)

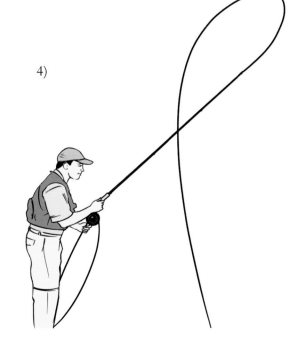

1)

2)

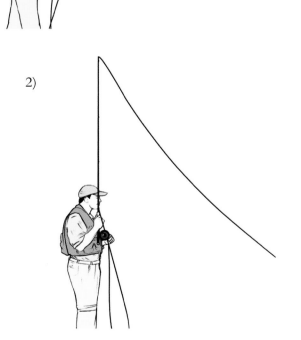

4)

5)

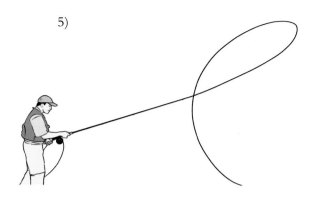

thicker joints of peacock herl separated by a thinner band in between may also suggest a large carpenter **ant** to the fish. It has been one of the most popular dry flies in the world for three-quarters of a century.

standard overhead **back cast** and then a forward cast or **false cast**. The roll cast pickup is useful when picking up a short amount of line, where a standard back cast will not bend the rod enough to develop casting power.

It is not easy to change the direction of the line when making a roll cast because the loop may catch on the rod when rolling forward. In this case, a variation of the roll cast called **Spey cast** (actually a series of casts) is used. Roll casts are better with rods over 8½ feet long, and in the case of the Spey cast are usually performed with two-handed rods anywhere from 11 to 15 feet long.

ROYAL WULFF

The Royal Wulff, developed by **Lee Wulff** in the 1930s, is a variation of the traditional Royal Coachman **dry fly**. Instead of the white duck feather wings on a traditional Royal Coachman, the fly uses more buoyant, durable, and visible bucktail and about twice as much **hackle** as a standard dry fly. Because it floats well and is easy to see, the fly is most often used in fast water. With its white wings and green peacock herl and red floss body, the fly appears to mimic nothing in nature, but once the fly gets wet its tones become a subdued dark bronze-brown and probably imitates a number of **mayflies** and **caddisflies**, or even a flying **beetle** that has fallen into the water. The two

RUSSIA

OVERVIEW

There are most likely opportunities for fly fishing throughout this giant country, but the two areas that have been extensively explored—and have the infrastructure to accommodate the traveling fly fisher—are the Kola Peninsula in northwestern Russia and the Kamchatka Peninsula in the Russian Far East. Both of these peninsulas are of strategic interest and were heavily guarded military regions in the Cold War. As a result they are still wilderness areas with limited access.

The Kola Peninsula is known as the finest destination in the world for **Atlantic salmon** fishing, both in quantity and size of fish. It also has abundant populations of sea-run and resident **brown trout**, resident **grayling**, **Arctic char**, and **northern pike**, which get almost no fishing pressure because of the emphasis on salmon fishing. The main attraction on the Kamchatka Peninsula is **rainbow trout** fishing, but the rivers there are also filled with grayling, northern pike, Arctic char, **Pacific salmon**, and khundza, a large white-spotted **char** native to Kamchatka and Siberia. Of the two destinations, the Kola Peninsula is the most accessible, with regular commercial flights through Murmansk, and then transportation either by bus or helicopter to fishing camps on the rivers. Kamchatka Rivers are only reached via helicopter from the city of Petropavlovsk, but finding air service to this city is sometimes challenging.

FISHERIES

The largest and most famous salmon river on the Kola Peninsula is the Ponoi River. It flows parallel to and just north of the Arctic Circle and is nearly 250 miles long. Despite its wide river channel, it is quite shallow; although most of the fishing is by boat, it can be waded at most water levels. Fish here tend to run smaller than some other Russian rivers, but salmon are plentiful. The Kola River is one of the most accessible rivers on the peninsula and not as wild and scenic as others, but it produces big fish. 20- to 30-pound salmon are common, and 40-pound fish are caught every season. The Umba River is even more accessible than the Kola, because it can be reached via a five-hour bus ride from Murmansk, yet is still one of the most productive salmon rivers on the peninsula. Other famous salmon rivers on the peninsula include the Varzina, Yokanga, Rynda, Litza, and Varzuga.

Russian salmon rivers can be fished with double- or single-handed **fly rods**. Early in the season (April through June), the water is high and cold and a sinking or sink-tip line and a double-handed fly rod may be necessary. By the middle of June, many anglers switch to a single-handed rod and floating line. Russian salmon are quite aggressive and many **salmon fly** patterns from Europe and North America have been used with great success. The most popular salmon flies seem to be both tube flies from one to two inches long and hair-wing salmon flies in sizes 6, 8, and 10. Best colors are orange (especially those suggesting shrimp), green, and black.

Fishing on the Kamchatka Peninsula has been described as experiencing what fishing in **Alaska** was like 50 years ago. Flying into a fishing camp in this wild and volcanic land, it is amazing how few settlements or dirt roads are seen—just vast tundra, scrubby trees, and still-smoking volcanoes. Since Kamchatka is across the Bering Strait from Alaska, fish species and fishing conditions are similar. The same species of Pacific salmon—king, chum, coho, pink, and sockeye—are found in these rivers, plus Arctic char and grayling. Two species of salmonids not found in Alaska, cherry salmon and khundza, are also abundant. However, it is the magnificent fishing for rainbow trout, probably the finest in the world, which attracts most anglers. Besides resident rainbows, there is a coastal rainbow that supposedly goes to sea at age two, spends up to three years at sea before returning to fresh water, and then spends the remainder of its life in freshwater rivers. There are also **steelhead** in Kamchatka rivers, but it is a protected species and can only be targeted by anglers with a special collector's permit.

Rainbow trout in Kamchatka seem to be more surface-oriented than Alaskan rainbows, because Russian rivers are more fertile and have good populations of **mayflies**, **stoneflies**, and **caddisflies**. Thus at certain times of the year, especially during July and August, **dry fly** and **nymph** fishing is better than in Alaska. These fish are not picky and most general **attractor** patterns work very well. Rainbows in Kamchatka are also very fond of eating mice, lemmings, and other small rodents, and a floating mouse can elicit explosive **strikes** from large rainbows, up to 30 inches long. The rainbows, along with the khundza, char, and salmon, will also strike large attractor **streamers**, especially patterns with pink, orange, or purple in them. Like rainbow trout everywhere, if there are large numbers of salmon in the rivers, the fish will concentrate on eating their eggs, so flies that imitate salmon eggs become essential.

In Russia, the magnificent fishing for rainbow trout, perhaps the finest in the world, attracts most anglers.

Most opportunities for fly fishing throughout this giant country are still wilderness areas with limited access.

Most rivers in Kamchatka are low gradient, with large expanses of white water or canyons. Thus floating in a raft, finding new locations by jet boat, and **wading** are all possible without concern about finding dangerous conditions. Many of the rivers in Kamchatka have not been explored thoroughly, but two of the most popular rivers are the Zhupanova and the Sedanka, which exemplify the variety available on the peninsula. The Zhupanova is a large river with extremely large rainbow trout and salmon, and fishing with streamers and mouse patterns is the best way to catch these fish. The Sedanka, on the other hand, is more like a **spring creek**, with prolific fly **hatches** and better dry fly fishing, but with rainbows that average from 16 to 22 inches long. It is a high-volume river rather than a trophy river. Among the many other rivers that have been explored, the Pymta, Voyampolka, Opala, Kolpatova, Oblukinovina, Icha, and Medved also have excellent fishing for trout and salmon.

SEASON

Atlantic salmon fishing in the Kola Peninsula begins as soon as the rivers are free of ice, usually in late May. Until the middle of July, high water makes wading difficult and most fishing is from boats with two-handed rods. Once the spring floods subside, salmon run most of these rivers continuously throughout the summer, as there are five different runs of salmon during the season. The low water of July and early August can be quite warm, and fishing with a floating line and smaller flies usually draws the most strikes. August is a transition month, with small flies effective at times, and big, fresh fish entering the river as the water cools at the end of the month. The shorter days and inclement weather of September and October can be challenging, but the rivers are full of fish and biting insects are nearly absent.

The best time to visit Kamchatka for fly fishing is mid-June through September. Rainbow trout, grayling, Arctic char, and khundza are caught throughout this period, with the best dry fly fishing from mid-July through mid-August. King salmon run the rivers from mid-June through early July, coho from mid-August through October, Sockeye in July and August, and pinks from early August through September.

South fork spey

SAILFISH

Of the billfish species, sailfish are the smallest and most aggressive feeders on smaller **baitfish**, and are thus the easiest to hook with a fly. Although fly fishing pioneer **Lee Wulff** caught sailfish lying in shallow water from a small boat, today nearly all of them are caught by trolling live bait or plugs (or a combination of both), removing the "teaser" lure at the last moment, casting a big fly to the same spot, and hoping the sailfish will eat the fly. This technique relies every bit as much on the skill of the captain and mate as it does the angler, since there is an art to teasing the fish but not letting it grab the bait. According to **IGFA** rules and to generally accepted methods of fly fishing, the boat should be shifted out of gear before the fly is cast to a fish.

Rods and reels must be up to the task of playing a large fish and moving it up from the depths when it sounds. Although a 12-weight tarpon outfit is suitable for the smaller Atlantic sailfish, the bigger fish of Mexico and **Central America** call for big, thick rods that cast a 14-weight line, and are shorter (typically 8½ feet) than the traditional 9-foot saltwater **fly rod** because a shorter rod has better lifting power. These rods are not very precise casting tools, but the compromise is reasonable because casts to sailfish are usually less than 40 feet. **Fly reels** for sailfish should be massive—large enough to hold a 14-weight sinking line or **shooting head** plus running line and at

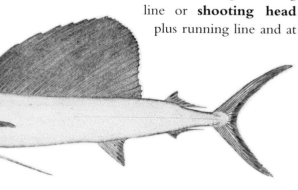

least 400 yards of 50-pound gel-spun polyester **backing**. This is not a place to save money on a fly reel. The reel should have a very strong, smooth drag mechanism and should be constructed so that the heat generated by the drag system during the fast prolonged runs of a sailfish is dissipated quickly into the frame of the reel. **Leaders** are usually made with a 16- or 20-pound class **tippet** and must have a 100-pound **shock tippet** because of a sailfish's abrasive jaws. Flies range the gamut from baitfish **streamers** to **poppers** but have one thing in common—they are big, probably the largest artificial flies tied today, anywhere from 7 to 12 inches long. A popular rig is to string a floating head of cork or foam on the leader in front of a large streamer tied on a 7/0 **hook**. The popper can then be added or removed as needed. The most popular color is all-white, but sailfish flies are used in every color of the rainbow.

Small sailfish of around 60 pounds are quite common off the east coast of **Florida** and off the Florida Keys, where they are often attracted to chum slicks set for other species. Winter months are best. The larger Pacific sailfish range from the northern coast of South America to the Sea of Cortez. The best places to chase these fish with a fly are Panama and Costa Rica in April and May, and off Baja **California** throughout spring and summer.

SALMON FLY

"Salmon fly" in the western United States refers to a giant **stonefly** that **hatches** in late spring for only a week but brings extremely large fish to the surface. But when the term salmon fly is used to refer to an artificial fly, it is for a fly made specifically to catch **Atlantic salmon**. **Pacific salmon** are also caught on flies, but most anglers use oversized versions of flies designed for **steelhead** for these species. On the other hand, the tying of flies for Atlantic salmon is an intricate art that sometimes approaches cult status for fly tiers.

Prior to the Victorian era, flies used for Atlantic salmon in England were large **wet flies**—not particularly ornate and sometimes quite subdued in color. In the nineteenth century, colorful flies became popular with Irish fly tiers, and once these gaudy flies were accepted by Victorian anglers the fly patterns reached a zenith of ornate excess. So-called full-dress featherwings might have three or four different feathers for the tail, a mixture of tinsel, floss, and more feathers for the body, and up to a dozen different feathers for the wing. Bustard, bird-of-paradise, toucan, blue chatterer, golden pheasant, and jungle fowl were just some of the more exotic feathers used. North American fly tiers, without access to the feathers brought to England for the millinery trade, took the same basic fly patterns and simplified them, substituting moose, fox, squirrel, and deer hair for the more exotic feathers. These simple hairwing patterns were just as effective as the featherwings, but even today fly tiers try to duplicate the Victorian recipes, substituting dyed chicken, pheasant, and goose feathers for the more exotic varieties. (Most of these intricate flies are tied to be showcased in shadow boxes and never see the end of a **leader**.)

Most anglers today use simple featherwing wet fly patterns like the Blue Charm or basic hairwing flies like the Hairy Mary or Black Bear Green Butt. Flies tied to imitate shrimp, such as Ally's Shrimp, are also widely used, especially in **Iceland** and **Russia**. **Tube flies** are very popular on European rivers; less so on **Canadian** waters. Using **dry flies**

for Atlantic salmon is a North American development, first practiced in the early twentieth century on Canadian rivers. Salmon dry flies look like very large, oversized trout flies and most are either large **Wulff**-type dry flies or patterns tied from spun and clipped deer hair, and patterns like the Buck Bug or Bomber look like cigar butts with **hackle**.

Most wet flies and all dry flies used for Atlantic salmon are tied on single **hooks**. However, double hooks (a hook with one eye but two points and two bends) are used on some rivers, although care should be taken because double hooks are not allowed on some rivers. Double hooks sink a fly quicker and are said to ride better in fast current. Although double hooks are thought to hold a fish better once hooked, they are not as efficient at hooking salmon, plus they make releasing a salmon more difficult, so the use of double hooks gets less popular each year.

SALMON, ATLANTIC

The Atlantic salmon, *Salmo salar*, is native to the North Atlantic. Most of them fatten on shrimp and **baitfish** as adults in the Davis Straight between Greenland and **Canada**, returning to freshwater rivers in North America and Europe to spawn. In North America, Atlantic salmon were historically found from the Connecticut River north to Labrador, but only remnant populations remain in some **Maine** rivers, where the fish are protected and only very limited sport fishing is allowed. In Canada, although salmon rivers are shadows of their former glory, fly fishing for salmon (the only legal method in all North American rivers) can still be productive if a trip is timed to the arrival of a run of fish.

In Europe, Atlantic salmon historically spawned in rivers from Portugal north to the Kola Peninsula in **Russia**. Although remnant populations remain in southern Europe, salmon only occur in number suitable for sport fishing in **Great Britain**, **Iceland**, **Norway**, and Russia. Their numbers on both

sides of the Atlantic have been decimated by pollution, dams, river netting, and especially by commercial fishery off Greenland and the Faroe Islands. Conservation organizations, especially the Atlantic Salmon Federation, have worked hard to restore Atlantic salmon to their native rivers, including a 2002 agreement with Greenland to reduce offshore netting, but Atlantic salmon populations are still in danger throughout most of their range.

Atlantic salmon return to the river where they were born between June and October, which is when anglers fish for them. The adult fish spawn in late fall and early winter in headwaters or small tributaries, and the female builds a series of **redds**, dropping eggs in clean gravel as a male fertilizes them. Some adults return to the ocean immediately, but if rivers are jammed with ice the adults may overwinter in fresh water, returning to the ocean the following spring, when they are known as black salmon or kelts. Eggs hatch into tiny salmon called parr, which are nearly indistinguishable from young trout. Parr spend from one to three years in salt water, and then, prior to migrating to the ocean, turn silvery and enter a

S

stage called a smolt. Atlantic salmon remain in the ocean for one to three years, feeding on sand eels, capelin, krill, and other baitfish and crustaceans. Unlike **Pacific salmon**, Atlantic salmon do not always die after spawning and may return to freshwater rivers multiple times.

A salmon that returns to its native river after only one winter at sea is known as a grilse. Grilse are smaller than multiple seawinter salmon (which are called simply "salmon") and run from 3 to 10 pounds. Grilse are mostly immature male fish and often arrive in a river prior to the larger salmon. Grilse are more eager to take a fly and the runs in some rivers are almost entirely grilse, providing great sport but not large salmon, which can reach 30 or even 40 pounds.

Atlantic salmon do not feed on their freshwater spawning run. Theories abound as to why they **strike** a fly, and include a reflex memory from when they fed in rivers as parr, pure aggression, or territoriality. It's a leap of faith to cast a fly over a fish that does not feed, expecting it to strike the fly—but salmon strike both **wet** and **dry flies** and will sometimes chase a fly 10 feet before inhaling it. Typical fly presentation is to cast above where a salmon has been seen or one is suspected, letting the current swing the fly over the fish. Salmon are more likely to take a wet fly if it is presented broadside to them. Unlike trout fishing, where the fly is most often fished **dead drift**, the most effective fly is one that wakes just below the surface, making a

disturbance that would send most trout bolting for cover. Fly speed is important and should be neither too fast nor too slow. In very slow water the angler may **retrieve** line to speed up the fly, and in fast water upstream **mends** may help. Dry flies can be fished dead drift, just as you would for trout; but in many rivers a dry fly is most effective when swung in the current on a tight line, making a large wake in the current.

Although most salmon fishing is done with a floating or intermediate **fly line**, if the water is very high or cold a full sinking or **sink tip** line is necessary to get the fly where a fish can see it. Where it is legal to fish for kelts in the spring, a sinking line is almost essential because salmon rivers in spring are usually swollen with snow melt.

Atlantic salmon may just make a pass at a fly, creating a big swirl on the surface but never touching the fly. A fish that moves for a fly like this can usually be caught after resting the fish for a few moments and trying a different fly. When a salmon takes a fly, the move is slow and deliberate, and it is best to wait until the salmon has turned with the fly before striking—which is easier said than done, especially for experienced trout anglers, who reflexively strike immediately when a fish rises!

Salmon that have just entered rivers from the ocean and are moving through a **pool** will strike a fly best. Once a school of salmon is "laid up" in a big pool, they become stale and are more difficult to entice. During low water times in midsummer, dry flies are often effective, especially if the **water temperature** is above 60 degrees. Very small wet flies and **nymphs**, down to a size 12 or 14, will also entice a salmon that has ignored conventional wet flies in the common sizes of 4, 6, and 8. **Streamer** flies will also catch salmon, especially in the fall and any time a river is swollen and discolored from rain.

Atlantic salmon also have landlocked populations in large, deep lakes and in rivers leading into these lakes. Maine and Labrador still have native populations of these wonderful fish, and "landlocks" have been introduced into the Great Lakes, mountain lakes in **Vermont**, **New Hampshire,** and **New York**, as well as small deep lakes as far away as **Michigan** and **Oregon**. Landlocked salmon behave just like trout in rivers, and eagerly respond to trout dry flies, nymphs, and streamers. In lakes, although they will also feed on insects, landlocked salmon are particularly fond of smelt, and streamers that imitate these baitfish are either cast or trolled to salmon cruising just under the surface.

SALMON, PACIFIC

Pacific salmon include six different species in the genus *Oncorhynchus* and are more closely related to the **rainbow** and **cutthroat trout** of western North America than they are to **Atlantic salmon**. Unlike trout and Atlantic salmon, Pacific salmon always die after spawning, an adaption to the nutrient-poor waters where they evolved. (Without the organic matter produced by dead adult salmon, insect life to support their young once hatched would not be enough to support the young fish.)

In North America, Pacific salmon spawn in rivers from the Rio Santo Domingo in Baja **California** north to **Alaska**. In Asia, Pacific salmon are found as far south as the Tachia River in Taiwan and north to the permafrost zone of Pacific Siberia. Pacific salmon have been introduced in **Chilean** and **New Zealand** rivers by accidental escapes from salmon farms, where they are not particularly welcome, as well as the Great Lakes, where they are popular as a sport fish. Best places to fly fish for Pacific salmon include **Washington, Oregon,** British Columbia and Alaska, **Russia**'s Kamchatka Peninsula, and tributaries of the Great Lakes.

All Pacific salmon enter freshwater rivers from the ocean with a silvery color, but most change into darker shades of red, black, or mottled olive within a week. Fresh "bright" fish, whether in an estuary or brackish water at the mouth of a river, are quite aggressive and may still feed on crustaceans or **baitfish**, so just before their spawning migration they take streamer flies well.

Once in fresh water, Pacific salmon other than coho do not take a fly as readily as Atlantic salmon or **steelhead**—but they will take a fly if presented properly. Pacific salmon seem difficult to take on a fly because anglers often fish for them with a swung fly as they would for steelhead, and species other than the coho respond better to a **dead drift** presentation than to a fly stripped through the water. The best way to catch most Pacific salmon is to cast upstream and across with a **sink tip line**, **mend** the line once or twice to keep the fly from swinging, and then let the fly drift through a pool. Getting the fly down to the depth the fish are resting is key: Unlike steelhead, which rest close to the bottom, Pacific salmon may suspend in the middle of slow current, so it pays to experiment with different depths.

SILVER OR COHO SALMON, *ONCORHYNCHUS KISUTCH*

Cohos are by far the most popular Pacific salmon with fly anglers. They are aggressive and will chase a **streamer** fly **retrieved** just under the surface and will even strike a large deer hair mouse skated across the surface. They have a lifespan of three years and spend a year in fresh water, enter salt water in their second year, and return to spawn in their third. Mature fish run from about 10 to 17 pounds. Best flies are streamers that combine bright colors with lots of flashy tinsel. Pink, white, and purple are the top colors.

S

KING OR CHINOOK SALMON, *ONCORHYNCHUS TSHAWYTSCHA*

King salmon are the largest of the Pacific salmon, and when fresh from salt water may range from 15 to 80 pounds. The young live in fresh water for one or two years and then spend four or five years on long feeding migrations in the ocean. When fresh and silver from the ocean, a mature king salmon is a freight train when hooked and serious fly anglers use fly rods from 10-weight to 12-weight **tarpon** rods when chasing them. When first in fresh water they will chase large, bright streamer flies or salt-water flies, but once they have migrated upstream and turned dark red, they are more often caught on dead drifted eggs flies or steelhead flies.

CHUM OR DOG SALMON, *ONCORHYNCHUS KETA*

Chum salmon live three or four years and because the young do not stay long in freshwater rivers they spend most of their life at sea. Chum salmon are very aggressive when they first enter rivers, and will still take a dead drifted fly after they have been in fresh water and developed the large canine tooth and blotchy olive and pink markings typical of a fish closer to spawning. Best flies for chum salmon are **Woolly Bugger**, White Marabou, and Egg-Sucking Leech streamers, as well as any fly with a bright pink marabou wing. Although chum salmon do not get as much press as cohos and kings, they put up a terrific battle on a **fly rod** and are the favorite of fly anglers throughout their range.

SOCKEYE OR RED SALMON, *ONCORHYNCHUS NERKA*

Sockeye live four to five years and spend the first two years of their life in freshwater lakes. Sockeyes sometimes become landlocked or are purposely stocked in freshwater lakes. (When landlocked they are known as *kokanee*.) Effective sockeye salmon flies are typically sparser than the big fluffy patterns used for other species of Pacific salmon, and hair-wing Atlantic salmon and steelhead flies seem to work best. Schools of sockeyes often stay suspended in the middle of the water column. Finding the right depth is important and a sink tip line is essential.

PINK OR HUMPBACK SALMON, *ONCORHYNCHUS GORBUSCHA*

Pink salmon live only two years and spend most of their life at sea. As a result, they don't grow as large as other Pacific salmon but in odd-numbered years in British Columbia and northwestern United States, and in even-numbered years in Alaska and Kamchatka they are abundant and eagerly take any small, brightly colored fly when fresh from the ocean. Pinks spawn close to the ocean, so look for schools of them close to salt water. Best flies are small streamers in shades of pink or blue that imitate shrimp or baitfish.

CHERRY SALMON, *ONCORHYNCHUS MASOU*

Cherry salmon are the only species of Pacific salmon found only in Asian rivers. Landlocked varieties, known as cherry trout, are common in Korea and Hokkaido and will strike standard trout dry fly and nymph patterns. Sea-run individuals can be caught on small, bright streamers or steelhead flies, especially those with pink colors.

SAWYER, FRANK (1906–1980)

For over 60 years, Frank Sawyer was the river-keeper on **England**'s River Avon, a productive spring-fed trout stream. As riverkeeper, he spent nearly every waking hour on the river, observing trout feeding behavior as well as the behavior of the insects they ate, particularly **mayfly nymphs**. Sawyer developed a number of extremely effective trout flies, all with the philosophy that flies should be made to simulate the appearance of life and suggest insects, rather than to be exact copies of the naturals. His most famous fly, the **Pheasant Tail Nymph**, is a perfect example. The only materials incorporated into the fly are copper wire and fibers from the tail of a ringneck pheasant rooster. There are no legs on the artificial fly, because Sawyer felt that the legs of a mayfly nymph are typically tucked under the body of the insect when it is drifting, and legs on the artificial fly would inhibit its sink rate. Although the color of the natural pheasant tail fiber is close to that of many natural mayfly nymphs, he always used the natural color because he felt it was close enough. Sawyer was also influential in developing many techniques for **upstream** nymphing, and although he developed other fly patterns similar to the Pheasant Tail such as his Gray Goose nymph, the Pheasant Tail is the only one still used regularly today.

SCHWIEBERT, ERNEST (1931–2005)

Ernest Schwiebert was a brilliant and precocious fishing writer, publishing his first book, *Matching the Hatch*, in 1955, while he was still an architectural student at Ohio State. By that time, he had already spent countless hours on the trout streams of **Michigan**, where the Chicago-born son of a religion professor spent summers. While in college, he was taken under the wings of the "**Letort** Regulars" like Charles Fox, **Vincent Marinaro**, and Ross Trimmer. While studying the behavior of **spring creek** trout with this group, he invented the **Letort Hopper**, the first really effective grasshopper imitation. While *Matching the Hatch* was not the first American book to use Latin names of trout stream insects, it was far more extensive and geographically diverse than earlier books by **Preston Jennings** and **Art Flick**.

Schwiebert went on to write other important books on fishing. His *Nymphs* (1973) was an amazingly complete study of immature trout stream insects, with some of the finest insect illustrations ever included in a fishing book. Schwiebert did all the art himself. His collection of stories of fishing around the world, *Remembrance of Rivers Past* (1984) was an eloquent travelogue of trout and salmon rivers around the world, as Schwiebert traveled widely in his career as an architect. *Salmon of the World* (1970) was a large-format, lavishly illustrated (again, by the author) review of the history of **Atlantic salmon** fishing. His largest and most complete book, the two-volume *Trout*, at over 1,700 pages, is one of the most complete books of trout fishing ever published.

SCOTLAND

OVERVIEW

Scotland offers perhaps the best fly fishing in Europe, certainly the greatest numbers of trout streams, salmon rivers, and salmon lochs. In addition, Scottish fishing is often done in near-wilderness settings in the highlands or more pastoral settings in the populated valleys. Scotland's most famous fly fishing resource is its **Atlantic salmon** fishing, which like salmon fishing everywhere else is fickle because of varying water levels throughout the season and the current health of the salmon population at sea. But the trout fishing in Scotland is

S

more reliable and productive, and wild **brown trout** are found in all of the salmon rivers as well—both resident and sea-run populations. Although **northern pike** are not as much as a glamor fish, they are common in most lochs and are a reliable species to chase with a fly. In addition, two non-native species, **rainbow trout** introduced from the United States and **grayling** introduced from England are popular game fish.

FISHERIES

There is good salmon fishing throughout Scotland, from the more settled valleys in the south to the wildness of the Outer Hebrides. Unlike many places in the world, salmon run the rivers of Scotland year-round, and in any month of the year there will be fresh salmon in at least some rivers. Beginning in the south, just south of Glasgow and Prestwick on the West Coast are a number of smaller salmon rivers in Ayrshire and Galloway. In the northern part of this range near the cities the rivers are more gentle and easily waded; in the very southwestern part they are wilder, in a more upland landscape. Productive among these small rivers are

the Luce, Dee, Urr, Ayr, and Doon. On the East Coast, south of Edinburgh, is the Tweed, one of the finest salmon rivers in Scotland and the river where more salmon are caught each season than anyplace else in Scotland—in fact, in most years this river produces more salmon than any other river in the European Union, despite being a popular salmon river since the seventeenth century.

North of Edinburgh is the Tay, Scotland's largest river. The largest rod-caught salmon in Scotland was captured in the Tay in 1922 by Miss Georgina Ballantine and weighed 64 pounds. The Tay is a productive river, running through the fertile farmlands of Perthshire, and its tributaries the Earn, Isla, Ericht, Tummel, Garry, Dochart, Lyon and Eden are all excellent rivers in their own right. Near Aberdeen is the Dee, one of the best rivers for producing salmon early in the season. The Dee, Tay, Tweed, and Spey are considered the "big four" salmon rivers of Scotland. And the Spey, inspiration for the **Spey rod**, **Spey casting**, and the **Spey fly**, is a river that should not be missed by any fly fisher with even a passing interest in fly fishing history. This river fishes well throughout the summer and fall, with nearly pristine flows from its alpine headwaters. Other excellent salmon rivers in Scotland include the Findhorn, one of the most scenic, the Beauly, a classic highland river, and the many small rivers of the Outer Hebrides, where salmon fishing is best during the summer in rainy periods when the small rivers gain enough flow to allow migrating salmon to head upriver. Trout fishing, both for resident brown trout and **sea trout**, is excellent in the Outer Hebrides as well. Unlike other places in Scotland, much of the fishing is done in shallow sandy estuaries before the fish head inland, which can be quite exciting because fish can be readily spotted in the clear water. Because rivers are generally short before they flow into lochs, much of the fishing here is done in lochs, although many of the lochs are shallow and fishing is often with **floating lines** and **dry flies**.

Many of Scotland's smaller salmon rivers can be

fished with a 9-foot, 8-weight rod, but for the true Scottish experience, and for its bigger rivers, a Spey rod will add to the enjoyment. The best all-round two-handed rod for bigger Scottish rivers is a 15-foot rod that handles a 9- or 10-weight line, and for smaller waters or low-water fishing in the summer a rod between 13 and 14 feet for a 7-weight line is standard. A floating line may be all that is needed for summer fishing, but for spring salmon it is important to carry a sinking or **sink tip line** as well. Popular **salmon flies** are Ally's Shrimp, Munro Killer, Stoats Tail, and General Practitioner in sizes 4 through 12. **Tube flies** are also very popular on Scottish rivers.

Great fishing for both brown trout and sea trout is available throughout Scotland. In late spring and early summer, there is excellent dry fly fishing on the lowland rivers of the south, especially the Tweed and its tributaries, the Tay, Don, Clyde, and Annan. These are not easy fish, as they have a rich food supply and encounter plenty of fishing pressure. Easier fishing is found in the upper reaches of these big lowland systems and in the rivers of the northern highlands, where trout do not have much choice in what they eat and will grab any reasonably presented fly.

Loch fishing for trout in Scotland is an experience that should not be missed. Traditional loch fishing is with a team of three **wet flies**, and as much water as possible is covered from a drifting or rowed boat. Such bright and traditional English wet flies as the Alexandra, Dunkeld, Soldier Palmer, Blue and Silver, Peter Ross, and Zulu are a joy to fish, as an angler seldom has a chance to catch wild brown trout on such whimsical flies. The most productive lochs are the shallowest, which also means that at times trout will rise to dry flies during a hatch of **mayflies**, **caddis** (called sedges here), or **midges** (known as buzzers locally). Because there are over 35,000 lochs in Scotland and most hold trout, this fishing is often more intimate and secluded than river fishing, and because most of the lochs are relatively infertile the fishing can be quite

easy, with trout taking flies within a rod's length of the boat. Of the bigger lochs, Loch Leven, Loch Awe, and Lake of Mentieth (the only one actually called a "lake" in Scotland) are the best for fly fishing, and Loch Rannoch is one of many lochs noted for its ferox, a strain of large predatory brown trout, that, unfortunately, are typically caught by deep trolling.

Sea trout fishing in Scotland is best on the gentle-gradient rivers of the East coast including the South Esk, Ythan, Deveron, and Nairn. Other productive rivers and lochs are found in the southwestern corner of the country and in the Outer Hebrides, especially in the East Lewis and Harris areas. Sea trout are quite light-shy, and unless rivers are high and dirty because of recent rains most fishing for them is done after dark with wet flies or dry flies skated across the surface. In lochs, sea trout are generally fished downwind of a boat. While the oarsman holds the boat in position against the wind, the angler casts a team of three wet flies and retrieves rapidly, allowing the upper fly to skim across the surface.

SEASON

In most rivers, the main runs of salmon begin in March, although the Tay fish can run earlier. April and May are the best months for large spring salmon, and by June the smaller grilse begin to enter most rivers. Large salmon continue to run the rivers through fall, mixed in with the grilse. Trout season opens in March, but April, May, and June offer the best fly fishing, particularly with dry flies. Later in the summer, fishing is best early and late in the day, but by September, when water temperatures cool, fishing returns to an all-day event. Trout season closes in October. Sea trout fishing is best during the summer months of June and July.

It is important to know that although fishing is allowed on Sunday in Scotland, it is frowned upon in some areas of the country.

SCUDS

Scuds are small freshwater crustaceans in the order *Amphipoda* that are imitated by small **nymphs** from size 14 through 20. They are abundant in alkaline, weed-filled **spring creeks**, **tailwater** rivers, and lakes, where a single handful of weeds may contain hundreds of them. At rest, scuds are flattened laterally with a curved body, but when swimming the body straightens. Live scuds are a dull gray with olive tinges, but after death they turn the color of cooked shrimp. Imitations of these invertebrates are both naturally colored and pinkish-orange, especially when used in tailwater rivers, because scuds are often killed after running through dam outflows and trout wait below in the current, eating dead as well as live scuds. Because scuds spend their entire lives under water and never **hatch**, trout feed on them throughout the year. Scud imitations are fished **dead drift**, but an occasional twitch can sometimes interest a trout that is reluctant to take the fly. Best patterns include the Flashback Scud, Bead Body Scud, and Oliver Edwards's Freshwater Shrimp. A similar freshwater crustacean, the **sow bug** (also known as a cress bug), is less common and can be distinguished from a scud by its dorsally compressed shape.

SCULPIN

Sculpin are small, bottom-dwelling fish of the family *Cottoidea* that are a favorite prey of large trout. Although most species of sculpin are marine dwellers, the freshwater species are very abundant in cold, clear streams with rocky bottoms. Sculpin are not as easy to spot as other **baitfish** because they dart from rock to rock along the bottom, but a quick swipe through a **riffle** in a trout stream will demonstrate their abundance. Sculpin range from one to four inches in length (fly size 2 to 10) and have a flat body with a large head and distinct, fanlike pectoral fins. The dorsal side of the body is a mottled brown with tones of olive or gray. The belly of the fish is a pearlescent white or gray. Any streamer fly with a large head will imitate a sculpin well—the famous **Muddler Minnow** and Woolhead Sculpin streamers are two of the most common imitations—but the most important aspect of fishing sculpin imitations is to fish the fly close to the bottom with an erratic stop–and–start **retrieve**, which imitates the darting behavior of the actual fish.

SEA TROUT

Although the term "sea trout" can refer to sea-run races of **brown trout**, especially in Europe, in North America it usually refers to the spotted sea trout, *Cynoscion nebulosus*, a popular gamefish of the Gulf and Atlantic Coasts of the United States. (They can be caught as far north as **North Carolina**.) They are also known as speckled trout, and large ones are referred to as gator trout. Although they can reach 15 pounds, the average fish caught on a fly ranges from 2 to 4 pounds. Sea trout feed on shrimp and small **baitfish**, and will be found feeding over grass beds and sand flats when water temperatures are between 60 and 80 degrees. Sea trout prefer a brisk, snappy **retrieve** of short strips followed by brief pauses. In colder weather they will be found in deep holes adjacent to shallow flats, where they can be caught on **streamers**

fished on a **sinking fly line** with a slow retrieve. Sea trout are not terribly picky about fly patterns, and most small saltwater patterns that imitate **shrimp** or small baitfish will be taken eagerly if they are in the neighborhood. Sea trout will also take small **poppers** on calm days.

SEDGE
See Caddis.

SHAD, AMERICAN

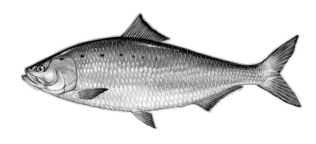

Often called "poor man's salmon" because of their inclination to leap when hooked, American shad, *Alosa sapidissima*, are excellent fish to pursue with a **fly rod**. Shad are anadromous and feed on plankton in salt water. They return to freshwater rivers to spawn in May and June along the North Atlantic coast and in November as far south as **Florida**. Although they do not feed when migrating, they will strike small, brightly colored flies. The best way to catch shad with a fly is to get above a school of them and cast a small white fly (**bonefish** flies with white wings are excellent, although flies tied especially for shad can be found) across the current, letting the fly sweep just above the bottom on a **sinking line**. The rod tip should be twitched throughout the drift, and shad are especially partial to taking the fly as it hangs in the current below the angler. **Strikes** are quite soft, but once a shad is hooked, these three- to eight-pound fish will jump and take a lot of line, especially in heavy current. After spawning, on their

S

return to the ocean shad will feed on insects and can even be caught on **dry flies** during a **mayfly hatch**.

American shad are native to the Atlantic Coast and best rivers to fish for them with a fly include the Merrimack River in **Massachusetts**, the Connecticut River in Connecticut, the Delaware River in **New York**, **Pennsylvania**, and **New Jersey**, the Potomac in **Virginia**, the Savannah in **Georgia**, and the St. John's in **Florida**. Shad were introduced to the West Coast of North America in the nineteenth century, and superb fly fishing is found in **California**'s Klamath, Trinity, Yuba, and American Rivers, the Umpqua and Rogue Rivers in **Oregon**, and the Columbia River in **Washington**.

SHARK

Sharks are an underrated but fun experience on a **fly rod**. They often provide big-game fishing when species like **tarpon** or **bonefish** are hard to find, and although sharks take a fly well, they are not as eager to grab a fly as it might seem. Fly rod fishing for sharks is usually done by casting to cruising fish on shallow flats, or by chumming them close to the boat in deeper water. On the flats, the most commonly pursued shark is the blacktip, a very aggressive shark that hunts in shallow water. Lemon sharks and small hammerheads are also commonly taken on the flats. When a shark is spotted slowly cruising through the shallows, the angler tries to get in a position so the shark is moving toward him. When the shark is in comfortable casting range, the fly should be cast a foot from the shark's head and then **retrieved** with a moderate strip past the shark's head. Sharks feed primarily by smell and their eyesight is not as keen as that of most other gamefish, so the fly has to be cast close to the fish. Anything big and bright will catch a shark, and they will strike surface **poppers** as well as **streamers**. The only requirement for a shark fly is that it has a strong **hook**, and sizes 2/0, 3/0, and 4/0 are most common. Of course, when

fishing for sharks it is absolutely essential to have a piece of **wire** between the fly and the rest of the **leader**. **IGFA** rules stipulate that a **shock tippet** can be no longer than 12 inches, but unless fishing for the record books most anglers make their leaders at least 20 inches long, because a shark can cut a leader with its abrasive skin as well as its teeth.

Chumming for sharks in deeper water is done with either a whole fish hung over the side, a bucket of ground chum, or pieces of cut fish thrown overboard, or to cover all the bases a combination of all three. Once a chum slick is started, it may take sharks anywhere from five minutes to an hour to come into the slick, and once they do, it's important to save some chum to keep them close to the boat. The fly should be cast into the chum slick and either just allowed to sink like the natural chum or twitched slightly. Sharks can be reluctant to take a fly even when fired up over a chum slick, so a hookless plug cast on a spinning rod is often thrown into the mix to tease the shark into chasing something and then pulling the plug out of the water as the fly is cast. The most common sharks that come into a chum slick are blue sharks, but the magnificent and spectacular fighting mako shark, with its thrilling leaps, is also commonly seen in the slick. Less common but perhaps the most exciting of sharks is the spinner shark, and they are often caught off the east cost of **Florida** on flies.

Sharks take a fly very slowly and deliberately, so it's best to wait until the shark turns its head to set the hook—and then the hook should be set multiple times so the shark realizes it is hooked. Sharks make long and powerful runs, and it can take anywhere from five minutes for a small blacktip on the flats to several hours for a large blue or mako to bring one to the boat. A 9- or 10-weight rod is fine for most flats sharks, but for the offshore species a 12-weight is minimum and many fly fishers use a beefy 14-weight. Reels should obviously be loaded with several hundred yards of 50-pound **backing** when fishing for the offshore sharks. Sharks caught on a fly are seldom brought into the boat. The wire tippet can be cut, or if not deeply hooked, the fly can be removed with a metal loop on the end of a long pole.

SHOCK TIPPET
See Leader.

SHOOTING HEADS
See Fly Line.

SIDE CAST
See Overhead Cast.

SINK TIP FLY LINE
See Fly Line.

SINKING FLY LINE
See Fly Line.

SKUES, G.E.M. (1858–1949)
G.E.M. Skues, an English lawyer by trade, was one of the finest fly fishers who ever lived. Truly the

father of modern **nymph** fishing, when all of Edwardian England was blindly fishing the **dry fly**, Skues observed that many of the "bulging" rises (rises that move the surface of the water but don't produce the bubbles made by a true surface-feeding fish) were made by trout feeding on nymphs just under the surface. At a time when the traditional **wet flies** were fished by swinging them over the fish, Skues developed a method of fishing his nymphs **upstream,**

dead drift, to visibly feeding fish. Thus began a great debate in English fly fishing circles, with Skues in the nymph fishing corner and **Frederick Halford** as the high priest of dry fly fishing. The debate continues even today, when a few British fly fishing clubs still place regulations on nymph fishing.

Skues was perhaps one of the most articulate fly fishing writers of the twentieth century; his books *Minor Tactics of the Chalk Stream* and *The Way of a Trout with a Fly* are as informative and enjoyable as they were in the first decades of the twentieth century.

SLATE DRAKE
See *Isonychia*.

SNAKE RIVER
The mighty Snake River, with its headwaters in Yellowstone National Park, flows through **Wyoming**, **Idaho**, **Oregon**, and **Washington** before joining with the Columbia. Although mixtures of trout, **steelhead**, and **smallmouth bass** are found **downstream** of Idaho Falls, it is the upper reaches of the Snake that appeal most to fly fishers. Most of the upper river is prime habitat for the native Snake River fine-spotted **cutthroat trout**, a race of cutthroats that grows bigger and is more selective to fly patterns than most other races of cutthroats. In Yellowstone the fishing is mainly small-stream fishing in a wilderness setting for small trout, but below Jackson Lake in Grand Teton National Park the rivers and the trout grow in size. A float through Jackson Hole on this stretch of the Snake is one of the most spectacular fishing trips in North America, and its large trout respond well to big dry flies and streamers. The river then runs into Palisades Reservoir in Idaho, and below Palisades (where it is now known as the South Fork of the Snake) the river flows full and cold throughout the summer and fall, keeping irrigation channels in

S

the Idaho farms full of precious water. The river here is a mixture of high desert and canyon water, and supports a very high density of native cutthroat as well as large **brown trout** and **rainbow trout**. Near Rigby, Idaho, the South Fork joins with the Henry's Fork of the Snake (also known as the North Fork). The Henry's Fork, **upstream** to Last Chance, Idaho, is a fine trout river as well, and is world-famous for its prolific fly **hatches** and large rainbow trout. The Henry's Fork is also a **tailwater** river and alternates between wide placid meadow stretches that look like a giant **spring creek** to whitewater canyon sections.

SNOOK

The word snook encompasses a dozen different species of saltwater fish, but they are difficult to tell apart and their behavior is almost identical. Snook are found in the Atlantic from central **Florida** down through **Central America** and South America, but are never found any farther north because they cannot tolerate **water temperatures** below 60 degrees Fahrenheit. Snook will always be found where fresh water meets salt, because they cannot tolerate either pure fresh water or pure salt water. Since they prefer to ambush their prey, small **baitfish** and shrimp, they will commonly be found in mangrove backwaters, edges of beaches, and along the edge of the current in channels. Snook feed mostly at night, and one of the best ways to catch them on a fly is at night near lighted docks because the lights attract baitfish and shrimp.

Nearly any saltwater streamer that imitates a baitfish will catch snook, and the best ones are between two and four inches long. The old adage "dark day, dark fly; bright day, bright fly" seems to hold for snook, so it is best to carry a range of light and dark flies in such patterns as the **Deceiver** and **Clouser Minnow**. **Poppers** will also catch snook when they are feeding near the surface. **Leaders** should be heavy because snook are very hard fighters and tend to dive into cover, and also because their gill covers are razor sharp. Many fly fishers use a straight 9-foot piece of 40- to 60-pound **monofilament** as a leader. Snook will nearly always ambush their prey close to cover, so the fly should be cast right next to mangrove roots, docks, logs, and shoreline rocks.

S

SOW BUGS

Sow bugs are small freshwater crustaceans of the order *Isopoda*. They are also known as cress bugs. Similar to **scuds**, they are flattened dorsal-ventrally, but unlike scuds, they are found in rich, alkaline waters. Smaller than scuds (most imitations are tied on size 16 and 18 hooks), sow bugs also have a fraction of the protein content of a scud; trout will typically gravitate to the most nutritious food, so where both scuds and sow bugs are found, trout prefer the scuds. Still, in some rivers sow bugs far outnumber scuds and are common prey for trout, so it pays to carry a sow bug **nymph** imitation such as the Fur Cress Bug.

SPEY CAST

Spey casts are a group of similar casts that can reposition long (over 60 feet) lengths of **fly line** with a single cast—without the effort of repeated **false casts** and with very little line going behind the angler. They are useful when fishing wide, powerful rivers, when wind is a problem, and when a high bank or a brushy bank is behind the angler. Spey casts are typically used when fishing **wet flies** for **Atlantic salmon** and **steelhead** with a double-handed or **Spey rod**, but they can be modified for single-handed use with a trout rod to good advantage. A Spey cast is a modification of a **roll cast**, and unlike the roll cast, where a single **power stroke** is made, Spey casts involve additional steps to reposition the line so that a change in direction can be made without tangling the fly on the line or rod.

SINGLE SPEY CAST

The single Spey cast is used when the current is running from your right to your left, or when a strong wind is blowing **upstream**. Allow the line to hang **downstream** in the current, and make sure there is plenty of tension on the line. (In fact, throughout the cast, the most important thing to remember is to always maintain line tension on the

rod). The idea is to fire the line straight across the river so the fly will once again swing in the current, so to begin, move your body so that the front of your body is facing the opposite bank. Turn your upper body to the downstream direction (toward the line) and raise the rod tip to about 50 degrees above the horizontal. When the rod reaches this position and as much line as possible is off the water, rotate your upper body to the front while swinging the rod in front of you to a position slightly upstream of you. The idea here is to hand the fly, **leader**, and the last couple feet of fly line about two rod lengths upstream and off to your right side. At this point, the line and rod should form a D shape, with the rod forming the straight line of the D and the line behind it forming the arc. Now it is a simple matter to fire the line across the river by pushing with your upper hand and pulling with the lower hand. With this cast, and all Spey casts, the power stroke should stop high, at about the 11:00 o'clock position, so that the line has enough elevation to straighten on its long cast across the river. The D loop is the most critical part of the cast, and it's important that the anchor point, or where the line touches the water, is 45 degrees upstream of the target and that the line is fired across the river just as soon as the anchor point touches the water.

1)

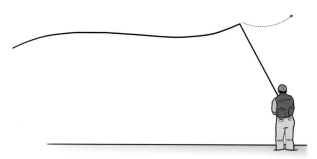

2)

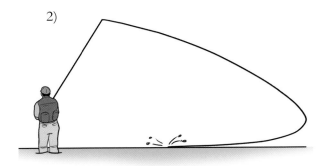

upstream of the rod and the fly is in the water about a rod's length out and slightly downstream of your position. The rod is then swept downstream so that the line travels over its original path, and then raised to the vertical so that a D loop is formed on the downstream side of your body. The line will rip across the surface of the water and make a lot of commotion, but this is desirable because tension has to be built up in the rod to complete the cast. Now the cast is fired across the river as in the single Spey.

3)

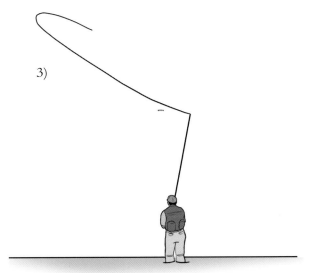

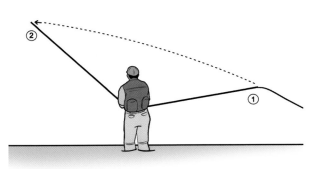

S

DOUBLE SPEY CAST

Now imagine that the current is running from left to right, or that a strong wind is blowing downstream. In this case, a single Spey cast would place the line downstream of your position or the wind would blow the fly into your body in the middle of the cast. Although the double Spey cast looks slightly more complicated, it is also slightly easier to perform correctly and is more forgiving because a slight pause in the middle of the cast will not ruin it, as it would for a single Spey cast. Allow the line to hang downstream, this time on your right side. Sweep the rod low in front of you from right to left (upstream) until the line above the water is

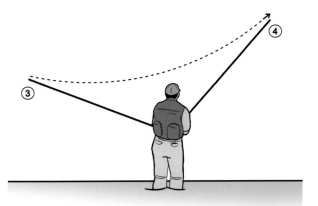

SPEY FLIES

Spey flies are **wet flies** with long, flowing **hackles** that move enticingly in the current. The bodies of these flies are slim, so not only do they breathe and give an impression of life in slow currents, the lack of bulk in the dressing of the fly allows them to sink quicker than flies with a bulkier dressing. Developed in Scotland on the River Spey in the nineteenth century for **Atlantic salmon**, Spey flies have also become very popular with **steelhead** anglers. Modern Atlantic salmon and steelhead anglers use these flies as much for their beauty as for their utility.

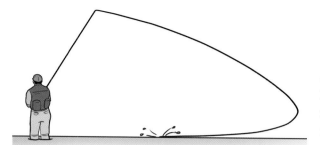

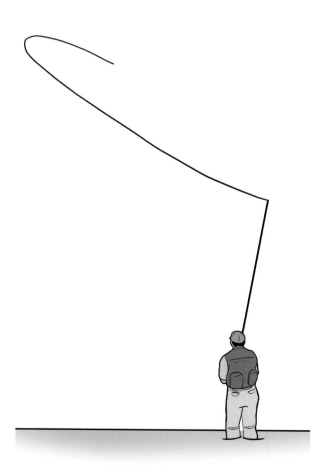

SPEY ROD

Spey rods (also called double-handed rods or two-handed rods) are long rods with extended grips so that the rods can be cast with both hands. Most Spey rods are between 11 and 16 feet long, for line sizes 6 through 11. The advantage of a Spey rod is that a fixed length of line from 60 to 100 feet can be easily propelled across a river even in a strong wind, without a lot of effort and repeated **false casts**. The disadvantages of Spey rods is that they are heavier than single-handed rods, they are not efficient for shorter, more delicate casts, and that when fish are landed they either must be "beached" on a gravel bar or netted by another person; it is impossible to land a large fish in the middle of a river without assistance with a rod that is 12 feet long.

For most North American fishing for **Atlantic salmon** and **steelhead**, a 12½-foot rod for a 7- or 8-weight line is standard, where on European salmon rivers a longer, heavier rod like a 14-foot 9-weight is the norm. Although most anglers choose a Spey rod for **Spey casting**, they can also be used with a traditional **overhead cast**.

S

Switch rods are a type of Spey rod designed for lighter lines, used for summer steelhead or trout fishing, and can be comfortably cast double-handed or single-handed. Traditionally a large double-taper **fly line** was mated to a Spey rod, but with modern Spey rods modified weight-forward lines and **shooting heads** are also used.

SPINNER
See Mayfly.

SPLIT SHOT
Split shot are small sinkers that crimp onto a **leader** to help bet a **nymph** or **streamer** deeper in the water column. Traditionally made from lead, most split shot used for fly fishing has moved to various alloys of tin and tungsten, because lead shot lost in a snag on the bottom of the river poisoned loons and other waterfowl that picked up the shot when ingesting gravel for their gizzards. Split shot is generally split on one side and attached to a leader by crimping the shot to the leader with a pair of pliers. In some cases a rubber grommet around the shot holds the leader in place. Split shot is typically placed above a knot in the leader to keep it from slipping, anywhere from 6 to 20 inches above the fly. When using split shot, it is essential to cast with a wide, open loop, otherwise the shot will tangle with the fly. In addition, the line should be cast to one side, as shot hitting the back of an angler's head is painful, and shot hitting a **graphite fly rod** on the **forward cast** can shatter a rod.

SPRING CREEK
Spring creeks are trout streams that derive most of their flow from groundwater. They are known as chalk streams in England, where vast underground deposits of calcium carbonate hold water like a giant sponge and release it to streams like the River Test and River Itchen where faults in the bedrock allow the spring water to bubble to the surface. Spring creeks are most often found in fertile valleys, where groundwater under pressure from surrounding hills or mountains forces water to the surface, or in areas with rich limestone deposits, where groundwater dissolves the bedrock and allows the water, enriched with nutrients from the limestone, to seep to the surface. Spring creeks usually run clear throughout the year, regardless of the amount of rainfall. Aquatic weed growth is usually heavy because of the stable flows and rich nutrients in the water.

Trout in spring creeks are notoriously difficult to catch and often quite large. One large trout from a spring creek is often more exciting to an angler than a dozen from a more forgiving **freestone** stream. Long, fine **leaders**, careful approach, and delicate flies are precursors to success in spring creeks. Since food is plentiful and trout don't have to exert themselves to capture it, they feed at their leisure and inspect every morsel carefully. The most common trout foods in spring creeks are **scuds**, **midges**, and small **mayflies** like the **Pale Morning Dun** and **Blue Wing Olive**.

Famous spring creeks in the United States include the **Letort Spring Run** and Falling Springs in **Pennsylvania**, the Nissequogue and Connetquot on Long Island in **New York**, Mossy

S

Creek in **Virginia**, Flat Creek near Jackson Hole in **Wyoming**, the spring creeks of the Paradise Valley near the **Yellowstone River** in **Montana**, and Hat Creek, Hot Creek, and Fall River in **California**.

STEELHEAD

Steelhead are **rainbow trout** (*Oncorhynchus mykiss*) that spend part of their life cycle fattening on the ocean's rich food supply. Their natural range is from Baja **California** to southern **Alaska**, and across the Bering Strait to Kamchatka. All steelhead spawn in freshwater rivers, and young steelhead spend between one and three years in a river as smolts before they return to the ocean. Adult fish then spend between one and four years fattening at sea on **baitfish** and shrimp before returning to freshwater to spawn. Steelhead can spawn multiple times during their life, but the size of an adult steelhead in a river is totally dependent on how many years it spends at sea before returning to fresh water: A steelhead that spends only one year at sea returns as a "half-pounder" that will weigh from one to three pounds, whereas a fish that spends four winters at sea before spawning could weigh as much as 40 pounds.

Exactly what constitutes a steelhead is a matter of speculation. In some populations there are individuals that never return to the ocean, and for the past 100 years, hatchery strains of nonmigratory rainbow trout and steelhead have been mixed with wild populations so the gene pool of any population is of questionable ancestry. In addition, strains of steelhead have been introduced to large freshwater lakes like the Great Lakes; although these fish never see the ocean they act and look like sea-run steelhead.

Unlike other anadromous salmonids like **Atlantic salmon** and **Pacific salmon**, steelhead do feed when migrating in freshwater rivers. Typically, the smaller the fish, the more actively it will feed. Summer-run steelhead are typically smaller fish and will feed on insects and baitfish; they are regularly taken on **dry flies** as well as the traditional **wet fly** patterns. Winter-run fish are harder to entice to the fly, but will eat salmon and steelhead eggs—and may also strike a fly out of aggression or a territorial response.

FISHING FOR SUMMER-RUN STEELHEAD

Summer-run fish enter spawning rivers from April through October. Because they will not spawn until January, they spend a long time in freshwater, feed often, and migrate long distances. Summer-run fish are more aggressive and easier to catch, and also are available when fishing conditions are more comfortable for the angler. Although summer-run fish can be taken by standard trout-fishing techniques with **nymphs**, dry flies, or **streamers** when feeding, the traditional way to catch them is by swinging a wet fly through a lie where steelhead have been spotted or where they have historically

S

been caught. Although local knowledge is best (because steelhead just seem to prefer certain places year after year), they will most often be found along the edges of fast, deep currents and in the tails of **pools**, where they will rest after negotiating the rapids below. Look for water that is between two and six feet deep, with a moderate current—about the speed of a casual walk.

Steelhead do not like bright sun, and during the summer it is best to be on the water early or late in the day; if fishing in the middle of the day it's critical to look for deep runs or tails of pools in the shade. When fishing a wet fly, the presentation is relatively simple in theory: to swing the fly through water that might hold a steelhead. In contrast to most trout fishing, here you want the fly to **drag**— but not too fast and not too slow. In very slow current, the fly is cast directly **across-stream** to help speed up the swing, and the fly speed can also be picked up by stripping line as it swings. In very fast current, the cast is angled more **downstream** to slow down the severity of the swing. Some runs might be perfect for simply making a cast and letting it swing, while others require careful presentation and numerous **mends**.

Summer steelhead will also rise to a dry fly, but not often to the classic **dead drift**. Instead, the fly is cast across and downstream and allowed to drag in the current, creating a wake behind the fly that steelhead often find impossible to ignore. This is known as "fishing the damp fly," "waking," "riffling," or "skating." Many of the flies used for waking are imitations of a large orange **caddis** common to summer steelhead rivers, and an orange version of the Bomber Atlantic salmon **dry fly** is one of the most popular patterns.

Because steelhead rivers are often wide and frequent mends will be made, the most popular rods are single-handed, 10-foot rods that call for line sizes 6 through 8. Light **Spey rods** are often used, and the most popular two-handed configuration is a 13-foot rod for a 7- or 8-weight line. On big British Columbia rivers where flies as large as 2/0 are sometimes used, rods as heavy as a 9-weight may be necessary.

FISHING FOR WINTER STEELHEAD

Winter steelhead prefer a slow-swinging fly close to the bottom. They will not rise for a dry fly, nor will they chase a wet fly fished just under the surface. The challenge is to get the fly to a steelhead's lie just above the bottom, and the problem is compounded by the high, fast water of the winter rainy season. Fast-sinking **fly lines**, a cast made slightly **upstream** to help sink the line, and weighted flies all help get the fly down. Steelhead usually take the fly at the deepest part of the swing, just as the fly begins to rise from the bottom. Numerous upstream mends are made so that, at the end of the drift, when the fly rises toward the surface on a tight line, it is as close to the bottom as possible. Winter steelhead will also take flies that look like salmon eggs or **stonefly nymphs**, and these are usually fished dead drift, just as you would for trout. On West Coast rivers this technique is frowned upon in some circles, as it is not as elegant as a swung wet fly because often **split shot** and **indicators** are often added to the leader. However, in Great Lakes rivers, where a tradition of swinging the wet fly was not present when steelhead were stocked in the mid-twentieth century, this technique does not have the dark reputation it does in other parts of the country.

BEST STEELHEAD RIVERS

In the United States, the most productive West Coast rivers include the Klamath, Eel, and Smith Rivers in northern **California**; the North Umpqua, Deschutes, and Rogue in **Oregon**; the Kalama, Skagit, Sauk, Hoh, Sol Duc, and Grande Ronde Rivers in **Washington**; and the Clearwater, Salmon, and Snake Rivers in **Idaho**. British Columbia is home to perhaps the best steelhead fishing in the world, and its best rivers include the Thompson, Dean, and Skeena, including Skeena tributaries like the Babine, Kispiox, Bulkley, and

S

Morice. There are also smaller steelhead rivers in southern **Alaska** and **Russia**'s Kamchatka Peninsula. Steelhead have been introduced very successfully in the Great Lakes, where most of the fish are of the winter-run variety. Best rivers include Lake Ontario's Salmon River and Oak Orchard Creek, plus the mighty Niagara below the falls. Lake Erie hosts a number of small but productive tributaries, including the Grand River on the **Canadian** side, Walnut and Elk Creeks in **Pennsylvania**, and the Chagrin River, Grand River, Rocky River, and Conneaut Creek in **Ohio**. Best Lake Michigan tributaries are the Peshtigo in **Wisconsin**, the Muskegon, Pere Marquette, and Little and Big Manistee Rivers in **Michigan**, and Trail Creek in Indiana. The best Lake Huron tributaries are mostly in Canada, and the steelhead runs of the Nottawasaga, Maitland, and Saugeen are the most productive, although the lower **AuSable** and Ocqueoc in Michigan also have good runs of fish. Best Lake Superior tributaries are the Nipigon in Ontario, the St. Mary's and Big Huron in Michigan, and the Knife and Temperance Rivers in **Minnesota**.

STEELHEAD FLIES

In the early to mid-twentieth century, flies used for steelhead were big **wet flies** with bright red and orange tones and wings made from white or black hair. These flies looked much like **Atlantic salmon** wet flies, but the wings were bigger and bulkier and the colors brighter. Traditional wet flies like the Brad's Brat, Skykomish Sunrise, Skunk, and Polar Shrimp are still effective and used today. Steelhead anglers were not satisfied with the same old patterns, and during the last part of the twentieth century steelhead pioneers like Harry Lemire, Roderick Haig-Brown, and Syd Glasso began to experiment with **dry flies** and slim, elegant, and sparsely tied wet flies in the **Spey fly** style of Atlantic salmon fishing. Later, giant black **streamers** like the articulated leech, rubber-legged **nymphs**, foam-bodied skaters, and flies of almost every description joined the steelhead fly collection found in most **fly boxes**.

STILLBORN INSECT

Not all aquatic insects **hatch** successfully. Often, an **emerging** fly gets stuck in its **nymph** case, and these "stillborn" flies appeal to trout because the fish knows the insect cannot escape and fly away just as the trout opens its mouth. These insects may also be found on the water after a hatch is over, so imitating them presents opportunities for **dry fly** fishing long after a hatch is over. This is especially important in lakes and ponds, where crippled insects may be pushed by the wind and concentrate along the leeward shore. Although flies designed as "cripples" or "stillborns" have been designed, an emerger pattern or just a standard dry fly trimmed down a bit with a pair of sharp scissors will fool most trout when they are feeding on stillborn insects.

STILLWATER
See Lake Fishing.

STONEFLY
Stoneflies are aquatic insects of the order *Plecoptera* and are found in temperate zone rivers throughout the world. Stoneflies need a greater concentration of dissolved oxygen than other aquatic insects like

S

S

mayflies and caddisflies, so in rivers they are found in fast tumbling water and seldom in slow pools or weedy spring creeks. In lakes, stoneflies will only be found along rocky shorelines where constant wave action keeps the dissolved oxygen level high enough to support them. Stonefly larvae are flat, drab-colored insects that superficially resemble mayflies, but can be identified by their two thick tails, two pairs of wing cases, and two claws on each leg. Large stoneflies have feathery gills along the underside of the thorax, where mayflies always have gills along the abdominal segments. Adult stoneflies at rest carry their wings low and hugged to the body and the wings lie flat as opposed to the tent shape of a caddisfly adult. In flight, the body of a stonefly adult hangs below the wings so that the insect appears ready to crash land at any moment.

Stoneflies do not have a **pupa** stage and do not undergo complete metamorphosis. When the nymphs **hatch** into adults, they crawl onto streamside and midstream rocks until a foot or two above the waterline, then the nymph splits its skin and the winged adult flies away. The body of the adult looks almost identical to that of the nymph, so the size and color of the adults that may hatch can be determined by the color and size of the nymphs found under submerged rocks, or by looking at the empty shucks of recently hatched insects on streamside rocks. Adults live a **terrestrial** existence for up to a week, followed by mating above the water and either falling to the water or crawling underwater to lay their eggs. Trout feed on stonefly nymphs prior to hatching when they get dislodged from their secure spots underneath rocks, or when they crawl to shore to hatch. Although the adults do not hatch on the surface of the water like mayflies and caddisflies, stoneflies are clumsy fliers and get knocked to the surface on windy days. They are most vulnerable to trout, however, when they return to the water to lay their eggs.

Stoneflies range in size from about a size 20 up to the giant **Salmonfly**, which is a full two inches long when it hatches, matched by a size 4 or 6 **hook**. Most are brown or black with tinges of orange or yellow, but the abundant Yellow Sally stonefly is a pale yellowish green. One of the stoneflies most relished by trout is the Golden Stonefly, a brownish yellow insect in size 8 through 12 and perhaps the stonefly most commonly eaten by trout. The Salmonfly, however, gets the most notice because of its giant size and the way it brings very large trout to the surface. Unfortunately, the Salmonfly hatches for only a few days in any given place in a river, usually in late June or early July, and the hatch is hard to predict. But when it does occur, trout will eat very large dry flies for weeks after the hatch, even after all the natural insects are gone.

Trout west of the Mississippi are far more likely

to eat adult stoneflies than their eastern counterparts, even though many species of stoneflies are found in eastern rivers. Eastern rivers don't seem to have the concentrated hatches of stoneflies seen on western rivers; also, eastern stoneflies tend to hatch when mayflies and caddisflies are hatching and the fish obviously prefer the insects that hatch on the surface, where they are easier to capture. Thus although the fly fisher will find fly shops in **Montana** with entire display cases dedicated to stonefly dry flies and nymphs, a fly shop in **New York** State might carry just a few imitations of the common nymphs. Effective stonefly nymph imitations include the venerable Prince Nymph, Montana Nymph, Kauffman's Stone, Bitch Creek, and Bead Head Stonefly. Popular stonefly adult imitations are the Stimulator, Yellow Sally, Turk's Tarantula, and Bugmeister.

STREAMERS

Streamers are long, skinny flies used to imitate **baitfish**, although some streamers may be eaten by gamefish that think they are crustaceans, leeches, or other large prey. In the past, trout anglers distinguished between streamers, which were tied with feather wings, and bucktails, which were tied with hair wings. However, many modern baitfish imitations are made with a combination of both feathers and hair, and many are made with synthetic materials that are neither. The term streamer is now used as a catch-all term for all kinds of baitfish flies.

Types of streamers include:

BUCKTAILS

Bucktails, first used in the late nineteenth century, are streamers tied with deer tail or other similar fine hairs like squirrel tail. For trout streams they are usually tied small and slim, size 8 through 12, and are most popular on smaller streams or on ponds. Bigger sizes, up to size 2, are used for salmon, **pike**, and bass. Bucktails are best when the water is clear and fish are feeding on small baitfish like blacknose dace. The Mickey Finn and Blacknose Dace are two of the most popular examples.

FEATHERWING STREAMERS

Featherwing streamers, like bucktails, are slim flies best for clear water or for fishing in tumbling current where the action of the water brings out their lifelike qualities. Big featherwing streamers are used in New England for **brook trout** and landlocked **Atlantic salmon**, typically tied with very long wings and sometimes on tandem **hooks**, especially when trolled behind a boat. Chicken **hackles** are used for many featherwings, and marabou, a very soft, fluffy feather from the under wing of a turkey, makes streamers that pulse with every tiny movement of the current or by the angler stripping the fly. These are very attractive to aggressive fish like large **brown trout**, **Pacific salmon**, and **steelhead**. Popular trout streamers include the Gray Ghost, White Marabou, and Platte River Special. The Popsicle series, tied almost entirely with marabou feathers, is one of the best examples of featherwing streamers used for Pacific salmon and steelhead.

SCULPIN

Because **sculpin** are such common trout prey, and because they are not shaped like other baitfish, many streamers have been developed to imitate them. Sculpin imitations have broad, flattened heads made from spun deer hair or coarse wool. The most famous sculpin fly is the **Muddler Minnow**, first tied almost 50 years ago and now fished in its original form in addition to hundreds of different variations.

STREAMERS

Woolly Buggers

Woolly Buggers are simple streamers with fuzzy bodies and long, flowing tails of marabou feathers. They are not meant to imitate any specific prey item but are probably eaten because they look like large nymphs, leeches, tadpoles, **crayfish**, or sculpin.

Zonkers and Matukas

Zonkers and matukas are streamers with an imitation of a prominent dorsal fin. In the case of the zonker, the back of the fly is made from a strip of rabbit fur and the matuka's high dorsal fin is made from a chicken hackle lashed to the dorsal side of the fly. These flies have a lot of action in the water and are best when fish are feeding on deep-bodied baitfish like **shad**.

Saltwater Streamers

Because most saltwater gamefish eat other fish, most saltwater flies are really oversized streamers. Saltwater streamers are often tied longer than freshwater versions, and with the exception of some older (but still deadly) patterns like the **Deceiver**, are often tied with synthetic materials. Natural materials six to eight inches long are rare, and synthetic fibers are more durable when exposed to the sharp teeth and harsher conditions encountered in salt water. Translucent **nylon**, polyester, Mylar tinsel, and acrylic fibers are just some of the materials used. Saltwater streamers are also likely to be coated with strong epoxy at the front end of the fly for durability, and large plastic or glass eyes are added to imitate the large eyes of baitfish. Saltwater streamers are tied on strong, stainless or plated hooks to resist rust and corrosion when exposed to salt water.

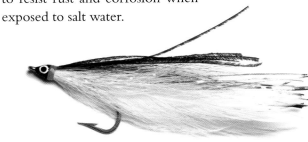

Streamers with weighted eyes and cones

Brass and tungsten cones and dumbbell-shaped eyes are often added to streamers. The extra weight at the head of the fly makes it sink quicker, and also gives a fly a darting motion not unlike the jigs used by spin fishers. Weighted dumbbell eyes are the essential component of the deadly **Clouser Minnow**, and metal cones have been added to just about every popular streamer pattern over the years, particularly sculpin imitations, because these baitfish live among the rocks on the bottom of a river. These flies are great for fishing fast, deep water—even when a **sinking line** is used, an unweighted streamer may swim too shallow, and with **floating lines**, weighted streamers give the angler the ability to fish deeper without changing fly lines.

How to pick the right streamer

Unlike picking the right dry fly or nymph, picking a trout streamer is often a matter of whimsy or of trusting the advice of another angler. Some patterns do seem to work better on certain rivers, but it's not necessary to find out what kind of baitfish are in a river before picking the right streamer pattern. In low, clear water, a small, sparse streamer will work best, and in fast, deep water a bulkier streamer will catch a trout's attention better. Bulkier flies are not only more visible in tumbling or discolored water—fish can "hear" the vibrations set off by these flies and can find flies like the Conehead Marabou Muddler in water that seem impenetrable. In waters where crayfish are abundant, a bulky fly in shades of orange, brown, or olive may offer some advantage. And the old fisherman's adage "bright fly, bright day, dark fly, dark day" is a guideline that has often brought action to a slow day.

In lakes and in saltwater fly fishing, where one species of baitfish may be prevalent to the exclusion of others, fly selection is more critical. The most important consideration is length, so if **striped bass** are eating three-inch baitfish a smaller or larger fly may be ignored.

S

S

Shape may also be critical—**tarpon** feeding on deep-bodies mullet may turn away from a slim bait-fish pattern but will eagerly accept one with more bulk. Trout or landlocked salmon in big lakes feeding on smelt may key into the length and pastel shades of this slim baitfish and pass up a bulkier Woolly Bugger or Muddler Minnow.

STREAMER FISHING TECHNIQUES

In trout fishing, knowing *when* to fish a streamer pattern is more important than fly selection. Trout may ignore baitfish when the water is clear and the sun is bright because they can't catch the more nimble prey in the middle of the day. Early morning and after dark are times when trout are more likely to chase streamers. When a sudden rainstorm

darkens the sky and discolors the water, baitfish and crayfish become disoriented and trout will ravage them as long as visibility stays low. Although salt-water gamefish are also more likely to chase baitfish aggressively at dawn and dusk, daily tide movements also trap baitfish along structures, so fishing a streamer can be effective even at high noon.

The most common way to fish a streamer is by moving the fly through the water by stripping line. Strips can be anything from long, slow pulls to fast, jerky movements; it's often necessary to experiment with different kinds of **retrieves** until the right combination is found. In current, whether in fresh or saltwater, an effective technique is to cast the fly across the current and merely let it swing on a tight line until it swings below the angler. The swing can be combined with occasional strips or pulses of the rod to introduce an erratic movement. Streamers are also effective fished **dead drift**, just like a nymph to imitate a dying baitfish tumbling in the current. The fly is cast upstream and allowed to drift back to the angler with no added motion, and a strike is made if the line hesitates.

STRIKE

See Hooking Fish.

STRIKE INDICATOR

See Indicator.

STRIPED BASS

Striped bass, *Morone saxatilis*, are one of the finest **fly rod** fish in salt water. Because this schooling fish prefers to feed in shallow coastal areas and estuaries, stripers are caught on flies hundreds of miles from the ocean when they ascend large rivers to spawn in the spring, off sandy swimming beaches throughout the summer, in bays and harbors, and on near-shore rips and reefs. They are native to the Atlantic Coast from Nova Scotia to northern **Florida** and also to the Mississippi Delta region of **Louisiana**. They have been introduced into many large freshwater reservoirs and river systems throughout the United States, and populations have also

been established by stocking on the Pacific Coast, most notably in the San Francisco area and in some of the larger estuaries in **Oregon**.

Although striped bass have been caught in nets in weights close to 100 pounds, the average fish caught on a fly is between 5 and 15 pounds. Stripers up to 40 pounds are occasionally caught on flies, especially from **North Carolina** to **Maine**, where their numbers are strongest, but most of the larger specimens are caught on bait and plugs. Giant stripers have also been caught on flies in estuaries in northern **California** and southern Oregon. Smaller fish from 12 to 24 inches, called "schoolies," are very abundant in estuaries and harbors throughout the year, especially from Chesapeake Bay north to Cape Cod. These little fish take small **streamer** flies with abandon, and it is great fun to take them on a light trout rod in protected harbors.

Striped bass fishing with a fly rod begins in earnest in April and May, when the larger fish leave their spawning grounds in the Chesapeake and Hudson River estuaries and move north to fatten on the abundant food on the mid-Atlantic and New England coasts. Smaller schoolies appear first, followed by larger fish in a few weeks. Prime time in New England is late May through early July. Although fish are present all summer long the bigger ones will move slightly offshore for cooler water or feed primarily at night. In the fall, the fish reverse their migration and although the action can be hit-and-miss, hitting the right

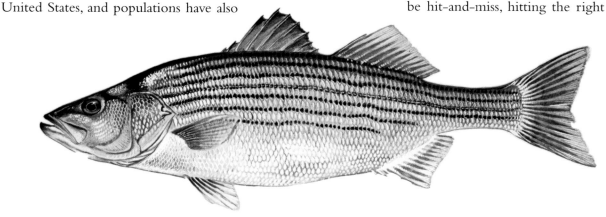

beach in the fall when migrating schools are chasing **baitfish** on their way south can be an amazing experience, with thousands of stripers herding baitfish on the surface. The beaches of Long Island are especially famous for these runs of striped bass in October and early November.

Once striped bass have reached an area, they can be caught almost anywhere. Sandy beaches, especially those with "bowls" or deep bays are especially good in early morning and at night. **Jetties** will hold fish that are attracted by the baitfish concentrated around the rock structures. Steep, rocky beaches will hold stripers all day long, where they feed in the white water where waves crash up against the rocks. Sand and mud flats, especially near estuaries, will hold feeding bass at all hours of the day, and fish up to 30 pounds can sometimes be found cruising these shallows for crabs, shrimp, and baitfish, even in the middle of the day in bright sunlight. Offshore rips hold the biggest bass during the summer, as water temperatures stay cool and the rips hold great quantities of baitfish and squid.

Fly fishing for striped bass is productive with a myriad of different techniques. At night, in harbors and estuaries and off calm beaches, stripers can be heard feeding on baitfish close to the surface, and it's a simple matter to throw an unweighted fly like a sand eel or **Deceiver** fly to the disturbance, retrieving with a very slow strip to imitate a crippled baitfish. **Poppers** are also great flies to use for stripers, and they work well during the day in spring and then at night and at dawn throughout the summer. Typically the best **retrieve** for a popper is to let the fly sit and make short strips followed by long pauses, but sometimes a fast, steady retrieve with lots of noise will interest one, especially in the offshore rips.

During the day, it's often necessary to go to fast-sinking lines, when fishing in the surf, in currents between jetties, or along deep dropoffs. Here, best flies include the **Clouser Minnow** or the Half & Half, a cross between a Clouser and a Deceiver. Typically, a fast retrieve works best when fishing

deep during the day. However, shallow flats should not be ignored during the day. There is more food on shallow flats than in deep water, and stripers will prowl these places on incoming and outgoing tides looking for food. Carefully stalk the flats looking for wakes or the shadows of fish as they slide through the shallow water, and cast well ahead of a cruising fish with a 12-foot, 12-pound **leader**. The fly can be either retrieved in mid-water or allowed to sit on the bottom until a striper cruises by—often just a one-inch strip will be enough to make a striper inhale a **crab fly**. The standard baitfish imitations can be used here, but success rates are much higher with **bonefish** or **permit** flies that imitate crustaceans.

Offshore, look for stripers anyplace currents form or rocks line the bottom, as those are the places where baitfish will congregate. Terns and gulls hovering over the water are a sure sign that striped bass are nearby, although the fish will not always be feeding on the surface. Sometimes, when birds are found it is necessary to fish with a **sinking line** 20 to 30 feet below the surface, as stripers will push baitfish close to the surface but may feed deep. Often, at the turn of the tide stripers will begin to feed close to the surface, so if birds are in the area it may be worth hanging around. Striped bass in freshwater lakes typically retreat to deep water during the summer and are best in spring and fall, when the fish herd schools of baitfish near the surface.

S

Schoolie stripers can be handled with a 7-weight line and a **floating line**, but the preferred outfit for striped bass is a 9-foot, 9-weight rod. An intermediate or slow-sinking line is the best all-around option, but knowledgeable striper anglers always carry a fast-sinking line on an extra spool in case the fish are deep. Productive flies may be anything from a 6-inch Cowan's Magnum baitfish when the bass are chasing large herring or menhaden in the spring to a size 6 bonefish fly on a shallow flat. However, day in and day out a baitfish pattern three or four inches in length will probably interest a feeding striped bass.

The very best places and times to catch striped bass on a fly include the coast of Maine in late June, Cape Cod, Martha's Vineyard, Nantucket, and Block Island in June and July, Long Island in June and September, the Chesapeake region in spring and fall, the Roanoke River in North Carolina in April, and San Francisco Bay in September and October.

STRIPPING BASKET

When frequent long casts are made, especially where the **fly line** is stripped onto rocks, brush, or a crowded boat, a stripping basket is an essential piece of gear. Line is stripped into the basket, and when the next cast is made, the line shoots easily from the basket, rather than catching on sharp rocks, kelp, or boat cleats. A stripping basket can be made from a plastic dishpan, with slots cut in the

side of the basket to accommodate a **wader belt** to keep it handy around the angler's waist. However, the best stripping baskets also have tapered cones lining the bottom of the basket, which keep coils of line separate and aids in the ability of the line to shoot cleanly from the basket. A two-handed **retrieve**, with the rod tucked under the arm, is often used with a stripping basket because this method places the coils of line more precisely than stripping with one hand.

SUBIMAGO
See Mayfly.

SUNFISH
See Panfish.

SUNGLASSES

Sunglasses are an essential item for fly fishers. They protect eyes from damaging ultraviolet rays and stray casts and also keep eye strain at a minimum through a long day of fishing. Because visible light that hits the water at an angle becomes polarized, polarized sunglasses, which block the polarized light, help remove glare and allow the angler to see fish and hidden structures under the water's surface. Nonpolarized sunglasses only block visible and ultraviolet light; since they reduce resolution without cutting glare, they are dangerous when **wading** deep, fast water because the angler cannot see hidden snags.

Glass sunglass lenses offer the best optics and scratch resistance but can be heavy and uncomfortable over a long day of fishing. Plastic lenses made from CR-39 or polycarbonate offer good optics and light weight, although they scratch more easily. Polarized lenses made from acrylic are inexpensive but they offer neither the scratch resistance or optical superiority of glass and the other plastics. More expensive sunglasses also add layers of anti-reflective

coatings to both sides of the lens, which make vision sharper by reducing glare.

The best polarized lens color for fishing shallow water is amber, or any of the similar tints like light brown or copper or vermillion that block blue light rays. Removing blue light makes contrast stronger and the definition between objects of different shades more pronounced, which is important for deciding whether a shape on the bottom is a submerged log or a fish. Gray polarized lenses work well over deep water, where submerged objects are too deep to be seen, and gray also has the advantage of preserving colors as they are seen with the unaided eye. Lenses with a green or blue tint should be avoided for fly fishing because they allow more blue light to reach the eye and make objects fuzzier.

SURGEON'S KNOT AND LOOP

The Surgeon's Knot and Loop are two very simple but effective knots, and when tied properly they retain nearly 100 percent of the weaker strand's strength. While not as clean and slim as knots like the Barrel Knot or **Perfection Loop**, they can be tied quickly, when darkness approaches or when hands are cold. In addition, the Surgeon's Knot is a stronger knot when joining two pieces of material that differ by more than .002".

SURGEON'S KNOT
- Overlap the standing part of the **leader** and the **tippet** for about three inches. From a simple overhand knot in the doubled section by bringing the tippet and the short end of the standing part of the leader through the loop.
- Bring the tippet and short end of the standing part around and through the loop a second time. Tighten the knot by wetting it, holding both the short and long ends on each side, and pulling with a quick, smooth motion. (In tippets smaller than 3X, many anglers use a three-turn Surgeon's knot.) Trim the short ends on both sides of the knot.

SURGEON'S LOOP
- Double the leader material at one end, overlapping by a few inches (figure 1). Make a loop with the doubled section by doubling it over itself and passing the top of the loop through the loop just made (figure 2).
- Pass the top of the loop through the doubled loop once more (figure 3). Hold the top of the loop in one hand and the tag end and standing part in the other. Wet the knot and pull firmly to seat it. Trim the tag end (figure 4).

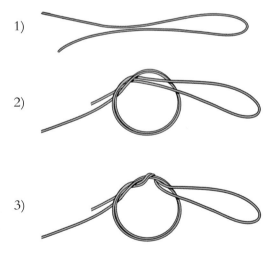

1)

2)

3)

4)

S

Tarantula

T

TAILWATER

A tailwater river flows below a dam, and is greatly influenced by the flows allowed through the dam. Dams tend to concentrate nutrients in the reservoir below, modify temperature regimes, and moderate flows. The concentration of nutrients makes tailwaters richer than other rivers, with a greater biomass of both aquatic plants (most often algae) and aquatic invertebrates below the dam. Temperature regimes can be modified positively when the water leaving the dam is a constant temperature throughout the year. This happens when dams are "bottom release," and the water in the river below the dam stays a constant temperature year-round, typically the temperature of groundwater in the region. Thus, tailwater releases are warmer in the winter than surrounding waters and colder in the summer. This, combined with a moderation in flows, preventing major flooding, creates an extremely stable environment that allows trout and other fish to maintain a high growth rate year-round, as opposed to trout in **freestone** streams,

which may only grow for a few months in late spring and early summer when **water temperatures** are optimum.

Not all dams are beneficial to trout populations. Those that allow releases from the top of the reservoir often release water that is too warm into the tailwater below. Dams that generate power by pulsing water daily through the dam create daily flow fluctuations can hinder aquatic life because of the constant instability. And of course, tailwaters that rise many feet in a matter of minutes can be dangerous to the wading angler. Thus, the best dams are those that release water from the bottom of the reservoir at a nearly constant rate throughout the season.

Tailwaters have enabled fishery scientists to create trout streams in unlikely places, especially in warmer states where natural river flows are far too warm for trout most of the season. Rivers such as the **White River** in Arkansas, the San Juan in **New Mexico**, and the Gunpowder in **Maryland** would not support trout without the cool waters from bottom-release dams. Many of the most beloved trout rivers in more temperate, trout-supporting regions of the United States are tailwaters as well, including The Bighorn and Madison in **Montana**, the Pitt and Sacramento in **California**, the Colorado and South Platte in **Colorado**, and the Delaware in **New York**.

Tailwater rivers are often more like **spring creeks** than freestone rivers. A rich food supply encourages both large trout and selective feeding, so the fish in tailwaters often require careful fly selection and long, fine **leaders**. And although the food supply is abundant, it is often less diverse than in freestone rivers. The most common insects in tailwaters are filter feeders like **caddisflies** and **midges** because of the vast amount of plankton that flows into tailwaters from reservoirs. Also extremely common in tailwaters are aquatic **worms** and **scuds**. As a result, although **dry fly** and **streamer** fishing in tailwaters can be excellent, day in and day out, the best tactic is fishing with **nymphs**. In some tailwaters, huge trout feed on tiny midge **larvae** almost constantly throughout the year and the best way to catch a trout over 20 inches long is to fish a fly smaller than a size 20.

TAIMEN

The fish known as taimen in Asia and huchen in Europe, *Hucho hucho*, is the largest salmonid in the world, approaching 200 pounds. Unlike other large salmonids such as **Atlantic** and **Pacific salmon**, taimen live entirely in large freshwater rivers. Their range includes part of the Caspian and Arctic drainages in Eurasia and some rivers in the Pacific drainage of

Mongolia and **Russia**. It is Mongolia where most fly fishers pursue this exotic and gigantic fish. Taimen eat mainly fish but will also swallow rodents and small waterfowl. Flies are necessarily large and tackle used is that more suitable for small **tarpon**, an 8- or 9-weight outfit with a large reel and plenty of **backing**. Because taimen feed eagerly on the surface, the most exciting way to catch one is with a hair mouse pattern; the dramatic **strike** is totally visible to the angler.

TANDEM FLY

A tandem fly is one with a second **hook** added behind the first, usually attached to the shank of the first hook with a piece of **wire** or heavy **nylon**. A tandem fly is useful when a fly longer than six inches is needed, as it will catch fish that may **strike** short or just strike the tail of the fly. Tandem **streamers** are often used when trolling for landlocked **Atlantic salmon** or **pike**, because casting a tandem fly is not easy and a fly trolled behind a boat is less likely to tangle. Tandem hooks are also used occasionally for flies used for **sharks** and **barracuda** because both of these species often nip at the tail of a fly.

TANDEM FLY RIGS

Fishing two flies at once on a tandem rig is a great way to test the effectiveness of two fly patterns at the same time. Sometimes fish may be attracted to a bigger fly but reluctant to **strike** it, so a smaller, more subtle fly is added to close the deal. Despite the attractiveness of this ability, it should be recognized that tandem fly rigs are very air-resistant and difficult to cast, and are prone to tangle, especially on windy days.

The most common way to create a tandem fly rig is to tie a short (6-inch to 20-inch) piece of **tippet** to the bend of the **hook** of the first fly with a **clinch knot**. Another way, more prone to tangle, is to leave one tag end of a **barrel knot** long when

attaching the tippet and to tie one fly to this piece and the second fly to the end of the tippet. In most cases, it's easiest to cast if the upper fly is larger or more heavily weighted than the lower fly.

Any combination of tandem flies is possible. The most common arrangements are two **nymphs** (often a larger and smaller one) or what is called a "dry **dropper**," with a highly visible **dry fly** as the upper one and a small nymph as the lower fly. In this situation, the dry fly can catch fish but it also acts a strike **indicator** when a fish takes the nymph. Two dry flies are sometimes used in a similar technique, where a large, highly visible dry fly like a Stimulator or hopper pattern is followed by a tiny dry that is difficult to see. Less common but still effective combinations are two different **streamer** patterns or a streamer and a small nymph. The latter is especially deadly when trout chase a big streamer but are reluctant to strike it— the smaller and more subtle nymph appears to be less suspicious than the big streamer pattern.

TAPER, LEADER
See Leader.

TAPER, LINE
See Fly Line.

TAPER, ROD
See Fly Rod.

TARPON

Tarpon, *Megalops atlanticus*, are one of the most highly sought gamefish on a fly rod. Their potential great size (fish up to 200 pounds have been caught on fly tackle) and their thrilling runs and acrobatic displays, with leaps up to 10 feet vertically and 20 feet horizontally, contribute to their allure. But tarpon offer more. A giant 200-pound fish is just as likely to eat a three-inch fly as a plug or live bait, and in many places in the world, especially in southern **Florida**, these giants are caught in clear, shallow water where every wiggle of the fish as it pounces on the fly is visible to the angler. Smaller fish are found along the Atlantic Coast of Mexico and northern South America. Giant fish roll in dirty water off Costa Rican rivers and on the coast of West Africa. But nowhere else in the world provides the combination of large fish and clear water like the Atlantic and Gulf Coasts of Florida—and especially the Florida Keys.

Resident tarpon, mostly smaller "baby" tarpon of 10 to 40 pounds, will be found year-round in brackish water in the Everglades and along both Florida coasts as well as The Atlantic coast of **Central America**. Navigation canals and hot water outflows of power plants are especially good places to find these smaller fish. They are often seen feeding on **baitfish** on the surface at dawn and dusk, and during the day will roll in deeper water. When the fish are feeding they are relatively easy to catch on bulky **streamers** and **poppers**, but when rolling in deep water they can be annoyingly difficult to tempt, probably because they are not actively feeding. The best tackle for these smaller fish is a 9- or 10-weight outfit with a **floating line**, plus a **sinking line** for trying to catch them in deep water during the day. Although baby tarpon are not especially picky about fly pattern and are not afraid of heavy **tippets**, they can be very spooky, especially the Everglades fish, so a careful approach with minimum disturbance will result in more strikes.

The larger fish that are seen in the Florida Keys and Gulf Coast from March through July are migratory. Some authorities feel that each major estuary along the Gulf Coast has a unique population, while others believe the same fish move from south to north during the season. What is known is that the giant fish move into the estuaries to "stage" prior to spawning, and that they eventually move far offshore to spawn. It is this annual migration of large tarpon, and their tendency to eat shrimp, small crabs, and palolo **worms** (an aquatic worm that comes to the surface for spawning) that makes them such ideal targets for the fly fisher.

Fishing for tarpon is a team effort, with the boat handler (a friend or a guide) being as important as the angler. Tarpon move along the shore in schools, and once the school is spotted, the boat must be in position so that the angler is able to cast to the fish as they are coming at the boat or crossing at some incoming angle to the boat. Casting to a tarpon or school of tarpon moving away from the boat means the fly will move toward the tarpon, and tarpon get nervous and don't eat when their intended prey appears to be rushing toward them. In most fisheries, experienced guides know exactly where the tarpon will pass each day, and boats will be "staked out" in a prime location so the angler gets as many shots as possible.

When casting to a school of tarpon, the best angle is at about 45 degrees to the fish, so that when retrieved the fly moves away from the fish rather than toward it. With a school of tarpon passing in front of the boat, this means casting to them when they are still 80 to 100 feet away, leading the fish by about 10 feet so the fly has a chance to sink to their level. Tarpon on their migration are not aggressive feeders, and the idea is to swim a fly that looks like a crab or shrimp right in front of one so it looks like an easy morsel to pick up on the way. Usually, foot-long retrieves of fly line with a short pause in between is the best way to move the fly, although at times a guide may ask the angler to speed up if a tarpon appears to lose interest, or slow down the **retrieve** if the fly is moving out of the strike zone in front of the fish too quickly.

Tarpon flies should be retrieved with the rod tip almost touching the water so that wind and waves don't affect the retrieve. Tarpon are quick to attack a fly but slow to clamp their jaws upon prey, so either wait until the guide says to **strike** or hit the fish once it is felt by tension on the line. Strikes should be low and off to the side, with two or three quick, hard jabs with the rod while yanking on the line in the opposite direction with the other hand. Tarpon

T

have extremely hard jaws, and "trout strikes" where the rod is raised when striking, do not put enough pressure on the hook.

It's often said that the most important part of a tarpon fly pattern is the **hook**. Hooks should be high quality, short-shank, and razor-sharp; most guides have a preferred brand and model number. (Pattern is secondary.) Traditional tarpon flies are mostly **hackle** with reds, blacks, yellows, and purples the favored colors. However, tarpon flies that are more imitative of crabs and shrimp are replacing the more impressionistic fly patterns favored in the twentieth century. Every tarpon spot has its favored patterns, so it is best to check with a guide or local anglers before buying or tying tarpon flies.

Tarpon tackle is heavy. Ten-weight **fly rods** are fine for smaller fish, but for fish over 100 pounds 11-weights and 12-weights are standard. These bigger, heavier rods are not as intimidating as they seem, because modern **graphite rods** are very light and tarpon fishing is mostly a matter of hunting and waiting with a few casts in between, as opposed to constant casting throughout the day. Rods larger than 12-weights are seldom used because the bigger 14- and 15-weights don't have the accuracy or delicacy needed for fishing to tarpon in shallow water. And whereas the **fly reel** is of secondary importance to the rod in most fly fishing situations, a strong, smooth reel capable of holding the line and 300 yards of 50-pound gel-spun **backing** is mandatory. Tarpon on the flats are usually fished with either a floating or intermediate-weight fly line, or a floating line with a clear intermediate tip. The later line is very popular because the floating line can be picked up quickly if a poor cast is made to the wrong direction, yet the slow sinking clear tip keeps the line below the influence of wind and waves.

TENNESSEE

OVERVIEW

Most of the fly fishing opportunities in Tennessee are found in the eastern end of the state. There are opportunities in the western part of the state for **largemouth bass** and **panfish** in ponds, and bass and **carp** in the Mississippi drainage. Even **smallmouth bass** are native only to the eastern half of the state and have not been established in western Tennessee because it lacks the cool, clear water and rocky habitat needed by smallmouths. Although some ponds in public parks in western Tennessee are stocked with trout during the winter, this is strictly a put-and-take artificial fishery and not popular with fly fishers. In fact, the most popular fly fishing destination for those living in western Tennessee is the **White River** in Arkansas.

Eastern Tennessee, however, offers some of the finest trout fishing in the Southeast. Trout fishing here is broken into three broad groups: Fishing on Tennessee Valley Authority (TVA) **tailwaters** below dams, fishing free-flowing mountain streams, and fishing on TVA reservoirs. The fish in the tailwaters are mostly stocked but grow fast in the rich food supply and constant temperatures of the dam releases. Wade-fishing is limited to times when dams are not generating, although fishing from a **drift boat** is productive when the river level rises several feet or more during power generation. Most of this fishing is with small **nymphs** (sizes 16–22), although **dry flies** work well during spring and summer **hatches**, and **streamers** produce in high water. In the mountain streams of the Smokies, many of the streams support populations of wild trout. The fish are spooky but not very selective, and a big dry fly may be all that is needed throughout the day. On the reservoirs, trout are far less abundant, especially for the fly fisher, but the average fish will be much bigger than from rivers and streams.

FISHERIES

The Caney Fork, east of Nashville, is a tailwater fishery in the center of the state and the furthest west of quality trout streams in the state. Its smooth flows serve up good hatches of **midges** and **caddisflies**, making it an excellent stream for dry fly fishing. Further west, the Clinch River, north of

T

Use bead-bodied scud imitations in Tennessee tailwaters.

Knoxville, is a moody river that holds large trout that are often quite selective; small caddis, mayfly, and midge **larva** imitations are the best flies on this river. An hour west is the Holston River: Midge dry flies and nymphs are the year-round staple patterns here, but caddisflies and mayflies hatch well during the summer months and **grasshopper** and **beetle** patterns also work well in late summer and fall. This river should not be confused with the South Holston in the extreme northeast corner of the state, which is a veritable insect and fish hatchery that supports populations of both wild and stocked **brown** and **rainbow trout** of all sizes. This river offers excellent hatches and frequent periods of great dry fly fishing with sulphurs, midges, caddisflies, and **Blue-Winged Olives** the most important. Nymph fishing with **scud** and **sow bug** imitations is also productive, and of course streamer fishing during the high water of power generation. Another tailwater, smaller and more intimate than the South Holston but less than 30 minutes away, is the Wautaga. The fish here are not as selective as on other tailwaters and **attractor** patterns work well.

All the best mountain freestone rivers in Tennessee are found along the border with **North Carolina**, in the higher altitude of Great Smoky Mountains National Forest and Cherokee National Forest. Trout in these streams do not have the rich food supply of fish in tailwater rivers, so the main determinant of success in these walk-in streams is careful approach and presentation. Any reasonable dry fly or nymph should interest the mixture of small wild and larger stocked trout in these streams. Best watersheds to fish, from north to south, are the Laurel Creek, North and South Indian Creeks, Paint Creek, Middle and West Prongs of the Pigeon River, Little River, Abrams Creek, and the Tellico River. Smaller wild trout, even native **brook trout**, will be more often found in the tiny tributaries of these streams. Although **lake fishing** for trout is not as popular with fly fishers as river fishing in Tennessee (and the fish are harder to catch), large trout can be found in some of the TVA impoundments, especially the three lakes that are part of the original Little Tennessee River watershed: Tellico, Chilhowee, and Calderwood Lakes.

SEASON

Trout fishing in Tennessee tailwater rivers is a year-round experience, and the nymph fishing, especially with tiny midge nymphs, is excellent all winter long. Dry fly fishing with midge imitations is also possible 365 days a year because of the stable temperatures and flows in these rivers. Best hatches of the bigger mayflies and caddisflies will be in April through June. Fishing on the mountain **freestone** streams is best in spring and fall. In winter, **water temperatures** may be too low for trout activity, and during the summer water temperatures may be too high. If fishing small mountain streams in midsummer, it's best to head into the smaller tributaries where water temperatures are cooler and trout may feed throughout the day.

TERRESTRIALS

When fly fishers speak of terrestrials, they mean either land-bred insects like **ants**, **beetles**, **grasshoppers**, and crickets (as opposed to aquatic insects like **mayflies**, **stoneflies**, and **caddisflies**), or the flies that imitate these insects. Although trout and other gamefish eat terrestrial insects throughout most of the season, land-bred insects become very important in late summer and early fall, when most aquatic insects have hatched and the **larvae** that will form next year's **hatches** are too small to be of interest to the fish. In small streams, which lack large expanses of insect-producing **riffles**, terrestrial insects can make up 80 percent of a trout's diet during the summer.

Although artificial flies designed to look like ants or moths were used for hundreds of years, it was not until the middle of the twentieth century that fly fishers began to study the behavior of insects that fall into the water and their effect on trout feeding behavior. In contrast to an aquatic insect hatch, where many flies appear on the water almost instantaneously, terrestrial insects fall into the water throughout the warm parts of the day when they are most active. As a result, trout feeding on these insects may only rise once every ten minutes or more and this kind of feeding often goes unnoticed by all but the most careful observer. Rises to terrestrial insects are typically soft and

subtle, because land insects ride low in the water and all a trout has to do is sip one gently from the surface film. It is important to look carefully for fish feeding on ants or beetles, especially where deep water runs along a grassy bank. Exceptions to this feeding behavior are sometimes seen when trout eat large grasshoppers or **cicadas**, because several trout may try to pounce on these big packages of protein at once, and the momentum developed by a trout rushing to intercept a big insect may manifest itself in a violent splash.

The best way to fish terrestrial flies is to fish from late morning through early evening, working **upstream** with a careful stalk so as not to frighten trout feeding in the clear water of late summer. Smart anglers scour the banks to find out which kind of terrestrials are most common and pick a fly accordingly. Trout seldom feed on a given species of terrestrial insect to the exclusion of others, but if no grasshoppers are seen along the banks but tiny black beetles are abundant, it's wise to stick with a beetle instead of a hopper imitation. Because terrestrial insects are clumsy when hitting the water, it often

T

helps to overpower the cast a bit so that the fly hits the water with a slight amount of commotion. Most anglers fish terrestrial imitations as dry flies because it is more fun, but fishing them subsurface like a nymph is often a deadly practice because terrestrial insects sink and drown after drifting only a short distance. A **dry fly** imitation of a beetle or grasshopper can be easily made to sink by pinching a small **split shot** to the **tippet** about 8 inches above the fly and fishing it with a strike **indicator**.

Besides the more common and obvious insects like ants, beetles, grasshoppers, and crickets, trout also feed on moths, inchworms, leafhoppers, house flies, bees, wasps, and cicadas. Although imitations of all these insects have been created by fly tiers, a box full of ant, beetle, and grasshopper flies will catch most trout feeding on terrestrials.

TEXAS

OVERVIEW

Although Texas has limited trout fishing, there are still many opportunities for fishing with a **fly rod** 12 months a year without leaving the state. There is good fly fishing for **largemouth bass**, **smallmouth bass**, Guadalupe bass, **striped bass**, and **panfish** in freshwater; plus saltwater fly fishing on the Gulf Coast for **redfish**, **sea trout**, jack crevalle, and even **tarpon**.

FISHERIES

The only good fly fishing for trout in Texas is in the tailrace of the Guadalupe River below Canyon Lake, about an hour west of Austin and San Antonio. This beautiful river, in the Texas Hill Country, is the southernmost trout stream in the United States. Although it regularly gives up **brown** and **rainbow trout** of over 5 pounds in weight, many of the bigger fish are caught on bait or plugs. In the 15 miles of trout water below the dam, 9 miles are special regulations water where only one trout of 18 inches or longer may be kept and only artificial lures may be used so there is still a good chance to catch a large trout on a fly. Like most **tailwaters**, **midges**, **scuds**, and **caddisflies** are the most common trout foods, although the river does support mayflies like the **Trico**, **Pale Morning Dun**, **Blue-Winged Olive**, and **Hexagenia**.

Other rivers in the Texas Hill Country offer wonderful fly fishing for largemouth bass, smallmouth bass, spotted bass, various species of panfish, and the native Guadalupe bass. Rivers like the Blanco, San Gabriel, Llano, and the Guadalupe below the cold water trout zone run through large stands of native pecan trees and limestone bluffs inhabited by large herds of deer and wild turkeys. For the most part, these rivers run clear and are easy to wade, which makes this region interesting for the fly fisher, and less artificial than the stocked trout water of the Guadalupe.

Texas has many reservoirs full of largemouth and landlocked striped bass, but two are the most popular with fly fishers. Lake Texoma, only an hour north of Dallas, is referred to as the "freshwater striper capitol of Texas." Unlike many lakes in the south, Texoma produces wild striped bass. Additionally, Texoma holds largemouth bass up to 11 pounds and smallmouths up to 7 pounds, which would be considered trophies for either of these species anywhere within their range. Lake Fork is a large impoundment two hours west of Dallas that that has produced 36 of the 50 biggest largemouth bass in Texas. Both sinking and floating flies are productive, and unlike many bass lakes, the fish here can be caught on a fly close to the surface all year long.

The Gulf Coast offers the most exotic and exciting fly fishing opportunities in Texas. The best fly fishing is south of Houston, where larger estuaries provide the food and habitat that inshore gamefish need. The Port O'Connor area offers great sightcasting for redfish over mud flats and oyster bars and large sea trout over grass beds. There is also an annual movement of very large tarpon off Pass Cavallo in early fall, before the tarpon then move south along the Gulf Coast. Unlike **Florida** tarpon fishing, this is mostly fishing for rolling fish over

The Gulf Coast offers the most exotic and exciting fly fishing opportunities in Texas.

deeper, dirtier water, but the potential for a tarpon close to 200 pounds on a fly is there. Further south, in the sheltered bays behind the barrier beach of San Jose Island near Rockport, the fishing is similar with even more shallow-water fishing inside the bays. Finally, the South Padre Island area on the border with Mexico adds **snook** to the mix, as well as greater numbers of jack crevalle and tarpon. In any of these areas, if weather permits and the fly fisher is able to get further offshore, there is great fishing for **false albacore**, Spanish and king **mackerel**, large redfish, and tarpon in the Gulf.

SEASON

Trout fishing in Texas is available year-round but most fly fishers prefer it during fall and winter because at other times the river is crowded with inner tubers and crowds of other fishermen. Fishing in the Hill Country Rivers is also year-round, but the best fly-fishing for bass is from March through June. For freshwater stripers in Lake Texoma, spring is the best time for large fish on a fly, when the fish run along rock ledges and channels as they head upriver to spawn. Summer brings big schools of fish to the surface chasing shad, and if a fly fisher is in the right place at the right time the streamer fishing can be spectacular. In fall, fish move into shallow

bays and coves and will take flies well until mid-November, when they head into deep water for the winter. For largemouth and smallmouth bass fishing in the big lakes like Lake Fork, fish are found around the mouths of creeks and on shallow flats during their spawning season, which is the best time to catch them on a fly. During the summer, smart anglers fish flies early and late in the day on the shallow edges of weed beds, and at night with big **poppers** and **streamers**. In the fall, the same tactics work better on the deeper edges of large weed beds, and fish will also be seen in shallow water chasing schools of shad on the surface. During the winter, bass can be caught with weighted flies on sinking lines around submerged structure like old road beds and dams.

THERMOMETER

Many fly fishers carry a small thermometer with them to find the optimum **water temperature** for the fish they are pursuing, and also to determine when insects will hatch on trout streams. For instance, an angler fishing a small mountain stream in spring might measure the water temperature and find it to be 38 degrees, too cold for active trout feeding. However, by moving to a lower altitude and in a valley that gets more sunlight, the lower reaches of the same stream might be ten degrees warmer and more productive for fly fishing. During the middle of the summer, in streams that approach the lethal limit of 75 degrees for trout, a smart fly fisher will take the temperature of small tributary streams and find cooler water and more cooperative trout.

Thermometers are also used to predict when various insects will **hatch**. Most aquatic insects have an optimum temperature at which they will hatch into adults and taking the water temperature may help an angler determine what fly to use. For example, the **Hendrickson mayfly** begins to hatch when spring water temperatures first hit 50 degrees. If a fly fisher arrives at a river on a sunny day and the water temperature measures 48 degrees, a smart move would be to fish a Hendrickson **nymph** during the morning and then switch to a **dry fly** or **emerger** in the afternoon when the temperature has risen a few degrees.

Ordinary medical and meat thermometers are not suitable for fly fishing because their accuracy is in the wrong range. Special stream thermometers are best for fishing, and both digital and analog alcohol-based versions are found in tackle shops.

TIDES

Currents concentrate food and attract gamefish in estuaries, shorelines and the open ocean, and tides are the most common source of these currents. Tides are formed by a complicated relationship between the gravitational pull of the sun and moon in relation to the earth and the inertia obtained by moving water. In most places on earth there are two high and two low tides per day, with the times of the tides advanced by 50 minutes each day.

The strongest tides, called spring tides, are formed when the sun and moon are in alignment and happen twice a month, once around the full moon and once around the new moon. Neap tides are when the sun and moon are at right angles to each other in relation to the earth and happen halfway between spring tides. Daily, tides are strongest in offshore areas at the extremes of high and low tides and are strongest close to shore halfway between high and low tide. Fly anglers often prefer times of lesser current because it is more difficult to fish a relatively lightweight fly in a strong current without the help of a fast-sinking **fly line**.

Fish can be caught on a fly in all stages of the tide, and the influence of tides on fly fishing will vary with every location. Offshore, where ocean currents flowing over humps on the bottom form turbulence or "rips," **baitfish** get trapped in the turbulence and fishing is best when the tide is moving. Whether baitfish or gamefish lie on the upcurrent or downcurrent side of a rip varies with each location, but if more fish are found on one side of a rip during a particular phase of the tide, when the tide turns it's often necessary to reposition the boat.

Sometimes fish feed best just after the tide turns or in the middle of a tide, but one certainty is that during slack water between tides gamefish will be spread out and more difficult to catch. This problem is particularly acute for the fly angler, as a **fly rod** cannot cover water as thoroughly as a spin rod fisher or trolled lure.

Inshore, tides create different circumstances. On shallow flats, during high tide fish are dispersed and it is often difficult to locate them. On **bonefish** flats, fish may move way back into mangrove swamps during high tide, making them inaccessible to anglers. However, during a rising (or incoming) tide, when gamefish are able to move onto a flat to prey on baitfish, crabs, and shrimp that were protected in shallow pools, the fishing is usually extraordinarily good, and most flats anglers prefer a rising tide. Fish also feed on a falling (outgoing) tide but since they are headed into deeper water it is a matter of finding the deeper channels where they travel. Blind-fishing off the edge of a flat into deeper water during a falling or low tide is often very productive as some of the plentiful food supply from the shallows gets washed into deeper water.

In estuaries, fishing is often best on a falling tide when water flowing out of marshes and very shallow flats brings food into the middle of the estuary or into the water outside of the estuary. However, fishing on an incoming tide will be excellent in places where the higher water levels allow gamefish to get into productive areas they cannot reach at lower water levels.

TIP
See Fly Rod.

TIPPET
The tippet is the part of a **leader** to which the fly is attached. In a leader with knots, the tippet may be a discrete piece of **monofilament** separated from the rest of the leader with a knot, but in knotless leaders, where the entire leader tapers gradually without a knot, the tippet may be difficult to identify exactly. In knotless leaders, typically the taper ends a few feet from the end, and when these leaders are extruded, about the last two feet are held to a constant diameter, and by carefully feeling the leader the transition between the tippet and the rest of the leader may be determined.

The tippet is the most critical part of the leader because it is closest to the fly. When fishing for saltwater species, bass, and salmon, the strength of the tippet is the most important consideration, so these tippets are often stated in pound-test. Thus a "9-foot 12-pound" leader is 9 feet long with a final piece that breaks at 12 pounds of force. In trout fishing, the diameter of the tippet determines how the fly

will behave on the water, and a difference of .001" in the tippet can mean the difference between success and failure. For these finer tippets an "X" nomenclature is used, with the following X sizes always referring to the diameter of the tippet, regardless of the brand or breaking strength of the tippet:

0X	.011"
1X	.010"
2X	.009"
3X	.008"
4X	.007"
5X	.006"
6X	.005"
7X	.004"
8X	.003"

Tippets are made from either **nylon** or **fluorocarbon** monofilament. Nylon floats better, is slightly more elastic and absorbs shock better, is less expensive, is easier to knot, and will eventually degrade in sunlight. Fluorocarbon or PVDF is denser than nylon so it sinks better, is more abrasion resistant, is impervious to the solvents in insect repellent and sunscreen, and because it has a refractive index very close to water, it is less visible when submerged. Knots in fluorocarbon should be tied carefully because this material is stiffer and does not draw down as easily as nylon. Because fluorocarbon does not biodegrade, it is extremely important for anglers to keep trimmings from knots and old

leaders in a pocket or other container and dispose of them in household trash, not in or near the water. Fluorocarbon and nylon can be knotted to each other with a surgeon's knot, and fly fishers often use a nylon leader combined with a fluorocarbon tippet knotted to the rest of the leader to take advantage of the beneficial properties of both materials.

TOWER CAST

See Overhead Cast.

TRICO

Trico **mayflies** are tiny insects in the genus *Tricory-thodes* that are extremely important to fly fishers. Although they may hatch from June through October, on most trout streams they **hatch** heavily in August and early September, providing great **dry fly** fishing at a time when most other aquatic insects have already hatched for the season. Despite their tiny (size 20–26) dimensions, Tricos often hatch and mate in vast clouds, stimulating active feeding by trout. Trico **duns** hatch either the morning before mating or very early in the morning of their mating swarms. The duns will bring some trout to the surface, but it is the concentrated swarm of mating **spinners** that all fall to the surface at once, usually in the middle of the morning, that provides the most exciting fishing. Often there will be so many insects on the water that it is difficult to determine whether a trout has taken the angler's artificial or a natural insect, and the competition from so many naturals at once makes repeated precision casting necessary. Nonetheless, trout often lose their normal caution when feeding on Tricos so the fishing can be easier than it might seem.

TRICORYTHODES

See Trico.

TRILENE KNOT

The Trilene Knot is very similar to the **Clinch Knot**, except two turns are taken through the eye of the **hook** instead of one prior to tying the knot. It is a very strong and secure knot to tie when the diameter of the **tippet** is much smaller than the diameter of the **wire** on the eye of the hook. For instance, if an angler is using a 5X tippet for **dry flies** and decides to tie on a big size 4 **streamer** without cutting back the tippet, a standard Clinch Knot will slip whereas the Trilene Knot will keep the fly securely attached.

- Pass the tag end of the tippet through the eye of the fly. Bring the tag end around in the same direction and go through the eye again. This forms a double loop in front of the eye. Do not tighten the loops (figure 1).

1)

- Wind the tag end around the standing end of the tippet four or five times. Bring the tag end back through the double loop formed in front of the eye (but not through the eye itself), (figure 1). Wet the knot and tighten by pulling the fly and the standing part of the tippet in opposite directions. Trim the tag end close to the eye of the hook (figure 2).

2)

TROUT UNLIMITED

Trout Unlimited is a North American organization (actually two organizations, a United States Trout Unlimited and Trout Unlimited **Canada**) dedicated to conserving, protecting, and restoring North America's coldwater (trout and salmon) fisheries and their watersheds. Trout Unlimited works with a combination of a national headquarters staff, scientists in the field, and grassroots local chapters, and accomplishes its work with a combination of full-time, professional staff and volunteer work. Formed in **Michigan** during the 1950s, Trout Unlimited has been a powerful and effective agent for change. Instead of just looking at short-term enhancements of fisheries for recreation, the organization looks at initiatives that benefit habitat from a watershed or species level, so that trout and salmon populations remain or become self-sustaining through natural reproduction rather than stocking. Trout Unlimited believes in using the latest in scientific information to accomplish its goals, whether it is restoring an eroded bank on a small trout stream with local volunteers or lobbying at the highest levels of government.

TUBE FLY

Tube flies are flies tied on hollow plastic, aluminum, or copper tubes instead of on a **hook**. The tube fly is threaded on the **leader** and a separate bare hook is tied to the **tippet** and is then secured to the rear of the tube fly with a small piece of soft plastic tubing, so that the hook stays in place during casting and throughout the drift of the fly, but can then separate once a fish is hooked. Tube flies were originally developed for **Atlantic salmon** fishing because the ornate **salmon flies** used in the early twentieth century were very expensive and time consuming to tie and the hook would often break or rust, making the fly worthless. In addition, once a fish is hooked the tube often slides up the leader and away from the sharp teeth of the fish, so tube flies greatly extend the useful life of a complicated fly pattern. Although early tube flies incorporated double or treble hooks, modern tubes flies use single hooks for lower mortality when catch-and-release fishing. (Multiple points tear up the mouth of a fish too much—and don't appear to be any better at hooking fish anyway.)

Once tubes became more popular, anglers realized other advantages. When tying a three- or four-inch fly in the standard manner, it's necessary to use a large, heavy hook. Big hooks are heavy and difficult to cast, and for all but the largest fish, hooks larger than a 1/0 are less likely to penetrate the jaw and are easier for a fish to throw because of the leverage a fish obtains against the long shank of a big hook. Multiple tubes can also be strung on a leader to get flies as large as 12 inches with a smaller hook that will penetrate and hold a fish better, so tube flies are popular when fishing for saltwater gamefish that prefer large flies like **sailfish**, **tuna**, and roosterfish. Large trout **nymphs** and **dry flies** are sometimes tied on tubes because when an eight-inch trout takes a two-inch dry fly the large hook in a standard fly will penetrate its eye or brain, causing high mortality. A two-inch dry **stonefly** imitation tied on a tube can be used with a size 8 hook instead of a size 4, which is far safer when a tiny trout eats the fly.

TUNA

Fly fishing for tuna can be either extraordinarily exciting or completely foolhardy depending on the size of the fish. Small tunas like **false albacore** and **bonito** provide exciting **strikes** and fast battles. Large tunas like bluefin and yellowfin tuna over 60

T

pounds are exciting at first but the battle soon turns into a long slugfest, and fly fishers who have caught yellowfin in excess of 80 pounds are usually quoted as saying they will never do it again. Tunas are amazingly stream-lined and built for speed, and they peel line off a **fly reel** as fast as any fish, literally causing inferior fly reel **drag** systems to smoke and melt. But the main problem with landing large tuna is that they are invariably caught in deep water, and after the initial runs the fish will sound straight down toward the bottom. The tuna must then be lifted up through the depths, and because tuna sport such hard, rigid bodies the angler cannot turn the head of a tuna in the same way that a large tarpon can be manipulated. This kind of fishing calls for a huge reel with a minimum of 400 yards of backing and a stiff, short heavy 14-weight **fly rod**.

Smaller tunas in the 20- to 60-pound range are within the arm strength limits of most fly anglers and the equipment can range from an 8-weight rod for bonito to a 12-weight for the smaller bluefins and yellowfins. Reels should still hold at least 200 yards of backing even for small tunas (and 300 yards is better). Flies used for tuna are often surprisingly small (from two to three inches long) and sparse because tuna have excellent eyesight and often feed on small **baitfish**. Tunas have tiny sharp teeth but will shy away from wire **shock tippets**, so the usual approach is to add a **monofilament** shock tippet of between 40- and 60-pound tests. If not fishing for **IGFA** records, many fly anglers just use a straight piece of heavy monofilament, which is easier to cast.

Tuna seldom stay in one place. Most conven-tional-tackle anglers troll for them, but for the fly angler it is a matter of finding fish herding baitfish on the surface, looking for wheeling birds and breaking fish, and then getting close to the school without running over it and spooking the fish. Schools may stay on the surface feeding for a few brief seconds or several hours, but a few minutes is the typical window of opportunity. Chumming for

Yellowfin tuna

tuna is one way to keep them close to a boat, but it is an expensive and time consuming process as it may take some time for the tuna to find the chum slick and once the chum runs out they will leave the area in a hurry.

Besides the two small tunas that most often inhabit shallow inshore areas, bonito and false alba-core, other tunas may require a boat run of from a mile to over 50 miles offshore. Bluefin tuna, found in seas throughout the world, may occasionally crash baitfish within sight of the beach, especially off the coast of New England and the Mid-Atlantic States. Once farther offshore, it is often a matter of finding bluefin small enough to catch on a fly, as bluefin grow to over 1,000 pounds. Skipjack tuna are found offshore on both Atlantic and Pacific Coasts, sometimes move close to shore, and are a manageable size on a fly rod. Blackfin tuna are commonly caught offshore on flies from Florida through the Gulf States and come to a chum slick readily. Yellowfin tuna are perhaps the most coveted trophy on a fly rod because they are reputed to be the strongest tuna on a fly rod. Bluefin tuna of over 100 pounds have been caught on the fly rod, but the 100-pound mark has yet to be reached with yellowfin. In addition, yellowfin are a deep-water tuna so it's necessary to run a long way offshore to target them with a fly rod. Other tunas like longfin albacore and bigeye tuna have been caught on a fly rod, but these species typically feed in deep water, well offshore, and are beyond the reach of fly anglers in most waters.

Ultra damsel

UPSTREAM

"Upstream" always refers to the direction from which the current in a river is coming. If you are standing in a river looking at the opposite bank and the water is flowing from right to left, upstream is to your right. Fish lying in a current always face into the current, which is usually in an upstream direction, unless a whirlpool is present. (There, fish could be facing any direction, depending on their position in the whirlpool.) Quartering upstream means to cast the **fly line** and fly about halfway between upstream and **across-stream**. When a fly line is cast directly upstream, there is very little **drag** on the line and fly because the angler is standing in the same current lane as the line and it does not cross conflicting currents. The term "upstream **dead drift**" is used to describe this presentation, and is most often used with **dry flies** and **nymphs**.

UTAH

OVERVIEW

Although it is the second-driest state in the Union, Utah offers some great fly fishing, including one of the finest trout streams in the world. Most of the best fly fishing in Utah is found in the north central to northeastern part of the state, but there is fishing for trout, **carp**, **panfish**, and **largemouth bass** in hundreds of water storage reservoirs throughout the state. Because most of these reservoirs are small and shallow, they can be easily fly fished from shore or from a small watercraft.

FISHERIES

The granddaddy of all Utah trout streams is the Green River. Located in the extreme northeastern corner of the state, the Green leaves giant Flaming Gorge Reservoir cold, clear, and fertile. This **tail-water** seldom fluctuates, so fishing conditions and **hatches** are dependable and trout grow quickly. The river's emerald waters flow through a spectacular canyon that is most often floated in a raft or **drift boat**, but there is public access just below the dam, at Little Hole about 7 miles downstream, and at Indian Crossings Boat Launch 15 miles below the dam. Anglers can walk from these access areas for many miles, although the terrain is rugged. Just **downstream** of the dam, **rainbow trout** are most common with some **cutthroat trout** mixed in. Below Little Hole fly fishers will find mostly fat, wild **brown trout** that regularly rise to small insects, plus big hoppers and **cicadas** in late summer. However, **nymph** fishing with small **midge larva** and **scud** imitations will produce the greatest numbers of fish.

The second most famous and productive trout river in Utah is the Provo. Because of its close proximity to Salt Lake City and Park City fishing pressure is high, but this little tailwater is often worth the effort. Divided into three sections, an upper section and two between a pair of reservoirs—Jordanelle and Deep Creek—the Provo is mainly a nymph river, with fish coming to the top for the occasional hatch. Because it is open all year long and is closer to civilization than the Green, the roads along the Provo remain open after snowstorms and nymph fishing can be excellent even in the middle of winter. The Logan River near Logan is a less demanding river to fish than either the Green or Provo, with easy access along Highway 89 and more reliable **dry fly** fishing. Wild brown and cutthroat trout are abundant in this river. But unlike the Green and Provo, spring runoff in May and early June make this river unfishable due to high, dirty water. South and east of Salt Lake City are a number of worthwhile trout streams. The Strawberry River is a meadow stream with a good population of brown trout and cutthroats below Strawberry Reservoir, and although fishing pressure is quite high there are plenty of good fish in this stream to make up for the lack of solitude. Less crowded is Current Creek below Current Creek Reservoir with a similar mix of large brown trout and cutthroats.

For the fly fisher willing to do some hiking to get away from the more popular tailwater rivers, the Uinta Mountains east of Salt Lake offer many opportunities for fishing in high mountain lakes and small **freestone** streams. Here, the trout are smaller. But in addition to the more common brown, rainbow, and cutthroat trout, many of the smaller lakes and streams have dense populations of small **brook trout**. The two best areas are probably the headwaters of the Duchene River drainage, including its North, West, and East Forks, and the Weber River drainage.

SEASON

Fly fishing on tailwater rivers is year-round, with stable flows and active trout even in the dead of winter. January and February can be slow months except for nymph fishing, although midge hatches might be seen on warm days. And although the Green River does fish well all winter, road closures in the dead of winter may make it impossible to get to the river even if the fish are feeding. **Mayfly**, **stonefly**, and **caddisfly** hatches begin in late March and early April and last through the summer, although many aquatic hatches taper off in midsummer, increasing the importance of **ant**, **beetle**, **grasshopper**, and **cicada** flies. Through it all, the ubiquitous midge hatches nearly every day. Fishing in the freestone mountain streams enjoys a relatively short season. Rivers are too cold or inaccessible in early spring, then runoff makes them high and unfishable. These smaller streams are at their best in early summer, because by the time August arrives they may already be too low for good fishing. Some of these streams pick up in the fall, especially those that have runs of spawning fish coming out of reservoirs.

Velvet crawfish

V

VERMONT

OVERVIEW

Vermont is a mostly rural, heavily forested state with a low population, so the water quality in the Green Mountain State is very high in most places. Vermont has few large rivers but many wild trout streams, and the best fishing is in the smaller mountain streams, where the fly fisher can go for days without seeing another angler. **Brook trout** are native to Vermont, but wild and stocked **brown** and **rainbow trout** are common in the lower reaches of many rivers. Fly fishers should not go to Vermont looking for impressive insect **hatches**, because Vermont's **free-stone** rivers are not very rich. And besides famous rivers like the Battenkill, upper Connecticut, and Winooski Rivers, most Vermont waters do not offer trophy trout. Vermont does offer some good fly fishing for both **smallmouth** and **largemouth bass**, especially in the larger lakes and the Connecticut River, and there is good spring and fall fishing for landlocked **Atlantic salmon** in tributaries to Lake Memphremagog on the state's northern border with **Canada**.

FISHERIES

The Connecticut River, which forms the border with **New Hampshire**, is one of the state's best fisheries. The northern section of the river, south to Bloomfield, Vermont, is excellent trout water, with a mixture of stocked and wild brook, brown, and rainbow trout with an occasional landlocked salmon. The Connecticut River in Vermont is a tailwater fishery, and thus hosts a richer insect life population than most other Vermont Rivers. **Caddisflies** and **stoneflies** predominate, but during the summer the river also has some good **mayfly** hatches, including the giant **Hexagenia** mayfly, which hatches in the long, slow silty pools that are found between areas of fast water. Best flies on this river are size 8–12 **nymphs** and size 14–18 **dry flies** that imitate stoneflies, caddisflies, and mayflies. The river is big enough to float and there are a number of excellent guide services in the area. It is also possible to wade the river, but this big river can be tricky in high water. Further **downstream** along the New Hampshire border, the Connecticut offers excellent fly fishing for smallmouth bass,

THE ORVIS ENCYCLOPEDIA OF FLY FISHING **275**

largemouth bass, and **pike**. There are also short stretches of water that host elusive populations of very large rainbow and brown trout, especially in the **riffles** at the mouth of the White River below White River Junction. The White River itself is an excellent trout river, with beautiful pools and many miles of cool, clear water that supports wild rainbows, stocked brown trout, and smallmouth bass.

To the north and east of the upper Connecticut, in the Northeast Kingdom of Vermont, are a number of rivers that flow into Lake Memphremagog. The Black, Barton, and Clyde Rivers have spring runs of **steelhead** and landlocked Atlantic salmon in their lower reaches, with decent fishing for small trout in their headwaters. The Willoughby River also has a famous run of small steelhead that run out of Lake Willoughby, and the fish stay in the river late enough that they sometimes feed on **dry flies** before returning to the Lake in May. On the other side of the state, two tributaries of Lake Champlain are popular with fly fishers. The Winooski River is a relatively large (for Vermont) river that offers excellent fishing for brown and wild rainbow trout from its headwaters **upstream** of Montpelier. Most fly fishers prefer the smaller upstream reaches, but during low flows the bigger stretch in the vicinity of Waterbury is manageable with a fly rod and has excellent fishing with small dry flies and nymphs for wild rainbow trout. Also not to be missed is a major Winooski tributary the Dog River, which is known for its good populations of wild brook and brown trout. The Lamoille River north of the Winooski is another popular northern river, with very productive wet fly and nymph fishing for brook trout in its upper riffles, and good fishing with dries and nymphs in the lower reaches below Hardwick Lake.

Giant Lake Champlain, on the western border of the state, has some occasionally good but spotty shoreline fishing for landlocked salmon, especially in the lower reaches of the Lamoille and Winooski Rivers. The lake is also one of the finest places in the northeast to catch large smallmouth and largemouth bass, especially in the shallow bays during May and June. Two other lakes south of Champlain, Lake Bomoseen and Lake St. Catherine, are also good bass fisheries, and these lakes are stocked with brown trout that grow quite large on the introduced and unwelcome alewife, a **baitfish** that is not native to these lakes. Best time to chase these very large brown trout is early morning, when they are found feeding on tiny midges or crashing baitfish on the surface.

Two rivers in southern Vermont, the Black River and Otter Creek, are marginal trout fisheries but are stocked by the state with large breeder fish. These trophy stretches are found between Danby and Wallingford on Otter Creek and along Route 131 in Cavendish and Weathersfield. Otter Creek also has good fishing for small wild brook trout in its brushy headwaters and smallmouth bass and pike north of Rutland.

The Battenkill is Vermont's most famous trout river. Its notoriously difficult brown and brook trout are all wild, and the river runs through a scenic Vermont valley, once the home of Norman Rockwell and Charles F. Orvis. The river has good but not heavy insect hatches, but the water quality is very high, and it is unusual to find wild brook trout in a river this size outside of northern **Maine**. The river's brown trout have experienced periodic declines due to a lack of overhead cover in the river, but it is still one of the best places to catch a wild brown trout bigger than 20 inches on a **streamer** or on a dry fly from late May to early June. The river stays cool in summer and fishing can be excellent when other rivers in the East suffer from high water temperatures, especially during August when the river has dense hatches of tiny **Trico** mayflies, perhaps its best hatch.

SEASON

Vermont has no winter fly fishing, and although trout season opens in early April, fly fishing is difficult in Vermont rivers until the first week of May on the Battenkill, when the **Hendrickson** mayflies hatch. Most other rivers in Vermont are just too high and cold for decent fly fishing until the middle of May, when caddis and **Pale Evening Dun** mayflies begin. Summer trout fishing in Vermont is excellent; in fact many of the small mountain streams are in their prime during the heat of the summer. Fall fly fishing in Vermont is spotty, with the best fishing on warm Indian summer days, but rivers are nearly empty of anglers when the season closes in late October. Bass fishing in Vermont is also good throughout the summer, with the best fly fishing in early June when the fish are in shallow water before and after spawning.

VEST

A vest is the traditional trout angler's repository for **fly boxes**, **tippet** material, **leaders**, extra reel spools, and all the gadgets that fly fishers accumulate. Vests come in many varieties, from minimalist vests with just a few pockets to complicated models with over 20 different pockets. Many anglers want to know exactly what should go in each pocket, but the best approach is to decide how many fly

boxes will be carried and how much other gear the angler wants to carry and then choose a vest with the right capacity. Some vests offer special pockets for tippet material, **sunglasses**, or **forceps**, but most of the pockets can be filled with whatever the individual desires. It's best to plan a vest layout so that the most-used items will be close at hand in the outside pockets, and less useful gear can then be loaded in the back or inside pockets. Cotton vests are cool and comfortable, but synthetic vests made from **nylon** or other synthetics are more durable and dry quickly. For hot weather, look for a vest with mesh panels. When carrying more than two fly boxes, look for a vest design with shoulder support to prevent back pain. A great alternative to a vest is a **chest pack** or **waist pack**, both of which offer slightly less capacity but more freedom of movement for long days on the water.

VIRGINIA

OVERVIEW

Virginia offers diverse opportunities for the fly fisher, from s**pring creeks**, **tailwaters**, and small mountain streams for trout to large rivers for **smallmouth bass**, large lakes for smallmouth and **largemouth bass**, and **striped bass** and **sea trout** in the Chesapeake Bay estuary. Although Virginia waters contain some wild trout, many of the waters are supported by an extensive stocking program. Many of Virginia's rivers are in private hands, or in a patchwork of public and private ownership, so it is important to check access before you fish a river.

FISHERIES

In the southwestern corner of the state, one of the best trout rivers is the South Fork of the Holston River near Wytheville. This freestone stream supports a good population of stocked rainbow and brown trout. Two different special regulations sections above Buller Fish Culture Station ensure that many large trout remain in the stream throughout the year, although fishing in midsummer can be difficult because of high water temperatures. South of the Holston on the North Carolina border upstream of Damascus is Whitetop Laurel Creek, a beautiful forested mountain stream with a few wild trout mixed in with stocked browns and rainbows. The river is paralleled by the Virginia Creeper Trail, and nice fishing in solitude can be obtained by mountain bike. The river has good hatches of yellow **stoneflies**, **caddisflies**, Hendrickson **mayflies**, **Pale Evening Dun** mayflies, and **Blue-Winged Olive** mayflies. In addition, the giant **Green Drake** mayfly **hatches** in early May and brings the largest trout in the river to the surface. Also not to be missed is Green Cove Creek, a productive tributary of Whitetop Laurel.

The Jackson River north of Covington is one of Virginia's best trout streams. The lower part of the river, below the dam on Lake Moomaw, is a **tailwater** that offers big-water fly fishing, a rare opportunity in Virginia. The crystal clear water flows over long **riffles** that produce good hatches of yellow stoneflies, Pale Evening Duns, Blue-Winged Olives, and caddisflies. Not to be ignored are the vast numbers of blackfly **larvae** that carpet the bottom of the river, and small black **nymphs** are a required pattern in this river, especially during the winter. Although some of the lower river has public access, one large stretch is completely private, and in an acrimonious Virginia Supreme Court Decision the landowners were granted not only ownership of the river bottom but also of the trout that live in the stream. This area is plainly marked and the landowners mean business. Upstream of Lake Moomaw the river is a **freestone** mountain stream, with plenty of public access and a more remote setting. Although the trout population is not as dense in this stretch, the river is not as crowded and wild **brook trout** can be found in Muddy Run, a tributary of the upper Jackson.

The Smith River near Martinsville is a weedy, cold tailwater below Philpott Reservoir. Although the river just below the dam fishes best in winter because the water stays warmer, the best fishing for the rest of the year is below Town's Creek, because more nutrients enter the river there so the insect life is richer and fly hatches are better. Close to the dam most of the fishing is with **midge** imitations, but lower in the river it has great hatches of Pale Evening Duns, Blue-Winged Olives, Hendricksons, green drakes, and caddisflies. All the large brown trout in the river are wild and all the rainbows are stocked.

Although small (8- to 12-inch) browns predominate, the river gives up very large brown trout each year. Water generation from Philpott Reservoir is pulsed every day, and the flow can go from 100 to 2,000 cubic feet per second in a short time period, so it is best to check water generation schedules before fishing. These schedules are published a week ahead of time so fishing trips can be planned. West of the Smith is Dan River, which offers great fishing for brown and **rainbow trout** in a near-wilderness setting. Although the river is a small tailwater, larger nymphs (size 10–16) than are normally needed to fish tailwaters will catch trout, so the river is relatively easy to fish.

The two best trout waters to fish in northwestern Virginia, Mossy Creek and the Rapidan River, could not be more different. Mossy Creek is a meadow spring creek with a silt bottom and extensive weed growth. It supports very large brown trout that can be caught on **dry flies** and nymphs—although the biggest fish are caught by fishing **streamers** along its undercut banks. The Rapidan is a wild brook trout stream in a forested mountain setting and is known as the best stream in Shenandoah National Park. However, for the adventurous angler, there are many brook trout streams in the park and along the length of the Blue Ridge Parkway.

Smallmouth bass are second only to trout in the eyes of Virginia fly fishers. Although most rivers in the state support populations of this great fighter, the best ones are the James from Eagle Rock to below Lynchburg, the North and South Forks of the Shenandoah down to their confluence with the James, and the entire length of the New River. Two of the best lakes for fly fishing for both smallmouth and largemouth bass are Philpott Reservoir and Smith Mountain Lake, and the latter provides the opportunity to catch landlocked **striped bass** in spring and fall, when the fish move closer to shore to feed on **baitfish** near the surface.

Striped bass fishing along Virginia's coast can be good, although much of the best fishing in the north must be accessed by boat. The islands along the Chesapeake Bay Bridge are some of the most productive places for stripers. Further south, there is more **wade** fishing in Rudee Inlet and Lynnhaven Inlet, where fly fishers can catch sea trout (called speckled trout locally), and small **redfish** known in Virginia as puppy drum.

SEASON

Virginia's trout fishing is best in April and May, when rivers have warmed enough to get a trout's metabolism in high gear and insect hatches are most abundant. Summer trout fishing can be productive with small flies during cooler weather, but during hot spells the only decent fly fishing will be found in cold tailwater rivers like the Smith or in the headwaters of tiny mountain streams. Fall brings back cooler water temperatures and better fishing, especially when the leaves begin to fall. At this time, hordes of **ants** and **beetles** fall into streams, and trout are found gorging on these **terrestrial** insects in between the floating leaves. Winter fishing is not very productive in freestone and mountain rivers, but fishing with streamers and small nymphs will bring strikes in the tailwater rivers and spring creeks. Smallmouth bass fishing is best from April through October. In the spring, bigger fish are caught on large streamers, but lower, warmer water

in summer brings bass to the surface and a lot of fun can be had with floating **poppers**. Although fish can be caught on flies throughout the year along Virginia's coast, spring and fall are the best times to catch larger striped bass, sea trout, and redfish.

VISE

Although some fly tiers can hold a tiny **hook** in one hand and tie a fly with the other (the great **Lee Wulff** could tie a diminutive size 28 Royal Coachman without a vise), most fly tiers use a mechanical vise to hold the hook while fly tying. A vise consists of small jaws that taper to a point, a stem that keeps the jaws above the working surface, and some method of attaching the vise to a table. Most vise stems are either *C-clamp*, where the vise clamps to the edge of a table, or *pedestal*, where the stem is attached to a heavy block of metal. The pedestal design is best for travel, because it is difficult to predict whether an appropriate table edge will be present in a lodge or hotel room. Many vises have adjustments for changing the angle of the jaws to suit both the tier and the type of fly being tied. A rotary vise has jaws that rotate 360 degrees on the same axis. Not only does this help the tier view the opposite side of the fly, it also allows the fly to be rotated while the tier feeds material onto the hook, rather than winding the material around the hook by hand. This rotary technique is most useful where the tier needs to wind a large quantity of **hackle** or fur on a hook, and allows quick, even distribution of the materials.

Wiggle frog

WADER BELT
See Waders, Wading.

WADERS

Waders are available in chest-high, waist-high, and hip-length (usually called hip boots). Hip boots are fine for very small streams, but even in a medium-sized creek, you'll often need to cross a deep spot and wish you had some protection above your waist. Waist waders are for situations where you'll need to wade a little deeper than with hip boots, and are cooler in hot weather and more comfortable because suspenders are not needed. Many chest waders feature a roll-down top and can be converted into waist waders for comfort when the extra protection is not needed, which makes them versatile for all kinds of weather.

Waders are also made in boot-foot and stocking-foot configurations. Boot-foot waders have a boot built into the waders. Stocking-foot waders feature a neoprene booty attached to the upper fabric with

a waterproof seam, and must always be used with a separate **wading shoe**. Boot-foot waders are quick to put on and take off, but the kinds with a plain rubber boot do not offer as much support for long walks or in rocky streams as do stocking-foot waders with a more substantial separate boot. Some boot-foot waders are made with integral laces and a fabric boot molded over the rubber boot, though, and offer almost as much support as a stocking-foot wader with a separate boot.

The "upper" on a wader is the material used to construct the upper body. The most popular upper material is a multilayered waterproof and breathable fabric, so that condensation that builds up inside the waders can be vented to the outside. These waders are lightweight, cool, and comfortable, and with proper layering can be used in cold weather as well. Another material used in waders designed for cold-weather use is neoprene, which is thicker, warmer, and more buoyant than breathable fabric. However, neoprene is bulky and does not breathe, so these waders should be used only where wading without insulation might be dangerous, such as where the water is extremely cold.

When choosing waders, the most critical choice you'll make is size. Tight-fitting waders make it difficult to walk and do simple tasks like stepping over a log. Loose-fitting waders also make it difficult to walk as the crotch on the waders might be too low, and in fast water extra folds of fabric add to your water resistance. Also, waders that are too large, particularly in the inseam, can chafe and wear out prematurely. Measure yourself carefully if buying waders over the internet or through a catalog and follow the retailer's measuring instructions. If buying waders in a fly shop, try on several pairs with the type of clothing you'll most often be fishing in, and with a heavy pair of wading socks. Walk around, bend your knees, and kneel to make sure the waders will be comfortable in all conditions.

Always store waders in a cool, dry place, and make sure they are dry before you put them away. Mildew can grow on waders thrown into a corner when wet, which can be an unpleasant surprise on your next fishing trip. Also, waders should be stored away from electric motors, as the ozone created by motors can break down the rubber compounds in the waders.

Leaks in waders can be detected by a variety of methods. One is to take the waders into a dark room with a flashlight and look for pinpoints of light that shine through, identifying them with a waterproof marker for patching later. Another way is to immerse the waders in a bathtub, keeping air inside by pinching them at the top, and then squeezing various parts of the wader until you see air bubbles emerge. A popular way to check for leaks is to fill the waders with water and hang them up, but this method puts a lot of stress on seams and leaves you with a wet pair of waders to dry.

Waders will require repair at some point. Most fishing guides are lucky enough to get a year's use out of a pair, whereas a casual fly fisher might get a half-dozen years. A quick repair can be made to a pinhole leak with a plain piece of duct tape, and may hold for several outings if the tape is applied carefully to dry waders. Rubber inner tube repair kits such as those used for bike tires can also be used, but the best repairs are made with a compound designed especially for wader repair, such as the one sold under the brand name Aquaseal. This gooey substance dries quickly, is completely waterproof, and sticks to neoprene, all kinds of fabric, and rubber boots.

For small leaks, merely coat the leak (either inside or outside the waders) and let dry. For larger tears, prepare the surface of the wader with a coat of Aquaseal, lay a thin piece of fabric over the top of the coated area, smooth it out, and then apply a second coat of Aquaseal over the entire patch. It's best to use a circular piece of material as a patch, as it won't offer any corners to pull up. Overlap the ripped area by about ½ inch for security.

WADING

Wading is done to enter the water in order to get an unobstructed **back cast**, or when you cannot reach the fish from shore. In general, the less wading you do the better. Wading disturbs the water and can spook fish that might otherwise feed with confidence. Wading is also best done slowly; not only is it safer, you'll also disturb the water less. In a still pool, the waves pushed ahead of you telegraph your movements to wary fish, so wade slowly enough to minimize your wake.

Learning to wade confidently makes days on the water safer and less tiring. Whether wading in rivers, lakeshores, or the surf, there are a few safety issues to remember.

- Always wear a wader belt. The belt should be tightened around your waist enough to prevent water from entering the lower part of your waders if you fall in. If you take a tumble, the trapped air inside your legs will give you some buoyancy and help you reach shore safely. In addition, if you take a quick spill, a wader belt will keep you relatively dry below the waist.

- If you cannot see the bottom, never wade with the current, always against it. If you wade into a deep hole and cannot make any upstream progress, the current may push you into a dangerous situation. If you wade against the current, you can always retrace your steps to safety.

- Shallow water can be as dangerous as deep water, because if you fall onto rocks you can break a bone instead of just taking a swim.

- The shallowest place in a river is usually the tail of a pool or a wide **riffle**. Use these places to get to the other side of a river.

- Never turn your back to the water when wading in the surf. An unexpected wave can knock you over.

If you fall and find yourself in water over your head, the best approach is to get your feet in front of you as quickly as possible. In this position, you can push off of rocks that might otherwise bang your head. Ride with the current this way, paddling with your arms to keep your head afloat, and then swim to shore as soon as you are out of fast current. Make sure you crawl out of the water slowly; if your waders are full of water you'll have a difficult time standing up.

If unsure of your wading skills, it's wise to wear a personal flotation device (PFD) and use a **wading staff**. PFDs can be either of the solid kind, made of foam and reliable but bulky and uncomfortable in hot weather; or the inflatable kind, which are available either as a belt or suspender type that inflate with a CO_2 cartridge when a ripcord is pulled. When using a wading staff, use the staff to feel the bottom ahead of you, and always plant the staff downstream of your position, so that you can lean into the staff for support.

The Rio Manihuales, Chile

WADING SHOES

Wading shoes are worn over stocking-foot **waders**. They range from lightweight canvas varieties that are easy to pack and dry quickly to full-support models that are built like hiking boots. The lightweight varieties are fine for quick walks to the river, when fishing mainly from a boat, or on sandy or gravel bottoms. However, when walking for miles in a day's fishing or when the bottom is covered with large rocks, the greater support offered by more substantial wading boots is a wise choice. When looking for support and stability in a wading boot, look for models with a hard midsole and foxing (an extra layer of rubber) around the toe and lower part of the boot. In a fly shop, you can check this by flexing the sole of the boot to make sure it does not bend easily.

Wading boots are typically sold by shoe size; they are already sized to accommodate the bulk of a pair of heavy wading socks and the neoprene booty of stocking-foot waders. However, some brands are made in a wider profile than others, so if you have a very narrow or wide foot you may have to try a few varieties before you find the boot that best fits your foot. Always try on a pair of wading boots with stocking-foot waders and a pair of wading socks, and bear in mind that all wading boots loosen up slightly when wet, so they should

be moderately but not uncomfortably tight when you try them on in a store.

Other than fit, the most important decision to make is what kind of sole to choose. Plain rubber cleat soles are only for wading in mud or sand, and are dangerously slippery in rocky streams. If you need a cleat sole, the best kind to choose are those made from sticky rubber, which do offer some traction on slippery rocks. The most popular use for sticky rubber soles is for winter fishing, because wet snow can build up underneath felt soles when walking to the river, making progress slippery and uncomfortable. Because sticky rubber is not quite as efficient as felt on some types of slippery bottoms, it is sometimes available with metal studs inserted into the rubber which greatly increase purchase on the bottom.

The most popular sole for wading boots is synthetic felt. This material grips onto slippery rocks and gives a better purchase than rubber soles. Felt can also be combined with metal studs which add even a greater measure of security. Be aware, though, that if you fish from a **drift boat** many guides look poorly on studs, as they can ruin the bottom of a wooden or fiberglass boat.

In order to be able to use metal studs on slippery or icy bottoms and still fish from a boat, sandals with metal cleats that are secured over a felt-soled boot may be necessary. Although they add weight to boots and are uncomfortable when walking long distances, they offer superb traction on the slipperiest stream bottoms and can be removed when fishing from a boat.

WADING STAFF

A wading staff adds security when **wading** difficult rivers, and is essential for older anglers, or those who are not strong waders. It can be used as a walking staff when negotiating streamside cobbles or steep banks, and once in the water adds a "third leg" for balance.

A wading staff can be as simple as a strong stick

WAHOO

The wahoo (*Acanthocybium solandri*) is a very fast, aggressive fish that is found in all tropical and sub-tropical seas. It is a *scombrid* (in the **tuna** and **mackerel** family), and in appearance and habits it is very similar to the king mackerel. The best way to tell the difference between a wahoo and a king mackerel is that wahoo have a fold of skin that covers the lower jaw, where the bottom teeth of a king mackerel can always be seen.

Like many fish of the open ocean, the best way to attract wahoo to the fly is either by chumming or by trolling a teaser fly to locate fish and get them closer to the boat. Best flies for wahoo are large, flashy flies that imitate either **baitfish** or squid, their preferred foods. Because of their sharp teeth, a **wire shock leader** is essential, and because they can grow to over 100 pounds, a 20-pound **tippet** is the minimum size that should be used, unless pursuing a world record on a particular line class. Rods used should be at least a 12-weight in order to lift them if the fish sound close to the boat.

Wahoo are spectacular fighters with blistering runs and spectacular leaps, but are most often caught on a fly rod when pursuing other open-ocean species like dorado, **marlin**, or **sailfish.** They don't travel in large schools, so going offshore a dozen miles and looking for wahoo is typically an exercise in futility, except in Baja **California**, where they seem to be very abundant and smaller ones are caught regularly on a fly.

found on the riverbank. Better yet is an old ski pole (with the basket removed) or a staff made especially for wading, as they are thinner, lighter, and have a special tip designed for gripping slippery bottoms. Wading staffs come in two basic forms. The wooden types cannot be collapsed and are difficult to stow for travel or when walking through the brush. The fiberglass, aluminum, and graphite varieties are often made in collapsible styles, where sections contract inside each other and lock in place, similar to a camera tripod.

A third style is the emergency wading staff, made from sections of aluminum or graphite bound together internally with an elastic shock cord. This type can be kept in a holster and extends instantly at the river bank or in the middle of a river when needed. This type is not as strong or rigid as the solid type, but is perfectly sufficient for moderate current and for people of normal weight.

A wading staff should always be secured to a wader belt or fishing **vest** with a lanyard. Once in position for fishing, the staff can then be left trailing in the current until it is needed.

WAIST PACK

A waist pack is a minimalist alternative to the bulk and constriction of a traditional fishing **vest**, with pockets full of **fly boxes**, **leaders**, and gadgets. Waist packs are obviously not a good choice when wading deep (in that case the alternative to a vest would be a **chest pack** or just a shirt with big pockets), but are perfect for walking the edges of a pond when fishing for bass, fishing saltwater flats where the angler seldom wades more than

W

whereas the lakes and reservoirs are stocked with brown and **rainbow trout**. The wild trout are smaller, more colorful, and more difficult to catch than the planted hatchery trout.

Some of the more popular rivers for trout, grayling, and sea trout are the Wye on the border with England, the Dee in the North, and the Teifi and Towry in the south. **Atlantic salmon** do run some rivers in northern Wales, but their numbers are small and a trip to Wales in pursuit of salmon is not recommended. Wales also offers fly fishing for **pike** in reservoirs and for sea bass on the coast.

knee-deep, or fishing small trout streams where most walking is done along the banks.

Waist packs are secured with a **nylon** belt, and most can be swiveled around to the back when fishing or walking to stay out of the way, and then slid back around to the front to access gear. Most will hold at least two fly boxes, leaders, **tippet** material, fly **flotant**, and essential tools like snips or pliers. Many of them incorporate water bottle holders, which are very important on tropical flats or when hiking long distances.

WALES

Wales offers a wealth of rivers and lakes with easier public access than England. The most popular species pursued with a **fly rod** are **brown trout**, **sea trout** (sea run brown trout), and **grayling**. The season for inland, resident trout is typically from March through October, and sea trout run the coastal rivers from April through September, with the bigger fish (up to 20 pounds) running early, followed in June by smaller individuals (¾ to 3 pounds).

The peak of the sea trout season is June–August. Most sea trout fishing is done at night, with brightly colored **wet flies**, **streamers**, and **tube flies**. Trout fishing is best in May and June, and best flies are small dark **nymphs**, **wet flies**, and **dry fly** imitations of **mayflies**, **caddisflies**, and **midges**. Most of the rivers offer wild brown trout fishing,

Wales offers a wealth of rivers and lakes with easy public access.

WALLEYE

The walleye, *Sander vitreous*, is a large, predatory, warm-water fish related to yellow perch. Native to **Canada** and the northern United States, it is not commonly pursued with a **fly rod**. However, walleyes eat minnows and **crayfish** and will respond very well to a fly under the right circumstances.

Walleyes are abundant in shallow water during their spring spawning period, when **water temperatures** reach about 47 degrees. Look for them where rock piles border deep water, in either lakes or large rivers. Although walleyes can be caught any time of day, they feed most heavily between dusk and midnight, and on dark days with a chop on the water. Best flies for walleyes are brightly colored **streamers**, especially ones that have red or yellow in them. The **Clouser Minnow** saltwater fly and a large Mickey Finn trout streamer are two of the best patterns. Unless walleyes are in very shallow water, they are best fished with a Class II or Class III **sinking line**, with a 6-foot leader of 12-pound **fluorocarbon** as their teeth are quite sharp. The fly should be retrieved slowly with an occasional fast strip to catch a walleye's attention.

WALTON, IZAAK

Izaak Walton (1593–1683) was the author of *The Compleat Angler,* considered a milestone of pastoral English literature. Although Walton has been celebrated by anglers over the centuries and taught in college English classes (over 400 editions of his book have been published), he was not much of a fly fisherman and admitted it in his writings. It was not until the fifth edition of his book included a section by Charles Cotton (1630–1687) entitled "Instructions how to Angle for a Trout or Grayling in a Clear Stream" that fly fishers truly had a portion of the book that gave

them clear and solid advice. Other than the fact that Cotton did not use a **fly reel**, as they had not been invented yet, his advice on approaching trout, presenting the fly, and fly selection is as valid today as it was in the mid-1600s.

WASHINGTON

OVERVIEW

Washington is a state of vast contrasts, from temperate rainforest in the west to high desert in the east. These vastly different areas, divided by the Cascade Range, ensure that Washington offers diverse opportunities to the fly fisher. In general, the coastal area offers superb fly fishing for **steelhead**, **Pacific salmon**, and sea-run **cutthroat**, both in coastal rivers and in estuaries. Eastern Washington is known for its rich, alkaline lakes with fast-growing **rainbow trout** and for its summer steelhead fishery.

FISHERIES

The most popular **fly rod** fish in Washington is the steelhead. Washington is blessed with superb coastal rivers that provide steelhead fishing in winter and early spring, and Columbia river tributaries in the east that offer some of the best summer steelhead fishing anywhere. Many of our traditional steelhead flies and fishing techniques originated in Washington, and to fish for these magnificent sea-run rainbows in their native rivers is a rite of passage for any serious steelhead angler.

Best steelhead rivers for fly fishing in western Washington include the Skykomish and Skagit of Puget Sound, as well as the Sauk, a tributary of the Skagit. In the Olympic Peninsula, the Hoh and Sol Duc are considered two of the most productive steelhead rivers. In eastern Washington, the Grande Ronde, a tributary of the Snake River, is considered the premier summer steelhead river.

Resident trout fishing is more popular in eastern Washington because its high desert lakes, such as Dry Falls, Chopaka, Lenice, Nunnally, Dusty, and Lenore have alkaline water chemistry, which encourages heavy populations of crustaceans and insects, leading to heavy, fast-growing trout and great **hatches**. Other trout lakes of note include Omak in central Washington and Pass Lake, considered the best trout lake in the coastal area. Although Washington does not have as many world-class trout rivers as other western states, the Yakima is an incredible river for wild rainbows, and Rocky Ford is a superb spring creek. The Kettle and Elwha rivers also have notable trout fishing, and the Cedar, close to downtown Seattle, offers excellent wild rainbow fishing.

The coastal areas, especially Puget Sound, host some of Washington's best fly fishing—estuary and near-shore fishing for king and silver salmon, plus sea-run cutthroat trout. All of these species feed heavily before they enter rivers to spawn, and are caught on imitations of shrimp and **baitfish**. Fly fishers pursue these species by wading, from prams, or from larger boats when they venture further from shore.

Washington's other fly rod fish are often overshadowed by salmon and trout, but many of the lakes in the western part of the state offer good fly fishing for bass, **panfish**, and **carp**, and there is a run of **American shad** in the Columbia River. However, perhaps the best non-trout fishing in Washington is the **smallmouth bass** fishing in the lower Snake, Grande Ronde, and John Day rivers.

SEASONS

In winter, steelhead fishing on the coastal rivers is prime, with the biggest wild steelhead arriving in February, March, and April. At this time, silver salmon in Puget Sound begin to feed on small crustaceans and the fly fishing can be quite good. March and April usher in the major insect hatches on lakes and rivers, with **mayflies** and **stoneflies** providing the first action, followed in the summer by **caddis** and **damselfly** hatches.

Summer steelhead fishing begins in June and peaks in October, when fish can often be caught with **dry flies** and **floating lines**, as opposed to the subsurface techniques needed most other times during the year. Sea-run cutthroat trout also feed heavily along beaches in June, and continue this activity until they ascend coastal rivers in October through the winter. Silver and king salmon also enter coastal rivers in October, although the best fly fishing for these species is in the estuaries, before they begin their spawning runs. June is the best time to fly fish for shad in the Columbia River.

WATER BOATMAN

Water boatmen or backswimmers are aquatic insects of the order *Hemiptera* (bugs) in the family *Corixidae* and are common in nearly all types of lakes and slow areas of streams. Feeding mainly on aquatic vegetation, they hover near the surface and then dive to the bottom with a strong sculling motion. Trout and **panfish** prey eagerly on water boatmen, and because these insects are active in colder water than many other species, they become an important food source in late fall and early spring.

Because water boatmen are active swimmers, the best strategy for imitating them is to cast out, begin retrieving the fly with short strips, then pause for a moment. If you see fish feeding close to the surface with aggressive swirls but don't see any insects **hatching**, they may be feeding just under the surface on water boatmen. **Nymphs** used to imitate water boatmen should be about a size 14, oval in shape, and should include some silver tinsel to imitate the air bubbles that surround these insects. It's difficult to find flies designed specifically to imitate water boatmen, but **scud** imitations and Prince Nymphs will usually do the trick.

Like all aquatic bugs, water boatmen can fly and during the summer will often take to the air like a Polaris missile, fly some distance, and then crash into the surface of another pond. If you ever

encounter this situation, fish your nymph by slamming it hard onto the surface of the water to imitate the behavior of the naturals and attract the attention of cruising trout.

WATER CONDITIONS

Water conditions in a stream are usually classified by describing the water's flow (low, high, or normal) and clarity. Flow can be determined by looking at the shoreline. If streamside trees and brush are underwater, the stream is higher than normal, and if the flow is restricted to a narrow lane in the center of a streambed it is low. When describing clarity, fly fishers may talk about the water as either clear or dirty, but a more precise description, typically used by fishing guides, is the depth at which you can see the oar of a boat or a rock on the bottom. A third dimension of water conditions is **water temperature**, which adds even more precision to the description and can help predict the behavior of the fish, and suggest fishing tactics and what flies to choose.

High flows in a river can create more difficulties than just dangerous **wading**. Water that suddenly turns faster and deeper will sometimes put trout out of reach. Trout are reluctant to feed on the surface in raging currents, as the energy requirements of rising to the surface and then getting back to a position near the bottom, where the current is manageable, are higher than the calories obtained by eating a tiny bug. But it is also difficult to get a sunken fly close to a trout in deep, fast water because the current constantly fights the **fly line** and **leader** and pushes them back to the surface.

Luckily, in strong flows, during spring runoff or when a summer cloudburst swells a river, trout respond by moving to the quiet water along the banks, in back eddies, and in side channels, all places where the velocity of the river is reduced. Thus, during high flows it's smart to look for trout or **smallmouth bass** in places that might have been dry before the water rose.

In high flows, the best approach to fly selection is to use a bigger fly than is customary in normal conditions. Fish don't have a chance to inspect your offerings carefully, and a bigger fly will draw their attention better. If a size 14 Adams **dry fly** is normally the recommended fly, use a size 10 or 12 **Royal Wulff** instead. If a size 8 Black **Woolly Bugger** catches fish during normal flows, try a size 4.

Clarity affects fishing conditions less than one might think. Trout have been observed countless times feeding on tiny **mayflies** in the surface film when visibility was only an inch or so. But, typically, dirty water is associated with high flows, so the concept of using a larger fly than normal is also valid here. When the water is turbid, popular colors for **streamers** and **wet flies** are black, white, yellow, red, and orange or any combination of these. The Mickey Finn bucktail streamer, with its silver body and red-and-yellow stripe is high on many anglers' lists of top dirty-water flies.

When fishing subsurface in dirty water, observe if there is any debris drifting with the current. If sticks and leaves are abundant in the drift, trout will have trouble picking out drifting insects amongst the debris and turn to chasing actively swimming prey like minnows and **crayfish**, which distinguish

themselves from the floating junk by their movement and get disoriented in the heavy current and poor visibility—making them attractive targets for marauding gamefish.

The best time to fish higher, dirtier flows is as the water rises. There is typically a feeding frenzy during the first few hours of rising water, whether it is due to a sudden thunderstorm or the normal augmented flows of a **tailwater** river below a dam.

Low flows and clear water, like high and dirty water, typically go hand-in-hand. The most important consideration in these conditions is stealth; it's much more important than what fly you choose. Trout and bass under these conditions can see their predators well, and have less water around them for shelter so are constantly on guard for the slightest movement. Keep your profile low. Slow movements, and long, fine leaders will ensure more successful days.

Fly selection for low, clear flows typically requires that you go small. Fish in clear water and in slow current get a better look at the fly, and are less suspicious of a size 18 **Pheasant Tail nymph** than they are a size 12 **Hare's Ear**. In addition, during periods of low flow most of the aquatic insects are tiny. The exception to this rule is when large **terrestrial** insects like **grasshoppers** or **cicadas** fall into a river. These insects make trout and bass lose their normal caution, but even so, when the water is very clear, try to resist the temptation to use a size 6 grasshopper as a size 10 might be accepted just as eagerly and won't frighten the fish as much.

WATER TEMPERATURE

Fish are cold-blooded and are thus strongly affected by water temperature. When fly fishing, it's even more important to look for optimum water temperatures: Unlike bait fishing, where a slow-moving fish might find your offering by smell and inhale it slowly, when fishing with a fly you are looking for actively feeding fish that take their prey aggressively. This is the main reason early season anglers fishing with worms catch trout while fly fishers often return home without a **strike**.

All fish have an approximate range where they will feed if the opportunity presents itself, and an optimum range where fish are insistent and constantly on the feed. Your best opportunities with a fly are within that optimum range, but you can catch fish at the lower and upper ends. Typically, this means using a smaller fly and a slower **retrieve**, or if drifting a **nymph** in a river, getting the fly close to the bottom on a **dead drift**.

If water temperatures are below the optimum for the species you're chasing, look for places where the water might be slightly warmer—near springs, on sandbars, over dark-colored weed beds, and in places with slower current. If water temperatures are too warm, fish in deeper water, look again for springs, and along shady banks, especially if there is ledge-rock along the bank that might be contributing some cool groundwater seeps into a river or lake. Also, because warm water inhibits feeding because of a paucity of dissolved oxygen (cold water holds more dissolved oxygen than warm water), look for places where the water is turbulent, such as **riffles** in a stream, below waterfalls, in windswept places, or in the surf in lakes and in the ocean.

The following is a rough guide to the feeding temperatures of fish most often chased with a fly. Be aware that local populations may adapt to lower or higher than normal water temperatures.

Species	Feeding Range	Optimum Feeding Temperature
Brown Trout	48–70	55–65
Rainbow Trout	40–70	52–64
Brook Trout	48–65	57–59
Smallmouth Bass	59–74	64–68
Largemouth Bass	49–85	63–75
Panfish	49–76	60–72
Northern Pike	49–80	60–70
Carp	60–88	82–84
Bonefish	68–88	72–80
Tarpon	64–104	82–88
Striped Bass	60–78	62–72
Snook	60–90	70–80
Bluefish	50–80	64–79
Redfish	60–90	72–78
Permit	65–90	70–78
Barracuda	55–82	74–80
Tunas	50–80	58–78

WATER, READING

Reading the water is the ability to look at a piece or moving water and determine where trout or other stream-dwelling fish will be, without seeing them in the water or observing them rise to the surface for floating food. Reading is much more than looking at the surface of a river and deciphering the swirls and ripples on the surface. It involves knowledge of what habitat trout require, where they do their feeding, what kinds of structures they prefer, and the effect the roughness of the banks and the bottom of a river has.

Trout prefer to lie in water that is moving about one foot per second (about the speed of a slow walk), on the edge of water that is moving slightly faster. They stay in the slower water to save energy, and dart into the quicker water to feed, because

swift currents bring food at a faster rate. The slower water might be along a bank, at the bottom of a deep pool, or close to a rock, log, or weed bed.

One of the best ways to find these places where fast water meets slow, commonly called seams, is to watch the progress of bubbles or other debris on the surface. You'll see a distinct edge where the bubbles slow down and here you'll find the most trout, other things being equal.

Trout also use deep water, jumbles of rocks, and submerged trees as protection from predators. Yet none of these places offers an efficient place to feed, because there is not as much insect activity in the bottom of a deep pool or in a logjam as there is out in the open current. Most insects live and hatch in shallow **riffles**, and this food drifts in the main current into slower pools. Thus you'll find the most trout close to protection, usually within 10 feet, but not necessarily tucked inside the morass of a fallen tree.

Knowing this, you can begin to refine your stream-reading skills. In a deep pool, look for places where the bottom suddenly gets lighter, which means a sharp decrease in depth. You'll find more trout feeding in this place than you would in the middle of the pool.

In pools, whether a six-foot-long plunge in a mountain stream or a mile-long depression in a big river, the best places to fish are the head and the tail of the pool. Fish at the head, where fast water dumps into the pool and creates a seam on either side, will be less wary and will have a shorter time to inspect a fly, so they are typically the easiest. Fish in the tail of a pool, where the current constricts both horizontally and vertically, enjoy having drifting food funneled to them but are often far more difficult to catch because the water there is smoother and shallower. But often the biggest trout in a pool will be at its tail.

In the middle of a pool, look for rocks breaking the surface or the telltale bulge of a submerged rock. Contrary to popular wisdom, you'll find just as many trout, if not more, in front of rocks and along their sides than you will in the eddy behind a rock. The spot immediately behind a rock is often barren of food because the rock deflects most of the current away from this place. The larger the rock, the less likely you'll find trout on its downstream side.

One of the choice places in the middle of a pool is a place where deep water runs against a bank. Here trout have protection plus a reduction in current as the friction of the bank slows it. A bank is even more attractive if it offers partially submerged logs that lie parallel to the current, jumbles of rocks, or little points and bays that break up the smooth outline of the bank.

WAVE

A wave is a moving shape on the surface of the water. The height of a wave is determined by wind speed, wind duration, and the fetch (the uninterrupted distance wind travels across water). Out at sea, the water is moving much slower than the wave form, but once waves hit shallow water and break, the forward movement of the water increases. Near-shore ocean fish like **striped bass**, **bluefish**, and **redfish** are perfectly capable of negotiating

heavy surf and waves close to shore, which provide an excellent opportunity for fly fishing. **Baitfish** and crustaceans, because of their smaller mass, are pushed toward shore and disoriented by breaking waves, which gives the predators an advantage.

The best way to fly fish in breaking waves near shore is to watch a sequence of waves and wait until a large one is just beginning to break. Cast beyond the breaking wave, then either strip very quickly or take three steps backward to tighten the line, and then begin stripping the fly. If a fly is cast to the near side of a breaking wave, the velocity of the wave pushes the fly at the angler, a tight line is difficult to maintain, and thus the fly is not under control by the angler.

WEAKFISH

A gamefish of the Atlantic Coast from Cape Cod to **Florida**, the weakfish is most abundant in the mid-Atlantic states. Looking very much like the spotted **sea trout** of the southern Atlantic and Gulf Coasts, it gets its name from a relatively fragile mouth, which tears easily when the fish is hooked. Weakfish are found in shallow bays, estuaries, and in the surf, but unlike **striped bass** they won't enter fresh water. Weakfish suffer from strong cycles of abundance followed by scarcity, so pursuing them with a **fly rod** is best reserved for years when they are known to be abundant.

Weakfish are a wonderful fly rod fish, because they feed in shallow water on small **baitfish**, shrimp, crabs, and squid. During the day, they are most often found over sandy bottoms in 6 to 20 feet of water and are best pursued with a **sinking line**. However, at dusk and throughout the night, weakfish often feed close to the surface with a distinctive popping sound that differs from the heavier smash of surface-feeding striped bass. Best flies for weakfish are from 1½ to 4 inches long, and they seem to prefer **Deceiver**-type flies with some yellow and/or green in them. Weakfish generally prefer a slow, steady **retrieve**, especially at night.

WEATHER

Fish are obviously affected by weather that changes physical **water conditions** and **water temperature**, but are also affected by terrestrial weather patterns in ways that are sometimes understood and sometimes mysterious. The most obvious is a darkening sky during the day. The drop in light levels encourages aquatic insects to become active and begin **hatching**. Most insects are genetically programmed to hatch at low light levels because birds, fish, and other predators have greater difficulty finding insects in low light. Crustaceans and **baitfish** are also more vulnerable to gamefish when light levels are low, and most gamefish feed more heavily when a sudden drop in light intensity catches their prey in a confused state.

On the negative side, cloudy weather can ruin sight-fishing or make it extremely difficult. Low light augments glare on the water's surface and makes it difficult to see below the surface. The best way to spot fish is by their shadows, which are typically more distinct than the fish itself. Without sun shining on the water, shadows are indistinct and spotting fish becomes an exercise in futility.

Wind can have a dramatic effect on fly fishing success. As with light levels, wind **riffling** the surface of the water makes fish-spotting difficult. Wind can also stir up debris and silt in shallow water, making it difficult for a fish to find the fly. Trout in smooth water often stop rising to small insects when wind riffles the surface. This effect on trout feeding happens almost immediately and when winds are erratic it can be used to your advantage. If a trout is spotted rising during a lull in the wind and then stops when the wind blows, placing a fly over the fish as soon as the wind stops can result in an instantaneous take.

A light breeze on the surface can also make fishing easier if gamefish are spooky. Nearly all fly fishing takes place close to the surface of the water. A perfectly flat surface makes the delivery of a cast difficult as fish can see or feel the line striking the surface. A light chop on the water turns the disturbance into part of the background noise. For instance, both **tuna** in the ocean and landlocked salmon in a lake are far easier to catch on a fly in a light chop than they are in flat-calm conditions. Once winds reach 15 miles per hour, though, boating, casting, and manipulating the **fly line** become difficult. Even if fish are still feeding close to the surface, it becomes a chore just to present the fly to them.

Rain or snow seems to affect fly fishing in a positive way, especially after a long dry spell. Rain washes **terrestrial** insects and **worms** into the water, putting fish on the feed. However, the main beneficial effect of rain or snow may just be the lower light levels that always accompany a storm. At the beginning of a rainstorm, fish will often go off the feed for a few moments until they get used to the disturbance on the surface, but soon resume feeding heavily. Thunder, even though it can be felt underwater when it is nearby, does not seem to affect fish feeding behavior.

The barometer is often said to influence the feeding behavior of fish. However, it's doubtful that fish can sense a change in the air pressure when moving just a few feet up or down in the water column changes the pressure on them at a magnitude greater than the difference between a Bermuda high and a hurricane. It's probably the accompanying changes in light levels, wind, and rise or drop in temperature caused by the movement of a weather front that trigger the change in feeding behavior. Thus the reason that a falling barometer generally means improved fishing and a rising barometer, with brighter sunlight and more wind, seems to decrease their interest in feeding.

WEED GUARD

Many fish caught with a **fly rod** are found in heavy cover, from **largemouth bass** in lily pads to **bonefish** in eelgrass to **redfish** over oyster bars. If a fly without a weed guard is fished in these places,

you risk ruining your presentation when a fly gets bogged down with weeds, or even losing a fly in submerged branches or coral. Weed guards added to flies protect them not only from weeds, but from any object on the bottom that might snag a fly.

A properly designed weed guard will keep the point of the **hook** from snagging, yet will flex when a fish **strikes** so the point enters a fish's jaw. Weed guards can be made of bent flexible **wire**, a loop of monofilament that covers the hook point, two pieces of **monofilament** that form a V-shape over the point, or even just a bulky bunch of hair used in the fly dressing that covers the point.

Weed guards cannot be easily added to a fly after it is constructed, so if you intend to fish for largemouth bass, **pike**, or saltwater species over eel grass, it's best to prepare and buy some weedless flies in advance. Weed guards often need to be adjusted and can be bent into position. (If your fly snags weeds or the bottom regularly, bend the weed guard down past the hook so the point is not exposed. If you miss fish often, bend the weed guard closer to the point or just cut it off and take your chances.)

WEIGHTED NYMPHS

Weighted nymphs are **nymphs** that have had weight added to the dressing of the fly to make it sink quicker. Although nymphs are tied on heavy-**wire hooks** that do help the sink rate, often extra weight is needed. One way of adding weight to a nymph is to wind the shank of the hook with heavy wire before the fly is tied. Traditionally lead fuse wire was used, but with increasing awareness of the toxic effects of lead on waterfowl, weighted nymphs sold by responsible fly manufacturers are wrapped with tin wire instead.

A more effective method is to utilize a brass or tungsten bead into the fly patterns. Using beads adds more weight than tin wire, and many patterns benefit from the added sparkle a metal bead gives them. If the sparkle, which imitates the gas bubble that coats the surface of some **emerging** insects, is not desired, the bead can be painted black or brown for a more subtle look. For very heavy flies fished in deep water, two beads can be used, or a combination of a bead and wire under the body of the fly.

It should be noted that some anglers feel that an unweighted nymph looks more natural in the water, and they prefer to add weight in the form of **split shot** to the **leader** to get the fly deeper. However, using a weighted nymph alone makes casting easier and the leader will suffer fewer tangles during a day of fishing.

WEIGHT-FORWARD LINE
See Fly Line.

WEST VIRGINIA

OVERVIEW

Although West Virginia is not well known for its fly fishing, this state offers many fine trout streams plus excellent fly fishing for **smallmouth bass**, **largemouth bass**, **panfish**, and **muskellunge**. Many of West Virginia's mountain streams suffer from acid mine drainage, but some rivers, like the Cranberry and Blackwater, have been fitted with acid neutralization stations that help to keep the pH of the water at a level suitable for trout. Many other West Virginia rivers run through limestone bedrock, which naturally buffers the water from adverse acidity. West Virginia's best streams often host both

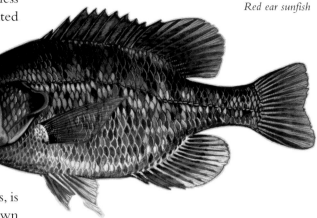

Red ear sunfish

wild and hatchery-raised **brown** and **rainbow trout**, but stretches of some rivers like the Elk are managed as quality wild-trout fisheries. Many of the headwater streams in the West Virginia mountains hold populations of small native **brook trout**.

FISHERIES

West Virginia's best and most famous trout stream is the Elk, located in the east central part of the state. This river is a rich, relatively large mountain stream that has both wild and stocked trout, and most of the famous **mayfly** and **caddisfly hatches** known to eastern trout streams. This river frequently gives up very large brown trout and fishes well all year long because natural limestone springs in its watershed keep the water cool in summer and warm in winter. Tiny **midges** and fine **leaders** are often necessary in the river, especially in late summer through winter.

The South Branch of the Potomac and its major tributary the North Fork of the South Branch, in the northeast corner of the state, are relatively remote rivers that offer near-wilderness fishing. The South Branch in particular is a large river with heavy but usually clear flows, and fishes better with **wet flies** and **streamers** than **dry flies**. It is also an excellent smallmouth bass fishery. The Blackwater River, also located in the northeastern part of the state, is one of the most scenic rivers. Although its headwaters flow smoothly through lowlands, further downstream near Blackwater Falls State Park it flows through a steep canyon, and inaccessibility keeps the crowds down.

The Cranberry and Williams Rivers, both in the southeastern corner of the state, are mountain rivers that have much access on public land and have mostly stocked trout along with some fingerling-stocked and wild fish.

West Virginia's best rivers for smallmouth bass fly fishing are the South Branch of the Potomac in the northeast, the Greenbriar on the eastern border, and the New River in the south central part of the state. West Virginia also gives the fly fisher the opportunity to catch muskellunge on the fly, especially in the catch-and-release sections on the Buchanon River in the north central part of the state and Middle Island Creek in the northwest. Muskies can also be caught on a fly in the Mud River in the southern part of the state and the Tygart River in the north.

Season

Because West Virginia's best trout streams are in the eastern mountains, lower flows and hatches may not be conducive to easy fly fishing until late April. Best hatches are through early June; once the heat of summer sets in, trout fishing on rivers that don't have a lot of spring influence will be difficult until fall. West Virginia has no closed season on trout fishing, and as long as the weather is reasonable trout can be caught on a fly all winter long.

Smallmouth bass fishing is best from April through early June when the fish are in shallow water, and then again in the fall. Smallmouth bass fishing can still be productive in the summer, but early and late in the day are best. The fishing then picks up in the fall, although once winter's colder temperatures set in, the fish settle into deeper pools and are reluctant to feed. Spring and especially fall are the best times to try for muskies with a fly.

WET FLIES

In a broad sense, a wet fly can refer to any fly that does not float, as opposed to a fly that is designed to float. However, most fly fishers use this term to refer to a fly that is designed to suggest a drowned or immature insect, or even a small minnow. In contrast, **nymphs** imitate aquatic insect **larvae** with a more specific profile, and streamers imitate **baitfish** more by design than by accident.

In trout fishing, a wet fly is a sinking fly that has either wings sloping along its body, or webby **hackle** that encircles the fly, serving the same purpose as the wings. These appendages suggest the wings of a drowned insect or the wing sprouts of an insect that is about to emerge from its larval shuck. Wet flies are usually fished on a tight line and swung through the current, where most nymphs are fished **dead drift**, or at the same speed as the current.

Wet flies were the first flies ever used. Some of the patterns that we fish today date back almost unchanged into Medieval times. (It's not that ancient fly fishers ignored fish feeding on the surface; they had no way of making hooks that were light enough to float a fly and the tackle they used was not capable of drying the water off a fly in between casts.) Wet flies up until the twentieth century were typically fished with multiple flies attached to a leader on **droppers**, where anywhere from 2 to as many as 15 flies were swung over the fish on a single cast. Today, fly fishers using wet flies might use 2 or 3 on one leader, but just as often a fly fisher will try one pattern at a time.

With wet flies, an angler can cover a lot of water with a single cast, because the fly is typically cast across the current and allowed to swing below the angler. Thus, on a 50-foot cast a wet fly will cover an arc of 50 feet below the angler. By taking a few steps **downstream** and repeating the cast, and angler can cover nearly every inch of productive water within casting range with very little effort. By casting the fly slightly **upstream** of an angler's position, a wet fly will swing deeper and slower in the water. This method works well in places with very fast water. In the same light, in very slow water the angler can cast at a more downstream angle to speed up the motion of the fly. These techniques are very important in **Atlantic salmon** and **steelhead** fishing, where the speed of the fly is critical. Another way to manipulate the drift of the wet fly is by careful **mends** of the fly line. By mending line upstream the fly will swing slower and deeper and by mending downstream the speed of the fly is increased and it will ride closer to the surface.

The most effective part of a wet fly drift is at the moment it begins to rise back to the surface under tension. This seems to imitate a hatching insect rising to the surface and happens about three quarters of the way through a fly's swing. A smart angler can exaggerate this motion by repeated upstream mends, following the fly's progress downstream with the rod tip, and then suddenly stopping the rod tip. This makes the fly sink deeper and suddenly rise to the surface when the rod stops tracking the fly. (The technique is often called the Leisenring Lift, after the **Pennsylvania** fly fisher who perfected it.)

Wet flies in lakes or reservoirs are often fished on droppers. The bottom (or point) fly is fished under the surface, the middle fly swims just under the surface, and the upper (or bob) fly skims the top of the water. By fishing three wet flies in this manner, the angler can imitate three different insect behaviors. Typically, three different patterns are used to give the trout a choice. The point fly should be the heaviest, the middle fly slim, and the bob fly should be relatively bushy.

Wet flies for trout are usually divided into two types: winged wet flies and soft **hackle** flies. Winged wet flies have short wings that slope along the back of the fly, and the wings are usually made from a wing or side feather from a duck, pheasant, or goose. Soft hackle flies dispense with the wings and instead a sparse amount of hackle encircles the head and slopes back along the body of the fly. Soft hackle flies seem to produce better in clear, shallow water and winged wet flies are best used in fast, tumbling currents, especially in mountain streams. Metal beads are sometimes incorporated into the dressing of wet flies, making them more appropriate for fast, heavy water.

Wet flies are far more popular in Europe than they are in the United States. European fly fishers, particularly those who fish reservoirs and lochs, rely heavily on wet flies for both resident and sea-run trout. British flies in particular run toward the more colorful patterns, and the most popular ones include the Alder, Butcher, Mallard and Claret, March Brown, Bibio, Soldier Palmer, and Invicta.

Popular American winged wet flies include the **Light Cahill**, Gold-Ribbed **Hare's Ear**, Royal Coachman, Hornberg, and March Brown. Soft hackle flies used commonly include the Beadhead Soft Hackle, Beadhead Pheasant Tail Soft Hackle, and Partridge-and-Orange.

WHIP FINISH

The whip finish is a knot used to finish off the head of a fly when the fly tier has completed the dressing. Without some type of knot, a fly would gradually unwind and become useless. In theory the knot is simple as it's merely a loop wound back over itself, after which the tag end is drawn tight. The structure of this knot is exactly the same as the **nail knot** used to attach a leader to a **fly line**.

Various clever tools have been designed to tie this knot, the most common of which is the Matarelli design, but the whip finish can be easily done by hand without the use of special tools, after some practice. After the head of the fly is whip finished, it is coated with head cement to increase the durability of the fly.

WHIRLING DISEASE

Whirling disease is an insidious parasite of trout that is native to Eurasia and was introduced to the United States in the 1950s through infected hatchery fish. The disease is caused by a microscopic metazoan, *Mixobolus cerebralis*, that penetrates the head and spinal cartilage of young trout and causes them to lose their equilibrium, giving them characteristic whirling behavior. The disease can prevent young fish from avoiding predators and in severe cases will kill or deform the young trout.

When a fish dies from whirling disease, millions of spores are released into the water. Unfortunately, the spores are resistant to freezing or desiccation and can survive for over 20 years in a dormant stage, only to be released when ingested by a small but common aquatic worm of the genus *Tubifex*. Anglers should always be careful to wash wading shoes and other fishing gear in hot soapy water when traveling from one watershed to another, but it's likely that whirling disease will continue to

spread on the feet of aquatic birds and other migrating animals.

Whirling disease is most damaging to populations of wild **rainbow trout**. The **brown trout**, introduced from Europe, has evolved with the parasite and does not show any ill effects from infection. **Brook** and **cutthroat trout** are only moderately susceptible to the parasite and seldom occur in rivers where it thrives. The most hopeful solution to the whirling disease problem is to develop resistant strains of trout, and research is being done in this area.

WHITE BASS

White bass, *Morone chrysops*, are closely related to **white perch** and **striped bass**. Originally native to the Great Lakes and Mississippi River systems, they have been transplanted throughout the country and do particularly well in southern reservoirs. Because white bass travel in large schools in shallow water and feed on small **baitfish** and crustaceans, they are a perfect **fly rod** fish.

Look for white bass in the spring in rivers leading into reservoirs when **water temperatures** hit the high fifties. They enter rivers to spawn and feed upon spawning baitfish, especially small **shad**. After the spring spawning season, look for them in lakes close to the surface over sandbars and gravel bars, in 10 to 30 feet of water. Schools of white bass can often be spotted chasing baitfish on the surface, and can even be found by looking for gulls that hover above the water waiting to grab injured baitfish. Unlike many **panfish**, white bass are more often found in open water, away from cover or structure.

Best flies for white bass are small white streamers with some silver flash in them. Suggested flies include White Zonker and White Marabou in sizes 8, 10, and 12. A 9-foot fly rod with a 5-, 6-, or 7-weight line is perfect, and anglers chasing white bass should have both a **floating line** and a full **sinking line** on an extra spool, in case the fish are deeper.

WHITE FLY

The White Fly is a medium-sized (size 12 or 14) **mayfly** that **hatches** in late summer on large rivers. Almost pure white, the **duns** hatch and molt into **spinners** in the same evening, and typically these flies hatch in such great numbers the water is covered with flies. The hatch may become so thick that nearby roads become slippery and fish are difficult to catch because they have so much food.

The **nymphs** of the Ephoron mayfly burrow in silt, so these flies will seldom by found in rocky mountain streams or fast **riffles**. They are most commonly found in the lower reaches of trout streams, where trout often share the habitat with **smallmouth bass** and **carp**. In fact, this hatch offers such an attractive food source that fly fishers have reported seeing not only trout and bass but channel catfish and even **walleyes** feeding on the tiny insects.

A white or very pale dry fly is all that is needed for this hatch. Two of the best are the **Light Cahill** and White Wulff, in sizes 12 and 14.

WHITE PERCH

White perch, *Morone Americana*, is closely related to the **striped bass** and **white bass**, but you can identify a white perch by its lack of horizontal stripes on its side. Mainly confined to the northeastern United States, the white perch can be found in brackish, salt, and fresh water. Because it feeds mainly in insects and small **baitfish**, and feeds eagerly year-round, the white perch is a wonderful **fly rod** fish that's available when other species may be absent or uninterested in feeding.

Look for white perch in the spring in brackish estuaries, coastal rivers, and in rivers that feed large freshwater lakes. At this time of year, white perch feed mainly on insects and crustaceans, so **nymphs** are a good choice. You don't need more than a size 10 **Hare's Ear Nymph** or any other popular trout nymph in a dark color. During the summer, white perch herd small baitfish over brush piles and other cover, or in small coves. When they are herding

baitfish on the surface, any small **streamer** (size 8, 10, or 12) should result in a **strike**. Any trout rod will suffice for white perch fishing, although a 9-foot length helps when making long casts in big lakes. Both **floating** and **sinking lines** should be on hand, because during the summer white perch feed near the bottom unless chasing baitfish.

WHITE RIVER

The White River of Arkansas's Ozark Mountains and its major tributary, the North Fork, offer some of the finest trout fishing in the world. Both rivers regularly produce world-class **brown trout**, especially in the fall, when brown trout spawn and the bigger fish move into shallow **riffles**. Both Rivers are **tailwaters**—the White below Bull Shoals Dam and the North Fork below Norfork Dam. The rivers offer wild and stocked brown and **rainbow trout**, but are also stocked with the exotic (at least for Arkansas) eastern **brook trout** and western **cutthroat trout**.

Cold-water releases below Bull Shoals Dam create over 90 miles of trout water on the White. This massive river has everything, from long slick pools to shallow riffles to heavy pocket water. Although because its large size and large trout **streamers** are very effective, there are places in the White where the best fly is a tiny **midge** fished on a light **tippet**, particularly just below Bull Shoals Dam. The North Fork is a smaller river and when flows are low it fishes more like a spring creek, with tiny nymphs and **dry flies** on light tippets the rule.

Nymphs and dry flies are effective on these rivers all year long, and fish will average between 10 and 16 inches. However, during the fall spawning run of browns and during the winter, when the famous winter "shad kill" (when thousands of small shad are sucked into the water outflows of the dams and flushed downstream) the average size of the trout is measured in pounds instead of inches.

Both rivers are used for hydroelectric power, and water levels can rise many feet in less than an hour, particularly on the North Fork, because of its short run between Norfork Dam and its confluence with the White. Not only do high flows make fly fishing difficult, they can be life-threatening, so it's advisable to fish these rivers with a knowledgeable guide or at least with someone who has knowledge of flows and high-water escape routes.

WHITEFISH

Fly fishers are more likely to catch the mountain whitefish, *Prosopium williamsoni*, than other species of whitefish because they live in shallow rivers in the same habitat as trout. Mountain whitefish are sometimes called trash fish, but they are in the same family as trout and salmon and are actually less tolerant of polluted water than trout. Although whitefish eat the same aquatic invertebrates as trout, food is seldom a limiting factor to fish abundance so their presence in a trout stream should be celebrated and not cursed. Whitefish are also the native salmonid in western trout streams, whereas no **brown trout** are native and **rainbow trout** are only native the western slope of the Rockies.

Whitefish are sporty gamefish on a fly rod and will feed more actively in cold water than trout, so they often provide great fishing during the winter when trout seem to be glued to the bottom. The most effective flies for whitefish are **nymphs**; although they will rise to a **dry fly** with a distinctive splashy rise, they are more difficult than trout to hook because of their small, inferior (downward-pointing) mouth. Best patterns for whitefish are small-to-medium-sized nymphs in sizes 12–18. Popular patterns like the Prince and **Hare's Ear**, especially the **bead head** varieties, are very effective for whitefish.

Whitefish can be found anywhere in a river, but are most abundant in deep pockets in moderately fast, oxygenated water. They spawn in the fall and their young are an important source of food for large trout, particularly brown trout.

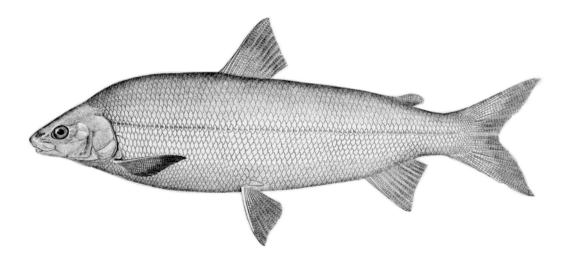

WHITLOCK, DAVE (1935–)

Dave Whitlock resigned his position as a research chemist in 1975 to devote his life to lecturing, teaching, photographing, and writing about fly fishing. He is also known as one of the best illustrators in fly fishing. Originally from Oklahoma, Whitlock resides on the **White River** in Arkansas, which is a perfect laboratory for his innovative fly designs.

Besides his work with trout flies, Whitlock has been at the forefront of bass fishing with a **fly rod**, and has developed many flies and techniques especially for bass fishing. He was instrumental in designing the Whitlock-Vibert Box System, which is a method of introducing fertilized trout eggs into a river and simulating wild trout production in rivers that cannot otherwise support wild trout.

Whitlock is the author of hundreds of magazine articles on fly fishing, as well as four books: *Dave Whitlock's Guide to Aquatic Trout Foods*, the *L.L. Bean Fly Fishing Handbook*, the *L.L. Bean Bass Fly Fishing Handbook*, and *Imitating and Fishing Natural Fish Foods*.

WIND, EFFECTS ON CASTING
See Fly Casting.

WINDOW

The window is a fish's view of the terrestrial environment. Because light rays that hit the water at a low angle are reflected, a fish sees a giant mirror above it, with a circular window to the world beyond. The size of the window varies depending on the fish's depth, because the window encompasses a cone of about 97 degrees, about 48 degrees on either side of the vertical. Because of the refraction of light rays when they enter the water, a fish can actually see below this angle to an effective distance of about 10 degrees above the horizontal.

All this is pretty academic because you never know exactly how deep a fish is lying in the water, and as you're watching the fish might shift positions anyway. The practical application is that if you keep your profile low you can get much closer to a fish before it spots you, and a fly fisher who is wading can get much closer to a fish than one standing on the bank, or a fly fisher in a **kayak** or float tube can get much closer than a flatboat with a poling platform.

Additionally, a fish in shallow water has a narrower window on the outside world, and although fish in shallow water can be spooky because they are exposed, with careful movement you can get closer to a fish feeding in a two-foot flat than you can to one at the bottom of a six-foot pool.

The window also affects how fish see a fly on the surface. Before a floating fly enters the window above the fish, all the fish can see is whatever part of the fly breaks the mirrored surface. Thus, when a **largemouth bass** sees a **popper** from 10 feet away, it only sees the bottom of the fly and perhaps the rubber legs breaking the surface film. It's only when the fly is directly overhead that a bass can see the color and shape of the popper above the surface. And because of the refractory properties of light, the wings of a fly that is drifting to a trout appear before the rest of the fly because they are the highest point on the fly and appear first in the window.

The effects of the window break down under most circumstances except perfectly smooth water. Wind and turbulence on the surface of the water turn the window into many smaller, distorted windows. Thus a trout in a **riffle** is easier to approach, and the profile and color of the bottom of your bass bug on a windy surface is far less critical.

WIRE

Wire is used as **tippet** material on **leaders** that will be used to catch fish with sharp teeth. **Pike** and **muskellunge** in fresh water; and in salt water **sharks**, **barracuda**, **bluefish**, Spanish **mackerel**, and **sea trout** require a wire bite tippet.

The type of wire you choose can be important. Fish with sharp eyesight like barracuda and Spanish mackerel are easier to catch with single-strand wire, which is thinner and far less visible in the water. However, single-strand wire often kinks, and once a wire is bent the fly does not swim properly and fish will turn away without **striking**. Braided wire does not kink easily but is more visible, so it is used for sharks or other species with poor eyesight. Bluefish have sharp eyesight but are often so aggressive that braided wire is sufficient.

Certain types of **nylon**-coated, flexible braided wire can be tied directly to the end of the leader with an ordinary **Surgeon's Knot** and tied to the fly with a **Clinch Knot** or **Loop Knot**. However, single-strand-wire requires special knots—typically a Haywire Twist to attach the wire to the fly and an **Albright Knot** to attach the wire to the rest of the leader. You may also buy pre-looped single-strand wire bite guards that have a loop on one end that is untwisted, the fly is threaded on the loop, and the wire is twisted back together. The other end of the wire is also looped and the leader can be attached with a simple clinch knot. Another method used with braided wire is to dispense with knots altogether and crimp the wire to itself using the same crimping tools used by conventional off-shore fishermen.

Wire on the end of a leader is difficult to cast so you should use just enough to protect the rest of your leader. For most species, 4 inches is plenty. For sharks or very large barracuda it might be wise to use a longer wire tippet of six or even eight inches.

WISCONSIN

OVERVIEW

With over 9,500 miles of trout streams, many thousands of miles of world-class **smallmouth bass** rivers, thriving river populations of **muskellunge**, plus the shorelines of both Lake Superior and Lake Michigan, Wisconsin has some of the finest **fly rod** opportunities in the country. In most of Wisconsin's trout streams, the upper reaches are the domain of native **brook trout**, and as you work further down most rivers **brown trout** will become more numerous. Stream-bred **rainbow trout** are not common, but stocked rainbows are available in some rivers, and large **steelhead** and **Pacific salmon** run the tributaries of Lakes Michigan and Superior in the fall and winter.

Smallmouth bass are found in the lower reaches of trout streams, where the water is warmer and richer. They are also abundant along the shores of the Great Lakes. Muskellunge are abundant in many of the larger rivers, and Wisconsin is one of the best places in the world to catch one on the fly. The Great Lakes and smaller lakes also offer lots of warm water opportunities for the fly fisher, and **largemouth bass**, yellow perch, bluegills, and **carp** are challenging and enjoyable quarry to chase with a fly.

FISHERIES

In the Driftless Area in southwest Wisconsin (named because the last glaciers bypassed this area) are a number of spring-fed meadow streams, known for their large, wild, and difficult trout. Small flies, light **tippets**, and a careful approach are needed on streams like the Big Green and Black Earth Creek. In west central Wisconsin on the edge of the Driftless Area, the Kinnikinnic and its tributary the Rush River are known for their productive fly **hatches** and large brown trout. Also in this region are some warm water streams that offer excellent fly rod fishing for smallmouth bass, including the Milwaukee, Chippewa, Grant, Platte, Wisconsin, and Black Rivers. The last two also are great places to catch a musky on a fly.

Northwestern Wisconsin is home to Wisconsin's most famous trout stream, the Bois Brule. This river has resident trout in its spring-fed upper reaches and runs of steelhead, lake-run browns, and Pacific salmon as it gets closer to Lake Superior. Besides the lower Bois Brule, Fish Creek and the Sioux River offer some of the better fishing for lake-run salmon and trout out of Lake Superior. The Namekagon is also a notable trout stream in this area, although most of the trout are stocked—but below Hayward the river offers some of the best fly rod musky fishing in the country. Notable smallmouth bass rivers in this area include the Flambeau and Chippewa rivers, and both of these offer musky fishing as well. And perhaps the best fly rod smallmouth fishing is in Chequamegon Bay, where the fish average almost four pounds.

Northeastern Wisconsin is notable for a diverse mix of smallmouth bass, musky, resident trout, and lake-run trout and salmon. Best smallmouth fishing is found in the Wisconsin and Menominee rivers, with some musky and northern **pike** mixed in. The Wolf River, like most of the rivers in this area, is a rocky wilderness trout river where you might even hear a wolf in the evening. The best Lake Michigan tributary is the Oconto, where steelhead, lake-run browns, and Pacific salmon enter the river in the fall.

The southern part of Wisconsin's eastern border, along the shores of lake Michigan, does not offer as much quality inland trout fishing as the rest of the state, but it makes up for that in lake-run trout and salmon. Best Lake Michigan tributaries include the Root, Milwaukee, Sheboygan, and Kewaunee. These rivers also fish well in midsummer for smallmouth bass.

SEASONS

Although some Wisconsin trout streams are open 12 months a year, you'll find the best fly fishing in May through September. Unlike many eastern states, Wisconsin offers excellent midsummer fishing, because many of its rivers are spring-fed and thus stay cool even on the hottest days. The lake-run Pacific salmon and brown trout are best in September through November, and steelhead fishing runs from November through April, although the best months for fish fresh from the lake are in November and then again in April. Smallmouth bass fishing is good from June through September, with the best fly rod fishing in the middle of the summer. Muskies on a fly are possible June through October, but June is the most productive month.

WOOLLY BUGGER

The Woolly Bugger is one of the most popular and effective flies ever developed. In the past 30 years, it has likely caught more trout than any other fly pattern, but it is also used effectively for everything from bass to **carp** to **tarpon**. Technically a trout **streamer**, it can be fished as a **nymph** or a saltwater fly as well.

The Woolly Bugger is a variation on the Woolly Worm **wet fly**, a pattern that has been used almost unchanged for hundreds of years. In the late 1960s,

a **Pennsylvania** fly tier named Russell Blessing added a wiggly tail of marabou feathers to a Woolly Worm in an attempt to imitate a hellgrammite. His original pattern was all black, but today you can find Woolly Buggers in white, black, orange, and every shade and combination of shades in between. However, the original black and olive shades, or a combination of these two colors, are the most popular colors. Metal beads and cones are often added to Woolly Bugger variations to give the fly a better sink rate and a jigging action in the water.

The Woolly Bugger is thought to imitate many other fish prey than just hellgrammites. It works when trout or other fish are eating leeches, **crayfish**, **sculpin**, tadpoles, and even squid in ocean waters. The most common way to fish a Woolly Bugger is to cast the fly across the current and strip in back in foot-long pulls. However, the fly can be deadly when fished dead drift like a nymph, or with a combination of dead drift and active stripping.

The Woolly Bugger is one of the easiest and most inexpensive flies to tie. Anyone with reasonable dexterity can learn to tie an effective Woolly Bugger in less than an hour, and it is often the first fly offered in fly tying lessons.

WORLD RECORDS

The International Game Fish Association (IGFA) is the accepted organization for accepting and validating world record catches. There are specific rules and a separate list of records for fish caught on a **fly rod**. The IGFA awards separate records in each "**tippet** class," which includes 2-, 4-, 6-, 8-, 12-, 16-, and 20-pound classes.

Fly fishers attempting to break world records must follow specific rules regarding tackle and techniques, and must submit carefully documented proof of the catch. The major rules for fly fishing are:

- Any type of **fly line** or **backing** may be used without strength restrictions, but part of the leader must include at least a 15-inch single strand that does not exceed the line class for which the record is entered. In knotted leaders, a **Bimini Twist** or Spider Hitch is usually used to double the tippet where it is connected to the rest of the leader in order to get the maximum strength out of a knot but still incorporate a single strand. This section is referred to as the **class tippet**.

- A **shock tippet** of heavy **monofilament** or **wire** may be used between the fly and the class tippet, but the distance between the fly and the single strand of class tippet must be no more than 12 inches.

- The rod used must be one designed for fly fishing and can be no shorter than 6 feet.

- The reel used must be one designed especially for fly fishing.

- The fly must be a recognized type of artificial fly. Fly rod lures that can be cast by a fly rod are not allowed. No bait or scent can be added to the fly.

- Gaffs or nets used must not exceed 8 feet.

- No one but the angler may touch the rod, reel, or line, during the fight, but other people may touch the **leader** when landing the fish.

- Trolling the fly is not permitted. A boat must be out of gear from the moment the fly is presented until the fish is landed.

- Applications for world records must be presented to the IGFA within 60 days of the catch, and an official IGFA entry form must be used.

- Record fish must be weighed on a certified scale and witnessed by a disinterested party if possible.

- The fly, entire leader, and one inch of the fly line beyond the leader connection must be intact and submitted with the entry form.

- Photographs showing the full length of the fish, the rod and reel used, the scale used to weigh the catch, and a photograph of the angler holding the fish must be submitted as well.

WORMS

Common earthworms get washed into trout streams during rainstorms, but many anglers don't realize that aquatic worms are also found in certain rivers and trout relish them just as much. These worms, of the family *Lumbricidae*, are closely related to common nightcrawlers and garden worms but they live their entire lives underwater, typically in weedy, silt-laden habitat along the banks of rivers. Because **tailwater** rivers below dams encourage this kind of habitat, aquatic worm imitations are most productive in flows controlled by dams, particularly the San Juan River in **New Mexico**, the South Platte River in **Colorado**, and the **Bighorn River** in **Montana**—but aquatic annelids may be found in most tailwaters.

Worm imitations are simple flies, typically just a piece of fine cotton chenille lashed to a **hook**. The most common colors are red, brown, and tan, to match the shades of various species of worms, but sometimes bright orange and pink variations will interest a trout. The most common imitation is the prototypical San Juan Worm and its many variations.

Worm flies should be fished close to the bottom, **dead drift**, without any added motion from the angler to imitate the free drifting behavior of the natural worms. Because worm flies are not usually weighted, weight must be added to the leader. Worms are most effective during a rise of water, after a rainstorm or during a water release from a dam, as the added flow washes the worms from their normal habitat and into trout feeding lanes.

WRIGHT, LEONARD (1923–2001)

Leonard Wright was an advertising executive, a P-51 fighter pilot in World War II, and one of the most iconoclastic trout-fishing authorities. His most important contribution to fly fishing techniques was a technique used to make a **dry fly** flutter across the water in a natural manner, as opposed to uncontrolled **drag** on the fly. This technique, The Sudden Inch, was first explained in his book *Fishing the Dry Fly as a Living Insect*. It utilizes an **upstream** curve cast, followed by a short movement of the rod tip that moves the fly upstream an inch, followed by a **dead drift**. The technique was designed to imitate the fluttering behavior of **caddisflies** but can be used with any dry fly to catch a trout's attention.

Wright had a house on the Neversink River in the Catskills, where he did much of his research on trout habitat and feeding behavior. In his later years, he moved to Islamorada in the **Florida** Keys and enjoyed the challenges of flats fishing. His books include *Fishing the Dry Fly as a Living Insect*, *The Ways of Trout*, *Trout Maverick*, *The Fly Fisher's Reader*, *Fly-Fishing Heresies*, *First Cast*, and *Neversink*.

WULFF, LEE (1905–1991)

Lee Wulff was one of the most famous and influential fly fishers of the twentieth century. Born in Valdez, **Alaska**, he studied art in Paris in the 1930s

and then moved to Brooklyn, where he became interested in fishing the Catskill and Adirondack trout rivers. It was on **New York**'s **AuSable River** that Wulff developed his famous Gray Wulff, White Wulff, and **Royal Wulff dry flies**, characterized by lots of **hackle** and with wings and tail from deer hair, so the flies would float well in the heaviest water. Wulff also invented the fly fishing **vest** while living on the New York stretch of the Battenkill in the 1930s. He was an inveterate tinkerer, with an engineer's brain combined with an artist's sensitivity and an outsized ego.

Wulff did much to popularize fishing in northern **Canada**, especially in Newfoundland and Quebec. He first went to Newfoundland to fish in tournaments for giant bluefin tuna with conventional tackle, and soon after fell in love with **Atlantic salmon** fishing in Newfoundland's productive rivers. He learned how to use a movie camera and fly floatplanes, and soon began to fly to remote salmon and **brook trout** rivers, making movies for the Canadian government to help promote sport fishing tourism. In the 1960s, Wulff became a host of the legendary *CBS Sports Spectacular* and *American Sportsman* TV series, bringing exotic locations into the homes of ordinary fishermen with the help of fellow hosts Curt Gowdy and Bing Crosby.

Although many anglers before him had urged that most game fish be released instead of kept for the frying pan, it was Wulff who really began the modern catch-and-release movement with this statement from his 1938 book *Lee Wulff's Handbook of Freshwater Fishing*: "There is a growing tendency among anglers to release their fish, returning them to the water in order that they may furnish sport again for a brother angler. Game fish are too valuable to be caught only once."

In his later years, Lee and his wife, tournament caster Joan Salvato Wulff, taught fly fishing to hundreds of students in their school in the Catskills. Lee Wulff died of a heart attack at the age of 86 while piloting a light plane.

WYOMING

OVERVIEW

Wyoming offers some of the most unspoiled and spectacular trout fishing in the lower 48 states. The fishing scenery alternates between rugged mountain rivers and lakes and sagebrush river valleys. The native trout of Wyoming are the Yellowstone **cutthroat** and the Snake River fine-spotted cutthroat, but equally abundant are introduced **brown** and **rainbow trout**. Most of Wyoming's rivers are managed for wild, stream-bred trout, although many lakes and reservoirs receive plantings of stocked trout.

Most of the best trout fishing in Wyoming is in the western half of the state. Once the land drops into the plains in the eastern side, rivers become warmer and filled with silt, and although these warmer rivers provide excellent sport for bass and **carp** on a **fly rod**, it's the trout streams in the east that get the most attention from fly fishers.

FISHERIES

The most famous trout stream in Wyoming is the **Snake River**, on central eastern border of the state and centered around Jackson Hole. A float on this river from Teton National Park through Jackson Hole is perhaps one of the most scenic trout-fishing experiences in the world, with the spectacular Teton Mountains framing an ever-changing dramatic backdrop. The trout in this river are almost all Snake River fine-spotted cutthroats, which are considered more wary and harder-fighting than other strains of cutthroat. Because this river hosts an abundance of large **stoneflies** and **grasshoppers** during the summer, very large **dry flies** in sizes 4 through 12 are the exception rather than the rule.

Just north of Teton National Park is Yellowstone National Park. It is a vast trout fisherman's paradise, with the headwaters of famous rivers like the **Yellowstone** and the Madison, as well as smaller rivers famous in their own right, like the Gibbon and the **Firehole**. Surprisingly, the trout fishing within Yellowstone Park is less crowded than the rivers outside the park, and no guiding or **drift boats** are allowed in the Park, which makes it a paradise for the wading fly fisher.

The best place for a large (over 20 inches) trout on a fly is probably the North Platte River in southern Wyoming, from the Colorado border downstream 150 miles to the city of Casper. It's a rich **tailwater** river with abundant aquatic life and mostly gentle flows. Because it is used heavily by irrigators, flows are irregular and the water is seldom very clear—but most times it is clear enough for the trout to see a fly. Although it offers good **hatches** at times, the best method for catching the large trout in this river is with **nymphs** and **streamers**.

Other trout rivers of note include the New Fork and Green Rivers near Pinedale, the upper Bighorn near Thermopolis, and the Shoshone and Clark's Fork of the Yellowstone near Cody. Wyoming also offers some of the finest alpine lake fishing, particularly in the Wind River Range, where it is possible to catch a rare **golden trout**, introduced from **California**.

Most of the best trout fishing in Wyoming is in the western half of the state.

Seasons

Fishing in Wyoming can be good all year long, and even in the bitter days of winter, trout can be caught on a fly in tailwaters like the North Platte. However, the best fishing begins in March. Rivers are typically low and clear because mountain snows have not yet begun to melt, and on warm days **midges**, **caddisflies**, and **mayflies** will bring trout to the surface. Summer crowds have not yet arrived and most rivers are lightly fished at this time of year.

When snowmelt begins in earnest in late May, many of the rivers in Wyoming become raging, muddy, and impossible to fish. This is the time to fish tiny meadow streams, tailwater rivers below dams, or mountain lakes (if they have thawed). Runoff season in Wyoming can be long. For instance, the **Green River** is usually low and clear enough to fish by mid-June, but the Snake River, which drains from the high peaks of the Tetons, may not be clear enough to fish until mid-July or even early August. But summer is the time of big dry flies and nymphs in Wyoming, and clearing rivers usher in the most exciting fishing of the season.

September is a great month to fish in Wyoming. The crowds have left, the aspens glow yellow, elk bugle in the meadows, and trout feed heavily in anticipation of the cold winter. By October, snow may fall in the high regions of Wyoming but fishing will remain good until the mercury really plummets.

X hopper

X

Yellow bass diver

Y

YELLOWSTONE RIVER
See Wyoming and Montana.

Z

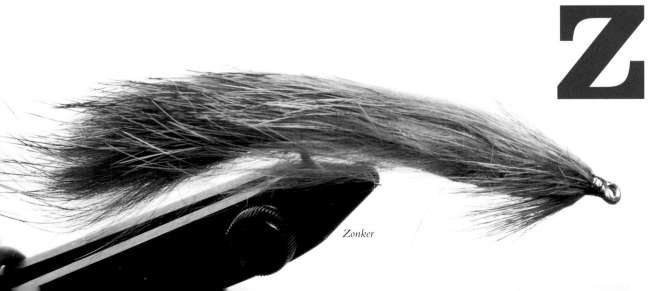

Zonker

ACKNOWLEDGMENTS

I've learned something from everyone I've ever fished with. Over many years of visiting new places and learning new techniques I've met hundreds of new friends, and in the typical manner of good fly fishers, they have been generous with their knowledge. To list them would take an entire book. But for this encyclopedia, I'd like to single out the following people for extra special help: Barry Beck, Robert Bryant, Jeremy Cameron, Chris Champine, Joe Codd, Kevin Devine, John Edstrom, Jason Elkins, Tom Evenson, Robert Harrison, Jonathan Jacobs, Ian James, Patrick Keller, Jim Lepage, Larry Mann, Ian Maclean, Jimbo Meador, Leland Miyawaki, Dave Norling, Manfred Raguse, Dan Small, Doc Thompson, Kip Vieth, Bob White, and Keith Wilson.

To my editors F-Stop Fitzgerald, Leigh Grossman, and Mie Kingsley: Thanks for your very generous patience and support with a manuscript that took almost two years longer than I thought it would.

To my wife Robin, son Brett, and daughter Brooke: Thank you for patiently waiting on many weekend afternoons and late evenings while I pounded the keyboard. You never complained even though we gave up a lot of family time.

—Tom Rosenbauer

BAND-F LTD. ACKNOWLEDGMENTS

We would like to thank the Orvis Company, Leigh Perkins, Perk Perkins, and Tom Rosenbauer for allowing us to create this book under the Orvis brand, which we value highly. Our sincere thanks to Thomas Nelson Publishers for believing in this project and agreeing to take it on.

PHOTOGRAPHERS ACKNOWLEDGEMENTS

We would like to thank the author Tom Rosenbauer for allowing us to collaborate on this project and Kristen Parrish and Kristen Vaasgard at Thomas Nelson for their vision in developing this book with us.

While there are too many great folks to thank individually, key individuals at several of the Orvis lodges include: Ben Turpin and Mike Ramos at Pocono Manor Lodge, Kay Maghan at Nemacolin, Damon Newpher and Charles Zeran at Glendorn, Carol Wightman at The Marquesa, Alexandra and Michelle Hanten at Morrisons, Richard Carroll of Chatham Bars Inn, Matt Batschelet at West Branch Resort, and Lannie Johnson at Oasis Springs.

Thanks to Bill Pekala of Nikon Professional Services, for allowing us the use of lenses, 35mm and compact cameras. Thanks to Maria Fernandez for her great work designing and producing this book. Thanks to Chris Champine for the exacting illos. Thanks to Otto Beck for a wonderful supply of flies to shoot.

Thanks to the Otto Beck Company which gave us hundreds of flies to shoot for this book, and to the following individuals who helped get our photographers on the water: Ralph Megliola at Pocono Manor; Nina Zappala, Joe Frunzi, Capt. Charlie Buldo, and Robert Baldaserri at Skytop Lodge; and Chris, Dave, and Capt. Mike Andolina at Fishing The Cape.

There are many local and state tourism agencies that were extremely helpful in photographing this book: Bill AuCoin of AuCoin Associates Inc., in St. Petersburg/Clearwater; James Raulerson of St. Petersburg/Clearwater Convention and Visitors Bureau (CVB); Lisa Humphrey, Public Relations (PR) Representative for the Tampa Bay CVB; Josie Gulliksen from Newman PR; Jonell Moodys, PR & Communications Manager of Naples, Marco Island, Everglades CVB; Everglades National Park; Big Cypress National Preserve; and Margaret Marchuk, Director of Media Relations, Lake Placid Essex County Visitors Bureau. Thanks to Visit Florida, the state tourism agency, especially Paul Kayemba and Cassie Henderson. For help photographing fly fishing in Florida, thanks to Capt. Mark Ward of Everglades Angler, Capt. Bruce Hitchcock in Chokoloskee, FL, Capt. Dan Malzone, Capt. Ralph Allen, Capt. John Miller, Capt. Glen Hales and Nick Pujic of *Canadian Fly Fisher* magazine, and Capt. Les Hill.

While shooting in Florida, generous accommodations were granted by Best Western Waterfront, Fishermen's Village, Harbor Pointe Condominium Resort, and Palm Island Resort. Additional accommodations were provided by Rob DeCastro and Jane Watkins, of the Lemon Tree Inn, Naples; Sasha Hlozek at the famous Cheeca Lodge in Islamorada; the Spring Hill Suites in Tampa; the Innisbrook Resort & Golf Club in Palm Harbor; and Cathleen Casper at Key West's magnificent Casa Marina Resort.

Special thanks to Judith, Weston, and Genni for watching the waters with us.

PHOTO CREDITS

The producers of this book would like to thank Bruce Curtis for his vision in bringing this book to our attention, and for working so quickly with us throughout the photographic process.

Two photographers who have helped make this book visually stunning, with their wonderful work are John G. Miller, who is responsible for the aquatic/insect imagery herein, and Cathy and Barry Beck, who helped with great imagery from many locations shown in the book.

Photos on the following pages are copyright 2009 by Bruce Curtis: All alphabetic fly photos in vise; 2, 3, 13, 14, 17, 19, 21 bottom, 25 bottom, 31 top, 33, 38 bottom, 49 bottom, 52 top, 53, 54, 56, 59 top, 62, 63, 64, 65, 67, 70, 74 bottom, 77, 78 top, 79, 80, 82, 83, 86, 89, 90, 97 bottom, 99, 101 top, 103, 105, 106, 107 bottom, 117, 124, 128, 146 top, 150, 151, 154 top, 161, 177, 187, 191, 194, 197 bottom, 202, 204, 205, 210, 213, 217, 220, 225 right, 228, 232, 237, 245 right, 251, 252, 257, 264, 268, 269, 270 bottom, 278, 279, 285, 286 top, 289, 291, 294, 295, 296, 303, 305 left, 307, 308.

Photos on the following pages are copyright 2009 by f-stop fitzgerald: iv-v, vi-vii, viii, 1, 11, 12, 22, 23, 30, 36, 38 top, 43 bottom, 58, 66, 74 top, 75 top, 76, 78 bottom, 95, 98, 100, 108, 112, 116, 118, 119, 127, 134, 144, 162, 165, 166, 172, 182, 184, 196, 197 top, 199, 200, 201, 209, 212, 214, 218, 219, 221, 234, 235, 239 bottom, 242, 247, 253, 255, 256, 261, 265, 273, 280, 288, 290, 292.

Photos on the following pages are copyright 2009 by John G. Miller: 6 bottom, 28 bottom, 37, 68, 72, 97 top, 102, 115, 125, 126, 130, 146 bottom, 147, 148, 152, 153, 160, 168, 181, 195, 198, 211, 229, 230, 238 bottom, 249, 250, 258, 270 top, 307, 308.

Photos on the following pages are copyright 2009 by Barry and Cathy Beck: 7, 8, 15, 45, 47, 50, 69, 123, 171, 186, 262, 283, 298.

Photos on the following pages are copyright 2009 by Tom Rosenbauer: 51, 138, 170, 193, 276.

Photo on page 39 is copyright 2008 by R. Valentine Atkinson.

Thanks to Joe Codd at Frontier Travel for photos on pages 41 bottom, 113, 175, 179, 226, 227, 287.

Thanks to the U.S. Fish & Wildlife Service division of the Department of Interior for photos on pages iii, 4 bottom, 16, 34, 35, 59 bottom, 92, 136, 157, 158, 169, 223, 233, 267, 277, 299.

Thanks to the U.S. Fish & Wildlife Service for photos on pages i, 4 top, 10, 18, 20, 21 top, 28, 29, 32, 34, 41 top, 43 top, 55, 59 bottom, 93, 96, 104, 107 top, 125 top, 125 bottom, 129, 137, 139, 142, 155, 173, 205 bottom, 206, 207, 216, 231, 236, 238 top, 239 top, 254, 260, 272, 295.

Illustrations by Chris Champine on pages 5, 26, 27, 48–49, 61, 149, 164, 188–190, 203, 224–225, 243–245, 257, 270–271.

Thanks to The Orvis Company for photographs on pages 24 bottom, 42, 46, 84, 85, 87, 122, 133, 140, 246, 281, 282, 284, 297.

Thanks to the Catskill Center for Fly Fishing for use of the following photographs: 24 top, 25 top, 52 bottom, 75 bottom, 94, 101 bottom, 120 top, 121, 141, 241, 287 bottom, 301, 305 right.

Thanks to the Kreiger family for use of the photograph on page 120 bottom.

Thanks to the Anglers of the Au Sable for use of their logo on page 6 top.

Thanks to the Atlantic Salmon Federation for use of their logo on page 11.

Thanks to the Federation of Fly Fishers for use of their logo on page 74.

Thanks to Trout Unlimited for use of their logo on page 271.

Thanks to Rhion Pritchard for the photo on page 286.

Thanks to Tourism Ireland for the photo on page 113.

Thanks to Manfred Morgner for the photo on page 110 top.

Thanks to the Bureau of Land Management for use of the photos on pages 111, 156.